S0-ARO-534

MAKSIM GORKY

MAKSIM GORKY

SELECTED LETTERS

SELECTED, TRANSLATED, AND EDITED BY

ANDREW BARRATT

AND

BARRY P. SCHERR

CLARENDON PRESS · OXFORD
1997

Oxford University Press, Great Clarendon Street, Oxford OX2 6DP

Oxford New York

Athens Auckland Bangkok Bogota Bombay
Buenos Aires Calcutta Cape Town Dar es Salaam
Delhi Florence Hong Kong Istanbul Karachi
Kuala Lumpur Madras Madrid Melbourne
Mexico City Nairobi Paris Singapore
Taipei Tokyo Toronto
and associated companies in
Berlin Ibadan

Oxford is a trade mark of Oxford University Press

Published in the United States
by Oxford University Press Inc., New York

© Selection, translation, and editorial material
Andrew Barratt and Barry P. Scherr 1997

All rights reserved. No part of this publication may be reproduced,
stored in a retrieval system, or transmitted, in any form or by any means,
without the prior permission in writing of Oxford University Press.
Within the UK, exceptions are allowed in respect of any fair dealing for the
purpose of research or private study, or criticism or review, as permitted
under the Copyright, Designs and Patents Act, 1988, or in the case of
reprographic reproduction in accordance with the terms of the licences
issued by the Copyright Licensing Agency. Enquiries concerning
reproduction outside these terms and in other countries should be
sent to the Rights Department, Oxford University Press,
at the address above.

British Library Cataloguing in Publication Data
Data available

Library of Congress Cataloging in Publication Data
Gorky, Maksim, 1868–1936.
[Correspondence. English. Selections]
Letters of Maksim Gorky / selected, translated, and edited by
Andrew Barratt and Barry P. Scherr.
Includes bibliographical references.
1. Gorky, Maksim, 1868–1936—Correspondence.   2. Authors.
Russian—19th century—Correspondence.   3. Authors, Russian—20th
century—Correspondence.   I. Barratt, Andrew.
II. Scherr, Barry P. III. Title.
PG3465.A38   1997   891.78'309—dc20   [B]   96–24311
ISBN 0–19–815175–6

1 3 5 7 9 10 8 6 4 2

Typeset by Hope Services (Abingdon) Ltd.
Printed in Great Britain
on acid-free paper by
Bookcraft Ltd.
Midsomer Norton, Somerset

PREFACE

'Few names have aroused more passion—of hatred or admiration—than that of Maxim Gorky.'[1] It is some sixty years now since Alexander Kaun wrote these words in his thoughtful obituary of the writer, yet the problem of which they speak is in all main respects as real today as it was at the time of Gorky's death. Of course, the passion abated with the passing years, the hatred gave way to a studied indifference, the admiration to ritual obeisance before the shrine marked 'A. M. Gorky'—a creature as mythical as the name invented by Soviet scholars to speak of their subject.[2] But the fact remains that Gorky—perhaps more than any other major figure in the history of Russian literature—has been very much the victim of his own reputation. It was as an attempt to rescue him from this sad fate that the present volume was first conceived.

Until quite recently, the state of Gorky studies was easily described. Whilst critics in the Soviet Union were effectively obliged to endorse an officially sanctioned image of the writer as the voice of the rising proletariat, the friend and ideological comrade of Lenin (and/or Stalin, as historical circumstances dictated), and—above all else—the founding father of Socialist Realism, scholars elsewhere displayed a determination either to uncover the distortions and evasions which underlay the sanitized Soviet portrait, or else—and this has been far more common—simply to dismiss him as a figure unworthy of serious or detailed attention.

But times, as we all know well enough, have changed. The advent to power of Mikhail Gorbachev, with his much-publicized policies of glasnost and perestroika, and the subsequent collapse of the Soviet Union itself, have ensured that the life and works of Maksim Gorky, like everything else to do with modern Russia, stand in need of a fundamental reexamination. The task is a daunting one. Although it is not so very difficult to dismantle the officially approved portrait—indeed, recent Russian commentators have demonstrated an almost unseemly relish in emulating their foreign colleagues in this endeavour—the larger issue of constructing new, more sophisticated, and more illuminating accounts of the career of this extraordinary man remains as intractable as ever.[3]

The main problem is one which besets most areas in modern Russian studies: a paucity of reliable documentary materials with which to work.

---

[1] A. Kaun, 'Obituary: Maxim Gorky', *Slavonic and East European Review*, vol. 15, 1937: 440.

[2] Gorky's real name was Aleksei Maksimovich Peshkov. Maksim Gorky (literally 'Maksim the Bitter') was his pen-name. The hybrid construction 'A. M. Gorky' passed into common usage after the writer's death.

[3] For a review of recent developments in Gorky scholarship in Russia, see Andrew Barratt and Edith W. Clowes, 'Gor'ky, glasnost' and perestroika: Death of a Cultural Superhero?', *Soviet Studies*, vol. 43, 1991: 1123–42.

Although it is true that recent years have witnessed the publication of many important documents relating to Gorky's life and works (some of which have made their way into this collection), it will be a long time until we are in a position where truly comprehensive new biographical studies are possible.[4]

In putting together this selection of Gorky's letters we have therefore recognized its 'interim' status, yet we hope that it will serve the larger task by promoting new interest in a writer whose career is still too little known, even among Russian specialists, in the English-speaking world. We have sought to do this by allowing Gorky—albeit through the medium of translation—to tell the story of his life in his own voice. It is only by listening carefully to that voice, in all its many modulations, that a proper understanding of this strange and contradictory man is likely to ensue.

We have been aided in the preparation of this volume by the generous support of a number of institutions and individuals. The University of Otago's research fund enabled us to employ a research assistant, whilst its William Evans Fund provided the opportunity for Barry Scherr to visit New Zealand for a period of intensive collaboration. The International Research and Exchanges Board (IREX) awarded a grant to Barry Scherr so that he could work in Moscow at the Gorky Archive, a branch of the Institute of World Literature (IMLI).

Turning to the individuals, thanks are due to Stephen P. Brown and John Beebe who, as undergraduate students at Dartmouth College, provided valuable assistance in the collation and organization of the published letters from which our selection was made. John Beebe also helped by preparing draft translations of a number of letters. To our colleagues, Richard Sheldon and Lev Loseff at Dartmouth, Alex Krouglov and Alexei Vikulov at Otago, we express gratitude for their expert advice and information. It is with particular pleasure that we acknowledge the contribution of Russian scholars. Feliks Feodosievich Kuznetsov, Director of IMLI, and Vladimir Sergeevich Barakhov, Head of the Gorky Archive, aided our work by providing access to necessary materials and giving permission to translate passages censored from a number of letters when they were published in Soviet Russia. Lidiia Alekseevna Spiridonova was also most generous with advice and assistance.

We reserve our special thanks for two people. Lynne Knapp, a graduate of Otago's Russian Department, provided admirable service as a research assistant, creating first versions of many of the letters contained in this volume. Her quiet diligence and cheerful good humour were a source of inspiration to us both. And to Nick Luker we owe a debt of gratitude for his willingness to find the time to cast an expert, and highly

---

[4] See, however, L. Spiridonova, *M. Gor'kii: dialog s istoriei* (Moscow, 1994). A new biography of Gorky by Geir Kjetsaa has also just been published in Norway.

attentive, eye over our final draft, making many invaluable suggestions for its improvement.

Finally, the inventors of electronic mail deserve mention for providing a highly convenient means of instant communication between two hemispheres.

Every effort has been made to obtain the necessary permissions. Any omission will be rectified in future editions.

CONTENTS

ABBREVIATIONS

AG
Arkhiv A. M. Gor'kogo, various volumes. Vol. 4: *Pis'ma k K. P. Piatnitskomu* (Moscow, 1954); vol. 5: *Pis'ma k E. P. Peshkovoi, 1895–1906* (Moscow, 1955); vol. 7: *Pis'ma k pisateliam i I. P. Ladyzhnikovu* (Moscow, 1959); vol. 8: *Perepiska s zarubezhnymi literatorami* (Moscow, 1959); vol. 9: *Pis'ma k E. P. Peshkovoi, 1906–1932* (Moscow, 1966); vol. 10. bks. 1 and 2: *M. Gor'kii i sovetskaia pechat'* (Moscow, 1964, 1965); vol. 11: *Perepiska A. M. Gor'kogo s I. A. Gruzdevym* (Moscow, 1966); vol. 13: *M. Gor'kii i syn* (Moscow, 1971); vol. 14: *Neizdannaia perepiska* (Moscow, 1976)

Chekhov
M. Gor'kii i A Chekhov. Perepiska, stat'i i vyskazyvaniia (Moscow, 1951)

Chteniia
Gor'kovskie chteniia 1958–1959 (Moscow, 1961)

Izv Ts K
Izvestiia Tsentral'nogo Komiteta KPSS

Kontekst
Kontekst 1978 (Moscow, 1978)

Korolenko
M. Gor'kii i V. Korolenko. Sbornik materialov (Moscow, 1957)

Lenin
V. I. Lenin i A. M. Gor'kii. Pis'ma, vospominaniia, dokumenty, 3rd enlarged edn. (Moscow, 1969)

LG
'Dva pis'ma Stalinu', *Literaturnaia gazeta*, 10 Mar., 1993: 6

Lit.-est. kontseptsii
Literaturno-esteticheskie kontseptsii v Rossii kontsa XIX–nachala XX v. (Moscow, 1969)

LN
Literaturnoe nasledstvo: vol. 70 *Gor'kii i sovetskie pisateli. Neizdannaia perepiska* (Moscow, 1963); vol. 72: *Gor'kii i Leonid Andreev. Neizdannaia perepiska* (Moscow, 1965); vol. 95: *Gor'kii i russkaia zhurnalistika nachala XX veka* (Moscow, 1988)

MI
M. Gor'kii. Materialy i issledovaniia: vol. 1 (Moscow, 1934); vol. 3 (Moscow–Leningrad, 1941)

N Zh
Novyi zhurnal, vols. 30, 31

Perepiska
Perepiska M. Gor'kogo v dvukh tomakh, 2 vols. (Moscow, 1986)

PSS
M. Gor'kii, *Polnoe sobranie sochinenii v 25-i tomakh* (Moscow, 1968–76)

SS
M. Gor'kii, *Sobranie sochinenii v 30-i tomakh*, vols. 28, 29, 30 (Moscow, 1954–6)

NOTE ON TRANSLITERATION

The system of transliteration used in this book is that proposed by the Library of Congress, with the following modifications: -y has been substituted for -ii and yi in the endings of family names (hence, Dostoevsky, not Dostoevskii; Bely, not Belyi); and the soft sign mark (') has been omitted from all personal names in the body of the text. Concessions have also been made to conventional usage in such cases as Ehrenburg, Tolstoy, Chaliapin, Yalta, and so on.

SPECIAL NOTE

Passages marked off with asterisks (*thus*) have been restored after consulting the originals of letters held in the Gorky Archive.

THE LIFE AND WORKS OF MAKSIM GORKY
A SHORT CHRONOLOGY

1868   Aleksei Maksimovich Peshkov born on 16 March in Nizhnii Novgorod (renamed Gorky, 1932–91), a major manufacturing and port city on the Volga River.

1871   Family moves to Astrakhan. Father dies of cholera. Aleksei returns to Nizhnii with his mother. Lives mainly in the care of his maternal grandparents.

1879   Mother dies of consumption. He is apprenticed to work in a shoe shop.

1880–4   Apprenticed to V. S. Sergeev, a building contractor. Does occasional work elsewhere, notably in an icon painters' workshop, and as a chef's assistant on Volga river steamers.

1884–8   In Kazan. Works in various bakeries. Becomes involved with radical political groups.

1887   Death of grandmother (February) and grandfather (May). Attempts suicide on 12 December.

1888   Spends summer in Krasnovidovo, near Kazan, with Mikhail Romas, a revolutionary activist. Sets off on first journey on foot through southern Russia.

1889   Returns to Nizhnii. Works as a lawyer's clerk. Meets the writer Vladimir Korolenko.

1891   Leaves Nizhnii for long journey on foot. Wanders through Ukraine, the Caucasus, and the Crimea.

1892   In Georgia. Publishes first story, 'Makar Chudra', in Tiflis newspaper (12 September) under *nom de plume* Maksim Gorky. Common-law marriage to Olga Kaminskaia.

1893–4   Gorky's stories appear in various Volga newspapers.

1895   Separation from Kaminskaia. Moves to Samara to work as newspaper columnist. 'Chelkash' is published in a major Moscow journal.

1896   Returns to Nizhnii to join staff of local newspaper. Marries Ekaterina Pavlovna Volzhina (30 August).

1897   Birth of son, Maksim (27 July). Goes to Crimea for health reasons.

1898   Arrested because of revolutionary connections. Imprisoned briefly in Tiflis (May). Two-volume collected stories published in St Petersburg with great success.

1899   First novel, *Foma Gordeev*, published. Meets Chekhov in Yalta. First visit to St Petersburg. Becomes literary editor of Marxist journal *Zhizn'* [*Life*].

1900   Meets Tolstoy in Moscow. Joins the Znanie publishing collective.

1901   Witnesses Kazan Cathedral demonstration in St Petersburg (March). Arrested and imprisoned for a month in Nizhnii. Birth of daughter Ekaterina (26 May). Publishes the novel *The Three* [*Troe*].

1902   Election to membership of Academy of Sciences blocked by Tsar Nicholas II. Production of *The Petty Bourgeois* [*Meshchane*] at Moscow Art Theatre (March). Exile to Arzamas. Second play, *The Lower Depths* [*Na dne*], is highly acclaimed (December).

1903   Separates from wife. Mariia Fedorovna Andreeva becomes common-law wife. Takes over Znanie firm with Konstantin Piatnitsky.

1904   First Znanie miscellany appears. *Summerfolk* [*Dachniki*] causes furore on opening night (November).

1905   First Russian Revolution. Witnesses Bloody Sunday massacre (9 January). Arrested for composing letter of protest. Imprisoned in Peter and Paul Fortress, then released on bail. Engages in many revolutionary activities. Possibly meets Lenin (November). Involved in Moscow armed uprising (December). Leaves Russia to evade arrest.

1906   Trip to America to raise funds for Bolsheviks. Scandal erupts over his relationship with Andreeva. Writes *Enemies* [*Vragi*] and *Mother* [*Mat'*] in upper New York State. Death of daughter in Russia (August). Returns to Europe. Sets up home on Capri (October).

1907   Special guest at Fifth Congress of Russian Social Democratic Party in London (May). Interest in 'God-building' and close collaboration with its ideologists, Bogdanov and Lunacharsky.

1908   Publishes *Confession* [*Ispoved'*], a novel reflecting ideas of 'God-building'. Lenin visits Capri, then condemns 'God-building'.

1909   Organizes political school for Russian workers on Capri. It quickly closes, having been opposed by Lenin. Gives up control over the Znanie miscellanies (September).

1910   Begins publication of *The Life of Matvei Kozhemiakin* [*Zhizn' Matveia Kozhemiakina*].

1911   Serious health problems.

1913   Publishes *Childhood* [*Detstvo*], first volume of autobiographical trilogy. Returns to Russia under amnesty marking the three-hundredth anniversary of the Romanov dynasty (December).

1915   Organizes a new journal *Letopis'* [*The Chronicle*].

1916   Publishes *Among People* [*V liudiakh*], the sequel to *Childhood*.

1917   Helps found newspaper *Novaia zhizn'* [*New Life*]. Begins publication of *Untimely Thoughts* [*Nesvoevremennye mysli*], a series of articles often strongly critical of the Bolsheviks, both before and after the October coup.

1918   *Novaia zhizn'* closed by Bolsheviks (July). Starts to organize the World Literature publishing house.

1919–21 Undertakes various initiatives to assist intellectuals engaged in cultural and scientific work.

1920   Mariia (Moura) Budberg becomes his common-law wife.

1921   Increasing difficulties with Bolshevik leaders, especially Zinoviev. Leaves Russia (October), ostensibly for health reasons.

1922–3 Lives in Germany and Czechoslovakia.

1923   Helps establish journal *Beseda* [*Dialogue*], an abortive attempt to bring Soviet and *émigré* writers together. Publishes *My Universities* [*Moi universitety*], the third volume of autobiography.

1924   Settles in Sorrento.

1925   Publishes *The Artamonov Business* [*Delo Artamonovykh*] in Berlin. Begins work on *The Life of Klim Samgin* [*Zhizn' Klima Samgina*], a tetralogy which remained unfinished at the time of his death.

1928   Celebration of sixtieth birthday. Returns to USSR for first visit (27 May).

1929   Second Soviet trip during the summer. Returns to Sorrento in poor health.

1930   Writes the play *Somov and Others* [*Somov i drugie*].

1931   Visits Moscow (May–October).

1932   Visits Moscow (May–October). Première of *Egor Bulychev and Others* [*Egor Bulychev i drugie*] (September).

1933   Leaves Sorrento for permanent residency in USSR (May). Première of *Dostigaev and Others* [*Dostigaev i drugie*] (November).

1934   Death of son (11 May). Delivers opening address at First Congress of Soviet Writers and is elected its Chairman (August).

1935   Travels the Volga and Crimea. Health deterioriates.

1936   Returns to Moscow (May). Dies on 18 June.

INTRODUCTION

Maksim Gorky was truly a prodigious writer of letters. More than 9,000 of them are currently known to scholarship, the first dating from April, 1889, the last from the middle of 1936, shortly before the writer's final illness.[1] It is also known that many other letters have been lost, either through mischance, negligence, or deliberate intent.[2] No less remarkable than the sheer size of this correspondence is the number and variety of Gorky's correspondents. On one occasion or another, he exchanged letters with almost all the leading Russian writers of his day and with a great many of the minor ones, too. Not that his epistolary activities were limited to the literary community or his fellow countrymen, of course. Scientists and journalists, politicians and workers, the famous and the anonymous, men and women at home and abroad—the full list of Gorky's correspondents speaks both of his extraordinary energy and an equally extraordinary range of interests, intellectual and practical.

Although a handful of Gorky's letters did appear in print during the writer's lifetime, the publication of his correspondence began in real earnest only after his death.[3] It would appear that the major impediment to this venture was the author's own unwillingness to have such materials pass through the doors of the archives to which they were already being consigned in large numbers during the 1920s and 1930s. There was more to this than the natural desire to preserve his personal privacy, however. As his letter to the editors of the newspaper *Izvestiia* makes clear (Letter 133), Gorky was even more sensitive to the fact that his unique status in Russian literary life meant that his private correspondence had become a piece of intellectual property which many people were all too eager to turn to their own advantage.

Gorky also knew full well that the Stalin regime was itself intensely concerned with the ways in which his letters (as indeed his literary heritage as a whole) might be used to promote its own interests and ambitions. The writer's triumphal return to his native land in the spring of 1928 coincided with a concerted effort on the part of the authorities to promote his image as a great proletarian writer and the natural elder statesman in the cultural life of Stalinism. The extent to which he became a willing participant in this process of canonization must remain a subject for speculation. What is certain, however, is that by the time of

[1] *Perepiska* 1: 6.

[2] Further information about Gorky's letters can be found in K. D. Muratova, 'Epistoliarnoe nasledie M. Gor'kogo', *Russkaia literatura*, no. 2, 1988: 216–28.

[3] Letters from Gorky to his first publisher, S. P. Dorovatovsky, appeared in *Pechat' i revoliutsiia*, no. 2, 1928: 68–88; letters to Andreev, Briusov, Balmont, and others, and letters to him by young Soviet writers were published in *MI* 1 (1934).

Gorky's death, a large number of his letters had become the closely guarded preserve of a small group of trusted scholars whose task it was to fashion a mythic portrait of the writer consistent with Stalinist doctrine.[4] Thus it is that the subsequent history of the publication of these letters has come to provide one of the most interesting and revealing case-studies in Soviet (and post-Soviet) cultural politics.

It was obvious from the outset that Gorky's correspondence would prove the most controversial part of his literary heritage, more controversial even than the publicistic writings which caused such embarrassment to his Soviet commentators.[5] The main problem was that by the late 1930s a great number of his correspondents had already entered the ranks of the politically unmentionable, be they writers such as Babel, Pilniak, and Platonov, or politicians such as Bukharin, Zinoviev, and Rykov. No less serious was the fact that a great many other letters contain comments which, had they been published in the Soviet Union, would have readily undone the entire project of constructing an officially approved 'Gorky'.

Such considerations explain why the publication of Gorky's letters was such a slow and tentative affair throughout the Stalin period. Even though a great deal of work had been done by scholars and archivists, only a very small and carefully edited selection of these letters found their way into print. The most significant early publications were the second and third volumes in the series *M. Gorky. Materials and Investigations* [*M. Gor'kii. Materialy i issledovaniia*] which contained letters to major writers, including Tolstoy and Chekhov (vol. 2), and to the critics Miroliubov, Vengerov, and Ovsianiko-Kulikovsky (vol. 3). But for the most part Gorky's correspondence was available only in the most tantalizingly incomplete form, much of it being presented to a wider readership through brief extracts carefully chosen to illustrate popular and scholarly studies of the writer's career. Towards the end of the Stalin era there were signs, however, that things were about to change. The first major breakthrough came in 1937, with the publication of Gorky's correspondence with Chekhov, an epistolary dialogue which is perhaps the most important single source for an understanding of the younger writer during that crucial period at the turn of the century when he first emerged as a major celebrity on the national literary scene.

A new Chekhov volume appeared in 1951 when Gorky scholars were already well advanced in their work on a three-volume selection which, for better or worse, has been destined to serve for forty years as the

---

[4] Nina Berberova's biography of Moura Budberg, Gorky's mistress during the 1920s, contains an interesting story which demonstrates the lengths to which the Soviet authorities were prepared to go in their efforts to have all the writer's letters surrendered to Soviet archives (N. Berberova, *Zheleznaia zhenshchina*, 2nd edn. (New York, 1982)).

[5] The most notorious of these were *Untimely Thoughts* and 'On the Russian Peasantry'. See Sections 4 and 5 for details.

'standard' general collection of the writer's letters in Russian. As it turned out, these three volumes were to prove significant in another way. The final part of a thirty-volume collected works which had begun publication in 1949—one of the darkest years of post-war Stalinism—these letters, 1,195 in all, actually appeared only after Stalin's death. As a result, the final product is a curiously hybrid affair. Predominantly 'Stalinist', in terms both of its contents and its editorial style, it nevertheless displays clear signs of the long-awaited post-Stalin 'Thaw'. Particularly revealing in this respect are the differences between a mock-up pre-publication edition of the three volumes which circulated in fifty copies in 1954 and the final versions which eventually appeared in print. Noteworthy first of all for the fact that the original selection was supplemented by a further sixty or so letters, several of which, like that to A. S. Shcherbakov of 19 February 1935 (Letter 172), contain highly uncomplimentary remarks on the state of Russian literature under Stalin, these volumes also attest to a growing scrupulousness on the part of the editors. Although the letters in all three volumes have been abridged at critical junctures, the excisions are far more consistently indicated in volume 30 than they are in volume 28.

Over the following decade and a half the situation improved dramatically as scholars took full advantage of the post-Stalin liberalization to publish a number of substantial collections. Gorky's correspondence with Konstantin Piatnitsky, his business partner in the Znanie publishing house, appeared in 1954, whilst the following year witnessed the publication of the first volume of his correspondence with his wife, Ekaterina Peshkova. Next in line were the writer's letters to Vladimir Korolenko, the leading representative of Russian Populism and one of the most significant influences on Gorky during his early years in the Russian provinces. A long-awaited compilation of letters and other materials relating to the writer's troubled relationship with Lenin followed in 1958, and this was succeeded, in turn, by other major collections, which included his correspondence with Russian writers and the publisher I. P. Ladyzhnikov (1959), with foreign writers (1960), and with M. F. Andreeva, his common-law wife for many years (1963).

Amidst all these fruits of the 'Thaw', two volumes stand out in particular. The first was the seventieth issue in the scholarly *Literary Heritage* [*Literaturnoe nasledstvo*] series. Containing selections from Gorky's correspondence with a large number of Soviet writers, many of whom had been *persona non grata* during the Stalin period, it provided a potent antidote to the extremely over-simplified accounts of the writer's involvement in the development of Soviet literature which had prevailed hitherto. Even more fascinating in many respects was the seventy-second volume in the same series, which comprised the complete correspondence between Gorky and his most famous contemporary writer, Leonid

Andreev.[6] Accompanied by a wide variety of other materials and volu-
minous notes, it charts the entire course of their turbulent relationship
from the close collaboration with which it began to the complete enmity
with which it ended. Nor was this all. Further important publications of
the 1960s included a two-volume collection of his correspondence with
Soviet journalists and editors (1964, 1965), the second volume of letters
which passed between the writer and his wife (1966), and his correspondence with Ilia Gruzdev, his official biographer (1966).

These various publications represent a rich resource which amply displays the new possibilities opened up by the Khrushchev 'Thaw'.
Certainly, there is more than enough material in these volumes to help
fill many of the 'blind spots' in the Stalinist record, thereby enabling
alternative readings of Gorky's life and works. Yet it was still obvious that
Soviet editors were obliged to operate within severe constraints. To take
the most striking example, the Lenin collection was selected most judi-
ciously, so that it could promote the new official line which had it that
Gorky's initially hostile reaction to the Bolshevik take-over was just a
temporary mistake, an error of judgement from which he was rescued by
the friendly advice of Lenin himself. Interestingly enough, although
Gorky's 'mistakes' were now readily acknowledged by the editors, they
were far less ready to present the truly controversial documents for direct
inspection by the reader, even as the volume passed through successive,
expanded editions. The degree of sensitivity to such issues can be gauged
from a note sent by the directors of IRLI following the publication of the
second volume of the Gorky–Peshkova correspondence in 1966.[7]
Referring to Gorky's letter of 2 December 1917 (Letter 91), the authors
of this note complained bitterly that the volume contained 'only a single,
very sceptical response to the events of the October Revolution'. And the
evidence we now have of editorial intrusions is eloquent in its own way.
The excision from a letter to Slonimsky (Letter 116) of a pointed reference to the importance of artistic freedom in post-revolutionary Russia is
typical in this respect. Consider also the rather cryptic postscript to the
letter to Peshkova of 15 November 1922 (Letter 108), scribbled upside-
down at the top of the page and alluding quite plainly to the writer's less
than positive view of the Soviet regime at the time.

The limits of the permissible were betrayed most clearly of all, however, by two events—or rather non-events—which were also symptomatic of the renewed conservatism which followed the ousting of
Khrushchev. The first was the decision not to proceed with the publication of Gorky's massive correspondence with Romain Rolland, an

---

[6] Most of these letters came from the B. Bakhmetieff archive at Columbia University, New York.
They were published in English by P. Yershov (see n. 13).

[7] See *Voprosy literatury*, no. 1, 1993: 20–3.

exchange which contains many intriguing insights into the real nature of the Russian writer's attitude to political and literary developments under Stalin. Like Solzhenitsyn's *Cancer Ward*, perhaps the greatest *cause célèbre* of Brezhnev's cultural policy, the two volumes containing these letters were apparently already typeset before the word was received from on high that they were not to be printed. The second key moment of the Brezhnev years concerned the fate of Gorky's complete works. Begun with a great fanfare in 1968 to coincide with the centenary of the writer's birth, the venture eventually ground to a halt, none too mysteriously, in 1982, by which time the first series, containing the artistic works and their variants, had been published. As for the promised second and third series, which were to comprise the publicistic works and the letters, respectively, not a single volume was issued.

There were, of course, a number of positive products of the Brezhnev period, but these were by and large as unspectacular as the era itself. Despite its promising title, *Unpublished Correspondence* [*Neizdannaia perepiska*], the fourteenth volume in the *Gorky Archive* series contained very little of real interest. Like its predecessor, *M. Gorky and his Son* [*M. Gor'kii i syn*], it was remarkable more for the issues it avoided than for what it contained. For example, the potentially controversial correspondences with Anatolii Lunacharsky, the first Soviet Commissar of Education, and Petr Kriuchkov, Gorky's secretary and NKVD 'minder', were very carefully selected indeed. And, for all its imposing bulk, volume 95 of *Literary Heritage*, which included many hitherto unpublished letters to prominent journalists (most notably A. V. Amfiteatrov), proved a major disappointment when it finally appeared in 1988 as a sort of posthumous testament to what is now called the 'era of stagnation'. Whilst it provides an extraordinary record of the mundane detail with which Gorky was burdened through his editorial work, it adds nothing of substance to what we know of his life and attitudes during the periods in question.

The most obvious sign of the impasse in Gorky studies was the selected correspondence in two volumes which appeared in 1986, on the historic eve of glasnost. The coincidence could hardly have been more ironic, as the collection gave little indication indeed of what lay ahead. Although it did contain a number of fascinating new items from the early years, this selection reverted to a safe and predictable pattern as it reached the more sensitive periods of the writer's career. (The statistics tell it all, in fact: whereas the first volume, covering the years 1889–1911, contained seven previously unpublished letters by Gorky and forty-eight new letters to him, the second volume (1912–36) had no new letters at all by the writer, and only thirteen written by others to him.)

When one surveys the full array of Gorky's letters published during the Soviet period, several features emerge. The most obvious—and predictable—has been the marked imbalance in favour of the years before

1917. Even as early as the mid-1960s, the reader had access to a wide variety of letters from which to form a detailed impression of more or less every aspect of Gorky's life and opinions in the pre-revolutionary era. But the later years received greatly inferior coverage, a fact which may be explained both by Gorky's ambiguous attitude towards the Bolshevik regime, and by the continuing reluctance on the part of the Party ideologists in the post-Stalin years to open up large tracts of Russia's political and literary history to direct scrutiny. Even so, for those willing and able to read between the lines (and what intelligent Soviet citizen was incapable of doing that?), there was still a vast amount of published evidence to confirm what everyone had always known by hearsay—that Gorky's real significance in the history of his country was quite other than what they had been told by their teachers in school and university.

But what can be said of the post-glasnost scene? As yet, one cannot pretend to speak with full authority on this subject, although certain trends are already apparent. Most significant, perhaps, is the fact that the publication of previously unknown or suppressed Gorky materials has been a relatively slow and sporadic business. Given the central place of Gorky in the cultural iconology of the Soviet regime (where it was second in importance only to the cult of Lenin), it is not surprising that it was not until glasnost was quite well advanced that the more controversial pieces began to emerge. The publication in 1988 of *Untimely Thoughts*— a series of articles written in 1917 and 1918 in which Gorky had mounted a spirited attack on the Bolsheviks and their policies—signalled the degree to which the old taboos could now be broken. The following years witnessed the first in an entire series of publications of Gorky's letters to prominent Party leaders (including Stalin), whose names had been more or less unmentionable even during the headiest days of the Khrushchev 'Thaw'. In the meantime, a number of articles in specialist journalists contained new items from his correspondence with important Russian writers.[8]

It would appear, therefore, that there are no longer any ideological or political barriers to the full publication of Gorky's letters. Nevertheless, progress to date has been frustratingly slow. Despite promises that publication of the complete works would be resumed in 1991 (and even finished by 1995), not a single volume has yet appeared.[9] Only at the time of this writing (February 1995) are substantial new collections finding their way into print.[10] Given that such scholarly publications now have to face the harsh realities of the new commercial environment in Russia,

[8] For details, see Barratt and Clowes, 'Gor'ky, glasnost'and perestroika: Death of a Cultural Superhero?', *Soviet Studies*, vol. 43, 1991: 1123–42.

[9] We understand that most of these volumes have been fully prepared for publication and that the hold-up is due to financial constraints.

[10] The most recent publication is *Neizvestnyi Gor'kii* (Moscow, 1994) which contains a substantial collection of letters, mostly to political figures.

it seems likely that it will be many years yet before we are in possession of anything like the complete epistolary record. As to what these new materials will reveal, only time will tell, but to judge from what we have seen to date, it seems unlikely that they will substantially alter the broad picture.

The present volume has been designed to fill what we perceive as a major gap in the works of Gorky currently available in English. Although a number of the writer's letters have been translated into English before, this is the first attempt to produce a comprehensive selection organized chronologically. Hitherto, the English-speaking reader has had to rely on a slim volume issued by the Soviet 'Progress' publishing house in 1966, a work highly conservative in its selection and curious in its organization.[11] The Gorky–Lenin correspondence published by the same firm in 1974 suffers from the same severe editorial constraints as the Russian work on which it was based.[12] Far more useful and illuminating, although necessarily specialized in focus, are the only two Western collections of note. P. Yershov's *Letters of Gorky and Andreev* is a substantial work, even though it is less complete than the *Literary Heritage* volume mentioned above and somewhat unreliable in its dating of certain letters.[13] Hugh McLean's earlier publication of the correspondence of Gorky and Khodasevich was all the more interesting in that it presented a significant, though smaller, body of letters which could not be published in the Soviet Union at all.[14]

Given that the 177 letters contained in this book represent only a small fraction of those currently available in Russian (and an even smaller fraction of the total corpus), it would be foolish to claim that this is anything more than a most highly selective sample of Gorky's output as a letter writer. Nevertheless, the process of putting together a small collection which might still adequately reflect the full range of Gorky's activities and opinions was not quite so difficult as the bare statistics might suggest. To begin with, there is a large number of letters which, although of undoubted interest to literary scholars (the correspondences with Piatnitsky, Amfiteatrov, and Ladyzhnikov are prime examples), deal almost exclusively with fine details of editorial work and hence reveal little of Gorky other than his monumental capacity for sustained hard work. There is also a high degree of repetition in these letters—a mark of Gorky's somewhat obsessive personality—which means that one letter can easily serve for many others in terms of what it shows about the writer. There are, for example, literally dozens of letters of the Capri

[11] M. Gorky, *Letters*, trans. V. Dutt (Moscow, 1966).

[12] *Lenin and Gorky. Letters, Reminiscences, Articles*, trans. B. Isaacs (Moscow, 1974).

[13] *Letters of Gorky and Andreev*, ed. P. Yershov, trans. L. Weston (New York, 1958).

[14] 'The Letters of Maksim Gor'kij and V. F. Xodasevič, 1922–1925', *Harvard Slavic Studies*, no. 1, 1953: 279–334.

period which express Gorky's concern at the decadent state into which Russian letters had fallen in the years following the abortive revolution of 1905. By the same token, his many letters to beginning writers, both before and after the 1917 Revolution, contain comments and advice which are more or less identical, even down to points of linguistic formulation.

Turning to the specific criteria which have governed the present selection, our first concern was to include letters in which Gorky describes certain crucial events in his life, such as his reaction to the Kazan Cathedral demonstration of 1901 (Letter 24), the première of the play *Summerfolk* (Letter 35), his first-hand experience of the Bloody Sunday massacre (Letter 37), or his initial impression of the Soviet Union on his first return there in 1928 (Letter 147). We have also deliberately chosen letters which reveal the more intimate side of his life, for which reason we have drawn heavily on Gorky's correspondence with his wife. These letters have the additional benefit of providing this volume with a central 'thread'. Finally, given continuing interest in the vexed issue of Gorky's dealings with the Soviet government, we have translated a considerable number of the recently published letters to which we have already referred.

After giving the matter a great deal of thought, we decided to include the selected letters in their entirety. Despite the obvious attraction of including interesting excerpts from a greater number of letters, and also of avoiding a certain duplication of ideas, we felt that only the complete letters properly capture the spirit of Gorky the man and the writer. It is only by reading the letters in full that one can experience the characteristic play of his mind at different times of his life. Jumping as they do from topic to topic, from personal confessions to business matters, from philosophical abstractions to practical concerns, the letters serve above all to reveal the sheer *tension* of a life which was lived quite literally at the extreme limits of human endurance.

The organization of the book is self-explanatory. The letters are presented in strict chronological order. They have been divided into six sections which correspond to the main 'periods' of Gorky's life. Each section is preceded by a brief introduction containing the necessary information, biographical and historical, for the letters themselves to make ready sense.

The act of translation is inevitably also an act of interpretation, and in rendering these letters into English we have been constantly aware of the many ways in which we have felt obliged to modify the flavour of Gorky's original Russian. Whatever else one might like to say of them, these letters are no models of elegance. Written often in large numbers (even up to fifteen or more at a single sitting) and at the end of days devoted to his own writing and editorial work, they tend to reflect the circumstances of their composition in disjointed syntax and awkward expression. This is especially the case—as Gorky himself is ready to admit to many of his correspondents—when he ventures into the realm of abstract ideas.

Whilst we have obviously striven on all occasions to be faithful to the sense of the original, we have also allowed ourselves considerable latitude, particularly with regard to matters of syntax. In so doing, we hope that we have made the letters read as naturally as possible in English, even though this may have resulted in the smoothing out of certain rough edges in the originals. In pursuit of the same readability we have also felt obliged—albeit reluctantly—to use different English expressions when rendering certain important key words which crop up regularly in these letters, such as 'strength' [*sila*] and 'necessary' [*nuzhnyi*] and their cognates. There have also been a few occasions where, like the native speakers to whom we have turned for help, we found the sense of Gorky's Russian to be so obscure as to warrant a footnote to this effect.

What, finally, might the reader expect to discover from the pages which follow? Gorky's letters provide a unique insight into the mind of a strange, obsessive, and (at times) clearly disturbed individual. Most striking, perhaps, are the contradictions which crop up with quite extraordinary regularity at all periods of his life. Gorky was a man who could marvel at the raw power of the United States, yet abhor its materialist ethic; who could idealize Europe as the source of the rationalist tradition, yet complain of its fundamental decadence; and who could entertain the most utopian hopes for the history of his native land, yet speak volubly of the dark Russian 'peasant' force which he so feared. The letters also show the extent to which he was capable of major changes of heart, thereby giving credence to Vladislav Khodasevich's suggestion that Gorky was a somewhat fickle friend. The letters contained in this volume provide ample evidence of his shifting attitude to Posse, Andreev, Skitalets, Piatnitsky, and others, betraying a characteristic pattern (again identified by Khodasevich) of initial enthusiasm and eventual disillusionment. Even more disturbing at times is Gorky's capacity for extreme belligerence in the expression of his views and his tendency to think in terms of simple binary oppositions.

Oddly enough, Gorky's correspondence with family members and close friends is often far less revealing in a personal sense than 'one-off' letters to people with whom he was unacquainted at the time of writing, such as Volynsky, Rozanov, or P. Kh. Maksimov. There may also be rather less of politics in these letters than one might expect. Although this may be explained above all by Gorky's awareness, before and after 1917 alike, that his correspondence was always likely to attract the attention of the secret police, there are reasons to believe that a degree of self-censorship was also involved in this. During the latter part of his life in particular, Gorky was very much aware of his own 'biography' as a mythic construct over which he wished to exercise as much personal control as possible. Symptomatic of that concern was the agreement between the writer and his wife to destroy a part of their correspondence which they both evidently found too personally revealing.[15]

In the end, of course, what one makes of these letters is very much a matter of individual interpretation, especially those written during the writer's final years. Consider, for example, the following extract from a letter to E. I. Khlebtsevich of 24 February 1928:

I do not believe that man is bad in his essential nature—by nature, he always wants something better than what there is, and he always wants to be better than he is himself. Man has been made bad—and he continues to be made bad—by the class structure of society. This has restricted his possibilities in every way, it has distorted his powers of reason, it has allowed him no freedom of imagination in his work or in the quest for conditions which might alleviate his work. It has taught him only submissiveness and subordination to the ruling class.[16]

How are these words to be read? As a sincere statement by Gorky and the sign of a naïve willingness to adopt the political vocabulary of Bolshevism? Or is it Gorky the pragmatist at work here, a man who understands the need to earn the trust of the Stalin regime by such small acts of calculated mimicry?

If Gorky will thus always elude those who wish to understand him completely, he is also remarkable for his seemingly endless capacity to surprise. No matter what conception one might have of him, there will be elements in these letters which will inevitably serve to confound the reader, whether it be the gruesome account of suicide and madness in the letter to Chekhov of October 1900 (Letter 22), the existentialist flavour of his philosophical musings in the letter to Voronsky of April 1926 (Letter 126), the admission of his personal unhappiness in the letter to Furmanova of May 1926 (Letter 127), or his extraordinary constraint when talking of the death of his son in the letter to Rolland of May 1934 (Letter 168). This quality of 'unexpectedness' is, in the end, perhaps the most revealing feature of a writer who is surely destined to remain one of the most intriguing figures of Russia's revolutionary era.

---

[15] *Perepiska* 1: 63.   [16] *SS* 30: 77.

1
IN THE PROVINCES
1889–1899

INTRODUCTION

'How am I? The same as ever, Mariia Zakharovna—restless.' These are Gorky's own words in a letter of 1899 to his friend Mariia Basargina (Letter 17) and they serve as a useful epigraph to any account of his early life. Whilst one might suspect a degree of youthful posturing here—'restless' was certainly one of the writer's favourite terms of self-definition at this time (see Letter 7, for example)—the bare facts of his biography speak for the aptness of the epithet.

As any reader of Gorky's autobiographical trilogy will confirm, the future writer's childhood, youth, and adolescence make for a tale of extreme and virtually unrelieved deprivation, both material and emotional. Born Aleksei Maksimovich Peshkov on 16 March 1868, Gorky was only three years old when calamity first struck. His father, a carpenter and cabinet-maker by trade, died after contracting cholera during one of the epidemics which were the scourge of the Volga region at the time. As a result, his mother returned to Nizhnii Novgorod, to the home of her parents, the Kashirins, in whose care the young Gorky was to be left. In effect, the boy was abandoned by his mother, for he saw very little of her from that time onwards except for a short period before her death from tuberculosis in 1879.

Life with the 'Kashirin tribe' (as his grandparents' family is so unflatteringly described in the autobiography) was a harsh and often desperate affair. The root of the trouble was the rapid decline of the family business, a dye shop, which was losing custom to competing enterprises of greater technological sophistication. As their fortunes worsened, so too did relations among the family members. Disharmony gave way to physical violence, which in turn inspired Gorky's grandfather to agree to the division of such assets as the family possessed, which act itself only precipitated the financial ruin of them all. Given the circumstances, it is easy to see why the young Gorky was viewed by his grandfather as an unnecessary encumbrance and how it was that, shortly after the death of his mother, the boy was sent away at the age of eleven to work for a living.

Although he returned to the Kashirin household on a number of occasions over the following years, Gorky spent the bulk of his time away from his family. His first job—as an assistant in a shoe shop—was succeeded by a series of equally menial, and sometimes degrading occupations. These experiences were truly soul-destroying and far worse in most respects than life had been at his grandparents', where he had at least known some degree of love and care. Now that he was out in the world, he witnessed the Russian provinces at their very worst. Venal, brutal, and insular, this was a world of quite senseless cruelty which he was later to describe so memorably in his autobiographical writings and in such fictional works as *Okurov Town* [*Gorodok Okurov*] and *The Life of Matvei Kozhemiakin*. The only bright spot during these years was supplied by his reading of literature, to which he was introduced by a man named Smury, the head cook on the *Dobryi*, a Volga paddle-steamer on which Gorky was employed for a while as a kitchen hand. It was through literature—first in the rather humble form of popular romance, later the classics of European and Russian literature—that he was enabled both to take temporary refuge from the rigours of his daily routine and to feed a youthful imagination which craved models of a better, more heroic life.

If these early experiences bred an intense idealism, they also developed in the young Gorky an equally intense spirit of resistance, which slowly matured into a conscious determination to work towards the creation of a better Russia. It was this determination which lay behind his decision, at the age of sixteen, to move to Kazan. Attracted in the first place by the thought that he might be able to study at the university in that city, he soon abandoned this idea, becoming involved instead in the dissident political life for which Kazan had long been famous. Over the next three years or so, he had dealings with a wide variety of underground groups, engaging both in the endless debates which animated the radical intelligentsia at that time and in the practical work of disseminating forbidden literature.

But if Gorky responded positively to the intellectual stimulation of his new life in Kazan, he was also sorely disappointed by what he found there. To his misfortune, his sojourn in the city came at a time when the Russian Populist movement—the dominant force in oppositional politics—was rife with the internal disputes which were to lead inexorably to its decline. Instead of encountering a family of rebels united in the common struggle against the evils afflicting their nation, Gorky came into contact with a heterogeneous collection of study circles and discussion groups which—or so at least it seemed to him—had allowed themselves to be diverted from the real task of revolution by engaging in arcane theoretical debates for which he had neither sympathy nor aptitude. He was also annoyed by the condescension with which he was often treated by those who looked upon him as a self-educated 'man of the people'.

Gorky's adolescent years were particularly influenced by his involvement with two men, both of whom were active in the revolutionary underground. The first was Andrei Derenkov, who operated a Kazan bakery which doubled as a secret library for books officially banned by the Russian government. Gorky went to work in the bakery, where he also participated in the illicit activities which went on behind the scenes. Although he evidently found this environment far more satisfying than the more intellectual circles to which he had been exposed, it was at

Derenkov's that he experienced the personal crisis which led him, on 12 December 1887, to make an attempt on his own life. It is, of course, impossible ever to plumb all the reasons for such desperate acts, but 1887 was significantly also the year in which both of Gorky's grandparents died. It would appear, however, that unrequited love for Derenkov's sister Mariia was the most direct stimulus for his suicide attempt.

Whatever the case, Gorky recovered quickly from the self-inflicted bullet-wound which had nearly killed him, and he soon left Kazan for the village of Krasnovidovo. He went there with the specific purpose of joining Mikhail Romas, a man of humble origins like Gorky himself, who had opened a village store in an effort both to serve the local peasants at large and to spread socialist ideas amongst those of their number open to persuasion. This was grass-roots revolution of a kind that Gorky would always relish, yet it all came to a calamitous end when a group of local peasants burned down the store and killed one of Romas's associates.

The Krasnovidovo débâcle was a terrible blow for the young Gorky. There can be little doubt that his enduring hatred for the Russian peasantry—both as a class and an *idea*—drew much of its power from the memory of this event. The immediate effect on his life was no less striking. Quite devastated by the appalling destruction he had witnessed, Gorky left the region for the first of his famous journeys on foot through the south of Russia, drifting from place to place before taking a job on the railway near Tsaritsyn (the latter-day Volgograd). It was from here that he wrote the letter to Tolstoy which opens this collection and which provides ample testimony both to his idealistic frame of mind and the particular restlessness of his life at this time.

In the end, however, Gorky returned to his native Nizhnii Novgorod, where he renewed his acquaintance with a number of his friends from the Kazan underground. These activities did not pass unnoticed by the authorities. Gorky was already a marked man, as were his associates, and it was little surprise that they were all arrested in October 1889, in connection with an investigation into the operation of a clandestine printshop in Kazan. Imprisoned briefly in Nizhnii, the future writer was released soon afterwards for want of conclusive evidence against him. But once again it was an affair of the heart which had the most decisive impact on his life at the time. The woman in question was Olga Kaminskaia. Ten years Gorky's senior, she was married with a four-year-old daughter. Even though Gorky found at least that his love was reciprocated on this occasion, Kaminskaia (rather wisely, one feels tempted to add) was unwilling to enter into a permanent liaison for the time being. This time too the young man sought an escape from his disappointment by setting out to tramp the south of the Russian Empire.

Gorky's nomadic existence came to an end in 1892. As it turned out, the year was significant in a number of respects. On 12 September, the

Tiflis newspaper *Kavkaz* [*Caucasus*] carried his first published story, 'Makar Chudra', thereby laying the foundation for the remarkable career of 'Maksim Gorky'. It was also in Tiflis that Gorky again encountered Olga Kaminskaia. Now divorced from her husband, she declared her willingness to set up house with the young writer, which the couple did on their return to Nizhnii Novgorod soon afterwards.

In the event, their relationship was not destined to last; indeed, the two years they spent together proved no more settled in many ways than the months of wandering that had gone before. Together with Kaminskaia and her daughter, Gorky took up residence in a converted bath-house which offered only the most primitive of comforts. The place soon achieved considerable local notoriety because of the wild gatherings which regularly took place there. Although one can easily imagine that this bohemian existence appealed to Gorky's rebellious urge simply to shock the local populace, it was not too long before he began to see that his relationship with Kaminskaia was, in the words of Filia Holtzman, an 'emotional fiasco'.[1] Highly sociable (not to mention flirtatious) by nature, she took no interest at all in Gorky's intellectual or literary interests. Indeed, it would be no injustice to say that what he did manage to achieve by way of writing at this time was done despite Kaminskaia's influence. Not that he could devote much time to writing anyway, as a great deal of his time had to be given over to his work as a clerk for the law firm of A. I. Lanin, which was the couple's main source of income. Things clearly could not go on this way for long, and pressure began to mount upon the young writer to extricate himself from a relationship which many of his acquaintances believed would be the ruination of him. Of these acquaintances the most noteworthy by far was Vladimir Korolenko, the Populist writer, whom Gorky had first met in 1889 and who now began to work behind the scenes to persuade the young man to move away from Nizhnii and Kaminskaia.

Korolenko it was who finally organized Gorky's departure from his native town for Samara, where he took up a post in March 1895 on one of the local newspapers, *Samarskaia gazeta* [*The Samara Gazette*]. This was a major turning-point for the young writer in every sense. Gorky himself summed things up well when he looked back on his life in 1930: 'I began to publish in 1892, but up until 1895, I did not believe that literature was my proper business.'[2] There can be little doubt that this final act of faith in his vocation was prompted above all by the publication that year (again through the active assistance of Korolenko) of his story 'Chelkash' in the prestigious Populist monthly *Russkoe bogatstvo* [*Russian Wealth*]. Over the next fourteen months he published more than two dozen other stories, an output which seems all the more remarkable when one realizes

[1] Filia Holtzman, *The Young Maxim Gorky 1868–1902* (New York, 1948): 23.
[2] *Kak my pishem* (Leningrad, 1930): 24.

that his journalistic commitments meant that he had to write upwards of 600 articles and *feuilletons* during the same period. Little wonder, then, that he spoke of journalism as 'hard labour',[3] or that the constant daily grind should have eventually undermined his health so completely that his friends came quite literally to fear for his life.

But if the move to Samara signalled a major change in Gorky's attitude to himself as a professional writer, he did not stay in the city for long. Before leaving Nizhnii for his new post, the writer had met Ekaterina Pavlovna Volzhina, who was working at the time as a proof-reader for *Nizhegorodskii listok* [*The Nizhnii Novgorod Sheet*]. The two conducted an intense correspondence during their enforced separation and Gorky took the first opportunity to return to Nizhnii, where they were married on 30 August 1896. Their son Maksim was born the following year, and their daughter Ekaterina in 1901.

Whilst marriage also contributed to Gorky's growing self-confidence— one memoirist speaks of how the young writer 'seemed somehow to draw himself up to his full height' in his new role as husband[4]—there are signs (not least from the letters included in this volume) that not all was well between the two young people. Even before their marriage, it is apparent that Volzhina had doubts about her future husband's faithfulness (see Letter 8). One also suspects, from the occasional irreverent references in Gorky's letters of various periods, that his mother-in-law was less than enthusiastic about her daughter's choice of mate. But the real problem clearly lay much deeper than this. As early as October 1897 Gorky was already experiencing real doubts about their relationship (Letter 9), and by May the following year he was all but instructing his wife to put an end to the relationship herself (Letter 12). But, for the time being, their marriage survived; it was actually to limp on into the new century. Only in 1903 did Gorky himself finally take the initiative to separate from his wife. Even though he was to live with a number of companions in subsequent years, the two were never officially divorced.

Gorky's troubles during these years were compounded by ill health. He was diagnosed as suffering from tuberculosis in 1896, and by the following year his condition was so bad that an application was made on his behalf to the St Petersburg Literary Fund for a grant to enable him to travel to the Crimea for treatment under the supervision of Dr A. N. Aleksin. Despite the jocular tone, Gorky was actually not joking when he later wrote to Mariia Basargina that he 'nearly made his final trip to the cemetery' on that occasion (Letter 17). This was only the first of several occasions in his life when Gorky was to come close to death from the effects of physical and emotional exhaustion on his frail constitution.

[3] Letter of 6 June 1896 to E. P. Volzhina, *Perepiska* 1: 66.
[4] A. A. Treplev, 'Kak M. Gor'kii nachal svoiu kar'eru', *Biulleteni literatury i zhizni*, no. 3, 1913: 162.

But the trip to the Crimea had the desired effect. After undergoing treatment, Gorky moved to the village of Manuilovka near Poltava for a period of convalescence. The relief from the stresses and strains of the previous year was reflected in his literary output: in 1897 he wrote far fewer stories, but they were much longer and included a number of pieces which remain among his most significant early works, such as 'Konovalov', 'The Orlovs' ['Suprugi Orlovy'], 'Varenka Olesova', and 'Former People' ['Byvshie liudi'].

By the end of 1897, Gorky already had a considerable body of published work to his name and he began to make approaches to publishers with a view to putting out a selection of his stories in book form. Although he received a number of rebuffs, the St Petersburg firm of Dorovatovsky and Charushnikov eventually agreed to publish his *Sketches and Stories* [*Ocherki i rasskazy*] in two volumes in 1898. What nobody could have predicted—all the more so as it was an event quite unprecedented in the history of Russian literature—was the enormous success this publication was to enjoy. The initial printing was sold out almost immediately; further editions followed in swift succession, as did a third volume containing more short stories.

The impact of this event was truly momentous. Almost instantly, Gorky emerged from provincial obscurity to occupy the spotlight of national celebrity. His name was almost literally on everybody's lips. He began to make much-publicized trips to Moscow and St Petersburg, where he attracted the sort of attention associated nowadays with the world of Hollywood. He also came to meet his great contemporaries Chekhov (in 1899) and Tolstoy (in 1900). In short, it was an extraordinary time for the young writer and he reacted to his new-found fame with a typical mixture of gaucheness and arrogance. But there were signs from the outset that he had already understood that his new position in Russian life offered him the opportunity he had been waiting for. For now, at long last, he had a real chance to make his mark on the intellectual life of his country.

The letters in this section provide considerable insight into Gorky's troubled personal life, his literary 'apprenticeship' in the provinces, and his rise to national celebrity. Yet much as they might have to tell us about the early life of this eternally 'restless' man, two questions will continue to loom large for the would-be biographer. The first concerns politics, the second literature. In each case, it is a matter of trying to 'place' Gorky in relation to the great debates of the age.

With regard to politics, one thing at least was clear from the outset. In Gorky's person, the Russian government had found an implacable enemy, a man sworn from an early age to work actively for revolutionary change. Far less clear, however, is where exactly the young writer stood in relation to the competing groups striving for supremacy within the revolutionary movement itself. Gorky's engagement with radical politics came at a crucial moment in the history of political opposition in Russia. His first encounters, as we have seen, were with the Populist groups which still dominated the scene in the 1880s. The Populists promoted a broadly socialist philosophy which centred on the peasant commune as the primary means through which the radical transformation of Russia could take place. This position came under increasing attack by the end of the decade, especially from the growing band of Russian Marxists who believed that the coming Russian revolution would have to be a proletarian, not a peasant one.

Gorky encountered both Populists and Marxists during his years in the provinces. And, as we already know, he was involved actively enough with these groups to be identified as politically 'unreliable' from a very early age. But if we are to understand the precise nature of his involvement with radical groups at the time, we would perhaps do best to begin with a statement made in 1899 to the artist Repin: 'I do not belong anywhere as yet, not to any of our "parties". I am glad of that, for it is freedom' (Letter 18). These words are revealing in a number of ways. Striking first of all for their obvious scepticism (the use of inverted commas tells it all), they suggest that Gorky's distaste for the actual conduct of oppositional politics was still quite strong. Even more revealing in this respect is a remark made earlier in the same year in a letter to Chekhov, to whom he had confessed: 'I think that all these political parties of theirs have little to do with real life' (Letter 15). In retrospect, however, it is the phrase 'as yet' in the Repin letter which is the most suggestive of all. For what this implies is that Gorky already realized that his new prominence in Russian life meant that some choice of allegiance would have to be made in the future. Indeed, that choice was very soon to be made.

It would be best to say, then, that the century closed with Gorky caught in a no man's land between Populism and Marxism. Yet there is nothing in these letters to tell us about the precise nature of his feelings towards either movement at this time. We may be sure, however, that he was suspicious of Populism for its faith in the Russian peasantry. (The memory of Krasnovidovo would have made sure of that.) As for the Marxists, it seems likely that their insistence upon the 'laws' governing social development, together with the consequent diminution of the role of the individual in human history, was ill-designed to appeal to the mind of this essentially romantic young man.[5] In fact, it is quite evident that Gorky was really very poorly attuned to the realities of political life and its attendant intellectual debates—witness his suggestion to Chekhov that the journal *Zhizn'* was striving to achieve 'a *merging* of Populism and

[5] Vladimir Posse later remarked in his memoirs: 'Gorky had no sympathy at this time for Marxism, which demeaned the human personality, in his view.' V. A. Posse, *Moi zhiznennyi put'* (Moscow–Leningrad, 1929): 126.

Marxism into a single harmonious whole' (Letter 15, emphasis added). No wonder so many of his contemporaries (including Lenin himself on a later occasion) were inclined to speak most dismissively of his political acumen.

If the great debate of the 1890s in Russian revolutionary politics was between the Populists and the Marxists, the crucial issue in literary life was the rise of new, Modernist trends to challenge the dominant tradition of so-called 'civic' writing. The latter tradition was associated in particular with the works of such Populist writers as Vladimir Korolenko, who sought quite consciously to appeal to the social conscience of their fellow citizens by composing sketches and stories depicting (often in the starkest tones) life as it was lived in the Russian village. Gorky read all the major works by Korolenko and other Populist writers during the 1880s. He even met many of these writers in person during his early manhood. But it was Korolenko who had the biggest part to play in promoting the younger writer's career by providing him with advice and support of every kind. Gorky later wrote to Korolenko himself: 'you were my teacher and you did me a lot of good' (Letter 14), an admission which he was to repeat publicly in an autobiographical notice written at the same time. Once again, however, we would do well to attend carefully to the implications of a statement which suggests that, at the time of writing (November 1898), Gorky already looked upon Korolenko's influence as something which belonged—like the Populist movement itself—very much to the *past*. Whilst he remained grateful to a man whom he saw as a living embodiment of the ideal of committed writing, Gorky was already determined to define his own independent position as Russian literature entered its 'post-Populist' phase.

Gorky was encouraged in his quest for new directions by the emergence of a whole generation of writers who had begun to question the vitality of Russian literature. This position found its most celebrated expression in Dmitrii Merezhkovsky's pamphlet *On the Reasons for the Decline in Russian Literature* [*O prichinakh upadka v russkoi literature*]. Published in 1893—the year after Gorky's début as a writer—it gave voice to a complaint which was to be repeated by many other early spokesmen for the 'new aesthetics'. The crux of their argument was that the Russian Populists, with their emphasis on the naturalistic depiction of *realia* and their determination to appeal to the civic conscience of their educated audience, had converted literature into a mere offshoot of journalism. The answer, they believed, lay in the invigoration of Russian literature with an injection of the 'new trends' which were already sweeping Europe, such as French Decadent poetry.

Gorky's early letters display the extent to which he was embroiled in these developments. His interest in the 'new currents of feeling and thought' is announced in a letter to B. V. Ber, where he refers in particular to contemporary French literature and the works of d'Annunzio and Maeterlinck (Letter 6). Other letters show that he was reading both Merezhkovsky and Nietzsche, who was perhaps the most important single influence on the development of the new literary movements (Letter 11). More interesting still—surprising even for those who have been accustomed to look upon Gorky as one who stood resolutely against the rise of Modernism in Russian literature—is his admiration for the Decadent poems of Zinaida Gippius and his declaration to Akim Volynsky (another of the prime movers in the new literature) that he looked upon the opportunity of collaboration with him as a personal honour (Letter 10).

But in the world of literature, as in the world of political opposition, Gorky was to find it necessary to align himself clearly with one side or other in the debate which was already threatening to divide Russian literature. In fact, there were already clear signs by 1900 that the choice had effectively been made. In his own writing, Gorky had abandoned the short story in favour of the novel. *Foma Gordeev* was published in 1899; it was followed by *The Three* in 1901. Morcover, the latter year was also significant in that it marked Gorky's début as a dramatist with his writing of the play *The Petty Bourgeois*. As critics at the time were quick to appreciate, there was much more to this than a mere shift of genre. The 'Maksim Gorky' whose novels and plays were to stand at the forefront of politically purposeful writing throughout the first decade of the twentieth century in Russia was quite different from the 'Maksim Gorky' who had achieved fame with his short tales of romantic protest and yearning in the 1890s. Equally significant was his growing involvement in editorial work, first with Viktor Miroliubov's *Zhurnal dlia vsekh* [*Journal for All*], a publication which (as its very name suggests) was directed at a democratic audience, then with Vladimir Posse's *Zhizn'*, a 'progressive' journal of Marxist orientation. Gorky had thus already taken a major step in the direction of organizational work designed to promote the cause of revolution amongst a broad readership. It was very much the shape of things to come.

Writing in 1914, the critic S. A. Vengerov reported that he had first heard of Maksim Gorky in 1897, at which time he 'was told that [he] was a man of talent, although he was very unbalanced'.[6] The letters translated here provide ample support for this view. What we see here is a young man trying—quite desperately at times—to orientate himself in politics, in literature, and in life itself. There is a story here for those who wish to find it—the story of a troubled young man whose insecurity and sense of inferiority undergo a characteristic reversal as he comes to speak with greater certainty, even belligerence at times. It is also an Oedipal

---

[6] S. A. Vengerov, *Russkaia literatura XX veka 1890–1910*, vol. 1 (Moscow, 1914): 189.

story of sorts; his initial reliance on father figures—Tolstoy and Korolenko, in particular (see Letters 1 and 4)—being displaced by a fierce determination to strike out on his own, and even to serve as a 'father' to others. The same process of inversion is displayed by another typical gesture: the man who regularly speaks disparagingly of his lack of education ('I consider it necessary to tell you that I am an ignoramus, for I am a self-taught man'—Letter 11) is equally capable of displaying his utter disdain for those more fortunate than himself ('I cannot bear the "educated" and "cultured" public'—Letter 17).

In the light of these examples, it is little wonder that Gorky himself should have been moved to say of himself: 'My God, I am so full of contradictions' (Letter 7). But of all these contradictions there is none so revealing as that between scepticism and faith. Here, for example, is what Gorky had to say in 1897: 'About myself I know only one thing for sure—that I was born an idealist, but now I am becoming a sceptic, because people are vulgar and petty, whilst life itself is dreary and dark' (Letter 11). Yet in 1899 he was to write to Repin, again on the subject of man: 'He is everything. He even created God [. . .] I am convinced that man is capable of perfecting himself endlessly' (Letter 18). Tempting though it might be to adduce this as evidence of Gorky's 'development' from scepticism to faith, the attentive reader will see that these are perhaps more properly seen as the extremes between which he was to vacillate at various stages of his long career.

1. To L. N. Tolstoy, [25 April 1889]

[Moscow]

Lev Nikolaevich!

I called at your homes at Iasnaia Poliana and in Moscow; I was told that you were ill and could not receive visitors.[1]

I have decided to write you a letter. The point is this: a number of people who work for the G.–Ts. rlwy.[2]—including the writer of this letter—have been taken with the idea of independent, personal labour and of living in the country. We have decided to devote ourselves to agriculture. But although we all receive a salary—about 30 roubles a month, on average—our private savings are quite paltry, and we would have to wait a very long time until they reached the amount necessary for setting up a smallholding.

And so we have decided to turn to you for help. We have heard that you have a lot of land which is not being worked. We are asking you to give us a piece of this land.

Also, besides assistance of a purely material kind, we are hoping for your moral assistance, for advice and instructions which would facilitate the successful achievement of our goal. We also trust that you will not refuse to give us copies of your books *Confession, My Faith* and so on, which have been prohibited from sale.[3]

We hope that whatever you might think of our endeavour—whether you find it worthy of your attention and support or simply empty and extravagant—you will not refuse to answer us. This will not take much of your time. If you would like to learn more about us and what we have already done towards the realization of our endeavour, one or two of us would be able to come and visit you. We are relying on your help.

On behalf of everyone,

Yours sincerely,

Aleksei Maksimov Peshkov,
Nizhnii Novgorod *meshchanin*[4]

SOURCE: *SS* 28: 5–6.

---

[1] Gorky visited Tolstoy's Iasnaia Poliana estate on 14 April, but the writer was in Moscow.

[2] Gorky was writing on behalf of a study group at the Krutaia station on the Griaze–Tsaritsyn railway.

[3] *Confession* [*Ispoved'*] and *What I Believe* [*V chem moia vera?*], like other writings by Tolstoy on religious subjects, were prohibited under the conditions of church censorship and were available only illicitly.

[4] Gorky was officially a member of the *meshchanstvo*, or lower-middle class.

2. *To I. A. Kartikovsky,*[1] *[beginning of 1892]*

[Tiflis]

[. . .] In short, this is my outward life: from 9 till 4—work, from 4 till 5—rest, from 5 till 9—reading (I'm free from this only on Wednesdays and Sundays), from 9 till 11 or 12—discussions, debates, and so on, and from 12 till 3 or 4—I read and write for myself. It's all very lively, as you can see!

Three weeks ago I went completely mad. I was put in hospital and released after ten days. I'm fine now.

What is this life of ours? Is it something final or a transition towards some better condition? This question will be the end of me. I will end up either putting a bullet in my forehead or else going totally mad. I would prefer the former, of course. Well, even if it is to be the end of me, I will not give in to it, no matter what!

I want to live, my dear friend! I want love, there's [. . .][2] I want to bow my head before it and rule over it; I want friendship which is pure, honest, and deeply understanding; I want beauty and everything that is good.

And I have nothing! I am destitute and wretched.

I do have you, of course, but how seldom I hear from you! I have a letter now, but then I'll have to wait six months before I get another.

In any case, I know what people are like—because I know myself—and their affections change so often.

You are a person, and I have the right to think that our friendship, like everything in life, will quickly die.

M.I.M.?[3] She doesn't understand me. But oh, how good and humane she is! So here I am alone. Solitude is itself a great and wonderful thing, it indicates a profound nature; and yet man will always thirst for earthly things, no matter how high he might be in the heavens. What a beast he is, my friend.

When man [soars] with his head in the heavens, his legs dangle in the air, where they are at the mercy of the winds. Every life is vile, my son, if you look into it deeply enough. Love alone is great and sacred, but given the present-day knack for debasing everything, it too has been soiled by all kinds of filth and has fled from our lives. So just enjoy its ghost and don't kick up a fuss!

The animate objects which masquerade as people and populate the town of Tiflis are no worse than those of Kazan or any other place. They are just as false, proud, hypocritical—and infinitely pathetic. They are just the same in not wanting to understand life and themselves, just the same in their 'striving'—but a striving for what? For anything which promises some recompense.

You say that I'm a dilettante and that this is why I feel bad. Perhaps that is so.

But long live dilettantism! For although it is agonizing and short-lived, it is all-embracing and beautiful! In my opinion it's better to experience more than to live longer.

A specialist is a dull, long-living brute who knows nothing except his own corner. He is a worker and a slave. A dilettante is sometimes a worker but never a slave.

My son! 'Life was given to us for living'[4]—that means take all that you dare to take. But those idiot rigorists think that life is either a battle, or a duty, or the devil knows what other sort of rubbish. Life is simply pleasure, and if we have ruined it to such an extent, then it is our duty to give it a form which inspires [. . .]

SOURCE: *Perepiska* 1: 36–7.

[1] Ivan Aleksandrovich Kartikovsky (1869–1931), student at Kazan University and a friend of Gorky in his youth. This letter is preserved in an incomplete form.
[2] Defect in the original.
[3] M. I. Metlina, a Nizhnii Novgorod acquaintance.
[4] A line from I. P. Kliushnikov's poem 'Life' ['Zhizn''] of 1840.

3. *To N. K. Mikhailovsky,*[1] *[end of October 1894]*

[Nizhnii Novgorod]

Dear Nikolai Konstantinovich!

You know how difficult and humiliating it is to be in need, and I hope you will look upon my request simply and favourably.

I'm asking you for a cash advance[2]—I need to pay fifty roubles by the tenth. No one here will lend me anything, since I'm already in debt to them all as it is. I feel awful asking. But I need the money . . . I need to live. Fifty roubles then!

Yours,

A. Peshkov
[N. Novgorod, Polevaia, Prilezhaev House]

SOURCE: *Perepiska* 1: 42.

[1] Nikolai Konstantinovich Mikhailovsky (1842–1904), critic and theorist of the Russian Populist movement, editor of the monthly *Russkoe bogatstvo*.
[2] Gorky had submitted two stories—'Chelkash' and 'By the Sea' ['U moria']—for publication in *Russkoe bogatstvo*. Only the former work was eventually published there.

4. To V. G. Korolenko,[1] [beginning of March 1895]

[Samara]

Dear Vladimir Galaktionovich!

As usual, I have a favour to ask.

Asheshov[2] has charged me with making the following request of you. Be so kind as to undertake the task of indicating the faults of *Samarskaia gazeta* and give us an outline of what you would like it to be.

Conditions at the newspaper are sufficiently favourable at present for such improvement to seem quite possible.

The publisher loves the business and is not sparing with money.[3]

Censorship is quite mild at the moment.

The chief editor, Asheshov, seems to me a very intelligent and energetic man.

Your advice and instructions would be of enormous importance to the newspaper . . . So be so good as to answer this letter as soon as possible.

I run the newspaper's 'Sketches and Essays' section.

Tell me, what do you think of the way I deal with facts? And what do you think of the value of facts as such? And what about the tone? Asheshov says that I need to write in a more lively manner.

I'm trying to do so. But it's obviously not my speciality, and I think that at times I lapse into a vulgar-mocking tone—*à la* 'His Mother's Son'.[4] What do you think? I try to restrain myself, but then everything turns out so dreary.

I'm begging you please to help both the paper and me with your advice and criticism.

I await your answer. Give my regards to Avdotia Semenovna and the Annenskys.[5] I left their books back in Nizhnii and I've already written to say that they should be returned to their owners. Be so good as to ask whether they've been received.

Well, goodbye for now.

I wish you all the best.

Yours,

A. Peshkov

N.B. Have you forgotten your promise to send me a photograph and the first book of your stories? Don't forget, Vladimir Galaktionovich!

What about my 'Mistake'?[6] Have you sent it off yet?

Good heavens! How I must be getting on your nerves! But what am I to do? . .

Please answer this letter as quickly as you can! It's very important for me to receive some instructions from you right now. When I said that Asheshov is energetic and intelligent, I forgot to tell you that he's young as well. In such an important enterprise, an enterprise of major social sig-

nificance, youth is scarcely a virtue. Asheshov's position is important—
he's the conductor of the orchestra. Outside instructions are essential for
him. Your instructions are more valuable than anyone else's. You live in
the provinces and you're well acquainted with the provincial press.
Address:

Samara,

The editor's office,

Samarskaia gazeta

SOURCE: *Perepiska* 1: 47–8.

---

[1] Vladimir Galaktionovich Korolenko (1853–1921), the outstanding writer of Russian Populism.
See the Introduction to this section for further details.

[2] As Gorky explains later in this letter, Nikolai Petrovich Asheshov was chief editor of *Samarskaia gazeta*.

[3] The merchant Semen Ivanovich Kosterin had acquired the newspaper in 1894.

[4] Gorky has in mind the style adopted by V. M. Doroshevich, who wrote under a number of *noms de plume*, including the one mentioned here.

[5] Korolenko's wife. On Annensky, see Letter 14, n. 5.

[6] Gorky submitted a story with this title ['Oshibka'] for publication in *Russkoe bogatstvo* in March 1895. It was rejected.

5. To V. G. Korolenko, [23 June 1895]

[Samara]

Dear Vladimir Galaktionovich!

I still haven't thanked you for your last letter. I've been constantly
unwell and in an awful temper.

My dear Vladimir Galaktionovich, I'm very depressed, for I feel that
I'm beginning to lose my way.

You probably saw three *feuilletons* with the signature 'Paskarello' in
Samarskaia gazeta—they are all my work, great sinner that I am.[1]

In these *feuilletons* I wanted to explain simply and sincerely everything
I have endured through my association with the provincial press. I
wished to point out its fatal dilettantism and its bad influence on society.
I also wanted to point out that an awful lot of people are worming their
way into the press who have no sense of vocation. In itself this is of no
matter, but these are people without honour or conscience—that is
what's so dreadful.

I see many other sad things in our press. This is new for me, and I
thought that I'd be able to say this in a new way, or at least 'in the old
way', but better. But the good intention simply remained inside me,
whilst what came out in my *feuilletons* was filth.

The censor cleaned them up, the editor shortened them and removed the more serious passages out of a desire not to disturb the general tone.

This would have been of no matter, but just at that very same time *Samarskii vestnik* [*The Samara Messenger*] made a coarse, base attack on Asheshov, Bulanina, Gusev, and myself. The devil must have prompted me to make a reply. Yesterday they, in turn, replied to me.

Well, I have lost forever any desire to 'polemicize'. They've knocked it out of me. It was a good lesson, and one that I won't forget. But it is all done in such a terribly coarse and dirty fashion.

And do you know what? The gentlemen who once left *Samarskaia gazeta* on 'a point of principle'—Klafton, Tsimmerman, Grigoriev, even Chirikov,[2] I hear—are all contributing to *Vestnik*, which is a base newspaper whichever way you look at it!

Perhaps they're embellishing it with their presence?

Alas, these are the very people who polemicize with us, calling Asheshov Balalaikin,[3] and pointing out that he's 'been to court several times', and so on in the same vein. They attack Gusev time and time again.

They write *feuilletons* full of hints and *double entendres*. I can't believe that Chirikov is also there, but they claim that the *feuilletons* signed 'A Tourist' are his!

All this torments me greatly.

What is more, it's all very petty, base, and quite without talent.

Our newspapers are insufficiently serious in their attitude to life. The people who stand 'at the helm' say that the public loves a 'light style' and that this is what it must be given whether we like it or not.

That's the way it is! And what about offering 'society' a guiding light? That task has been rejected, you see, because of its insoluble nature.

Where are we to lead people? Everything has been shaken loose.

It seems to me that the soul has come adrift from its moorings. Everything is the same as it always was, but now man's soul is frightened and exhausted; it has gone astray in the darkness of life.

All right, I know this isn't news to you.

I'm very sad, Vladimir Galaktionovich!

Somehow I'm sad about everything. I was in Nizhnii about a month ago, but I couldn't call on you—I only had three days and I was there on demanding and difficult business.[4] And I wasn't well either.

Please don't consider this a mark of disrespect for you.

Dear V. G., I'm asking you seriously to send me your photograph and your first book. I'd like to receive these from you while you are in Nizhnii, because, once you have left for Petersburg,[5] I may not see you again, since I'll probably be leaving Russia for somewhere or other myself.

Be so good as not to forget this request of mine.

Goodbye for now!
Give my respectful regards to your family and friends.
Yours,

A. Peshkov

SOURCE: *Korolenko*: 40–1.

[1] 'Several Days in the Role of Editor of a Provincial Newspaper' ['Neskol'ko dnei v roli redaktora provintsial'noi gazety'], a series of satirical articles which sparked a sharp exchange between *Samarskaia gazeta* and its rival, *Samarskii vestnik*.
[2] Evgenii Nikolaevich Chirikov (1864–1932), writer who later became closely involved in the Znanie miscellanies (see pp. 49–50 for details). His relations with Gorky soured after the 1905 Revolution.
[3] A comic name, derived from 'balalaika'.
[4] i.e. the breakup of his relationship with Olga Kaminskaia.
[5] Korolenko actually left for the Russian capital in January 1896.

6. To B. V. Ber,[1] [about 1 October 1895]

[Samara]

I received your letter and was most surprised by its passionate tone. What's the matter with you? To be honest, enthusiasm doesn't suit you. You've got to be more of a sceptic, for that is more valuable, and the main thing is it's more beautiful. Forgive me for giving you advice . . . I did, of course, enjoy reading your letter—I am human, after all. Your praise is all the more pleasant since I have no cause to doubt its sincerity. Thank you, my dear friend! It's really bad for me here. There isn't a single person who is familiar with the new currents of feeling and thought. And there are no followers of the old truth either, at least no sincere ones. The city is 'not intellectual' as the radicals say. There are no interesting people in the city is what I would say. There are neither men nor women with whom it would be possible to live or experience things in any full or proper way. Everything and everyone is boring.

Have you read Annunzio's *The Triumph of Death*?[2]

It's a good book. Do you happen to know anything about the new literary school in France—the school of someone called Hello?[3] Can you lay your hands on any sources on the history of the new literature in France? I love that country, it's always on the boil and they're always cooking up something original over there. If I were in your position, I'd go to Paris.

So you predict that I have a future. . .

Well, you should know that you do so in vain. I'll have a job to dance my way any further than where I've got to right now. The newspaper will devour me. That is a fact. I've also started to drink. And my chest is weak. These are three large boulders which stand in my path. And if I were to add that I have no desire either to jump over them or to walk around them—then it should be clear that I have no future whatever.

I don't need one either. Everything is vanity of vanities and vexation of spirit![4]

That's the truth. It's the best truth of the entire assortment which is at man's disposal. It does not demand that you submit to it. Once you have mastered it, it doesn't require that it be served. It is cold and impassive, and nothing more.

In your letter you don't say a word about yourself or your intentions. What are you up to? Don't forget that I find this all very interesting.

Are you writing and, if so, what are you writing? What's happened to your translations of Maeterlinck?[5] If possible, please send them to me— I really need to read them for a certain reason.[6]

I'm not writing any more for the time being. I'm acting editor of the paper for a while and I get very tired. This newspaper work is like an Egyptian plague! I'd really like to escape from here but I'm up to my neck in debt.

Goodbye for now.

Yours,

A. Peshkov

SOURCE: *Volga*, no. 5, 1966: 129–30.

[1] Boris Vladimirovich Ber (1871–1921), poet and translator with whom Gorky became acquainted in 1890 in Nizhnii.

[2] D'Annunzio's novel *Il trionfo della morte* appeared in a Russian translation in 1894.

[3] Ernest Hello (1828–85), founder of *Revue du monde catholique* and author of critical and philosophical essays often strongly mystical in tendency.

[4] A favourite phrase of Gorky's and a conflation of motifs from *Ecclesiastes* (1: 2; 5: 17; 11: 10; etc.).

[5] Ber is known to have been translating Maeterlinck's collection *Serres chaudes* in 1893.

[6] In connection, perhaps, with his work on the article 'Paul Verlaine and the Decadents' ['Pol′ Verlen i dekadenty'].

7. To E. P. Volzhina,[1] [25 May 1896]

[Nizhnii Novgorod]

It's night, and it's windy and raining. I am alone and I cannot sleep. My heart is filled with melancholy, so I have got up to write you a letter. I am, God save me, a very restless man and a most incomprehensible one. My God, I am so full of contradictions. Davydov[2]—a very clever fellow, let me say—maintains that, were I to allow myself to be sincere, I would be impossible to love. Perhaps he's right, Katia . . . For the sake of your own self-preservation, you ought to think what it is you actually like about Aleksei Maksimovich Peshkov. I know him well. Would you like me to talk to you about him?

Above all, Peshkov is insufficiently clear and simple, he is too convinced of the fact that he is unlike other people and plays on this too much, all the more so as it's an open question whether he really is unlike other people at all. This may be sheer affectation. But that affectation enables him to make unreasonable demands of others and to treat them somewhat haughtily. It's as if Peshkov were the only intelligent one and all the others were idiots and dolts. Overall, Peshkov has raised to perfection the fault of holding an exaggerated opinion of oneself. He is rude and uncultivated too, which you must also take into account. He is irritable. He is even malicious sometimes. These are certainly not qualities of the finest sort. Such is his psychology.

Now for his social position. What place in life can you be guaranteed by a wandering writer, a man whose pockets are full one day and empty the next? A vagrant life, full of reverses and deprivations—that is what awaits you. His writing for the [thick] journals, as you know, is still just a pipe-dream. He has no time to devote to such writing. Irregular income creates irregular needs. Such is his sociology.

His physique. He will, I believe, kick the bucket before too long. Acute rheumatism is an ailment which kills people when it recurs. His chest is weak. His back aches. Overall, he is an old devil who needs a nursemaid, not a wife. My darling, that is not for you at all. But the main thing is that he is difficult to understand; he doesn't even understand himself in actual fact. He is a broken and confused figure. As well as these very serious shortcomings, there are others, some of which I have forgotten, others which I don't know about, and others still which I don't want to talk about—it would be tedious to do so and anyway I feel sorry for Peshkov, whom I love. I am the only one who really does love him, in fact. Overall, I am warning you in all seriousness, Katia, that this is a man with many peculiarities. At times I am inclined to think that he is oddly intelligent, but more often I think that he is just curiously stupid. The main thing is that he is too incomprehensible, that's his misfortune.

For all these reasons, you should think hard about Peshkov, Katia.

I will return to this subject again. But that's enough for now! It's depressing to tear pieces of meat from one's own heart.

Marakuev[3] will be here in a week. Asheshov[4] will be able to tell him all sorts of vile things about me. I don't know what Asheshov has against me, but he holds me in extremely low regard. Anyway, let them think what they like! They flatter you to your face, then slander you behind your back, as people generally do. That doesn't bother me. They are all such clever folks here—it even makes you laugh to look at them. Katia, Katia, how bad my life is, how lonely I am here.

Regards,

Your Aleksei

SOURCE: *AG* 5: 22–3.

[1] Ekaterina Pavlovna Volzhina (1878–1965) was soon to become Gorky's wife. For further details see the main Introduction and the Introduction to this section.

[2] Dmitrii Iakovlevich Davydov, journalist with *Samarskaia gazeta*.

[3] Vladimir Nikolaevich Marakuev (d. 1921), publisher and editor of *Odesskie novosti* [*Odessa News*] in the mid-1890s.

[4] Contributor to *Samarskaia gazeta*, see Letter 5.

8. To E. P. Volzhina, [27 July 1896]

[Nizhnii Novgorod]

As if to spite me, she still hasn't come![1] I just wish she would arrive soon and then go away again. I was sitting at home this morning doing some writing—and extremely *déshabillé*—when, instead of her, two uncharitable Samara women appeared in my room—a red one and a yellow one.[2] They appeared and—God bless them!—they handed me a letter from you. The most important thing I learned from this was that you have not received a single one of my letters, even though, to date, since the Sunday after you left, I have written some eight letters to your two addresses—this is the ninth. And then it turns out that you sent me a telegram which I didn't receive. I doubt that you received mine either. What does all this mean, Katia?

Ponomareva & Co. have set themselves up for the time being on Zeveke's floating hotel.[3] I'll move them over here tomorrow. I would have done so even today, but when I first read your letter, I overlooked your suggestion that I do this, and by the time I had read it properly they had already left.

Once again, I am glad that you are getting back to normal.

It is said of me that I am too readily attracted to women, Katia. But the first thing is, who says so? Women themselves. Think about that, Katia. Perhaps they say so for the following reason.

When women meet me, they see in me a romantic vagrant, eternally dissatisfied with everyone and everything, eternally engaged in a melancholy quest for something and always singing of women, always filled with a feeling of reverence towards them for the tenderness of their souls, for the beauty of their bodies, and the gentleness of their minds. They are proud and ambitious, like all people. Every one of them without fail wishes to do something for this vagrant tormented by melancholy, to show him a little feeling out of their own generosity, to ease his hard and difficult life, to inspire his love and gratitude towards them. His attitude towards all women is equally calm and assured, and his admiration for them is purely abstract. And when he sees that they wish to offer him alms, he walks away—again quite calmly—taking not the slightest offence at their honourable intention. For he has long known that people are stupid and coarse. The charitable women are surprised. What? He has gone, and so coldly too? They are quite unable to explain such strange behaviour to themselves. To begin with, this man was close and intimate, but as soon as he was given to understand that even greater intimacy was possible, he walked away.

And because they are unable to explain this in any other way, they say: 'Oh, look how he is attracted to women!' They say this and believe that it is actually true. In reality he carries his ideal within him and says nothing. This is precisely what happened with El[ena] Mikhail[ovna].[4] You see, she believed that I needed love, like everyone else, and that I was inclined to treat love the same way as everyone else too. But although I like to write romances, conducting them is not my speciality.[5]

Basically, I am more serious than I seem.

Goodbye for now. Don't think too much about my passion for women—honestly, there is no truth in it. It is just a story which is being put about, like so many other things.

Mar[akuev] has still not come, nor has he sent the money. Give everyone my regards.

Ever yours,

Aleksei

SOURCE: *AG* 5: 41–2.

[1] Presumably a jocular reference to an expected visit by Volzhina herself.
[2] The sisters M. D. and F. D. Rozenblium, both friends of Volzhina; Gorky's description of them as 'uncharitable' is, of course, ironic.
[3] Elena Efimovna Ponomareva, an employee of *Samarskaia gazeta*.
[4] Chernova, the wife of Vladimir Aleksandrovich Chernov. Gorky was friendly with the entire family in Nizhnii in 1893–5.
[5] A play on the word *roman*, which in Russian means both 'romance' and 'novel'.

9. *To E. P. Peshkova,*[1] *[12 October 1897]*

[Manuilovka[2]]

I was quite startled by your letter, Katia.[3] I understand your mood and I knew that it was bound to arise. It is not your mood that startles me, but the fact that you can only talk to me like this from a distance of a thousand miles. I am unable to explain this to myself.

In essence I'm replying to say that your fear is unfounded because, if you have the desire to do so, it is always possible to create for yourself the kind of life that you want for yourself. I will gladly help you to learn to respect yourself—which is something you're unable to do at the moment. I love you not only as a man and a husband, I love you also— and perhaps above all—as a friend. There's no doubt that you're right— life is not given to us for kissing, embracing, bearing children, and constraining our souls. It has spiritual needs which are sacred. So what are you afraid of? Our relations? Although they're not good, at least they're better than those of other people. Just wait, we'll drop anchor somewhere after all. Then we'll have a talk about how to make you more free. Maksimka[4] won't get in the way of anything, and so long as you don't lose your way trying to understand yourself, you'll be all right. I always find it good to be with you, even if I'm sometimes irritable, etc. It will always be like this, I think. It's my nature, and anyway I don't really want to be calm at all.

Let's talk about something else. I received a letter from Korchagin with a firm proposal to publish a book.[5] I refused, but promised to call on him when I'm in Moscow. Perhaps I should publish with him though? The thing is that this winter I'll get some good things done. So far I'm pleased with 'the novel'.[6] When I've finished it, I'll start another very original work.[7] So should I wait?

And another thing. I get the impression from your letter that you're not happy in Kamennoe. Think about it and tell me whether on the whole it really would suit you to spend the winter there. Don't worry about me. I'm into the swing of work right now, and it will make no difference to me—I could even write in a chimney. But why are you so touchy with Zina, and is it really impossible to get her out of the way? I don't know Zina well, but she has always seemed intelligent to me.[8]

The letter with the request for money went off just yesterday to *Novoe slovo* [*New Word*].[9] Orlovskaia[10] very rarely posts mail to Galeshchina,[11] just to spite me. Yesterday I caused her to have a real fit.

It's started raining here. I'm in a hurry to finish so that I can catch the post. I ask you to calm down and to be more easy in your dealings with me. I'm yours alone, just as you are mine.

Yours.

SOURCE: *Perepiska* 1: 72–3.

[1] Gorky and Volzhina were married on 30 August 1896.

[2] A village in the Crimea, where Gorky was staying after undergoing treatment for tuberculosis under the direction of Dr A. N. Aleksin (1863–1923).

[3] The letter has not been found. It was almost certainly one of those 'personal' letters destroyed by mutual consent.

[4] The couple's son, born on 27 July 1897.

[5] Korchagin wanted to publish a volume of stories by Gorky.

[6] *Foma Gordeev*, Gorky's first novel.

[7] Possibly a reference to 'The Career of Mishka Viagin' ['Kar'era Mishki Viagina'], an unrealized plan for a novella.

[8] Zinaida Vladimirovna Vasilieva.

[9] Gorky published his story 'Former People' in the October and November issues of this journal for 1897.

[10] Aleksandra Andreevna Orlovskaia owned the estate where Gorky stayed in 1897 and 1900.

[11] A post-station on the railway, 20 km. from Manuilovka.

10. To A. L. Volynsky,[1] *[no earlier than 29 October 1897]*

[Kamennoe]

I have already told you, Akim Lvovich, how I view you personally[2]—now your letter prompts me to say something of the journal.[3] Yours is the best Russian journal, for it has something new to say which is genuinely Russian and necessary for life. If people were to stop being idealists, what would distinguish them from wild animals? I regard collaboration with you as an honour for myself, and even if you hadn't invited me, I would have come to you anyway, although perhaps not so soon. My talent is slight and very crude—that is what accounts for the artificiality of my descriptive passages, by the way—but it seems to me that I am still just learning to write. Everything I have written is insignificant and ugly; there is no other way of putting it if one loves the truth.

Are you really upset by all this silly fault-finding against you? Are you really pained by all this liberalism which is hampering freedom of thought? After all, this liberalism is itself merely the shadow of a major misunderstanding which has already disappeared—at least that's how it is in the domain of literary criticism. Nowadays it is something which bears a closer resemblance to a chronic nervous disease than to a sincere passion of a heart taken up with the great idea of freedom.

I curse when those in my company laugh at the quiet, sad groan of a man who declares he wants 'that which is not of this earth'.[4] But these blind people exasperate me only for the first minute, after which one feels mere pity for them. By the way—tell Gippius[5] that I really like her strange poetry.

I will soon be leaving Malorussia for Tver province. That is so close to where you are that I may perhaps pay you a visit in the winter.

Please note my change of address:

Kamennoe. Tver province. Novotorzhok district.

Well, goodbye for now! I wish you strength of spirit and courage. I wish you this from the heart, for you are involved in a difficult business.

A. Peshkov

SOURCE: *Lit.-est. kontseptsii*: 357–8.

[1] Akim Lvovich Volynsky (real name Flekser) (1863–1926), literary critic and philosopher associated with the rise of Decadence in Russia.

[2] In an earlier letter Gorky had told Volynsky: 'I look upon you as a thinker who is completely original and as a courageous man' (*Lit.-est. kontseptsii*: 355).

[3] *Severnyi vestnik* [*The Northern Messenger*], a literary and political periodical published between 1885 and 1898. Under Volynsky's editorship strongly identified with Modernism.

[4] A line from Zinaida Gippius's poem 'A Song' ['Pesnia'].

[5] Zinaida Nikolaevna Gippius (1869–1945), writer and critic. Together with her husband, Dmitrii Merezhkovsky (1865–1941), prominent in Russian Modernism.

11. To A. L. Volynsky, [December 1897]

[Kamennoe]

I don't know the era that [da] Vinci lived in and I don't know anything about him—I've never even seen any reproductions of his paintings. I would read Korelin's *Renaissance Sketches* with pleasure, but I haven't been able to find the book.[1] I consider it necessary to tell you that I am an ignoramus, for I am a self-taught man.

I am reading your articles about da Vinci first of all as a work of literature, and—this will probably surprise you—with the same enjoyment as when I read Poe.[2] What is there in common between the two of you? Poe was a man captivated by the mysteries of life, he inspired terror through his love of those mysteries, he was a slave to the troubled emotions of his spirit, but his slavery was more sublime, pure, and precious than any free analysis of those mysteries, for such 'free analysis' has always struck me by its coarseness and complacency. Everything that this sick genius of a man could and did say reveals him as a being gripped by a holy passion to understand his own soul, to reach its very depths. In my conception of you, apart from having a unity of aspiration, you are also similar to Poe in style. When I read pages 195–202 of your second article,[3] I felt the same thing that I felt while reading 'Ligeia', for the subject-matter of these pages is love, and when love is so sacredly pure it makes absolutely no difference whether it is God or a woman that you love. In your articles there is something undying—a sadness about the meaning of life, and an objection to its being so empty nowadays, a passion for the mysteries of existence, and much beauty and pain, much seeking. It is most likely that this comparison will make you laugh a great deal, but I can't concern myself with that. You ask, and I answer, you will say no, and I will go on thinking yes, because I want to think about you *in this way*. It is my right to think like this and to see in a person what I want to see, and not what others show me, nor what they might try to make me see.

As I have already told you what I feel about you, I will now say something about your task. If you should die tomorrow and our liberal bigwigs were to come out the following day with an appraisal of your work, this is what I would say in response to their patter of dull words and worn-out ideas, and all the other things in which they indulge: 'Gentlemen, this was a man to whom you did not listen and whom you did not want to understand. But if you had understood him, you would be ashamed of yourselves, for it was he, not you, who had a solid knowledge of that truth which people need if they are to be more noble, and which life itself needs if it is to be more beautiful and rich in feeling. And he was the one who was really convinced that he was right, who had the courage to go against the flow. What is more, there were many other things in him which could never be accommodated by you.' Believe me, I would say this, although I would say it perhaps not out of respect for you, but out of abhorrence for them.

You can believe me, for I speak without having met you and without knowing anything of you except as a thinker. Were we to meet in person, it is possible that we wouldn't like each other at all, in which case I would not say to you what I've just said—which means that it must be said now, for it seems to me that it will be as agreeable for you to hear as it is agreeable for me to say it to you.

Am I a shadowy figure in your eyes? I am shadowy in my own eyes as well. About myself I know only one thing for sure—I was born an idealist, but I am now becoming a sceptic because people are vulgar and petty, whilst life itself is dreary and dark.

I know your opinion of Merezhkovsky's talent, but I thought that it did not extend to *The Outcast* [*Otverzhennyi*].[4] I like this work, because I like Nietzsche too, as far as I know him. And that is because, being a democrat myself by birth and feeling, I can see only too well how democratism is destroying life, and I realize that its victory will be the victory not of Christ, as some think, but of the belly.

Warm regards,

A. Peshkov

I think that I will send you a work in January, or perhaps in February.

SOURCE: *Lit.-est. kontseptsii*: 359–61.

---

[1] Possibly M. S. Korelin's *Sketches of the Italian Renaissance* [*Ocherki ital'ianskogo vozrozhdeniia*].

[2] Volynsky's articles on Leonardo appeared in *Severnyi vestnik* between September and December 1897.

[3] The page references are to *Severnyi vestnik*, no. 10, 1897.

⁴ Volynsky had written that Merezhkovsky's lyrics displayed 'neither power nor originality' (*Severnyi vestnik*, no. 3, 1896). *The Outcast* was the original title of Merezhkovsky's first novel *The Death of the Gods. Julian the Apostate* [*Smert' bogov. Iulian Otstupnik*], a historical work set in fourth-century Rome.

12. To E. P. Peshkova, [17 May 1898]

[Tiflis]

Today I received four of your letters at once. Thank you, Katerinka, but why write to me daily? Like everything in this world, even frequent writing has its funny side. Don't take offence, but it really would be better if you were to write less often but at somewhat greater length.

Please don't worry about me—I assure you, I'm living quite well. The external conditions, my health, and state of mind are all quite satisfactory; truly, I've lived in immeasurably worse conditions [. . .]¹

I will probably be released on bail [. . .]

Let's talk seriously. It's a tiring and restless business living with me, isn't it, Katia? Remember everything you've experienced, think about it and rest assured that I will accept without the slightest protest your every decision, no matter how unexpected and difficult it might be for me. I find it necessary to tell you this because I am ashamed before you, I feel guilty for not letting you live in peace, with ease and joy. The worst thing, the most difficult and sad thing in my situation is the consciousness of this guilt. But let's change the subject.

I will tell you how I'm living. I think I get up early, but perhaps it's just that the days at this latitude are twice as long as our northern days. I go for a wash, then I drink tea, read, write, and look out of the window until dinner-time. Dinner is brought at midday. I'm given two dishes—the first is something of a general nature. These comestibles are a combination of all manner of groats and vegetables, there is meat, pepper, sometimes salt, but never any cockroaches or other insects—and it is precisely this last (and unusual) circumstance which is the most important thing about the food. Then they give me cutlets, wonderful cutlets designed for the punishment of gluttons! I eat them because I realize that we mortals are put in prison so that we can experience something unpleasant. I also buy eggs, white bread, cheese, and, to be quite serious, I am eating well in general. My state of mind is also satisfactory, it is even better than it was of late in Nizhnii. I will soon have finished reading Gibbon.² I really regret that I didn't bring Plutarch³ with me. By the way, please don't give my books to anyone. Please take care of them. If you go to the dacha, pack them up well, lock them away, cover them with an oilcloth or something waterproof and put them in a dry place. I owe Getz three roubles for binding. Also pick out some books at Lanin's. The behaviour of the birds makes me happy—what dear creatures they are! I'll be sad not to find them on my return, and I will miss the bullfinches and blue-tits especially.

I'll continue the description of my day. After dinner I repeat the morning schedule. At about six o'clock I drink tea. Again I read, write, look out of the window. I go to bed late, as usual. In the cell the lamp burns all night until the morning. I think they do this so that the gaoler can see at a glance through the little window in the door if I am sawing through the grating on the windows or about to hang myself. I don't want to do either, all the more so as the gratings are devilishly thick, there is a guard under the window, and there is nothing I can hang myself from.

The castle stands on a cliff above the Kura and the distance from its walls to the edge of the steep cliff is no more than two yards. The Kura is as filthy as a stoker and roars like mad. Its current is so fast that I'm surprised it doesn't destroy the foundations of the houses it washes over or erode the cliff which serves as the base of the castle. It is not wide: from my window I can discern the faces of people on the opposite bank. Across from my window there are tanneries, stone buildings of a regular cubic form, and houses with flat, cement-covered roofs. The tanners work on the roofs for days on end. There is also something like a coaching inn where the locals bring sheep, donkeys, and mules loaded with this and that. Sometimes people fish in the river with tacking thread. The first row of houses opposite my window stands in the water and, gradually ascending the mountain, the houses climb to the height of the castle roof. They are most unusual and filthy, some have been painted blue—they have their own aesthetics here—and all of them have terraces. Oriental people relax on the terraces, and sometimes figures of women appear in broad white shawls. I also see children, but I hear nothing other than the fierce sound of the Kura and sometimes the doleful music of the zurna.[4] There is probably much noise and movement and a lot of life among these clumsy houses in the narrow streets which creep across the mountain. This whole part of the city seems like a pile of rubbish which has been thrown out of a sack and scattered all over the mountain from its summit down to the waters of the river. It could have been enlivened and adorned by the presence of churches (there are two churches here, in fact), but the local church architecture is awful. In the churches here—I am talking only of the architecture—there is nothing majestic or ceremonial to elevate the spirit. What is more, they are painted a clay colour, not white like ours. The bells are small, and their chimes insipid, they are almost drowned out by the noise of the river and the street life. The only beautiful thing in this part of the town is the ruins of the Tiflis fortress. This is a very majestic building which reminds one a bit of Khersones[5]—do you remember?—but it is more massive and the brickwork is more solid. In its time this was probably an impregnable for-tification due both to its construction and its location. That is all I can see from the window. I watch the work of the tanners and the life of a girl who has been pottering about for days on end on the balcony of one of those gloomy houses.

If I'm released on bail and if I leave here in a different manner from the way I arrived, I'll buy a photograph of this part of the city and of the castle. I'll also go to the local museum, which is full of the most inter-esting things.

Thank you for the note you sent me from *Kur'er* [*The Courier*] about my books,[6] but don't send printed reviews, just ask the editor of *Listok*[7]—and please ask in your own right—to put aside everything that concerns me, or else to hand it on to you.

I approve of your decision to go to the dacha—I'm very glad for you and Maksim. Please keep a close eye on his nutritional needs. If you find it necessary, you can thank the nurse on my behalf for not leaving at the critical moment; in any case, give her my regards. Try to get the money from *Severnyi vestnik*;[8] ask Posse[9] to help you with this, I think he will man-age better than anyone else in Petersburg to force *Vestnik* to pay up. It would be a great shame right now to lose such a lot of money, let them pay at least 75 roubles, damn them! No longer will I ever associate with people who are so openly familiar, although candour can also be a good quality. Well, I think that's enough writing for the present.

Goodbye for now, Katia! Take care of our son, take care of him.

Love,

Aleksei

Demand the money from *Zhizn'* and *Zhurnal*,[10] and when you get it from the publisher, send me 25–30 roubles.

Goodbye for now. Look after yourself, keep calm and try to look mis-fortune straight in the eye.

How are the flowers? See that the palms always have damp soil; water them from the top and also by putting a little water in the saucers.

Today is Sunday. When will you get this letter?

SOURCE: *SS* 28: 26–9.

[1] This letter was written in Tiflis Prison, where Gorky was held during an investigation into his revolutionary activities. Parts were deleted by the prison censors.

[2] *The Decline and Fall of the Roman Empire.*

[3] Plutarch's *Lives.*

[4] A type of flute.

[5] i.e. Kherson, a town on the lower Dnieper in modern Ukraine.

[6] This was a positive review of *Sketches and Stories*, which appeared on 7 May 1898.

[7] N. P. Asheshov.

[8] Gorky had published 'Varenka Olesova' in *Severnyi vestnik*.

[9] Vladimir Aleksandrovich Posse (1864–1940), editor of *Zhizn'*.

[10] i.e. *Zhurnal dlia vsekh*, a popular St Petersburg periodical, which, like *Zhizn'*, aimed at a progressive democratic readership.

13. To F. D. Batiushkov,[1] *[19 or 20 October, 1898]*

[Nizhnii Novgorod]

Dear Fedor Dmitrievich,

I have already returned your splendid essay to you—thank you![2]

As for my fantasy[3]—you can publish it. If they curse me for it, then let them! I have already heard enough praise. In the end, the point is not how they treat me, but only whether I have struck home where I intended, and if I *have* struck home, with how powerful a blow. This particular blow is rather weak, that I know. I also know that some people will enjoy using this stick to beat me about the head and the soul. But that doesn't matter.

I will not regret having published this work, for my thoughts and feelings will never achieve a balance, they will never arrive at a common denominator—there is no room in my soul for God.[4] I also have neither the time nor the desire to strive for inner peace and lucidity—for I am as a wave of the sea, reflecting the sun's rays and singing of life with anger and praise. I know that a writer should be a prophet and even an Isaiah among prophets, but I am too small for such a role. I am a self-taught man, did you know that? Do not think that I am speaking out of pride. No, I say this out of bitterness. I am a self-taught man, constrained by the chains of my ignorance. I do not have the time to slacken my chains, nor do I have the strength to do so. Your observations are sensible and sharp-sighted, and I accept them without hesitation. Send the proofs, and I will correct what you have indicated. I thank you warmly for your letter, it is very dear to me.

I would like to hear your opinion of my language. Sometimes it seems crude, at others it seems colourless, and it always seems insufficiently simple, even fanciful. In particular, what might have you to say about the language of my 'fantasy'?

But you must also tell me straight out if I am getting on your nerves with my requests and questions.

So—publish it!

If anyone laughs at me for this work, I will retaliate with all my heart and mind, and I think I'll manage to inflict some good deep wounds upon my opponents.

Goodbye for now!

Yours sincerely,

A. Peshkov

[Nizhnii, Grebeshok 17]

I have not read Lessing and I do not know his theories.[5]

SOURCE: *SS* 28: 38–9.

¹ Fedor Dmitrievich Batiushkov (1857–1920), literary critic and scholar.
² Gorky had asked Batiushkov to send him a copy of his 'In the World of the Tramps' ['V mire bosiakov'], a review of *Sketches and Stories* which had just appeared in the journal *Kosmopolis*.
³ 'The Reader' ['Chitatel''], which Gorky had sent to Batiushkov in September.
⁴ In a letter of 4 October 1898 Batiushkov had expressed enthusiasm for 'The Reader' but noted that some of his older colleagues felt that Gorky might later regret publishing it (*Perepiska* 1: 87–9).
⁵ Batiushkov had identified Gorky's thoughts on the purpose of art with the aesthetic views of G. E. Lessing (*Perepiska* 1: 89).

14. To V. G. Korolenko, [end of November 1898]

[Nizhnii Novgorod]

Dear Vladimir Galaktionovich,

Yesterday I sent my books to you.[1] Once, when you were giving me one of your books, you said to me: 'Be sure you give me yours when you have some to give.' Well, I do have some now, but I am not confident that they are needed. Believe me, I say this without pretence—why should I pretend? I know which people are better, and which ones worse than I, and in general I have perhaps rather less modesty than I ought to. All I want to say is that since reading through everything I have written, I have begun to feel awkward. I am somehow depressed or perhaps I am offended or sorry about something. Maybe you will understand what this feeling is like, it is very unpleasant and saps one's courage.

I have called myself your pupil: tell me honestly whether you find this unpleasant.[2] I think that my wandering from journal to journal has given you an impression of me which is anything but flattering. I don't know how you regard me now, but all the same, you were my teacher and you did me a lot of good. I have not forgotten this and I will not forget it in the future. I thank you warmly: when all is said and done, I think I serve the same God as you do.

When I found out that N[ikolai] K[onstantinovich] [Mikhailovsky] had written something about me, my heart missed a beat.[3] 'This is it,' I thought. 'Retribution has come.'[4] But it turns out that he sees something in me which merits attention and even approval. That is good but, you know, I find it hard to understand. I thought he would treat me more severely.

I'm going through some very bad days at the moment. Bad thoughts weigh heavily on my heart. My destiny has caused me injury by not giving me the opportunity to study at the proper time, and now it takes away the time I need for this.

Forgive me for this sour letter—my soul is really in a bad way at present.

I wish you all the best—health, courage, inspiration. Give my regards to your wife and to Nikolai Fedorovich[5] and Nikolai Konstantinovich.
Goodbye for now!
Yours,

A. Peshkov

I would like to say something very good to N. K., but I am unable to. Should I say thank you? But why would he need my thanks? And besides, I don't need that either.

A. P.

SOURCE: *SS* 28: 47–8.

[1] The two volumes of *Sketches and Stories*.
[2] In an autobiographical note published in *Sem'ia* [*The Family*] in 1899 Gorky acknowledged that Korolenko had taught him how to write (*Korolenko*: 181–2).
[3] Mikhailovsky's lengthy review of Gorky's *Sketches and Stories* appeared in the September and October issues of *Russkoe bogatstvo* for 1898.
[4] Gorky is no doubt thinking of the awkwardness caused by his article 'How great men fall out' ['Kak ssoriatsia velikie liudi'] (*Samarskaia gazeta* on 18 April 1895). The article contained a reference to Mikhailovsky which Korolenko had interpreted as an unnecessary attack. See Korolenko's letter to Gorky of 23 April 1895 and Gorky's reply to it (*Korolenko*: 34–8).
[5] N. F. Annensky (1843–1912), statistician and publicist. A friend of Korolenko and a fellow Populist.

15. To A. P. Chekhov, [about 13 January 1899]

[Nizhnii Novgorod]

Things are going well for me! Your splendid letter contains an awful lot of subject-matter which I find both flattering and sad. I can sense the shape of your soul in it, a soul which seems stern to me and adds to my sincere admiration for you. I wish you health and good spirits.

It is depressing but true what you say about *Zhizn'*,[1] Chirikov, and 'Kirilka'. Yes, it is so: *Zhizn'* is not yet serious, Chirikov is naïve, and of 'Kirilka' one could safely say that it merits no discussion whatever. As regards Veres[aev]—I do not agree. He is not an author whom I consider either rich or strong in spirit. Since 'Pathless' ['Bez dorogi'],[2] 'Andrei Ivanovich' seems to be the best thing he has given us so far. Nevertheless, for *Zhizn'* that is not enough. Anton Pavlovich, do submit something to it! I ask you most earnestly to do this because *Zhizn'* is very dear to me. Why? You see, it is because I know someone who works for it—V. A. Posse. He is a man of great energy who could prove very productive for our life in Russia, a life so lacking in everything that is good. He will need to be supported to begin with, and he should be given his head. Besides this, the main thing for me is that *Zhizn'* inclines towards a merging of Populism and Marxism into a single harmonious whole. Such was its task, at least at first. But the Marxists who promised to participate in it pulled a fast one on Posse and founded their own journal, *Nachalo* [*The Beginning*].[3] I do not understand all these matters. And I can tell you frankly that I don't have a favourable impression of Petersburg journalists. I think that all these political parties of theirs have little to do with real life. They are concerned far more with the personal vanity of some not very talented people than they are with souls which have been inflamed by the desire to build a new, free life for all on the debris of the old, cramped one. You know, sometimes I want to shout at them with a lustiness which comes from a heart enraged by their pettiness. You see the sort of menacing fellow I am? But if you were to submit something of yours to *Zhizn'* right now, it would accept whatever conditions you cared to impose. Just think, with a stimulus from you and the concerted efforts of others, a journal could arise which would actually be interesting and serious. That would be wonderful! . . If it happens. But now—if you'll forgive me!—I am going to respond to your letter by talking about myself. You see, I need to speak about myself for some reason, and although I don't think you really need to hear this, I will tell you anyway.

You said I misunderstood your words concerning coarseness.[4] Perhaps I did. If I am elegant and talented, then the devil can take me! I would not believe in my elegance and talent even if you were to tell me this twice or even ten times over. You said I'm intelligent—that made me laugh. It made me both happy and bitter. I am as stupid as a steam-engine. Since the age of ten I have had to stand on my own feet. I had no time to study, I just guzzled life and worked, whilst life itself warmed me with blows of its fists, feeding me with all things good and bad, so that it finally got me so completely warmed up that it set me in motion, and now I am flying. But I have no rails beneath me. I feel things in a way which is fresh and anything but feeble, yet I am incapable of proper thought, and I sense that disaster awaits me up ahead. Not a bad comparison, by God! The day when I might bury myself nose first in the ground is still far off, but even if it should come tomorrow, I don't care— I neither fear nor blame anything. However, there are moments when I feel sorry for myself—as is the case now—and at such times I will talk about myself to someone I like. I call such conversations an ablution of the soul with tears of silence, because, you see, even if you talk a lot, you say foolish things and you will never really manage to express what the soul cries over. I am speaking to you because, besides liking you, I also know that you are a man for whom one word is enough to create an image and a single sentence enough to create a story, a wonderful story which penetrates to the depth and essence of life, like a drill into the earth. If we ever meet, I will not dare speak a word to you about yourself, for I would be unable to say things as I would wish. But now, from a distance, it is easy for me to give you your due. You have no reason nor do you have the right to refuse the tribute which I bring you as a man who has been captivated by the power of your talent. I am a dreamer by nature, and there was a time when I imagined you standing high above life, your face impassive, like the face of a judge, your huge eyes reflecting everything: the whole earth, the puddles on it, the sun which shines in the puddles, and human souls.

Then I saw your portrait—it was a print from a photograph. I looked at it for a long time and I did not understand a thing. Well, all right, that's enough. Believe me. I can write, but I am unable to lie and I never flatter anyone. But if you excite my soul so strongly, I am not to blame for that, and why should I not tell you how much you mean to me?

And so, Anton Pavlovich, please be so good as to send me your portrait and one of your books. That would do me good.

Please!

I send you warm regards and I wish you health—health, good spirits and the desire to do more work.

A. Peshkov
[Nizhnii, Polevaia, 20]

SOURCE: *SS* 28: 55–7.

[1] Posse had asked Gorky to encourage Chekhov to publish work in the journal. In his letter to Gorky of 3 January, Chekhov gave his opinion of the January 1899 issue, which contained, among other items, Evgenii Chirikov's 'Foreigners' ['Chuzhestrantsy'], Vikentii Veresaev's 'The End of Andrei Ivanovich' ['Konets Andreia Ivanovicha'] and Gorky's own 'Kirilka'. Of the latter work, he wrote: 'In your "Kirilka" everything is spoilt by the figure of the *zemstvo* chief; the overall tone is sustained well' (*Chekhov*: 30–1).

[2] Vikentii Vikentievich Veresaev (1867–1945), writer who became closely involved in the Znanie miscellanies. 'Pathless' (first published in 1895) marked Veresaev's controversial entry on to the national literary scene.

[3] Journal organized by the so-called 'legal Marxists'. Began publication in January 1899 but was soon closed down by the censorship.

[4] In his first long letter to Gorky of 3 December 1898, Chekhov had spoken of the younger writer's 'undoubted talent', but also of his lack of 'restraint', which was especially manifest in his nature descriptions. In reply, Gorky spoke of his fear of 'being coarse', which prompted Chekhov to answer that he had said nothing about 'coarseness' at all and that he found Gorky's writing quite 'elegant' at times, especially in stories like 'In the Steppe' ['V stepi'] and 'On the Rafts' ['Na plotakh'], which he found 'exemplary' (*Chekhov*: 26–30).

16. To A. P. Chekhov, [28 April 1899]

[Nizhnii Novgorod]

There is something wonderful about our letters having crossed in the post. And your letter is wonderful too.

You know, I had never thought that Lev Nikolaevich felt that way about me![1] You did well to chat with him about Gorky and then to tell Gorky about it. I have wanted to know what Tolstoy thought of me for a long time now, but was afraid to find out; now I know and I have tasted another drop of honey. Only two *such* drops have shown up in the barrel of tar that I have drunk: his and yours.[2] I don't need any others. I would like you to read Volynsky's article about you in the latest issue of *Severnyi vestnik*—that for October, November, and December. I liked it, even though the language is typically inflated. A Galician named Franko has also written about you in his paper; the piece is said to be written with amazing sincerity.[3] The paper is being sent to me; if you like, I'll pass it on to you.

I cannot come to Moscow. Having found out that I spent a night in Moscow, the authorities are making a fuss; however, most likely nothing will come of it, since the case for which I was brought to trial will soon be over.[4] At worst they'll send me to Vologda or Viatka for a couple of years; more likely still, they won't send me anywhere at all. The impossibility of arranging to come to Moscow before Thursday both vexes me to the point of tears and makes me furious. You can't believe how vile it is to live under surveillance. A policeman comes to visit you; this sordid duty embarrasses him as well—it is as difficult for him as it is for you. He has the right to ask you about whatever he pleases: 'Who visited you? Where was he from, where was he going, and why?' But he doesn't ask anything, because he is convinced that you will tell him lies, whilst you find this conviction of his offensive and insulting. But enough of that.

It grieves me even to think that if I were to come to Moscow, you and I might go to see *The Seagull* together. Nothing could induce me to sit beside you in the theatre! What you should do is chase everyone away and watch the play on your own—be sure to be alone. And then, my dear Anton Pavlovich, you should write to me afterwards with your impression of the play—please write! It doesn't matter that the play's your own work; you should write and tell me whether or not you liked it on the stage and what—which part—you liked most of all. I beg of you! And tell me how the acting was. For some reason I think that you will view *The Seagull* as though it were someone else's play, and that it will affect you powerfully.

And another thing, Anton Pavlovich, why don't you come down here to Nizhnii? It's so pretty here now the river has flooded its banks so mightily! Come and visit! I have a large apartment, and you could stay with us. My wife—a small, unpretentious and sweet person—likes you terribly, and when I told her that you were alone, she considered that a shame and an injustice; her eyes even shone with tears for you. Come and visit; we would treat you like one of the family. I do hope you'll come. And bring me the watch—it is not nice of me to remind you, but so what?[5] Be sure to have your name engraved on the case. Why? I don't know, I just want you to for some reason.

SOURCE: *SS* 28: 74–6.

[1] In his letter to Gorky, Chekhov said that Tolstoy had praised Gorky highly, that he liked the stories 'The Fair in Goltva' ['Iarmarka v Goltve'] and 'In the Steppe', but did not like 'Malva'.

[2] A play on the Russian saying which talks of 'a spoonful of tar in the barrel of honey' (i.e. 'a fly in the ointment').

[3] Ivan Iakovlevich Franko (1856–1916), Ukrainian writer and publicist. The article has not been identified.

[4] A reference to Gorky's arrest the year before.

[5] Chekhov had promised to buy Gorky a watch.

17. To M. Z. Basargina,[1] [June 1899]

[Nizhnii Novgorod]

How am I? The same as ever, Mariia Zakharovna—restless. In the course of ten years I managed to traverse almost the whole of Russia, and even now, as a married man, I cannot stay in one place for long. Come August, I will have been married for three years; I have a son who will be two in July. And during that time I have lived in Samara, Nizhnii, Yalta, Tver, Tiflis, again in Samara and Nizhnii, and again in Yalta—I left there only at Easter. I have been staying here since then. In the autumn I will go to Smolensk and Petersburg. About a year ago I nearly made my final trip to the cemetery, for I had an attack of pulmonary tuberculosis, and could barely stand on my feet.

What am I doing? I am writing. Have you read my stories? They will come out in a second edition in the autumn and I will send you a copy then. I have been lucky in literature—my first story appeared only in 1895 and I'm already publishing a second edition of my works.[2] I have been translated into several foreign languages. I am earning a lot of money—about four to five thousand a year—and I never have a penny, I am always in debt.

On the whole I live a difficult and joyless life. I work a lot, I am tired, my health has suffered. I cannot bear the 'educated' and 'cultured' public. I prefer to keep the company of my brothers, the common people, the workmen, draymen, down-and-outs, etc. These are simple, sincere, good people, and I love to be in their midst. I drink vodka, of course. But what of it?

I am still the same as always, just as ridiculous and just as foolish.

When you write to your folk, please greet Zakh[ar] Efim[ovich] for me.[3] I have wronged him—there was a time when I made him suffer some unpleasant moments.[4] I know this, but I am the one who must forgive. I love

Zakh. Ef., he is an exceptional man with a good heart. Give my regards to everyone, I have not forgotten any of them.

The past is better than the present, although I say so perhaps only because I am already thirty years old, I have worked a lot, I have climbed high and I am tired. But for all that I am still a lively man and there are times when I am able to be happy. I do not complain about anything, I like to laugh at myself and I do not sigh with sadness. Ha! What is there to be sorry about?

I will send you a photograph as soon as I have one ready. Please send me yours.

Goodbye for now!

Warm regards. It is good to encounter an old friend, especially one who is still as young as you are.

A. Peshkov

SOURCE: *SS* 28: 85–6.

---

[1] Mariia Zakharovna Basargina, a member of the study group at Krutaia station. See Letter 1, n. 2.

[2] Gorky's first story, 'Makar Chudra', actually appeared in 1892. But 1895 was significant as the year in which he first published a work ('Chelkash') in a 'thick' journal.

[3] Zakhar Efimovich Basargin, Mariia Zakharovna's father and the station master at Krutaia station.

[4] Gorky described his experiences at Krutaia station in 'From the Past' ['Iz proshlogo'] (1928). The sketch contains a lively account of his 'belligerent relations' (*PSS* 18: 387) with Basargin, but says nothing of any 'wrong' committed by Gorky.

18. To I. E. Repin,[1] [23 November 1899]

[Nizhnii Novgorod]

Thank you very much for the photograph, dear Ilia Efimovich! Your attention is extremely important to me and I was deeply touched by your responsiveness to my request.

It is a pleasure to answer your questions.[2] I wrote 'The Reader' four years ago. 'The Reader' is I, the man, in conversation with myself, the writer. I, the man, am dissatisfied with myself, the writer, because I have read too much and books have robbed my soul. Through reading I have lost a great deal of my originality, of what is my own and given to me by nature. Now that I have become a writer, I am becoming convinced that, like many others, I am not free in my thoughts, that I sometimes work with facts and thoughts which I have *read into myself from the books of others* but which I have not experienced directly myself, with my own heart. That is most annoying. And, of course, it is bad. Is it a worthy business to illuminate man with reflected light? No, it is not. I think that everyone should be free in their thoughts and feelings, that they should speak only from themselves and for themselves, and take responsibility upon themselves for everything that they say. Indeed, it is bad if a man is asked, 'How did you arrive at this or that notion?' and he answers, 'I read it.' It seems to me that all our contemporary literature has been borrowed from somewhere; yet even so, there is something originally Russian in it, something particularly characteristic of the Russian spirit, apart from elements of our everyday life. I believe in the idea of a national character and consider Korolenko's Tiulin,[3] for example, to be an expression of the Russian national character. Tiulin on the Vetluga is the same as Minin in history.[4] He appeared, performed his heroic deed, then he disappeared, vanished, faded away. I also do not like our contemporary literature for its pessimism. Life is not as bad as they like to depict it in books, it is brighter. And man in real life is better than in a book, even an accomplished book. He is more complex. In my opinion writers insult man. Of course, I also cause such insult. What can you do? I have become a professional. That is bad, but it is probably inevitable.

'The Rolling Stone' ['Prokhodimets'] is a living being, he is one of your Petersburg citizens. This is one of my countless adventures, it was written in 1897. 'My Fellow-Traveller' ['Moi sputnik'] is also an adventure which is rather poorly done. This is a pity, because it's a good theme. A great writer might have made a classic work from it. 'One Day in Autumn' ['Odnazhdy osen'iu'] was written in 1895, and is also a real-life affair. 'Mates' ['Druzhki'] was written in 1898. The only thing that should be heard in all these works is a feeling of indignation and resentment on behalf of man.[5] I do not know anything better, more complex, more interesting than man. He is everything. He even created God. Art itself is only one of the highest manifestations of his creative spirit, and therefore it is only part of man. I am convinced that man is capable of perfecting himself endlessly. And along with man himself, all his activities will also develop from century to century. I believe in the infinity of life, and I understand life as a movement towards perfection of the spirit. But I also see that man's development has been going wrong for some time—our minds have been developing whilst our feelings have been ignored. I think that this is harmful for us. Intellect and instinct must be combined in a well-balanced harmony, and then it seems to me that we and everyone around us will be brighter, more radiant and joyful. I believe that this is possible.

I do not like people who are intelligent but unable to feel. They are all malicious, even basely malicious. Similarly, I do not like people who are preachers of morals, those who consider that they have been summoned to judge everyone and everything. When I look at them, I always see the conceit of the Pharisee and I am inclined to laugh maliciously at them.

And what am I myself, when all is said and done? I don't know. Whenever I ask myself this question, I feel good. For I see that I do not belong anywhere as yet, not to any of our 'parties'. I am glad of that, for it is freedom.

And man very much needs freedom, he needs freedom to think for himself more than freedom of movement. To be subject to no one: that is happiness, is it not? To be master of your own soul and not to admit anything alien into it, anything which might insolently besmirch what is one's own— is that not good?

I look upon you as such a free and happy man. And I have my reasons for this: when I look at the dying tsarevich, killed by Ivan the Terrible, and then at the Zaporozhian Cossacks who are roaring with healthy laughter, and at Nikolai who is ready to die in battle for man, and at the Tatar guide with his complacent, brutishly handsome face—to me this all seems talented, great, bright, and true, it all says to me: this is art![6] This is the breadth with which life should be portrayed! God creates the nightingale and the spider, the elephant and the flea, everywhere he is a great creator, and in everything he is an artist, everywhere one sees his love for life, and everywhere the intense striving to create a thing as good, as clever, and as radiant as possible. In all his activities, but in art most of all, man should be creative, i.e. beautiful and strong, like God.

Well, forgive me for what is perhaps a vague and, in any case, a very long letter. I wish you good health, I. E., and the desire, the burning desire to work.

Yours truly,

A. Peshkov

SOURCE: *SS* 28: 100–2.

[1] Ilia Efimovich Repin (1844–1930), famous artist with whom Gorky became good friends.

[2] In a letter of 17 November 1899, Repin gave his impressions of the third volume of *Sketches and Stories*, referring particularly to 'The Reader' and the other works which Gorky mentions later in this letter (*Perepiska* 1: 116–17).

[3] Central character in Korolenko's short story 'The River Plays' ['Reka igraet'].

[4] Kuzma Minin was a Russian national hero. A butcher by trade, he was a key figure, together with Prince Dmitrii Pozharsky, in the expulsion of the Poles from Moscow in 1612.

[5] Repin had written: 'In all these pieces one hears a profoundly spiritual note which beats in the heart of man' (*Perepiska* 1: 117).

[6] Gorky refers to a number of famous pictures by Repin: *Ivan the Terrible and his son Ivan: 16 November 1581*; *The Zaporozhian Cossacks reply with mockery to a high-flown letter from the Sultan Mohammed IV*, *St Nicholas of Myra delivers the three innocent men*; and *A walk with a guide on the southern shore of the Crimea*.

2
WRITER AND ACTIVIST
1900–1905

INTRODUCTION

Gorky's rise to fame coincided with the beginnings of a new period of social and political unrest which eventually culminated in Russia's first revolution. Indeed, the 'Gorky phenomenon' was immediately identified by the writer's contemporaries as both a symptom and a product of the changing times. With his pronounced Volga accent, his romantic past as a 'vagabond', who had tramped the highways and byways of the Empire, and his reputation as a political oppositionist, who had already suffered for his beliefs, he was seen as the very embodiment of the rising spirit of protest in the land. Although Gorky was to complain of his new celebrity to his first biographer, V. F. Botsianovsky ('my biography is hindering a correct understanding of me'—Letter 21), one suspects a certain disingenuousness on his part. To be sure, he contributed in no small way to his own flamboyant image by the adoption of leather boots and a high-collared black peasant shirt as a sort of personal trade mark, which was seized upon with delight by the caricaturists of the day and even copied by some of Gorky's associates. And his often belligerent public behaviour throughout the early years of the century ensured that he was a perpetual talking-point among Russians from all walks of life.

Even though he was to describe his life in a letter to Chekhov of 1900 as being as 'fantastic and absurd' as ever (Letter 22), there is an energy and purpose to his activities over the following years which was altogether different from what had gone before. This difference is nowhere more evident than in the growing tone of optimism which characterizes many of the letters in this section. At times, there is real elation here, as in the following passage from a letter of 1901:

come what may, a revolution is happening in Russia. It is not the sort where people fight in the streets and chop off the heads of kings, but another sort, which is more serious. We are witnessing the breakdown of the philosophical and ethical basis on which the well-being of the petty bourgeoisie is founded. (Letter 27)

The contrast with the often pessimistic tone of his earlier letters could hardly be more pronounced. Indeed, one might even suggest that the rise of revolutionary sentiment in Russia enabled Gorky at last to feel that he had discovered his purpose in life. As he put it himself in a letter towards the end of 1904: 'How important, how marvellous to have a sense of one-self!' (Letter 35).

Gorky responded to his new position in the intellectual life of his country by redefining the task of writing in a way which was to prove quite crucial not only for his own work as an author but also for his dealings with others. 'It is one thing to write, and another thing altogether to be a literary man, Leonid Nikolaevich.'[1] These words, with which Gorky began a letter of August 1900 to his colleague Leonid Andreev, speak for his conviction that the profession of writing carried obligations which extended far beyond the mere production of works of literature. The expression 'literary man' (which we use to translate the Russian *literator*) was to become something of a key term in his vocabulary, connoting an activity whereby literary composition has to be combined with a conscious sense of the duty of a Russian writer to serve the cause of political change and to provide the democratic movement with a positive personal example. As far as Gorky himself was concerned, this even came to mean that writing was to play a subservient role to these other considerations: he was certainly not speaking idly when he suggested to Piatnitsky in 1902 that it could be both 'agreeable and instructive' for the democratically inclined proletariat 'if M. Gorky, amongst others, were to be killed or injured before their eyes on the street during a fight with the police' (Letter 29). Melodramatic though this prospect might sound, it was not altogether unlikely. Over the following years Gorky was quite often to find himself in situations where his political activities were to place him in considerable personal danger.

Although Gorky already had a long history of revolutionary activism, the turn of the century witnessed a substantial change in his involvement in radical affairs, to which the government reacted in predictable fashion. The first sign of increasing vigilance on the part of the authorities was the writer's arrest in Nizhnii in 1898. As the charges against him concerned events in Tiflis a number of years before, he was dispatched to that city under police escort and imprisoned there briefly pending further investigation (see Letter 12 above). However, the case against him was weak and he was soon released. But now that he had become a famous man, Gorky continued to attract ever more intense interest on the part of the organs of internal security. Reports by the police in Nizhnii Novgorod reveal that he was in constant contact with a number of radical groups and that his new-found fame was making him a real focus for dissident opinion and activity in the city.

The real turning-point in Gorky's political life came in 1901. It was on 4 March that year that the writer witnessed a major demonstration outside the Cathedral of Our Lady of Kazan, on Nevskii Prospekt, the main thoroughfare of St Petersburg. The demonstration had been organized as a protest against the Draconian measures taken by the government in the wake of student disturbances at Kiev University the previous year. For their part in these events 183 students were conscripted into the army as common soldiers. But if this punishment was harsh, the subsequent demonstration provoked an even more fearful display of government

[1] *LN* 72: 72.

brutality. The demonstrators were charged by armed Cossacks and mounted police who left a number of dead and many injured in their wake. Gorky was an eye-witness to these events, which he described quite graphically in a letter to his wife (Letter 24). On his return to Nizhnii Novgorod, he was immediately placed under arrest for having signed an open letter of protest against the government's action. He was subsequently accused also of having gone to St Petersburg in order to acquire a mimeograph machine for the reproduction of subversive literature.

The case against Gorky resulted in the administrative decision that he be exiled from his native city to Arzamas, where it was obviously hoped he would be out of harm's way. In the first instance, however, he was permitted to go to the Crimea so that he could undergo further treatment for his tuberculosis. The journey south was to prove an interesting one, for Gorky's celebrity was now such that the measures being taken against him became the signal for further anti-government action on the part of his many sympathizers. In fact, his departure from Nizhnii on 7 November 1901 provided the occasion for a major student protest, which served to alarm the authorities to the extent that they changed Gorky's travel arrangements, thereby forestalling the possibility of further demonstrations in Moscow. But the effect on Gorky was in no way diminished, for these signs of popular support made him realize just how great was his potential value to the revolutionary movement because of his national (and even international) prominence.[2]

Gorky did eventually serve his period of exile in Arzamas, in which town he composed *The Lower Depths*, the most famous of all his plays. He returned to Nizhnii only at the end of August 1902. But even when he was cloistered in the depths of provincial Russia, he remained in the public eye, due primarily to a notorious scandal which once again cast the government in an unfavourable light. Early in 1902 the literary section of the Russian Academy of Sciences announced the election of Gorky to its membership. But when the tsar came to hear of this decision in March that year, he ordered his advisers to persuade the Academy to change its mind. Chekhov and Korolenko—both of whom were already members of the Academy—resigned in protest, thereby compounding the bad publicity for the government.

Although Gorky was to remain in Nizhnii until the end of 1903, his literary affairs brought him ever more regularly to Moscow and St Petersburg. He was thus very much at the centre of things. By this stage, he had already made close contact with the Bolshevik faction of the Social Democratic Party, to which he also began to make considerable financial contributions. In the meantime, the political atmosphere in Russia was becoming ever more highly charged, especially after the

---

[2] See his letter to Posse: *SS* 28: 195–9.

ill-judged declaration of war against Japan, an act which itself served to precipitate the Revolution of 1905.

The revolution began with an event of quite horrific violence to which Gorky was once again a personal witness. Bloody Sunday, as this event soon came to be known, began with a mass procession of some 150,000 workers to the Winter Palace with the aim of presenting a petition to the tsar requesting political reform. Although the government had been informed that this was to be a peaceful demonstration, the order was issued for the procession to be met with a display of force. Troops opened fire without warning on the unarmed men, women, and children in the crowd, causing the deaths and injuries which are described by Gorky in Letter 37. In all, hundreds of people were killed, and many more hundreds wounded. In the aftermath of the slaughter, he composed a revolutionary appeal to the citizens of Russia and foreign states, for which act he was subsequently arrested in Riga on 11 January. But the Russian government now found itself in a quandary. Even though Gorky was transferred to the Fortress of Peter and Paul in St Petersburg to await trial, public sympathy for the writer and for the revolutionary cause he represented had now reached such a pitch that the tsar came to appreciate the danger of the situation. Bowing before pressure both from at home and abroad, he agreed to have Gorky released on bail from prison on 14 February. Although the authorities continued to prepare the case against him—in fact, Gorky was himself keen to use the trial to create further embarrassment to the government (see Letter 39)—events rapidly overtook them as Russia plunged further into the chaos of the revolutionary year. Gorky took advantage of his temporary freedom to promote the revolution in every way. He wrote proclamations and took part in numerous public meetings in St Petersburg and Moscow. His political position was very much at the radical end of the spectrum: in line with the Bolsheviks, he believed in the need to continue the revolutionary struggle to a victorious end, even after the government had made what more moderate groups considered a substantial concession to democracy with its so-called October manifesto.

The final months of 1905 were filled with hectic activity. Apart from his other editorial commitments, Gorky was closely involved in the setting up of *Novaia zhizn'*, the first legal Bolshevik newspaper. Its first issue appeared on 27 October 1905 and it ran until 2 December, when it was closed down by the government. It was during this same period that Gorky may have first met Lenin. (The Bolshevik leader had taken advantage of the revolutionary chaos to make his way back to Russia from his European exile.) And at the very end of the year, he was in Moscow for what proved to be the final act of Russia's first revolution. On 7 December, the workers of Moscow declared a general strike, a decision which they knew would provoke a display of force from a government now determined to restore order at any cost. Barricades were erected on the streets and weapons distributed to the striking workers. Gorky was in the thick of things. He helped in many practical ways and his apartment became the operational centre for the insurrectionists (see Letter 42). Although the workers managed to fight off the government forces for some time, the turning-point came with the arrival of the crack Semenovsky regiment from St Petersburg. The last pitched battle of the 1905 Revolution, the Moscow armed insurrection was thus quickly put down. In its aftermath, Gorky was obliged to escape both from the city and from the country itself. He was to remain abroad for the next seven years.

If Gorky's political activities between 1900 and 1905 display most directly the turn of his career towards a style of militant radicalism which was to make him *persona non grata* in his native land, his work as a writer changed in ways which are no less significant. By the turn of the century, it was already becoming clear to readers and critics alike that Gorky's career had entered a new phase. The change was signalled first of all by a turn away from the short story towards the novel. In *Foma Gordeev*, the tale of a young merchant's thwarted revolt against his provincial environment, and *The Three*, another story of frustrated ambition, Gorky launched a career as a novelist which was to be resumed with even greater intensity in the post-1905 period. In both works he showed that he was not afraid to use literature for the purposes of social criticism and even political persuasion. Not that this was to earn him much in the way of praise, even from such friendly critics as Chekhov, who declared *Foma Gordeev* to be 'as monotonous as a dissertation'.[3] Gorky was evidently sensitive to such criticisms and his letters are peppered with self-deprecating remarks about his abilities as a novelist. 'You will have probably seen from *The Three* that I can't write,' he confessed to Briusov in February 1901 (Letter 23). More revealing still, however, is the fact that this comment is followed almost immediately by the declaration that all contemporary art should be designed consciously to serve social ends.

Gorky himself was as good as his word, and nowhere more so than in one of his most notorious works of this period, the 'prose poem' 'The Song of the Stormy Petrel' ['Pesnia o burevestnike'] of 1901. With its famous refrain, 'To the madness of the brave we sing our song', it was an unmistakable call to revolution which was immediately adopted as a slogan by many young radicals. By this time, however, Gorky was already experimenting with another literary medium—the drama.

Gorky was first drawn to the dramatic form as a result of his encounters with the company of the Moscow Art Theatre (MAT). He had met the actors and directors of the theatre in 1900 in Yalta, where they had come on a special visit to Chekhov. In the north, Gorky had already

---

[3] *Chekhov*: 186.

attended a number of performances at the theatre itself, of which he left enthusiastic reports in a number of his letters (see Letters 19, 20). Stanislavsky and Nemirovich-Danchenko, the directors of the Art Theatre, obviously saw in Gorky a writer with real box-office potential and they set about encouraging him to write for their theatre at the first opportunity. As for Gorky himself, he evidently looked upon the theatre as a potent forum for his new style of committed writing. Between 1901 and 1905 he wrote four plays—*The Petty-Bourgeois*, *The Lower Depths*, *Summerfolk* [*Dachniki*], and *Children of the Sun* [*Deti solntsa*]—which stand as a substantial testimony to his revolutionary purpose as a writer.

In the eyes of the authorities, Gorky's engagement in this new sphere of endeavour posed extra problems of vigilance. So seriously did they regard the possible impact of his plays that every possible censorship barrier was reinforced, from the scrutiny of the text to control over the number and nature of stage performances. These fears were well founded. In *The Petty-Bourgeois*, for example, Gorky continued his attack on the middle-class pillars of society and he also introduced, in the character of Nil, his first proletarian positive hero. Although the play was no great success, he clearly fashioned the work to undermine the status quo.

It was with his next two plays that Gorky was to leave a real mark on Russian theatrical history. The first—*The Lower Depths*—was undoubtedly the greatest triumph, both for the author and for the Moscow Art Theatre. A graphic and unrelenting portrayal of life as it was lived by Russia's poor and dispossessed, it became an instant classic and even gave rise to spontaneous demonstrations when it eventually played in some provincial towns. *Summerfolk*, although a work of considerably lesser dramatic power, achieved greater notoriety still. With its critique of those feckless intellectuals whose liberal talk is a substitute for proper revolutionary action, it introduced a new theme into Gorky's work on the eve of the 1905 Revolution. The play's première, at the Komissarzhevskaia Theatre in St Petersburg, was without doubt one of the great literary events of 1904, provoking what amounted to a pitched battle between Gorky's defenders and his detractors. Gorky described the proceedings in an excited letter to Leonid Andreev (Letter 35). Calling this 'the best day of my incredibly long, interesting life—a good life which I've made all by myself', he concluded in the belligerent vein which was by now quite characteristic of him: 'Overall, it was a battle royal with the petty bourgeoisie, and I thrashed them.'

Gorky's militant stance at the première of *Summerfolk* perhaps best defines the role he had come to occupy in Russian literary life on the eve of the 1905 Revolution. By this time he had made his name not only as an author, but also as the organizer of an entire 'democratic school' of writers. Gorky was first inspired to move in this direction through his association with *Zhurnal dlia vsekh* in the late 1890s. An illustrated monthly which aimed to broadcast scientific ideas in a popular style, it underwent a significant change of focus when it effectively passed into the control of Viktor Miroliubov in September 1898. Miroliubov immediately transformed the journal into a forum for writers of realist fiction. Gorky himself published a number of works in the journal and did a great deal to promote its success, both by encouraging others to contribute to it and by publicizing its contents in articles he wrote for the newspapers. But he was soon to be even more closely engaged with another democratic journal of the day. *Zhizn'* was a literary, scientific, and political journal which, under the editorship of Vladimir Posse, had moved close to Marxism. Posse invited Gorky to serve as editor of the journal's literary section, which he did until the journal's forced closure in April 1901. This was his first real experience as a literary organizer and under his editorship many of the *Zhurnal dlia vsekh* writers were to find a further outlet for their writings.

As the new century got under way there were further important developments in the same vein. The first was the 'Wednesday' group, so named because of their weekly meetings on that day in the Moscow apartment of N. D. Teleshov. Teleshov himself was a minor realist writer of revolutionary sympathies and his home served for several years as a regular meeting-place for many popular writers of the day, such as Bunin, Skitalets, Serafimovich, Chirikov, and Kuprin. Gorky himself attended these gatherings whenever he was in Moscow and he encouraged other young writers (most notably, the as yet unknown Leonid Andreev) to do the same. Although it had no clearly defined political or literary programme, the members of the 'Wednesday' group were broadly united by their resistance to the Modernist styles of writing which were becoming more influential in intellectual circles.

By 1902, then, Gorky had both editorial experience and a wide range of contacts in the writing community. This was to serve him well as he embarked upon a new venture which was destined to be even more effective in promoting the cause of democratic literature. The Znanie ['Knowledge'] publishing firm had been founded in May 1898 as a co-operative venture in which participating authors would hold shares and draw a substantial return from the profits on their publications. Like *Zhurnal dlia vsekh*, it began as an outlet for popular works on scientific subjects, but it underwent a similar change of direction once Gorky became involved in it. The writer joined the co-operative in 1900 and, together with Konstantin Piatnitsky, one of the founders of the firm and its business manager, he organized a take-over in 1902. It was an inspired move and an ideal partnership—to begin with, at least. Piatnitsky supplied the commercial acumen and Gorky the editorial experience which was to make Znanie one of the great success stories in Russian publishing. Works by Gorky, Andreev, Bunin, Skitalets, and others were published in large, reasonably priced editions which found a ready audience among the 'new' democratic readers whom Gorky himself identified as his main target (see Letter 32). So successful was this venture that Gorky and Piatnitsky were encouraged to expand their activities by issuing a series of miscellanies containing new works by Znanie authors. The first such miscellany appeared in 1904. With contributions by Gorky, Andreev, Bunin, Veresaev, and others, it was published in 41,000 copies—a massive number for the time—thereby further consolidating the reputation of Znanie as the voice of progressive Russia. Altogether, forty such miscellanies were produced between 1904 and 1913.

The success of Znanie contributed in no small way to Gorky's growing sense of self-confidence and optimism as Russia's first revolution approached. He clearly relished the opportunity to play the father-figure and mentor to writers like Skitalets and Andreev, both of whom achieved remarkable success as 'Znanie authors' (see Letter 27, for example). By now, of course, his own conception of the nature and purpose of democratic literature had already taken a clear shape. Most notable in the first place was his hardening attitude towards Russian Modernism. Although his letter to Briusov of 1900 reveals that he had not totally lost his interest in the new literary trends, he was nevertheless unable to endorse uncritically writing practices that served no apparent social end (Letter 23). By 1905 he was more outspoken still: witness his dismissive judgement on Remizov's novel *The Pond* [*Prud*] as 'something artificial, fanciful and affected' and therefore unworthy of consideration by Znanie (Letter 41). From this time onwards, any kind of Modernist writing was to be seen by Gorky as something quite inimical to the cause of revolution, a view which he was to express in a number of controversial articles of the post-1905 period.

Despite his turn against the new trends in Russian literature, Gorky was not content simply to endorse the old style of realism as practised in the 1880s and early 1890s. Most interesting in this respect—all the more so as it rehearses an argument which was to resurface later during the debates over Socialist Realism—is his famous statement to Chekhov: 'Do you know what you are doing? You are killing realism' (Letter 19). Although the precise point of this comment may not be immediately apparent, it is clarified later in the same letter, where Gorky adds that 'the time has come when we need something heroic'. This became a common refrain in his letters of the time. Only a few months later he was writing to Andreev of the new Russian readers who needed writers who could supply them with 'something cheerful, heroic, something with romanticism (within reason)' (Letter 27). But if Gorky now believed that literature should present heroic models which might inspire revolutionary ideas—and action—among the proletariat, he also accepted that this would necessarily mean that there would be occasions when purely aesthetic considerations might have to be disregarded. His comments on the poems of Skitalets are a case in point (Letter 29). Despite his disclaimer ('I'm an absolute ignoramus when it comes to poetry'), Gorky obviously knew that these verses were extremely primitive, yet he recognized—quite correctly, as it turned out—their potential effectiveness as propaganda. As he was later to say of his own *Summerfolk*, this is 'not art, but it is clearly a well-aimed shot' (Letter 35).

By 1905 Gorky's life as a writer and a political activist had undergone a radical change. His personal life had also taken a new turn. Although his marriage to Ekaterina Peshkova had never proved mutually satisfactory, they continued living together for a number of years, due no doubt in part to inertia but mainly to Peshkova's evident unwillingness to sever the tie. But their separation was really only a matter of time and that time eventually came at the end of 1903. Gorky had by now become involved with another woman, Mariia Andreeva, who was an actress with the Moscow Art Theatre. The writer had first met her in 1900, when the company had gone to Yalta to visit Chekhov. They encountered each other again in 1902, during rehearsals for *The Lower Depths*. Soon after separating from his wife, Gorky and Andreeva set up house together in St Petersburg, a move which, rather belatedly, marked the end of his 'provincial' days. The significance of this liaison was not only personal, however. Andreeva was a person of radical sympathies who had close links with the Bolsheviks and she may well have had some influence on Gorky's own choice of political allegiance at this crucial time. Certainly, in the years of exile to come, the two of them would devote themselves more or less exclusively to the service of the Bolshevik cause.

Gorky's letters reflect in many ways the changing circumstances in which they were written. More uncompromising in tone, they are also far less personal than his correspondence of the 1890s. Whereas he had previously looked upon his letter-writing as an 'ablution of the soul with tears of silence' (Letter 15) and upon his correspondents (especially Chekhov, as in the instance quoted) almost as confessor figures, there is a perceptible shift away from the highly self-conscious and analytical tone so evident in the early letters. It is an ever more militant and more opinionated Gorky who speaks here, a man whose mind returns repeatedly to a number of obsessive themes. Religion looms particularly large here, which is a sign of Gorky's already growing concern at the renaissance of religious thought which was so important a part of intellectual life in turn-of-the-century Russia. The names of Struve, Berdiaev, and Merezhkovsky—all key figures in this new movement—become the regular target of Gorky's ire (see Letters 25, 26, 27). Not only was he resolutely opposed to the idea of 'God-seeking', which these thinkers were seeking to explore, he was also deeply disturbed by the evidence that such notions could prove attractive to people like Miroliubov and Posse, both of whom, as he saw it, had thereby been seduced from the true path of social revolution. But if Gorky protested against 'God-seeking' it was not because he was fundamentally antagonistic to faith *per se*. On the contrary, he challenges the 'God-seekers' in these letters from a position already close to that mixture of socialism and religion which was later to be known as 'God-building'. The basic idea is that God is not a transcendent being who has to be *sought*, instead, he has to be *created* by the collective and concerted exercise of human consciousness. 'Only man exists, everything else is opinion,' he writes in his angry letter to Posse (Letter 25). Rather than worship the conventional Christian God, he says a little later, we human beings must 'create a great, beautiful, joyous God for ourselves, a God who will be a loving protector of everything and everyone in life!' (Letter 28).

The rise of 'God-seeking' and other trends in religious thought, together with the growing influence of Modernist styles of writing, were for Gorky the sign that the intelligentsia had finally turned its back on its historical mission to liberate the Russian people. His attack on the intelligentsia was conducted both publicly, in such literary works as *Summerfolk* and *Children of the Sun*, and in his private letters. The letter to Piatnitsky of January 1902 (Letter 29) is perhaps the most revealing in this respect, for here Gorky contrasts the discredited 'old' intelligentsia with a 'new' democratic intelligentsia which has yet to reach maturity and to whose service he is already pledging his allegiance. It was as the self-appointed spokesman for this latter group that Gorky composed his public riposte to Tolstoy in 1905 (Letter 40). Although the letter was not published at the time, it was a most significant gesture: in the coming years Tolstoy (together with Dostoevsky) was to be identified by Gorky as one of the main sources of the 'disease' afflicting contemporary Russia. The fact that he now had the courage to set himself against such an illustrious contemporary was a mark of how far the young man from Nizhnii Novgorod had come.

19. To A. P. Chekhov, [after 5 January 1900]

[Nizhnii Novgorod]

Happy New Year!

I am living as absurdly as always and feel desperately overwrought. I shall be going to Yalta at the end of March or in April, if I do not fall ill before that. I really want to live differently somehow—brighter, faster—the main thing is faster. I saw a production of *Uncle Vania* recently—the acting was amazingly good! (I am not a connoisseur of plays, however, and whenever I like a play I always seem to say that the acting was marvellous.) But this *Uncle* of yours has the power to make even poor actors perform well. That's a fact. There are plays which it is quite impossible to spoil in any way by the acting, and there are plays which can actually be spoilt by a good performance. I saw *The Power of Darkness* recently at the Maly Theatre.[1] There was a time when I used to laugh when I heard readings of this work—I even liked it a little—but now I find it offensive and grotesque: indeed, I will never go to see it again. For this I am indebted to the performance of good actors, who mercilessly exposed all the coarseness and absurdity in the play. The same is true in music: even a bad violinist plays Ernst's elegy well, but any trashy little piece becomes quite disgusting when it is played by a virtuoso.[2] I read your 'Lady'.[3] Do you know what you are doing? You are killing realism. You will soon have killed it off completely, and it will stay that way for some time to come. This form has outlived its time, and that's a fact! No one can go further along this path than you have done, no one can write as simply about such simple things as you can. In comparison with even your most insignificant story everything else seems coarse, as if it had been written with a block of wood rather than a pen. The main thing is that everything seems not simple enough, i.e. not truthful. That's how it is. (In Moscow there is a student, Georgii Chulkov,[4] who does a very good imitation of you—he may well be a most talented fellow.) Anyway, you are knocking realism on the head. I am extremely glad about this. We've had enough of it anyway! To hell with it!

Truly, the time has come when we need something heroic: everyone wants something stimulating, something bright, something which is not like life, you know, but more elevated, better, and more beautiful. It is quite essential that the literature of today should start to embellish life a little, and as soon as it starts to do this, life will embellish itself, i.e. people will start to live more quickly and brightly. But just look at them at present, they have such awful eyes—depressing, lacklustre, icy.

You are doing a great thing with your short stories—you are exciting an aversion for this sleepy, half-dead life—the devil take it! Your 'Lady' affected me so deeply that I immediately wanted to betray my wife, to suffer, to swear, and do other things in the same vein. But I remained faithful to my wife—I had no one to be unfaithful with—instead, I just quarrelled furiously with her and with her sister's husband, who is my close friend.[5] I'm sure you didn't expect to have such an effect, did you? I'm not joking, that's the way it was. And I'm not the only one this happens to—don't laugh! Your stories are elegant scent-bottles with all the smells of life in them, and, believe me, in their midst a keen nose will always detect that subtle, pungent, and healthy smell of the 'real', something truly valuable and necessary, and which is always found in all your scent-bottles. But that's enough of that, otherwise you will think that I'm simply paying you a compliment.

As regards a separate book of my best stories—what a wonderful idea that is of yours.[6] I will get this under way, although I definitely do not agree that 'The Fellow-Traveller' is a good story.[7] That was not the right way to write on this theme! Nevertheless, please give me a list of those stories which are worth anything. What do you think—'In the Steppe', 'Izergil',[8] 'On the Rafts', 'The Fellow-Traveller'—but what else? 'Chelkash'? Fine! What about 'Malva'?

You behave very curiously with me, i.e. not curiously, but in a way which is somehow surprisingly absurd; i.e. this is probably not your fault, but mine. Your letters make the strangest impression on me. I'm not just talking about now, when I'm terribly overwrought, but in general. I like them very much, and so on and so forth. You'll have to excuse me for all this prattle, but the fact is, you see, that every time I write to you I want to talk about something which you would find both cheerful and pleasant, and which would generally make life easier for you on this rather rotten earth of ours. Thank you for telling me about Sredin.[9] He is also an awfully good soul. Only I simply cannot understand why he likes Timkovsky.[10] There's a puzzle for you! Please give him my regards, Sredin that is.

They say that you are getting married to an actress with a foreign name.[11] I don't believe it. But if it's true, then I'm glad. It is good to be married, so long as the woman is not dull and not a radical. But the best thing is children. Ah, my son is such a mischievous boy! And very clever too. You will see this for yourself when I bring him in the spring. The only thing is that he has learnt to swear from me and he now curses everyone, and I can't get him out of it. It's very funny—but unpleasant too—when a two-year-old little charlatan shouts at his mother at the top of his voice: 'Get the hell out of here, you anathema!'

And you should hear how clearly he pronounces it, an-nathem-ma!

Well, goodbye for now! My regards. For some reason my *Foma* still hasn't come out yet.[12] Have you read how the Germans are praising you? Recently someone in Petersburg wrote that *Uncle* is better than *The Seagull*. Is that perhaps true, do you think? It's a tricky matter.

Please write.

A. Peshkov

SOURCE: *SS* 28: 112–14.

¹ Lev Tolstoy's drama about peasant life.
² G. W. Ernst, German violinist and composer.
³ Chekhov's story 'Lady with Lapdog' ['Dama s sobachkoi'].
⁴ Georgii Ivanovich Chulkov (1879–1939), poet and prose writer, soon to become a prominent Russian Modernist.
⁵ Adam Egorovich Bogdanovich (1862–1940), historian and ethnographer. Married to Aleksandra Pavlovna Volzhina (1879–99).
⁶ Chekhov had suggested that Gorky publish a single volume containing the best stories from the three volumes of *Sketches and Stories*.
⁷ i.e. 'My Fellow-Traveller'.
⁸ i.e. 'Old Izergil' ['Starukha Izergil''].
⁹ Leonid Valentinovich Sredin (1860–1909), a doctor with whom Gorky first became acquainted in Yalta in 1899.
¹⁰ Nikolai Ivanovich Timkovsky (1863–1922), writer, contributor to *Zhizn'*.
¹¹ Chekhov eventually married Olga Knipper of the Moscow Art Theatre on 25 May 1901.
¹² Gorky's first novel, *Foma Gordeev*, had been serialized in *Zhizn'* between March and September, 1899. It was published in book form in 1900 with a dedication to Chekhov.

20. To A. P. Chekhov, [21 or 22 January 1900]

[Nizhnii Novgorod]

Well, I've been to Lev Nikolaevich's.[1] Eight days have passed since then and I still can't form an impression of him. At first I was startled by his appearance: I'd pictured him quite differently—taller and bigger-boned. But he turned out to be a small old man and for some reason I was reminded of stories about that eccentric genius Suvorov.[2] But when he began to speak I listened and was amazed. Everything he said was surprisingly simple and profound. And even though he was at times quite wrong in my opinion, it was still awfully good. The main thing is that it was very simple. When it comes down to it, he's a complete orchestra in himself, it's just that not all the trumpets are playing in tune. And this is also very good, for it's very human, i.e. typical of a man. In essence, it's terribly stupid to call a man a genius. It's totally incomprehensible what a genius is. It's far simpler and clearer to say 'Lev Tolstoy', as this is both concise and totally original, i.e. definitely unlike anything else. What is more, it's powerful somehow, especially powerful. It's very important and useful to see Lev Nikolaevich, although I do not consider him a miracle of nature in any respect. When you look at him it's terribly nice to feel that one is also a man, to realize that a man can be Lev Tolstoy. Do you understand? It's nice for man in general. He treated me very well, but of course that isn't so important. It's not even important that he talked about my stories, somehow it's the whole lot taken together which is important: everything that was said, his manner of speaking, of sitting, and watching you. It was all of a piece, powerful and beautiful. I never really believed that he was an atheist, although I had felt it, but now, having heard him speak about Christ, having seen his eyes—which are too clever for a believer—I know that he really is an atheist, and a profound one at that. I'm right, am I not?

I sat with him for more than three hours, then I went to the theatre in time for the third act of *Uncle Vania. Uncle Vania* again. Again. And I will go on purpose to see this play more times yet, I'll even book a ticket in advance. I don't consider it a pearl, but I see more content in it than others do; its content is vast, symbolistic, and its form is completely original, quite incomparable. It's a pity that Vishnevsky[3] doesn't understand the uncle, but the others are a pure delight! Even so, Stanislavsky's Astrov is not quite as he ought to be.[4] But they all act marvellously! The Maly Theatre is amazingly crude by comparison with this company. What clever, intellectual people they all are, how much artistic sense they have! Knipper is a wonderful actress, a charming woman and a very clever person.[5] How good her scenes with Sonia are. And Sonia also acted beautifully.[6] Everyone, even the servant—Grigoriev[7]—was splendid, everyone had a fine, subtle understanding of what they were doing, and really, it's even possible to excuse Vishnevsky for his false conception of Uncle Vania because his acting was so good. On the whole, this theatre has given me the impression of being a solid, serious undertaking, an important undertaking. And how appropriate it is that there's no music, and that the curtain is not raised, but drawn back. You know, I couldn't even have imagined that such acting and such a set were possible. It's good! I even regret not living in Moscow: if I did, I would just keep going to this wonderful theatre. I saw your brother, he was standing and clapping.[8] I never applaud the actors—it's offensive to them, i.e. it ought to be offensive.

Have you seen *Cyrano de Bergerac* on stage?[9] I saw it recently and was in raptures over the play.

> Make way for the free men of Gascony!
> Sons of the southern sky are we,
> Beneath the midday sun are we
> All *born with the sun in our blood!*

I really like that 'sun in our blood'. That's how one ought to live, like Cyrano. And not like Uncle Vania and those of his ilk.

But I must have worn you out already. Goodbye for now!

I've got pleurisy. I cough with all my might and I can't sleep at night from the pain in my side. I'll definitely go to Yalta for treatment in the spring.

Warm regards. Give my best wishes to Sredin if you see him, and ask him to pass on my best wishes to Iartsev[10] and Aleksin.

Yours,

A. Peshkov

SOURCE: *SS* 28: 117–18.

[1] Gorky met Tolstoy in person for the first time on 13 January 1900 in Moscow.

[2] Aleksandr Vasilievich Suvorov (1729 or 1730–1800), famous Russian military commander and theorist.

[3] Aleksandr Leonidovich Vishnevsky (1861–1943), actor at the Moscow Art Theatre (MAT).

[4] Konstantin Sergeevich Stanislavsky (real name Alekseev) (1863–1938), actor and director, co-founder of MAT. He directed the play and took the role of Astrov.

[5] Olga Knipper played Elena Andreevna.

[6] The role of Sonia was played by Mariia Pavlovna Lilina.

[7] Mikhail Grigorievich Grigoriev was a member of the Moscow Art Theatre (MAT) in 1899 and 1900 only.

[8] Presumably Ivan Pavlovich Chekhov, who was a teacher in Moscow.

[9] By Edmond Rostand (1869–1918). Gorky saw the play in Nizhnii in 1900 and wrote an enthusiastic review of it.

[10] Grigorii Fedorovich Iartsev (1858–1918), artist and architect, close friend of Chekhov's in Yalta.

21. To V. F. Botsianovsky,[1] *[14 or 15 September 1900]*

[Nizhnii Novgorod]

Dear Vladimir Feofilovich!

I don't consider that I have the right to make any corrections to your work and I cannot permit myself to do so.

It's too late to mention this now, but I find it extremely unpleasant that a personal letter of mine found its way into print due to the indiscretion of the person to whom it was addressed,[2] and that many people are passing it off as my autobiography.

If you are interested in facts of a biographical nature, you can glean them from such stories as 'My Fellow-Traveller', 'One Day in Autumn', 'The Affair with the Clasps' ['Delo s zastezhkami'], etc.

As Mr Menshikov[3] has so rightly commented, my biography is hindering a correct understanding of me.

After all, the point is not who I am, but what I want.

Please don't send me the proofs of your book, for I'm overloaded with all sorts of work and I'd scarcely find the time to read them, unless I were to hang on to them for a long time, which is not in your interests, I think.

All the best!

A. Peshkov

SOURCE: *SS* 28: 129–30.

¹ Literary critic, author of the first book about Gorky, *Maksim Gor'kii: Kritiko-biograficheskii ocherk* (St Petersburg, 1901).
² Gorky's letter to D. M. Gorodetsky, which contained a number of autobiographical details, was published without the writer's permission in *Sem'ia*, no. 36, 1899.
³ Mikhail Osipovich Menshikov (1859–1919), literary critic close to the ideas of Tolstoyanism. His article was entitled 'Krasivyi tsinizm' ['A Beautiful Cynicism'].

22. To A. P. Chekhov, [between 1 and 7 October 1900]

[Nizhnii Novgorod]

Dear Anton Pavlovich!

I've just returned from Moscow, where I raced around for a whole week, enjoying the contemplation of all sorts of wonders, like *The Snow Maiden* and Vasnetsov, *The Death of Ivan the Terrible*, Chaliapin, Savva Mamontov, and Krandievskaia.¹ I'm very tired, quite stunned and glad I've returned to my Nizhnii. *The Snow Maiden* is charming. Ol[ga] Leon[ardovna] [Knipper] is the ideal Lel. Andreeva² isn't bad in this role either, but Ol[ga] Leon[ardovna] is a delight! She's sweet, sunny, and fairy-tale-like—and how well she can sing! The music in *The Snow Maiden* is so good it brings tears to your eyes—it's simple, naïve, genuinely Russian. Good Lord, how splendid it all was! Like a dream, like a folk-tale! Kachalov³ is wonderful in the role of the Tsar Berendei. He's a young fellow who possesses a voice of rare beauty and versatility. Both Snow Maidens, Lilina and Mundt,⁴ are good. Oh, I could write so much about this splendid theatre where even the carpenters have a greater and less selfish love of art than many 'famous Russian literary men'. The theatre, Vasnetsov, and the crazy Knipper family—everything gave me an awful lot of joy, but I fear, my good, dear man, that my joy will cause even greater sadness for you down there in Yalta, hellish, deserted, and cramped place that it is. I'd really like life to shower you with many sparks of joy. You should get away somewhere!

It's good to have been in Mos[cow], but it's tiring to spend a week there. I saw Mamontov—what an original figure he is! I really don't think that he's a swindler at heart, it's just that he has too great a love for beauty and he got carried away by this love. But is it really possible to love beauty too much? Art is like God: all the love in man's heart is insufficient to it, it demands divine homage. And when I see Morozov⁵ backstage at the theatre, covered in dust and all a-tremble for the success of the play, I'm prepared to forgive him all his factories—not that he needs this, of course. I love him for his unselfish love of art, and I can almost feel his peasant, merchant, money-grubbing soul.

Vasnetsov sends his best wishes. I have come to love and respect this great poet more and more. His Bard⁶ is a magnificent thing. And he has so many other lively, beautiful, powerful subjects in his pictures! I wish him immortality.

Krandievskaia. A simple, sweet, deaf woman. She loves you madly and has a good understanding of you. She's a splendid woman who isn't really like an 'intellectual' at all. You have to shout when you talk to her, but that doesn't matter—she has a passionate love for many things. I find that attractive too. Chaliapin is a simple fellow, huge and clumsy, with a coarse, intelligent face. You can sense the artist in his every judgement. But I spent just half an hour with him, no more.

On this trip, I took a great shine to that clever fellow, Danchenko.[7] I'm really glad that I've got to know him. I told him the plot of my play[8] and straightaway, with two or three comments both apt and true, he brought my play to life. He amended and rearranged it all and I was amazed myself how deft and well structured it all turned out to be. What a fine fellow!

My wife and I dined at the Knippers' house. Anna Ivanovna[9] sang with her daughter and on her own—it was lovely! Sredin's mother was there too—she's a fine old woman. It's amazing that all the good old women I know have ugly faces. It's good at the Knippers', simple and devilishly happy.

God knows how much I've endured this week. I left for Moscow with a bad impression. Two days before leaving I went over to Cheshikhin-Vetrinsky's[10] flat—perhaps you know his books about Granovsky and the forties? I went in and saw his wife's brother, a seventeen-year-old lad, lying in the entrance to the flat. His head was torn off and smashed to pieces, so that there was just the lower jaw hanging from his neck. Part of his forehead and a lump of cheek were lying nearby, and between them—an open eye. There were brains and blood on the ceiling and walls. There was a double-barrelled gun in the boy's hands. He'd shot himself in the mouth from both barrels. Because of love and a lack of justice in life.

That same day I received a telegram from Mos[cow]: 'Zina[11] has passed away.' Zina was a marvellous woman, the mother of four and daughter of the Pozern lady to whom I dedicated one of my books.[12] She was a person with a crystal-pure soul. One day she saw her husband unbuttoning the blouse of a seamstress who was living in their home, and when she saw this, she collapsed on the floor. From that night on she was sick for nine months and seven days. She lay in bed all the time and was moved around on sheets. Her whole nervous system was inflamed and something happened to her ganglions—is that possible? Everything caused her pain: her bones, skin, muscles, nails, and hair. Seven minutes before she died she said, 'I shall soon be dead—thank God! Wait a year before telling the children of my death, I implore you.' Then she died. I was in love with her once. Five years ago I thought I couldn't live without her. But now, on my arrival in Moscow, I accompanied her body from the Smolensk market to the Kursk Station and then I went to the theatre to watch *The Snow Maiden*. This is blasphemy, it's disgraceful. Am I a greedy animal or am I just stupid and callous? I feel ashamed as I tell you this now, but for the most part I don't even think about it. And it's the fact that I don't think about it which disturbs me. But now . . .

The other day, I woke up early in the morning and saw a girl in a night-dress sitting on my bed. She asked me if I believed in God. I thought it was a dream and spoke to her about God and many other things. Then she got up and went out into the other rooms. Suddenly there was a wild shriek from my mother-in-law, my wife, and the wet-nurse. It turned out that the girl was not a dream. She was the sister of our neighbour in the flat, a teacher by the name of Ilyinsky, and she had gone mad. Now everyone here is frightened and the door is kept locked, even though the patient has been taken away to hospital. But no one can take her from my memory.

You can see that I live a fantastic and absurd life. My head is spinning and I envy you your peace. It seems to me that life treats you like a sacred object, it doesn't disturb you in your seclusion, it knows your gentle love for people and it doesn't wish to disturb it by encroaching rudely upon you. Perhaps I'm wrong. Perhaps life doesn't spare you at all, but wounds you where you are most sensitive. I envy you because it's beginning to seem to me that life is perhaps rather too concerned to sate me with impressions. You know, sometimes everything swirls about in my head, everything becomes confused and I don't feel particularly well.

I also feel that people are stupid. They need God so that they can live more easily. But they reject him and laugh at those who have faith. Soloviev![13] I'm reading him at the moment. How clever and subtle he is! I'm reading Annunzio—it's beautiful stuff! But incomprehensible. Is God necessary? What do you think, Anton Pavlovich? But let's leave this matter. Forgive me for writing a coarse, incoherent letter which, I imagine, will burst in upon you like a flood of murky water. I'm sorry. I'm like a bull in a china shop.

I'll buy Danilin's[14] book tomorrow. I'll read it and let you know my impressions. I will do so quite calmly. I met Briusov[15] in Moscow. I liked him very much—he's modest, clever, and sincere. The publishing house 'Skorpion'—Briusov and other Decadents—is organizing the publication of a miscellany. They've asked me for a story. I'll give them one. Without fail. I'll be cursed for it, but that's why I'll do it.[16] Otherwise, I'll be just too popular. By the way, how right Menshikov was when he pointed out in his article that I owe the greater part of my popularity to the fact that my autobiography was published.[17] And he was right to accuse me of romanticism, although he was not right to say that my romanticism derives from the intelligentsia. What romanticism do they have? The devil take them!

I won't publish anything in *Nedelia* [*The Week*], I don't have the time. I don't like Menshikov for what he said about Viazemsky and Zhedenov.[18] He's malicious, that Menshikov. He's putting on the Tolstoyanism in vain, it doesn't suit him at all, and I think it is serving only to hinder the development of his outstanding, passionate talent.

I'm writing a novella.[19] I'll soon have it finished. Then I'll start immediately on a drama which I want to dedicate to Danchenko. But how about you, Anton Pavlovich? Have you written anything? Posse showed me the telegram in which you advised him that you'll be sending him something in October. Posse is as happy as a child. I'm happy too. You haven't been sending me the proofs of the Marks edition, even though you promised.[20] Well, never mind. It makes no difference, as I have no time to write an article right now. But in the summer I'll get away somewhere into the backwoods, I'll read everything and then I'll write something with pleasure and joy. It's good to work! I'm getting some writing done and I'm very satisfied, although the novella will be long and boring. It's most embarrassing: I simply can't think of a title for it.

Anyway, it's time to let you get some rest. Goodbye for now!

God grant you happiness—take a trip somewhere. I embrace you firmly.

A. Peshkov
Kanatnaia, Lemke House.

SOURCE: *SS* 28: 132–6.

[1] *Snegurochka*, fantasy play by A. N. Ostrovsky, which had its MAT première on 24 September 1900. The artist Viktor Mikhailovich Vasnetsov (1848–1926), designed the set. *Smert' Ioanna Groznogo*, tragedy by A. K. Tolstoy (1817–75) which played at MAT during the 1899/1900 season. Gorky first met Fedor Ivanovich Chaliapin (1873–1938) in August when the singer was on tour in Nizhnii. Savva Ivanovich Mamontov (1841–1918), industrialist and patron of the arts. A. R. Krandievskaia (1865–1938), contributor to *Zhizn'*.

[2] Mariia Fedorovna Andreeva (1868–1953), actress at MAT, later to become Gorky's common-law wife.

[3] Kachalov, i.e. Vasilii Ivanovich Shverubovich (1875–1948), one of MAT's most famous actors.

[4] Ekaterina Mikhailovna Mundt, actress at MAT.

[5] Savva Timofeevich Morozov (1862–1905), factory owner who gave financial support to MAT.

[6] 'Baian', a painting by Vasnetsov.

[7] Vladimir Ivanovich Nemirovich-Danchenko (1858–1943), dramatist, critic, and director, co-founder of MAT.

[8] Presumably *The Petty Bourgeois*.

[9] Olga Knipper's mother.

[10] V. E. Cheshikhin-Vetrinsky. His books *Granovsky and his Time* [*Granovskii i ego vremia*] and *In the Forties* [*V sorokovykh godakh*] were published in 1897 and 1899 respectively.

[11] Zinaida Karlovna Smirnova, daughter of Gorky's close friend from Samara, Mariia Sergeevna Pozern.

[12] The second volume of *Sketches and Stories*.

[13] Vladimir Sergeevich Soloviev (1853–1900), writer and mystical philosopher, a major influence on Russian Symbolist writers.

[14] Actually I. A. Danilov, the pseudonym of O. A. Fribes, whose collection *In a Quiet Haven* [*V tikhoi pristani*] was published in 1899.

[15] Valerii Iakovlevich Briusov (1873–1924), poet, translator, critic, and prose writer; a leading Symbolist.

[16] Briusov had requested a story for *Severnye tsvety* [*Northern Flowers*], a miscellany published by 'Skorpion'. In the end, Gorky did not contribute (see Letter 23).

[17] See Letter 14, n. 2.

[18] Chekhov had passed on an invitation to Gorky from Menshikov to publish in *Nedelia*. Menshikov had written an article challenging the idea that Prince V. V. Viazemsky was a precursor of Tolstoyan ideas, and had argued with a *zemstvo* official named Zhedenov concerning another of his articles.

[19] *The Three* began serial publication in November 1900.

[20] Chekhov's complete works were being published by A. F. Marks in St Petersburg.

23. *To V. Ia. Briusov, [4 or 5 February 1901]*

[Nizhnii Novgorod]

I'm writing with gratitude to inform you that I've received the excellent book of poetry by Bunin,[1] whom I consider the leading poet of our day.

I know that I'm doing something unforgivable by declining to contribute to *Sev[ernye] tsvety*, and I cannot even apologize to you or make any excuses for myself. But I will, perhaps, explain what the matter is. If I had no time to write anything tolerable earlier, I have even less time to do so now, in particular. My dear Briusov, you will probably have seen from *The Three* that I can't write. My mood is like that of a vicious dog which has been beaten and chained up. And if you are interested, sir, in things other than Assargadonian inscriptions, Cleopatras, and other such old things, if you love mankind, then I have to think that you'll understand what I'm saying.[2]

You see, I feel that it's an abomination to conscript students into the army, it's a vile crime against the freedom of the individual, an idiotic act by scoundrels who have gorged themselves on power.[3]

My heart is seething, and I'd be glad to spit in the impertinent faces of those misanthropes who will read your *Sev[ernye] tsvety* and praise it, just as they praise me.

This is disgraceful and offensive, to the point where I feel an inexpressible anger at everything—at *Tsvety*, at 'Skorpion', and even at Bunin, whom I love—and yet I don't understand why he won't take his talent, which is as beautiful as matt silver, and fashion it into a knife and stick it where it's needed.

I like you a lot; I don't know you, but there's something strong and firm in your face, a profound thought and faith.

It seems to me that you could stand up well for the oppressed, that's what.

That Balmont! Do you like his demonism in the book of Saturnalia?[4] I find it offensive. He's made it all up, he's putting it on. 'People are midges.' He's lying. People are no less unhappy than he is, and anyway, what if they are more deserving of attention and respect than he is?

Warm regards,

A. P.

SOURCE: *SS* 28: 152–3.

[1] Ivan Alekseevich Bunin (1870–1953), poet and prose writer. *Znanie* contributor who wrote a bitter memoir of Gorky in emigration.
[2] A reference to Briusov's poems 'Assargadon' and 'Cleopatra'.
[3] There was a student demonstration in Kiev on 11 January 1901, to which the government responded by having 183 of the demonstrators conscripted into the army.
[4] Konstantin Dmitrievich Balmont (1867–1942), poet and translator, leading representative of Russian Decadence. Balmont's poem 'The Artist-Devil' ('Khudozhnik-d'iavol') had the subtitle 'A Book of Saturnalia'.

24. To E. P. Peshkova, [4 March 1901]

[St Petersburg]

It's now 5 o'clock in the evening. I've just come from a demonstration at the Kazan Cathedral.[1] It started at 12 p.m. and is continuing even now. The crowd was huge, about twelve or fifteen thousand. Two to three thousand were demonstrators, the rest were sympathetic onlookers. I can't tell you anything about it at present, I'm too upset. People were beaten with whips in the cathedral and on the church porch; they say that two were killed. A great number of people were beaten up both inside and outside the cathedral.

We'll see each other soon, dear Katia.

Don't worry, for goodness' sake.

Yours,

Aleksei

SOURCE: *AG* 5: 78–9.

[1] A demonstration outside the Kazan Cathedral on Nevskii Prospekt in protest against the conscription of students into the army (see Letter 23, n. 3).

25. To V. A. Posse, [after 10 August 1901]

[Nizhnii Novgorod]

Dear friend!

I started to answer your letter several times, but I couldn't do it and decided not to answer at all. But there is one point in your letter which definitely requires an answer.

You write: 'You are, perhaps, friends with an imaginary me but not with the real me.' I love your lively, passionate soul, and I'm friends with a man who is able both to be captivated and to captivate. Sensitive, tender, a little jaded, he has a magnificent talent for detecting the living sounds of the new life which is to come and he's able to convey those sounds passionately to people. I love the fighter in you, the organizer, the man of intelligence, and I believe that I've sensed all these qualities in you. This is why it was all the more annoying and absurd for me to hear you exclaim: 'It's impossible to live without religion!' Without which religion? Struve and Berdiaev and others of their ilk are trying to create a religion.[1] Pathetic people! They have caught a whiff of the practical idealism which has been born in life, in real life, in the hearts of people—the idealism of healthy beings who feel that they are people in the proper sense of the word. And so, in order not to lose touch with life, P. V. Struve places under this finished building a starry-eyed bourgeois foundation in the form of an idealism borrowed from Fichte.[2] What the hell do I want with bitter-sweet jelly of this sort when I could supply Fichte himself with the idealism which is in my blood, my brain, my soul? I don't know Fichte, damn him, and I don't want to go back to anyone, not even if it were Plato himself! I want *my own* mood to be my philosophy, i.e. that guiding thing they want to call religion. I like life, I love to live, I get pleasure from living, do you understand? Explain this to me and a new philosophy will appear of itself, and then Fichte becomes unnecessary. What the hell do you want with a religion if you don't feel able to create your own? And how can you adopt something from others when you yourself are God, Kant, and the source of all wisdom and obscenity?

Only man exists, everything else is opinion. You say that 'a conscious being is a mistake of nature'. That may be so, but that conscious being exists, and therefore it is a fact of reality. It alone is conscious, and therefore free to create a life for itself as it wishes. Did not man create God in his own image and likeness? And he will create life as he wishes too. I'm not surprised that you've turned sour. If I had left Russia I might perhaps have hanged myself. But I endured the loss of *Zhizn'* in silence and I proudly spurned all regrets.[3] And even if my son, whom I love most of all, were to die, I would also keep silent and send to the devil anyone who might come with their condolences. I don't want to give pleasure to the petty bourgeois, and such condolences are a pleasure for them.

You will read this and you will be angry, perhaps, and think: 'He is preaching at me!' But I'm only trying to persuade you. You are dear to me, because in my eyes you are a great figure, a person who is necessary to life, you are a fire and therefore capable not only of creating a great deal of light and heat, but also of burning things. You've been struck a blow, you've grown weak. But you should have become angry, for this suits you far better and is much more valuable. To me your letter was like a knife in the back: I didn't expect you to howl from the pain the way you did and to show no pride. You will say: 'But I wrote this to a friend!' However, you should hide your wounds from your friends just as I've hidden mine from you on more than one occasion. One should be proud of one's wounds only in the face of death, not before.

This letter has turned out to be incoherent. I didn't want to reply, but I have done so unwittingly somehow. I regret it. I shouldn't have. Well, goodbye for the time being. I'll write again soon.

Write to me care of my wife. She sends her best to you.

What are you going to translate: Heine or Fichte? It would really be better if you chose the former! But I repeat that I know the latter only through the history of philosoph[ical] systems, and alas, even if he were to be translated ten times over, I still wouldn't bother getting to know him. I have no desire to. Truly, brother, the philosophy in German books is far from first-rate; first-rate philosophy is to be found in Russian life.

Are you working on your book?

Write, my friend, but don't shout at me. I will answer promptly.

Yours,

A. Peshkov

SOURCE: *SS* 28: 169–71.

---

[1] Nikolai Berdiaev (1874–1948), religious philosopher and writer. At this time Berdiaev was close to Petr Berngardovich Struve (1870–1944), a politician and theorist who had been active in the social democratic movement during the 1890s. Berdiaev's book *Subjectivism and Idealism in Social Philosophy* appeared in 1901 with an introduction by Struve.
[2] Struve was co-author of *Problems of Idealism* (1902). Johann Gottlieb Fichte (1762–1814), German philosopher, the first of the transcendental idealists.
[3] The journal was closed down by the censors in 1901.

26. To V. S. Miroliubov,[1] [December 1901]

[Oleiz]

Thank you, brother, for the book you sent me and for the interesting letter.

Merezhkovsky's behaviour once again confirms my opinion of him— not that it needed any confirmation. He's a swindler and a clever little beast. He uses his speeches about God and Christ as a way to secure some of life's blessings, as a means of satisfying his ambitious soul. You'll see! Don't you believe him. Even if he were to pour oil on himself and set himself alight and then praise God as he burns, it should make no difference—don't you believe him! He'd do this so that people would talk about him and erect a monument to him. A petty Herostratus![2] Just remember that it makes no difference to a petty Herostratus what he does to achieve fame: he'd not only burn the temple, he'd even betray Christ to do so.

I would like to have a good look at all these seekers of God you're spending your time with! I think that they're all little people who have taken to searching for God out of shame for the emptiness of their lives or out of fear before its contradictions. They see that man is being oppressed ever more severely by the arbitrariness of those swine who are intoxicated with power. They see that man is suffering unbearably all around them. They have some conscience, but it is that Russian sort of conscience which is lascivious and cowardly, like the imagination of a masturbator. And these people, who have neither the strength nor the courage to remake life freely and rise boldly to the defence of the human right to live—a right which has been trampled on by the powers that be—these people hide in their corners like hypocrites and calmly conduct their debates about Christ. He who believes doesn't debate; he who debates wants a peaceful and cautious life. My friend, they conduct their debates above all out of a sense of self-preservation, and nowadays it is only sons of bitches who debate because decent people are not allowed to debate, even when they are on their own.

Seeing you in their midst, I look upon this as a punishment which has been visited upon them for their falsehood and hypocrisy. And by now a feeling of indignation towards them should have taken root in your direct and sincere soul. You must not and cannot tolerate such outbursts as Merezhkovsky's.

'Consequently, there is nothing to discuss'—this is what the priests and he said to you when you realized that T[olstoy] does not consider Christ to be God. You were unable to argue against them. But I swear the time will come when you will say something like this to them: 'You swine! Is it really a question of who Christ is? Why are you wagging your cowardly, dogs' tails? Why are you lying, you lackeys of bigots and rapists? The question is this: are the teachings of Christ—whether he be God or man, and whom you say you love—compatible with the life you're living, with the social order you so obediently serve, and with the oppression of man which you support by not arguing against it? Where is it that your Christ laid down that one man should ride on top of another, and that you should teach meek endurance to those who carry the burden and have become brutalized due to exhaustion? What do you need Christ for when there are policemen? And why have the church as a disciplinary establishment for educating the oppressed, when there are Cossacks who can beat them and shoot them down, should they become restive?'

Having said something of this sort, you should give the most fervent Christians, like Mitka Merezhkovsky, two or three good slaps in the face and then go back to your huge task, a task which will give you peace of mind far sooner than conversations with these adulterers and life-fearing cowards. Warm regards!

Yours,

A. Peshkov

I spoke to An[ton] Pav[lovich]. He promises to have it ready soon.[3] I'll probably manage to get myself organized before long too.

SOURCE: *SS* 28: 211–12.

---

[1] Viktor Sergeevich Miroliubov (1860–1939), editor and publisher, associated at this time with *Zhurnal dlia vsekh*. For further details, see the Introduction to this section.

[2] Herostratus burnt down the temple in Ephesus in 356 BC so as to immortalize his name.

[3] Chekhov's story 'The Bishop' ['Arkhierei'] was published in *Zhurnal dlia vsekh* in April 1902.

27. To L. N. Andreev,[1] *[between 2 and 4 December 1901]*

[Oleiz]

My dear old friend!

If they're talking about 'a pretentious celebrity', it means they've started to get jealous:[2] ergo, as the Latins would say, they'll soon come to hate you. But for a good writer hatred is the pepper, the mustard, and all the other seasonings necessary for digesting the impressions of reality.

I would really like them to hate you, even a great deal, you see, for each time my soul's nose detects the smell of hatred, I become more intelligent and more talented as a result, and this is what you need too. You need it even more than I do. For I've had a good sniff of fame— fame smells sour in Russia!—whereas you haven't yet. Thou shouldst fear praise above all things, O Leonid! Whenever I hear praise, it seems to me that it comes from the mouth of some son of a bitch who is praising me because he fears that I might have told the truth about him, the wretch. Suspicious is the praise of the Russian philistine who has become accustomed to bribing everyone, from the local policeman to God.

This advice will not hurt you, my friend and comrade. I will also say this: for the time being, our young people love you by way of an advance because, sir, other than 'Dark Distance' you have given them nothing so far.[3] What they need nowadays is something cheerful, heroic, something with romanticism (within reason). One must therefore write something in that style—I mean that quite seriously. Because, come what may, a revolution is happening in Russia. It is not the sort where people fight in the streets and chop off the heads of kings, but another sort, which is more serious. We are witnessing the breakdown of the philosophical and ethical basis on which the well-being of the petty bourgeoisie is founded.

Nowadays it is not so much the Gringmuts, Meshcherskys & Co. who are our enemies,[4] but rather those plasterers who are puttying over the cracks in the old barn of our life, that is to say Messrs. Menshikov, Rozanov, Merezhkovsky, 'a Russian' from *Russkoe slovo* [*The Russian Word*] and others of that same devout spirit, whom it is simpler to call the scum of Christ.[5] Not of the real Christ, but of that church-police-state Christ who recommends that we render equally unto God and tsar. I don't approve of the real Christ either, because he came too soon. His time is about a thousand years from now, and for the time being we must settle our scores, hate one another, fight, and grow tired. And once we have grown tired, then we will start to love each other, because, as you know, this is a business which is handled much better lying down. Yes indeed. This means that you should strike Menshikov, that advocate of love,[6] because the only reason the scoundrel preaches love is to keep life from disturbing him with the tragedy of its contradictions. Strike the petty bourgeois!.. For he loves to erect fences everywhere. But you probably find me tiresome and tedious.

I wrote to Teleshov.[7] It's a wonderful idea.[8] Send a copy of your book to Evgenii Nikolaevich Chirikov. The address is Yaroslavl: there's no need to put anything else. Should you need money, ask Piatnitsky[9] if he has any of yours and if he doesn't, ask him for some of mine. Write and tell him, 'I'm getting married!', then he'll give you some. Once you've got married, you should come here. I'll lock you in a comfortable place, and you can write while your wife goes out for walks. I don't know her, but she has a splendid face and eyes. I would like her to be a woman of character who is able to take you in hand.[10]

'The Tocsin' ['Nabat'] is excellent! It's really excellent. But if Benvenuto Cellini were to start just making brooches for ladies and pins for gentlemen's neckties, we'd have to hit Benvenuto about the head with a stick. Forgive me, brother! You need to spread yourself wider and jump higher. As I say, 'The Tocsin' is amazing, but 'The Wall' ['Stena'] makes a greater impression, despite its obscurity.

Send 'Thought' ['Mysl''] to *Russkoe bogatstvo*. They say that N. K. Mikhailovsky *himself* wrote about you.[11] This doesn't happen to just anyone, my friend. This happened to me too, although it wasn't particularly propitious.[12] Funny, absurd, and unnatural though it might seem to say so, but Nikolai Konstantinovich's voice is not much heard nowadays. Nevertheless he is himself a man of merit, etc. Send him the story.

Muraviev has assembled a fine company:[13] Andreev, Chirikov, Shestov (author of the book *Good in the Teaching of Tolstoy and Nietzsche*), Nevedomsky (author of the preface to Lichtenberger and articles in *Nachalo*), Vasilii Iakovlevich Bogucharsky, the fiction writer Serafimovich, Posse of course, and who else?[14] I don't remember just now. I can tell you that Posse is a fine fellow. He's a man of intelligence, an organizer, a passionate heart who is able to captivate any man. I am quite convinced that if you were to meet him, you'd come to feel a strong and sincere love for each other. . .

Just one more thing, dear friend. Get some money from Feigin and buy me *The Notes of Volkonsky*, the Decembrist, and when you've bought it, send it to me.[15] Do so as quickly as you can, please. Take some more money and have a copy of your book bound and send that to me as well. I need it. Have it bound at my expense, you devil, and I'll get it from you later... Give my regards to your fiancée. How do you spell the word, by the way? I don't remember. So will you come? I'm expecting you.

A. Peshkov

Damn! A telegram from Kiev—my old friend Nik. Vasiliev, the senior laboratory assistant at the Polytechnic, has poisoned himself and died.[16] My wife is going to Kiev. This is quite a blow for me. A rare man has died, a rare man.

SOURCE: *LN* 72: 113–14.

[1] Leonid Nikolaevich Andreev (1871–1919), writer soon to rise to prominence through the Znanie school. For more details see the general Introduction.

[2] Andreev had complained to Gorky that some of his friends had turned against him following the success of his first collection of stories.

[3] 'Into the Dark Distance' ['V temnuiu dal''] was Andreev's most obviously 'revolutionary' work in Gorky's eyes.

[4] Vladimir Andreevich Gringmut (1851–1907) and Prince Vladimir Petrovich Meshchersky (1839–1914) were both editors of right-wing publications (*Moskovskie vedomosti* [*The Moscow Gazette*] and *Grazhdanin* [*The Citizen*], respectively).

[5] All writers associated with the right and with religious ideas. Vasilii Vasilievich Rozanov (1856–1919), philosopher and writer whose views on religion, race, and sexuality brought him considerable notoriety. Grigorii Spiridonovich Petrov was a priest who wrote under the *nom de plume* 'A Russian'.

[6] Menshikov had published a collection of critical articles entitled *On Love* [*O liubvi*].

[7] Nikolai Dmitrievich Teleshov (1867–1957), writer and contributor to the Znanie miscellanies.

[8] Teleshov had the idea of publishing books of stories in cheap editions.

[9] Konstantin Petrovich Piatnitsky (1864–1939), business manager of the Znanie publishing house. See the Introduction to this section for further details.

[10] Andreev married Aleksandra Mikhailovna Veligorskaia in February 1902.

[11] Mikhailovsky's review of Andreev's first collection of stories appeared in *Russkoe bogatstvo*, no. 11, 1900. Andreev's story was turned down by *Russkoe bogatstvo*; it appeared in *Mir bozhii* [*God's World*], no. 7, 1902.

[12] See Letter 14, n. 3.

[13] Nikolai Konstantinovich Muraviev (1870–1936), Moscow lawyer and publisher. An active figure of the left, Muraviev was planning to take over the journal *Pravda* at this time.

[14] Shestov, *nom de plume* of Lev Isaakovich Shvartsman (1866–1938), critic and philosopher, whose *Good in the Teaching of Tolstoy and Nietzsche* [*Dobro v uchenii Tolstogo i Nitshe*] was published in 1900; Nevedomsky, *nom de plume* of Mikhail Petrovich Miklashevsky (1886–1943), literary critic and publicist, later a Menshevik; Bogucharsky (1861–1915), historian, publisher, and editor; Serafimovich, i.e. Aleksandr Serafimovich Popov (1863–1949), writer, whose later novel *The Iron Flood* [*Zheleznyi potok*] became a classic precursor of Socialist Realism.

[15] Iakov Aleksandrovich Feigin (1859–1915), publisher, translator, and official editor of *Kur'er* between 1897 and 1903. *Zapiski Sergeia Grigor'evicha Volkonskogo (dekabrista)* was published in St Petersburg in 1901.

[16] Nikolai Zakharovich Vasiliev (1868–1901). Gorky depicted Vasiliev in a later autobiographical work, 'On the Harm of Philosophy' ['O vrede filosofii'].

28. To L. N. Andreev, [7–9 January 1902]

[Oleiz]

Don't give them anything![1] You should not have made any promises. The very fact that you're wondering whether to write or not obviously indicates that you have nothing to write for *that* journal and that you will never write anything good for it. And for such publications—contrary to the accepted norm—one must write the very best one can. In this matter I advise you to wait until you really want to write yourself, until your soul feels fit to burst.

Even though you're no critic, what you wrote about *The Three* was good. But you don't understand Ilia the way I do.[2]

Ilia doesn't repent before people; he speaks to them out of contempt. He cannot accept judgement either from people, whom he has himself condemned, or from God, whom he has lost.

There's no God, Leonidushka. There is only the dream of him, an eternal, unquenchable yearning somehow to explain oneself and life. God is a convenient explanation for everything which is going on around us, and that is all. Tolstoy—who seems to be a believer in God—actually preaches the necessity for some sort of pantheistic hypothesis. In the mean time, God is not needed because, if we were to give him to them, the petty bourgeois would use him to hide from life. Today God is slipping away from the petty bourgeois, and the sons of bitches are left without a shelter. Serves them right! Let them hop about naked through life with their empty souls and let them rattle like broken bells. Once they have died from the cold and an inner hunger, then we will create a great, beautiful, joyous God for ourselves, a God who will be a loving protector of everything and everyone in life! So there!

Even if God did exist, we shouldn't give him up to the petty bourgeois.

Get married soon and then come for a visit. Don't get depressed, just work! If you're in poor spirits, don't go out visiting people, they won't cheer you up anyway. Just sit down and write, write, write; it makes no difference what you write as long as it's sincere. Really and truly! I am greatly looking forward to seeing you.

Get some money from Feigin, use it to buy *Miroliubov's book about Sakhalin* and send it to me quickly.[3] I really need it. Don't have anything to do with Viktor Miroliubov and his *Zhurnal*. Don't do it, I'm telling you straight! Do some writing, by all means, but don't have anything to do with him.[4] Goodbye for now.

Al. Peshkov

SOURCE: *LN* 72: 128–9.

[1] Andreev had asked for Gorky's advice on whether to write something for an 'illegal, strongly revolutionary journal' (*LN* 72: 128).

² Andreev's views on the novel and its central hero, Ilia Lunev, are contained in a letter of 30 December 1901 (ibid. 126).

³ Miroliubov, *nom de plume* of Ivan Pavlovich Iuvachev (1850–1936), a member of the terrorist People's Will organization. His book *Eight Years on Sakhalin* [*Vosem' let na Sakhaline*] appeared in 1901.

⁴ Because of Miroliubov's growing interest in religion and mysticism.

29. To K. P. Piatnitsky, [between 7 and 11 January 1902]

[Oleiz]

It was foolish of me not to hang on to Skitalets's poems.¹ If I had, I'd probably have been able to polish up 'The Diamonds' ['Almazy']. Send me the proofs, I'll try again. If it doesn't work out, we'll put 'The Bell' ['Kolokol'] first. It has a good sound to it. As far as the contents of Skitalets's book are concerned, the final say is yours. I must say that I'm an absolute ignoramus when it comes to poetry, as I am in grammar, and also in logic. I can't distinguish iambic verse from trochaic, and for a long time I thought that an amphibrach wasn't a verse form at all, but an antediluvian monster like ichthyosaurus.

When you send the proofs, would you be so good as to indicate in detail where things are wrong and what is wrong with them. As for Stepan's² lyrics, I am of the opinion that the whole lot should be sent to the devil so that people's impression of him might remain intact. What do you think? 'Don Quixote' is better in manuscript than in print because the censor has altered it somewhat. In the manuscript this work was called 'The Knight' ['Rytsar'']. It does have an idea in it but by no means do I insist on its inclusion in the book. I know that it's bad.

Your assumption that the book will be a success makes me very happy. I really thirst for such success with the public, and if it's accompanied by disapproval from the critics, I'll be beside myself with delight!

I'm busy proof-reading my books. Most disagreeable it is, to be sure! 'It does not befit the dog to return to his vomit.' L[ev] N[ikolaevich] [Tolstoy] and I once said these words at exactly the same moment and the coincidence was so touching that it made us both laugh heartily. But we didn't laugh as augurs, no!—we laughed as people who were ashamed of themselves. 'As you read you see how many superfluous words and pages there are, how much rubbish!' he said. 'I cannot bear to read Tolstoy's compositions!' 'And I can't bear to read Gorky. . .' your humble servant confessed sincerely. I'd like to tear out many of my writings by the roots but it's too late! If the public were to see that my books had become thinner, they would cry out, 'Fraud! Help! My neighbour's book is thicker than mine!'

Our mutual friend, who's living on Green Erin, continues to needle me by sending messages which seethe with impatience.³ He invites me

to join him. . . and summons me to death. He's apparently quite convinced that we can successfully set up a game of Herzen-Bakunin.[4]
Essentially there is a tiny little mistake in all this but it's a mere trifle, of
course—why shouldn't we test the strength of the wall with our heads,
after all? And, of course, 'poor is the soldier who. . .', etc. But who is all
this for? The point is that there are at present two groups of people in
our Empire who need free speech. What is more, whereas one of them
needs speech alone, the other also needs an example of that speech. The
first group is large, diverse, and lacking any sort of unity, even a unity of
desire. These people are usually ahead of the masses and, as always, they
stand apart from the needs of the people, from those vital needs which
they still haven't acknowledged. They are clever. But cowardly. Seeing
the rise of democracy, they have become frightened by this phenomenon—although they should have found nothing surprising about it—they
have become frightened for culture, claiming that in the event of victory
the democrat would show it no mercy. So now they preach the necessity
for 'aristocrats of the spirit', idealism, and other such things. If only you
knew how offensive I find this turning *back* to self-perfection![5] I mean
what I say—this is a step backwards! Nowadays we don't need the perfect man, we need a fighter, a worker, an avenger. We'll perfect ourselves
later, once we have settled the scores. There is another part of the intelligentsia which seeks God, behind whom it would like to hide its
incapacity for life, its fear of life's contradictions etc. The majority, as
always, are neither here nor there but they are quite willing none the less
to warm themselves at someone else's fire and to ride onwards on their
neighbour's back. For the sake of this intelligentsia it's not worth organizing anything on Green Erin.

  The other intelligentsia has only just hatched from the egg, it's in the
adolescent stage, but it already senses instinctively what it needs. This
intelligentsia enjoys a unity of aspirations even now, when its consciousness of its human rights is comparatively little developed. These people
do not have to be pushed forward, they need rather to be held back,
offensive though this might be. For them examples are far more important than words. They hear all sorts of words. Only yesterday they were
being told that they were the most important, the most joyful and mighty
thing in life. But today they are told that 'the spiritual achievements of
the aristocratic intelligentsia of the past display psychological traits which
are more lofty and in some respects closer to the future than the bour-
geois-democratic intel[ligentsia] of the capitalist age with its spiritual
poverty and anti-idealist spirit'.[6] Being literate, the democratic intelligentsia will read these lines—which are far less applicable to them than
to the first group, the bourgeois group—and take offence at their shrewd
eloquence, believing these lines to refer to themselves. And they are right
to take offence. But as long as they only take offence, it's of no matter!

This is what's bad: nowadays they sense that yesterday's teacher has become their enemy, a traitor to their interests. This intelligentsia needs examples of stability, it needs an active demonstration as well as words. For example, it would be most agreeable and instructive for them if M. Gorky, amongst others, were to be killed or injured before their eyes on the street during a fight with the police, whilst it would be extremely disappointing, vile, and of no pedagogic value if the selfsame Gorky, sitting in some foreign cell in the shade of an elm tree, were to begin to 'unleash the revolution' from there with words alone, no matter how eloquent those words might be. This is what we're talking about!

No, one ought to live at home. It's more interesting and useful to live at home.

Incidentally, I can agree about the 'closeness to the future of the spiritual achievements of the aristocr[atic] intellig[entsia]'. . . even though I do have a slight reservation. Close to the future, you say? Very well! But would you be so kind as to convince me that the 'future' must be built according to the old recipes, and that democrats—people who have not even lived as yet—are bound to follow the paths recommended down the ages, that they are unable to produce a culture of their own and their own understanding of the world which would run directly counter to the bourgeois-Christian view of the business of life, a view which seems not to be an indisputable axiom. As I understand it, the reverend wise men who have taught about life have tended more and more to teach about the means by which it is possible to achieve peace and comfort in this life. However, I haven't encountered any philosophers who have dared to argue that life is joy and music, that work is a duty which is far from pleasant, and that life is only good when work is pleasure. You know, for some reason it has seemed to me from the days of my youth, as it seems even now, that these gentlemen-creators of modern culture have always played much the same tune: work and endure, you'll never jump higher than your head, you will not know God. It's quite possible that this is true. But what if it isn't? What if I don't want to endure, what if I will work only when I'm able to find enjoyment in work, and what if I do jump higher than my head and create a most magnificent God for myself, a protector of everyone and everything, a God who is the source of joy and gaiety?

Man can do anything!

Please forgive me! I've got carried away by the grace of that devil [Viktor] Miroliubov. There's an impious individual for you! At first we quarrelled fiercely, but then we philosophized for quite a time and finished up philosophizing ourselves to the point where we almost began to quarrel again. In the end he gave me a splendid cane. . . It's obviously a symbolic gift. I think that with this very cane he has silently obliged me to correct his behaviour. What a ridiculous figure! But he has his virtues . . . it would be quite terrible if such a huge body contained only imperfections.

Having reread this letter, I can see that it is amazingly poorly written, confused, rough, and just plain nasty! No, it's evident that philosophy is not my speciality! Forgive me for all this chatter. The point is that this is something which is causing me more and more pain. I can see ever more clearly the gulf between two psychological types. There is the petty-bourgeois individual, cautious, adaptable, and cultured, a man who wants to pay a penny of his spirit for a shilling's worth of comfort for the body and soul, and then there is the straightforward, heroically inclined democrat who is prepared prematurely to bang his head against a wall. They are not getting on well with each other! I fear that they will drift even further apart, I fear that where there should be respect and trust, there is hate from one side and fear from the other. That's how things are.

Various people come to see me, mainly ordinary folk. The Tolstoys and various others come round. O Lord!

I'm waiting for you to come, but it seems it will be a long wait!

I received the telegrams concerning the money. Thank you. But don't transfer anything to the treasury, because I'm obliged by a signed statement not to leave Oleiz without the police chief's permission, and it would be quite unpleasant to have to ask for such permission. Send it to my wife in Koreiz.

Goodbye for now!

In my heart of hearts I still retain the faint hope of seeing you here.

A. Peshkov

SOURCE: *AG* 4: 65–8.

[1] Pseudonym (meaning 'Rolling Stone') of Stepan Gavrilovich Petrov (1869–1941), writer and protégé of Gorky. Znanie published his *Stories and Songs* [*Rasskazy i pesni*] in 1902.

[2] i.e. Skitalets's lyric poems.

[3] V. A. Posse was in Ireland at this time. He wanted Gorky to join him and revive the banned *Zhizn'* as an illegal journal.

[4] The celebrated radical journal *Kolokol* [*The Bell*; 1857–67] was published from London and then Geneva by Aleksandr Herzen and Nikolai Ogarev.

[5] 'Self-perfection' was a Tolstoyan belief that people should strive to perfect themselves rather than seek the radical transformation of society.

[6] A quotation from Nikolai Berdiaev's article 'The Struggle for Idealism' ['Bor'ba za idealizm'].

30. To K. P. Piatnitsky, [20 or 21 December 1902]

[Moscow]

Heartfelt thanks for the telegram, my dear friend. The play's success has been exceptional, I didn't expect anything like it.[1] And, do you know, this play will not succeed anywhere other than in this wonderful theatre. Vl[adimir] Ivan[ovich] Nemirovich[-Danchenko] interpreted the play so well and staged it so that not a single word was wasted. The acting is stunning! Moskvin, Luzhsky, Kachalov, Stanislavsky, Knipper, and Gribunin have accomplished something amazing.[2] It was only at the first performance that I realized and saw for myself the amazing advances achieved by all these people who have been used to portraying the characters of Chekhov and Ibsen. It's a kind of self-renunciation for them. The second performance was even more vivid in the harmony of its execution. The public roars and laughs. Just imagine, despite the great number of people who die in the play, there is laughter in the theatre during all four acts.

Moskvin plays with the public as if it were a ball. He says: 'Ah you scum!' and they laugh! 'You villain!'—they laugh even louder, and then, all of a sudden, 'He's hanged himself!' The theatre is suddenly like a desert. Faces drop, and I've been told several times: 'One can't help laughing, but you strive too hard for that laughter. It's unfair if you provoke it yourself'. Kachalov is remarkably good. Satin is splendid in the fourth act, devilishly so. Luzhsky too. It's the same with all of them. They're wonderful actors!

I'm leaving for Nizhnii tomorrow. I'm sending you a letter from Berlin.[3] *You* will receive the photographs in two days' time.[4] I don't trust sending them directly to the theatre, and think that perhaps I should get Scholtz to deliver them by hand.[5]

Well, goodbye for now!

Get hold of Sunday's *Novosti dnia* [*News of the Day*]; there are photos from *The Depths* in it.

Well, all the best.

A.P.

My wife sends her best wishes.

SOURCE: *SS* 28: 277–8.

[1] *The Lower Depths* opened at MAT on 18 December.
[2] These actors played the roles, respectively, of Luka, Bubnov, the Baron, Satin, Nastia, and Medvedev.
[3] A letter from the Kleines Theater in Berlin concerning the staging of *The Lower Depths*.
[4] The photographs were of the MAT production of the play.
[5] Avgust Karlovich Scholtz (1857–1923), translator of Gorky's works into German.

31. To K. P. Piatnitsky, [17–19 February, 1903]

[Nizhnii Novgorod]

Dear friend—things are bad. My nerves are so overwrought that I have become unwell, and my mood is disgusting. The reason is Andreev. In three days this fellow created such a hullabaloo with his unseemly goings-on that I was completely thunderstruck. It all began with his making a declaration of love, clearly because he was intoxicated, to a local girl, a good acquaintance of mine and simply a wonderful person. She informed me about this and was very indignant both about Leonid's ways and about the things he told her about his wife, who is unwell, by the way, having not yet entirely recovered from childbirth. I had it out with Leonid; he evaded matters rather abominably and ended up getting drunk. Not to the same degree of bestiality as the first time, but none the less quite thoroughly. When his drunken misbehaviour started, I suggested that he go to bed, but he didn't want to and said he was leaving. It was already 4.00 a.m. So I took off his boots and hid them. He got angry. He rushed at Aleksin with a knife, but he struck the door instead of the doctor.

We then decided to let him go off to any point of the compass. He left for his hotel in the company of Malinin,[1] and set off for Moscow that evening, without even looking in on me again. I sent a telegram to some acquaintances there so that they could meet him and sober him up. Such is the external aspect of the event. As for the inner aspect, it is as follows: I find the mere sight of Leonid Andreev disgusting; I find it so loathsome and vile that in all probability my attitude towards him will never be restored to what it was able to be before. It is sufficient to see a writer become like a beast just once for you to lose all respect for him.

Your report about the 'rights' and the events surrounding the history of their formulation inspires some very gloomy thoughts.[2] Send me a telegram to let me know whether I should inform V[ladimir] Al[eksandrovich] [Posse] of the new procedure with the addendum on the agreement. If so, send one word: 'yes' or 'inform'. I will write to him at once. To be frank, I doubt that we will succeed: they are angry with us and envious to the point of idiocy.

Send the money with mother.[3] If I remember correctly, I left 7,000. You have already sent 2,000, another 1,000 you should send off by money order, if you haven't done so already, so I must have 4,000 coming to me. But I don't remember: was it 7,000 or 6,000? My memory is getting awfully bad.

Upon receipt of this letter transfer 500 to my wife—this is something separate from what I have mentioned above.

I have a persistent desire to see you, in which regard I have a passionate adherent—my wife. It is quite probable that when mother returns, we'll both drop in on you. However, I would like to choose a time when you will be a little less busy.

Were I in your position, I would be in despair at the mass of petty details that bear in upon you from all sides.

I received the copies of my own books along with those of the new authors—thank you! But I no longer have any left. So I would like to ask for a dozen or so further copies of each volume. The demand in the countryside is increasing frightfully. How is the Chirikov going? I am more interested in his success than in anyone else's because his situation, as I have already described to you, is more difficult than that of the others.[4]

Warm regards,

A. Peshkov

I don't have Vladimir Aleksandrovich's address. So let me know his address, and in a letter (not a telegram) please answer the question: should I write to him?

SOURCE: *AG* 4: 121–2.

[1] An actor.
[2] Gorky and Piatnitsky had arranged to take over the rights of some members of Znanie who were leaving the co-operative.
[3] i.e. with Mariia Volzhina, Gorky's mother-in-law.
[4] In his previous letter to Piatnitsky, Gorky had written that Chirikov was depressed and had taken to drink (*AG* 4: 120).

32. To N. D. Teleshov, [19 or 20 February 1903]

[Nizhnii Novgorod]

Thank you, dear Nikolai Mitrich, for the book.[1] I wish it great success, and may this success stir in you the desire to work for the good of your native land and its new reader.

It is a great phenomenon, brother, this 'new' reader who devours books as if they were truly food for the spirit and not just a condiment for a tedious and grey life.

Give my regards to Aleksandr Serafimovich and let me know his address. He has also sent me a book and a letter, but he didn't tell me his address, so I don't know where to reply to.

I'm sending you *The Depths*.

Give my regards to your wife. I wish you all the best, and above all good spirits and the desire to write.

Yours,

A. Peshkov

SOURCE: *SS* 28: 281.

[1] The first volume of Teleshov's stories, published by Znanie in 1903.

33.　To E. K. Malinovskaia,[1] [February 1904]

[Sestroretsk]

Faith in the first instance is Faith in God—that is, an unshakeable conviction in the powerlessness of man. Faith in the power of Thought is a vibrant, proud, and free feeling, which grows constantly together with Thought; it means man having faith in himself.

Freedom, beauty, and respect for people are fundamental, and therefore undoubtedly need to be steadfast, but, of course—like everything—they need to grow and develop, changing their form while leaving their essence unchanged.

Harmony in a person is the merging of Thought and feeling into a single flame, into a single powerful essence. To live with a bifurcation in one's soul is complete agony, as you perhaps know yourself. For instance, you are in love with a man and yet the person in this man that you love is alien and even hostile to you, to your thought. The same thing happens with us men. Or a person may have attained a mental awareness of his inner freedom, but a feeling of affection, of love, or a habit, etc. prevents him from actually freeing himself from the fetters of those conditions which have hindered his spiritual growth.

As for my feelings towards Ekaterina Pavlovna, words cannot set them straight—they would only create a worse muddle.[2]

Her feelings towards me are abnormal at present—that is, new both for her and for me—and I have no way of responding to them. She is a bit too late, and at the present moment I want only solitude and rest. I would suggest that I have the right to that. I find it a little difficult to understand why I am the one who is somehow capable of preventing someone else—in this instance, Ekaterina Pavlovna—from living her own personal inner life. Or perhaps I have not understood you properly? For me the matter is clear in essence: of two people one has to sacrifice a part of himself for the sake of the other—right? I would not be true to myself or to others if I were to take this upon myself: to make a free sacrifice, without forcing myself, is something I just can't do right now.

Aleksei Vasilievich's death has shaken me.[3] My mood is rotten, for if you compare his life with mine, then mine is insignificant and unworthy. However, it has happened and tears have been shed. Farewell!

You are a most wonderful person and you treat people well, but I would advise you never to get involved as a third party. That is a difficult role, and it will inevitably cause one of the sides to be unfair to you.

A. Peshkov

SOURCE: *AG* 14: 306–7.

[1] Elena Konstantinovna Malinovskaia (1875–1942) met Gorky in Nizhnii Novgorod in 1900. A prominent figure both in Bolshevik affairs and in the theatrical world, she corresponded with Gorky throughout his life.
[2] Gorky had separated from his wife at the end of 1903.
[3] Aleksei Vasilievich Iarovitsky (1876–1903), writer and revolutionary, Gorky's close associate in Nizhnii Novgorod.

34. *To E. P. Peshkova, [11 or 12 July 1904]*

[St Petersburg]

Well, we've buried Anton Chekhov, my dear friend.[1] I am so oppressed by this funeral that I'm barely able to write sensibly to you about it. I walk, I talk, I even laugh, but there is a vileness in my soul, I feel as if I've been smeared all over with sticky, foul-smelling filth which has formed a thick crust around my heart and brain.

This wonderful man, this fine artist who fought all his life against vulgarity, finding it everywhere, illuminating all its rotten spots with a gentle, reproachful light, like the light of the moon, our Anton Pavlovich, who used to be upset by everything common and vulgar, was brought [back to Russia] in a wagon 'for the transportation of fresh oysters' and buried next to the grave of the Cossack's widow Olga Kukaretkina.[2] These are trivialities, dear friend, yes, but when I remember the wagon and Kukaretkina, my heart sinks, and I'm ready to wail, to howl, to lash out in indignation and anger. It would make no difference to him even if his body were to be carted about in a dirty linen basket, but I cannot forgive Russian society for that wagon 'for oysters'. That wagon is the very epitome of the vulgarity in Russian life, the boorishness which always so enraged the deceased. Petersburg didn't receive his remains as it should have. That doesn't bother me. At the funeral of a writer like Anton Chekhov I would have preferred to have seen a dozen people who sincerely loved him. What I saw was a crowd of 'the public', there were perhaps three to five thousand of them, and they all merged for me into a dense, viscid cloud of exultant vulgarity.

I walked among the crowd on the way from the Nik[olaevskii] station to the Art Theatre and heard them talking about me, about how I'd grown thin and wasn't like my portraits. They said that I had a funny overcoat and a dirt-spattered hat, that I shouldn't have been wearing boots, that it was hot and muddy, that Chaliapin resembles a pastor and looks ugly now he has cut his hair. They talked about everything, they were all going off to pubs to meet their friends afterwards, but no one said a word about Chekhov. Not a word, I assure you. There was an overwhelming indifference, a kind of unshakeable, rock-hard vulgarity—there were even smiles. When I stood near the theatre during the office for the dead, someone behind me recalled the short story 'The Orator'

['Orator']. You remember, it's about a man who delivers a speech about the dear departed over the coffin, but it turns out that the man is alive and standing next to him. That is the only thing they remembered.

People expected speeches to be made over the grave. There were hardly any. The public began to demand insistently that Gorky should speak. Wherever Chaliapin and I turned up, we both immediately became the subject of persistent scrutiny and inspection. And again, not a word about Chekhov. What kind of public was this? I don't know. They climbed up into the trees and laughed, broke crosses, and fought over seats, they asked loudly: 'Which one's the wife? And the sister? Look, they're crying!'; 'And do you know, he didn't have a penny to leave, everything went to Marks';[3] 'Poor Knipper!'; 'Why feel sorry for her, after all she makes 10,000 a year at the theatre', etc.

All this forced its way into my ears importunately, impudently. I didn't want to hear it. What I wanted was a beautiful, sincere, sad speech, but no one gave it. It was unbearably sad. Chaliapin began to cry and started swearing: 'To think that he lived for this scum, that it was for their sake that he worked and taught, that he made his reproaches.' I took him away from the cemetery. And when we had mounted our horses, a crowd surrounded us, smiling and looking at us. Someone—just one person out of the thousands who were there!—shouted: 'Gentlemen, get away from here! This is disgraceful!' But they didn't go away, of course.

Forgive me, this letter is incoherent, you will hardly manage to understand my mood, which is most melancholy and angry. I'm going to write an article about the funeral called 'The Monster' ['Chudovishche']: it will explain things to you.[4] We're thinking about publishing a book in memory of Anton Chekhov; this is still a secret for the moment. Only Kuprin, Bunin, Andreev, and I will contribute to this book.[5]

Chaliapin, Aleksin, and Eliz[aveta] Iv[anovna][6] send their very best to you.

Fedor [Chaliapin], the idiot, has gone and bought an estate. I'm very pleased for Aleksin. It seems that things are going well for him with El[izaveta] Iv[anovna]. But I'll write to you later about all of them, I can't do it now. I'll just say I was really moved by the way Fedor treated you, and Sashka [Aleksin] too. They're truly fine fellows. They are going to write to you. Fedor is going off to sing in Kislovodsk, Aleksin is going there too, but via the Volga. I'm going to Staraia Russa for three weeks or so, I'll be taking salt baths there.

Write to: Staraia Russa, Erzovskaia Street, Novikov House.

Aleksin talked about you staying in Yalta for the winter. I'll be there in October, but more about that later.

Love to Maksim. Regards.

A.

SOURCE: *SS* 28: 310–12.

[1] Chekhov died on 2 July 1904. His funeral was held on 9 July.

[2] Her name sounds close to the Russian for 'cock-a-doodle-doo' [*kukareku*].

[3] A reference to the notorious deal struck between Chekhov and the publisher A. F. Marks, the terms of which were very much in the latter's favour. See Letter 22, n. 20.

[4] The article was never written.

[5] The third Znanie miscellany was dedicated to the memory of Chekhov. It contained a poem by Skitalets, Gorky's *Summerfolk*, Andreev's 'The Red Laugh' ['Krasnyi smekh'], and memoirs of Chekhov by Bunin and Aleksandr Ivanovich Kuprin (1870–1938), a popular writer who broke away from Znanie after 1905.

[6] Aleksin's wife, whom he had just married.

35. To L. N. Andreev, [13–15 November 1904]

[St Petersburg]

My deeply embarrassed Markobrunner![1]

The letter has come, but not the story.[2] Is it coming? I'm pleased for you, I'm pleased in advance for I'm sure it's good. I can see even by the tone of your letter that it's good! And I can feel that it's good by your attitude towards the devil![3] Make all the angels of Znanie get a move on, hurry them up, the slowcoaches! Nothing has come in yet from Bunin, and I don't even know where he is. But this won't hold us up. As soon as you send your 'Red Laugh', we'll get it off to the press, don't worry! And it will fit perfectly: your story is about the war, and Kuprin's is about the military[4]—banzai! Kuprin's memoirs have been printed already, *Summerfolk* will also be ready soon, you've got yours done just in time, Bunin and Shatalets[5] will come after you—and the miscellany will be ready! We've enough material left for more than one miscellany, we may even publish two more. Write! Write, dear friend.

I'm not the least bit angry, on the contrary, I feel splendid. I hate every-one with a happy, tempestuous hatred: I say this quite sincerely! The day of the première of *Summerfolk* was the best day of my incredibly long, inter-esting life—a good life which I've made all by myself.[6] My dear friend, how wonderful I felt when, at the end of the third act, I walked right up to the footlights. I stood there and looked at the audience, I just looked without bowing to them, and a great, passionate joy burned within me.[7] I wish that you could experience such inexpressible, indescribable joy, such pride, such human power—the devil take it! It's good! Banzai!

Banzai, Leonid! They hissed when I wasn't there, but no one dared to hiss once I had made my appearance. They're cowards and slaves! Their names are Merezhkovsky, Filosofov, Diagilev, etc.[8] They consider them-selves free men, but they haven't the strength to stand up face to face with those they hate. Is this freedom? Is freedom really possible without courage? Without strength? People without strength and courage can go to hell.

I really recommend to you the articles in *Peterburgskie vedomosti* [*Petersburg Gazette*] and in *Svet* [*The Light*], the interview with Merezhkovsky in *Peterburgskaia gazeta* [*Petersburg Newspaper*], and the poem 'The Liberal' in *Rus'* [*Russia*]. The latter has nothing to do with *Summerfolk*, but it's interesting in itself.[9]

The *feuilleton* which you sent to *Nasha zhizn'* [*Our Life*] was about two years out of date, and after consulting with Nevedomsky, who loves you sincerely, we decided not to print it. Things are fine here. The weather is disgusting, I've got haemoptysis, and Mariia Fedorovna [Andreeva] is in hospital, she's had an operation. But one can endure all this, not even notice it, for that isn't what matters, my dear friend. We will all die one day, but you and I will not die completely, that's what matters.

They say that the audience swore a great deal during *Summerfolk*. Potapenko apparently abused the *Novyi put'* [*New Path*] people to their faces, someone shouted 'Vulgarians!' at them.[10] Overall it was a battle royal with the petty bourgeois, and I thrashed them! This was the first time I've thrashed them—get this right—it was the first time I *felt* I'd thrashed them.

No, life is good, I love life! I love you with a passionate love, deeply, sincerely, I love my noble Marusia [Andreeva], that beautiful woman-friend, I love Konstantin Piatnitsky whom nature has made firm and solid, like a knight's castle. There is a fine soul contained in that strong body of his, a soul which always burns quietly and constantly, like a solitary fire in the deserted steppe on a still summer night. I love everything else too. I even think I have a little love for those who offend me, because they allow me to have some sense of myself.

How important, how marvellous it is to have a sense of oneself!

Of course, *Summerfolk* hasn't risen in my estimation after this entire incident. *Summerfolk* is not art, but it is clearly a well-aimed shot, and I am as pleased as a devil who has managed to seduce the righteous into drinking themselves into a disgraceful condition.

Well, that's enough! On the 21st I'm doing a reading here for a charitable cause.[11] The cause is a good one. Will you come? Will you come tomorrow? Yes? Send a telegram if you agree. You can stay with us at 20 Znamenskii. My love and best wishes.

Miklashevsky [Nevedomsky] has arrived.

A.

SOURCE: *LN* 72: 239–40.

[1] A playful allusion to King Markobrun, a character in the folk-tale 'On Bova Korolevich' ['O Bove Koroleviche'].

[2] 'The Red Laugh', which was to be included in the Chekhov miscellany. See Letter 34, n. 5.

[3] Andreev had written to Gorky of his love for reason, adding that 'The devil is by no means evil. He is simply stupid' (*LN* 72: 236).

[4] Kuprin's novel *The Duel* [*Poedinok*] eventually appeared in the sixth Znanie miscellany.

⁵ A humorous reference to Skitalets.

⁶ See the Introduction to this section.

⁷ It was a tradition in the Russian theatre at the time for the author of a play to take a bow at the end of the penultimate act.

⁸ Dmitrii Vladimirovich Filosofov (1872–1940), essayist and literary critic close to the Symbolist movement; Sergei Pavlovich Diagilev (1872–1929), theatrical and artistic organizer, editor of the Symbolist-oriented journal *Mir iskusstva* [*World of Art*].

⁹ The first pieces named were all responses to *Summerfolk*. The poem was published as 'A Hero of Our Time' ['Geroi nashego vremeni'] in *Rus'* on 12 November.

¹⁰ Ignatii Nikolaevich Potapenko (1856–1929), writer. The '*Novyi put'* people' were Merezhkovsky *et al.*

¹¹ Gorky read his memoir of Chekhov and the story 'More about the Devil' ['Eshche o cherte'] at the Tenishchev Academy in St Petersburg.

36. *To M. Reinhardt,*[1] *[December 1904]*

[St Petersburg or Riga]

Dear Mr Reinhardt!

In a few days' time Konstantin Petrovich Piatnitsky will send you my play, *Summerfolk*.

I don't think you will like it and I don't think that it will interest the German audience: it's too much a purely Russian 'family affair', and it wouldn't surprise me at all if you were to find the play boring and pointless.

But for all that, I'll say a few words so as to facilitate your understanding of the life which I've tried to reproduce in the play.

I wanted to depict that part of the Russian intelligentsia which has risen from the democratic strata and which, having reached a certain level of social status, has lost touch with the people to which it is related by blood. It has forgotten about their interests, about the need to broaden their lives, and yet it has discovered no spiritual bond with the bourgeois and bureaucratic society, with which it is affiliated only in a purely mechanical sense and with which it has yet to merge into a single whole as a class having its own tasks and its own view of life.

Literature has instilled in these people a contempt for the petty bourgeoisie, and this contempt, which is purely cerebral and theoretical, prevents them for the time being from making close spiritual ties with the bureaucrat and the merchant, for whom, as the forest for the wolf and the pasture for the bull, the whole country serves merely as the place where they can eat.

This intelligentsia stands alone between the people and the bourgeoisie. Lacking any influence on life, lacking any strength, it feels terror in the face of life. It is rife with divisions, and wants to live an interesting and beautiful life—just so long as it is calm and quiet; all it seeks is the opportunity to justify itself for its disgraceful inertia, for its betrayal of its native stratum, the democracy.

Bourgeois society is degenerating quickly and rushing headlong into mysticism and determinism—anywhere it's possible to hide from the bleak reality which tells people: either you must rebuild life or I will cripple and crush you.

Many of the intelligentsia are following the petty bourgeois into the dark corners of mystical or other philosophies—it makes no difference where, so long as they can hide.

This is the drama as I see it. In my opinion, Mariia Lvovna's monologue in Act IV is the key to it.

I'm sending you Rubinstein's duet which is sung in Act IV.[2]

My friends who saw *The Lower Depths* in your theatre speak enthusiastically about the performance of the actors and the subtle understanding which you displayed in the staging of this play.

I wish you success and all the best!

M. Gorky

SOURCE: *SS* 28: 344–5.

[1] Max Reinhardt (1873–1943), German actor and director, whose Berlin Kleines Theater put on a number of plays by Gorky.
[2] A. G. Rubinstein (1829–94), composer, pianist, and conductor.

37. To E. P. Peshkova, [9 January 1905]

[St Petersburg]

You will read some amazing things, but you should believe them: they are fact.

This morning the workers of St Petersburg, about 150,000 strong, set out simultaneously from eleven places towards the Winter Palace in order to present the sovereign with their demands for social reforms.

Members of the 'Soc[iety] of Russian Workers', founded by Zubatov, marched from the Putilov Works with church banners and with portraits of the tsar and tsarina; they were led by the priest Gapon carrying a cross.[1]

They were met at the Narva Gate by troops who opened fire with nine volleys; ninety-three of the wounded are in hospital, and it is not known how many were killed or taken off to various apartments. After the first volleys some of the workers were on the point of shouting, 'Don't be afraid; they're blanks!' but about a dozen people were already lying on the ground. Then those in the front rows lay down too, whilst those at the back wavered and began to disperse. Six more volleys were aimed at them, and also at those who tried to get up and leave.

By some miracle Gapon escaped with his life; he is sleeping at my place right now. He says that there is no longer a tsar, there is no God or church; he spoke publicly to this effect at a meeting a little while ago, and he is writing the same thing too. He is a man who has tremendous authority among the Putilov workers; he controls more than ten thousand workers who believe in him as though he were a saint. He too believed up until today, but his belief has been shot down. I picture his future—he can only have several days of life left in his future, since they are already out looking for him—as being terribly interesting and significant; he will turn the workers towards the true path.

Our fellow townspeople, Olga and Anton, led the workers from the Petersburg Side.[2] They were shot at without warning near the Troitskii Bridge; there were two volleys, and about sixty people fell—I personally saw fourteen people wounded, including three women, and three killed.

Let me continue my description: the Winter Palace and the square in front of it were cordoned off by soldiers. There weren't enough of them: they even had to put a navy crew out on to the street, and a regiment was summoned from Pskov. As many as 60,000 workers and others had gathered around the soldiers and the palace. At first everything was peaceful, and then the cavalry unsheathed its sabres and began to hack away. There was shooting even on Nevskii. A man in the crowd which was scattering before the horsemen fell in front of my very eyes, and a mounted soldier shot him from the saddle. They were also hacking away on the Police Bridge; by and large, this was a mightier battle than many of those in Manchuria, and it was more successful too.[3] The figure for those killed and wounded in the districts has already risen as high as 600, and that's only for those outside Petersburg, at the gates. This is hardly an exaggeration; I speak as an eye-witness to the slaughter.

The workers displayed much heroism today, but so far this is still a sacrificial heroism. They stood before the rifles, bared their breasts, and shouted 'Fire! We don't care—our lives are intolerable!' They were fired at. Everything is on strike, except for the horse trams, the bakeries, and the power station, which is being protected by soldiers. But the entire Petersburg Side is in darkness; the power lines have been cut. The feeling is growing that the tsar's prestige has been shattered—that's what is significant about the day.

You will understand and believe this when you find out the details; as you see, I cannot write coherently, since the day has left me exhausted. There is nothing melancholy about the whine of bullets, but the wounded women are depressing and tragic.

The massacre was premeditated and organized on a grand scale. I have to tell you that on the evening of the 8th we—Arseniev, Semevsky,

Annensky, myself, Kedrin (a member of the city duma), Peshekhonov, Miakotin, and a representative from the workers[4]—tried to obtain an audience with Sviatopolk[5] to demand that he issue orders for the troops not to be brought out on to the streets and that he give the workers free access to Palace Square. We were told that he wasn't at home and they sent us instead to his deputy, Rydzevsky. The latter is a blockhead and an ignoramus, an irresponsible person. From him we went to see Witte;[6] we spoke with him for an hour and a half—to no purpose, of course—trying to convince him to influence Sviatopolk. He told us that he, Witte, was powerless and could do nothing; he then spoke to Sviatopolk on the phone and asked him to receive us, but Sviatopolk refused. We feel that we had fulfilled the task with which we had been entrusted: we notified the ministers of the peaceful nature of the demonstration as well as of the need to allow people to see the tsar and the need to remove the troops. Our signed declaration will inform all Europe and Russia of this.

And so, my friend, the Russian revolution has begun, on the occasion of which I offer you my sincere and profound congratulations. The deaths should not put you out of countenance; only with blood is history repainted in new colours. Tomorrow we are expecting events which will be more striking still, and a display of further heroism on the part of our supporters, although you cannot do much with your bare hands of course.

Here is a *word-for-word* copy of a letter from Gapon to the workers:

My dear comrade workers!

And so the tsar is no more! The innocent blood of our friends has fallen between him and the people. Long live the beginning of the people's struggle for freedom! I bless you all. I will be with you today. Right now I am busy with the cause.

Father Georgii

I enclose his letter to Sviatopolk.

I am very sorry that I cannot enclose his letter to the tsar, which serves notice that he and the workers are coming to request that they be received, or the list of Gapon's demands, which were drawn up under the guidance of the S[ocial] D[emocrat]s. These demands are the same as those of the *zemstvo* activists except that they are more democratic, of course.

As for me, don't worry. We'll see each other around the 20th. Please take care of yourself and of Maksim! And make a brave, honest man out of him.

The day after tomorrow, i.e. the 11th, I'll have to make a trip to Riga; my friend Mariia Fedorovna [Andreeva] is dangerously ill with peritonitis. The doctor and Savva [Morozov] have telegraphed to say that it is life-threatening. But right now personal sorrows and failures are no longer important, for we are living at the time of Russia's awakening.

I repeat, take care of Maksim and please take care of yourself.

So, keep well, and goodbye for now. Warm regards, my friend.

Pass on this letter to V[asilii] A[lekseevich].[7] Tell him that a future historian of the coming revolution will probably begin his work with a phrase like this: 'The first day of the Russian revolution saw the moral failure of the Russian intelligentsia.' That is my impression of its speeches and deeds.

A.

SOURCE: *SS* 28: 346–9.

[1] Sergei Zubatov (1864–1917), a police official who undermined the revolutionaries' efforts to organize workers by setting up legal workers' groups loyal to the government. Father Gapon (1870–1906) was active among the workers in St Petersburg and led the demonstration described in Gorky's letter. A strike at the Putilov Works, the largest factory in Russia, contributed to the revolutionary mood at the time.

[2] Anton Voitkevich and his wife Olga Ivanitskaia, active Bolsheviks from Nizhnii Novgorod.

[3] The Russians fought in Manchuria during the war against Japan.

[4] Konstantin Konstantinovich Arseniev (1837–1919), journalist and literary critic; Vasilii Ivanovich Semevsky (1848 or 1849–1916), historian; Venedikt Aleksandrovich Miakotin (1867–1937), historian and journalist.

[5] P. D. Sviatopolk-Mirsky (1857–1914), Minister of Internal Affairs.

[6] Count Sergei Iulievich Witte (1849–1915), statesman. At this time was President of the Council of Ministers.

[7] Desnitsky (real name Stroev) (1878–1958), Social Democrat who became a leading Gorky scholar in the Soviet era.

38. To A. V. Amfiteatrov,[1] [20 February 1905]

[Majorenhof]

Thank you for your letter, Aleksandr Valentinovich! I was profoundly affected by its sincerity and power. I send you warm regards; moreover, I shall venture to tell you that my recent reading of your daring and vivid articles has made me grow fond of you.

I received your letter only after I had been released, since it is a principle that no information from outside is allowed in gaol.[2] They adhere to it with strict severity: I was arrested in Riga on the 11th—I had gone there from Petersburg and had just returned from the hospital where I left Mariia Fedorovna [Andreeva] literally on the brink of death. I was not allowed to stop off to say goodbye to her, despite requests from myself and from the doctor treating her, and I left for the fortress with the agonizing conviction that I would never again see this wondrous person, who is so dear to me and whom I love and respect with all my heart. For nine days I received no news about Mariia Fedorovna's condition, which was something of a torture for me. I am not complaining, but a simple and distressing thought springs to mind: if they can treat me like that, then how do the authorities treat a male or female worker who falls into their hands? And I begin to feel afraid for people.

If you don't count the first days of my imprisonment, which were filled with worry for Mariia Fedorovna, then my month in gaol went well; during that time I even wrote a play, *Children of the Sun*, which has turned out quite successfully, I think, although it was taken from me by the Police Department 'for examination'. I am very concerned about the fate of this manuscript, since it seems to me that the aforementioned Department is staffed by savages of the sort who would not find it difficult to burn a manuscript. In prison I rested a little from my 'daily impressions' and pondered those I have received of late. On the 9th I was on the streets of Petersburg from morning till night, and I saw Russian soldiers kill unarmed people in defence of the 'throne of the fatherland'—thereby killing the autocracy's prestige in the process.

That last point is true, my dear Aleksandr Valentinovich. Knowing our people's attitude towards this prejudice,[3] I dare not exaggerate in the present instance. However, I heard a thousand voices curse the tsar; I heard old men, women, and children call him a murderer—people who, several hours before the murder of their relatives and acquaintances, were peacefully marching to their tsar and carrying in their hands banners and portraits of him and his wife. And they were being led by a priest. I was well informed that on the 7th and 8th the workers were loyally disposed, and on the night of the 8th I told Witte that this was a fact on which I was prepared to stake my honour. Amidst the tens of thousands in the general mass of people, the hundreds of revolutionary workers played no part right up until the 9th, until the shooting began; but after the murders they emerged at the head of the movement, which is only natural. It was a sense of loyalty which was destroyed by the defenders of the autocracy: that is the profound significance of what happened on the 9th of January. And the response to that event has been the same throughout Russia. A breach has been made in the 300–year-old Chinese wall of the autocracy, a breach that cannot be repaired by 50,000 roubles, not even if you were to increase that sum a thousand times over.[4]

About myself I will remark that prison has always had two negative features for me: it has somewhat aggravated my bad health and it has greatly increased my popularity. The latter—and I say this without trying to show off—gets in the way of living just as much as ill health does. I was released on a bond of 10,000 roubles and had to sign a pledge not to leave Petersburg, but straight after that I was exiled at Trepov's insistence.[5] They want to bring me to trial, and this makes me happy. I will make every effort to turn that trial into a merry wake for the autocracy, which I used to think of as just a senseless custom for ruling the land but which has now become a criminal association intent upon the oppression of Russia. I am expecting your letter for Jaurès; please send it to the office.[6] Again, my warm regards.

A. Peshkov

Majorenhof, Riga–Tukums highway, the Kevich boarding house. All my letters are opened, as are those addressed to Mariia Fedorovna. Write to K. P. Piatnitsky at Znanie.

Would you be able to thank the Italian people on my behalf for the concern they have shown me? Perhaps you could publish something like the following in a respectable Rome newspaper:

I am deeply touched by the concern the Italians have shown towards me; this concern enables me to believe that there will come a time when every act of violence against a person for his opinions anywhere on earth will give rise to a unanimous outburst of indignation and protest against the tyrants. Let there flourish in the world an awareness of the spiritual kinship of all people and a respect for mankind, for the freedom to think, for the right to love truth and to fight for its triumph!

M. Gorky

Pass on my profound and sincere regards to Georg Brandes and give him my warm greetings.[7] I love that man for his sharp mind. I remember reading his book at night in the bakery, standing in front of the stove after I had put the bread into it. It would happen sometimes that the bread would get burnt and the baker Konovalov would curse me as a result, but I never got angry at Brandes for writing so captivatingly, and to this day I am grateful to him for those moments of oblivion—those moments of happiness in my life at that time.

All the best, Aleksandr Valentinovich!

Be of good cheer!

SOURCE: *LN* 95: 64–6.

[1] Aleksandr Valentinovich Amfiteatrov (1862–1938), writer and critic of left-wing sympathies. On his correspondence with Gorky, see the main Introduction.

[2] Gorky was arrested on 11 January for his part in the events of Bloody Sunday and imprisoned in the Peter and Paul Fortress in St Petersburg. He was released on 14 February.

[3] i.e. the monarchy.

[4] The tsarist regime was trying to secure loans from various European states; Gorky and the Bolsheviks opposed these loans.

[5] Dmitrii Trepov (1855–1906), Governor-General of St Petersburg and Deputy Minister of Internal Affairs.

[6] i.e. the office of Znanie. Amfiteatrov's *The Franco-Russian Alliance and the 9th of January (A Letter for Jean Jaurès)* was being circulated illegally.

[7] Danish critic and literary historian (1842–1927), author of books on Shakespeare, Nietzsche, and nineteenth-century European literature.

39. To K. P. Piatnitsky, [27 February 1905]

[Majorenhof]

Dear friend,

There can be no question of my seeking to avoid a trial;[1] on the contrary, it is essential that I do go to trial. If they decide to stop this stupid business by administrative means, I will reopen the case immediately, but on a larger scale, in a brighter light, and I will secure a trial for myself (= disgrace for the family of Messrs Romanov and those of their ilk).

If there is a trial and I am convicted, this will provide me with an excellent basis for explaining to Europe just why I am a 'revolutionary' and what the motives are for my 'crime against the existing regime', a regime which slaughters peaceful, unarmed citizens of Russia, even including children.

And if I am acquitted, I will publicly ask the honourable royal family just why exactly they held me in the fortress for a month. This is my little plan.

You're right—it's imperative to put together a general appeal to Europe and, as you indicated, to send it to the main source of agitation— *Berliner Tageblatt*[2]—with a request that it be circulated amongst all the committees which have been campaigning for my release. I enclose the draft of such an appeal.

I'm thinking about going to the Crimea, but I'll do this when I have more precise information about the trial. I should let my lungs recover, to be on the safe side, and have a look at my son, who's probably succeeded in boring you thoroughly. We also need to make the trip for Marusia's [Andreeva's] sake. Although she is recuperating here, she should nevertheless have a breath of sea air in my opinion. She's as stubborn as Nikola Romanov,[3] but she's intelligent, and I hope to persuade her.

Please send:

100 roubles—to Mikhail Dmitrievich Galonen,[4] Nizhnii Novgorod, Napolno-Monastyrskii Street, Veselov House.

100 roubles—to the student M. Khiddekel, Technical High School, Nizhnii Novgorod.

Yesterday I read *Children of the Sun* to Marusia, Zakhar, and Lipa, but they're critics like Burenin,[5] only the other way round. Many compliments and sincere thanks to you for rescuing the manuscript so quickly from the jaws of hell.[6] I'm awfully glad and I'm settling down now to do some revisions.

A whole load of correspondence has piled up here. One ought always to be grateful for such things, but—can you imagine!—I don't feel gratitude to the extent that I should.

Thank you for sending the magazines and books published by

'Dzhalita'![7] But I didn't need the other books. Never mind! We'll find a place for them.

Things are wonderful here. Sometimes certain people come to our boarding house, but the landlady finds them suspicious and won't allow them on the premises. In general we are receiving excellent treatment. I am afraid to go to Riga, as a real scandal might result.

Your promise that 'we'll see each other soon' is nice, but nowadays notions of speed are so confused that I would like more precision.

Warm regards. I'm expecting you and wish you all the very best!

Bring the cartridges for the Browning with you if you have them, i.e. if I gave them to you.

Today we were out on the water, verily as upon the dry land, firing shots at Marusia's hand-muff. Fourteen shots were fired, but we all survived, no one was wounded and the muff remained intact.

There's a lesson in weapon-handling for you!

It would be better if you wrote to Majorenhof, Riga–Tukums.

Once again, goodbye for now!

I embrace you.

A. Pesh[kov]

Send the third volume of Shelley!

Leonid has been released—I'm glad! Efforts are being made on behalf of Skitalets.[8]

SOURCE: *SS* 28: 353–5.

[1] See Letter 38. Scheduled for 3 May, the trial was subsequently postponed.
[2] The German newspaper had protested strongly against Gorky's arrest.
[3] An irreverent reference to the tsar, Nicholas II.
[4] *Nizhegorodskii listok* correspondent preparing to enter university.
[5] Nikolai Evgenievich Burenin (1874–1962), active member of the Social Democratic movement. He met Gorky in 1905 and accompanied him on the trip to America the following year.
[6] See Letter 38.
[7] Publishing house specializing in classic works by foreign authors.
[8] Andreev was arrested on 9 February after an illegal meeting had been held in his apartment. He was released from Moscow's Taganka prison on 25 February. Skitalets was also arrested by chance at Andreev's apartment.

40. To L. N. Tolstoy,[1] [5 March 1905]

[Edinburgh[2]]

A letter to Count L. N. Tolstoy

Count Lev Nikolaevich!

Your name has an enormous appeal, all literate people the world over listen to your words, and there are probably many who believe them to be right, but what you have told the world concerning current events in Russia obliges me to raise some objections.

It seems to me that you've given too little thought to what you were asked by people abroad, that you were too quick to reject what is alien to your inner world and prevents you from concentrating on personal concerns. Your words could mislead both foreigners and Russians who want to come to terms with the significance of the events which our country is experiencing. This is what I want to say to you, Count.

I declare confidently both to you personally and to those who are capable of accepting your words on trust, that you do not know how the simple working people of our homeland live, you do not know their spiritual world, and you cannot speak of their desires, for you lost this right when you stopped listening to the voice of the people.

This is so, Count! On many occasions I witnessed personally the intolerance and irritation with which you rejected the opinions of peasants and workers who came to see you—the true representatives of the bold, young thought of our people—when these opinions did not harmonize with the ideas by which your once-free soul is now held captive.

For a long time now—I know this for a fact—you haven't wanted to hear what the representatives of the people, those who visit you from time to time, are talking and thinking about. Their speeches only irritate you. And now you arrogate to yourself the role of spokesman for the people's desires.

Once you had derived your philosophy from the peasants Siutaev and Bondarev, you were too quick to conclude that this passive philosophy is characteristic of the entire Russian people rather than being just a survival from the system of serfdom.[3] You are wrong, Count, there are millions more peasants who are simply starving, who live like savages, and who have no specific desires. And there are hundreds of thousands more peasants whom you don't know at all, for, I repeat, you have not wanted to listen to the voice of their hearts and minds.

For a long time now you've dwelt on high with your idea of salvation through personal self-perfection, but they have moved a long way ahead on the road to awareness of their human rights. You have lost sight of them, you do not understand them, and you do not have the right to speak about who their representatives are—you are certainly not one of them, Count!

You described as untimely and unreasonable the activities of those people for whom it is unbearably painful to see the Russian people starving, without rights, crushed by the weight of the oppression which bears down upon them, to see how the people, ignorant and intimidated, are capable of beating and killing anyone who is pointed out to them, even children, in return for a glass of vodka.

This is a mistake, Count. You described as unreasonable the work of people who want to see Russia adopt a system under which the whole nation might speak freely and openly about its spiritual needs, think boldly and hold beliefs consciously, without fearing that they might be beaten for this, thrown into prison, or sent to hard labour in Siberia, as it was in the case of the Dukhobors, the members of the Pavlovka sect[4] and thousands of other Russian people who were exiled from Russia, mutilated, and slaughtered by our ruling class, a class which has become brutalized through its attempt to maintain its control over the country.

This is unfair, Count.

Count Lev Nikolaevich! The name which you have earned quite deservedly as our greatest contemporary artist of the word does not give you the right to be unfair to people who love their nation unselfishly and sincerely and who work for it no less than you do.

They do so more than you, in fact, for you once said that to be completely happy you would like to suffer for your idea. Well, the people, whom you have so thoughtlessly and unfairly condemned, actually have suffered a great deal and continue to suffer, as you know.

These unknown, humble people are suffering steadfastly and silently, they perish by the hundreds and thousands in the struggle for the liberation of their people from the shame of spiritual slavery. It is your right not to agree with them, but you have no right not to respect them, Count!

You are wrong when you say that the peasant needs only land, and here you contradict the very Gospels which you consider one of the sources of pure wisdom. There it is said: 'Man lives not by bread alone,' and indeed you yourself know that the Russian people, besides owning land, also want to think and believe more freely, and you know that for this very reason they're being exiled to Siberia and driven out of Russia.

You are also wrong when you say that constitutional governments pay as little attention to their people as is the case with our government. You know that if people were to say to the King of England: 'You are wrong, King,' then the foremost gentleman of that country would not permit himself to throw anyone in gaol as a consequence. And you know that here in Russia there is only the government, whereas in the West there is the government, there are laws, and there is freedom of speech, which prevents the government from breaking those laws.

During these difficult days, when blood is being shed on your country's soil and hundreds and thousands of fine, honest people are perishing in the struggle for the right to live not like beasts, but as human beings, you—whose words the whole world heeds so avidly—find it possible simply to repeat yet again, and quite unnecessarily, the basic idea of your philosophy: 'The mission and meaning of life for all people lies in the moral perfection of the individual personality.'

But just consider, Lev Nikolaevich, is it really possible for a person to engage in the moral perfection of his personality when men and women are being shot in the city streets and the wounded are not allowed to be picked up for some time after the shooting?

How can one philosophize on the theme of one's attitude towards peace at a time when one sees the police cruelly beating children who are suspected of intending to overthrow the existing regime?

And is it possible to think about peace and one's own spiritual calm in a country where there are people who can be hired for the sum of 50 kopecks a day to slaughter the intelligentsia, that part of the Russian people which is the most unselfish and pure in its motives?

How can one overcome the feeling of anger and vengeance in one's soul, knowing that here, in the country where one lives, lackeys and liars set one family of people against another and incite bloody carnage in the city so as to exterminate in that carnage those people who have already discovered their human dignity and who demand recognition of their human rights?

Tens of thousands of people are perishing in this senseless battle, a battle which is both incomprehensible and unnecessary to the people and which is destroying the country. The newspapers are full of reports of the suffering of our soldiers: it is as if their pages were red and damp with human blood. The imagination pictures fields covered with the bodies of peasants forced to wear soldiers' greatcoats. . .

You must agree, Count, that a man who is able to concern himself with self-perfection at a time of misfortune for his country might create the disgusting impression of being a heartless Pharisee in the minds of all people to whom the ideals of truth, beauty, and freedom are precious.

Finally, Count, and to turn back upon you all the condemnations which you hurled at the best Russian people from the lofty summit of your world fame, may I be permitted the liberty of describing your letter to *The Times* as being not only unjust and unreasonable, but also harmful?

Yes, it is harmful. I can already see the pleasure with which the predators and parasites in our country are baring their teeth. In protecting the interests of the blind, crude power which oppresses our people, they defend lawlessness, they incite the people to hatred by insolently violating the truth, they spread vile lies and they corrupt in every possible way a Russian society which has become exhausted by recent events and has lost its way.

But with each day the means for protecting their servile positions are drying up. It is becoming ever more difficult for them to lie because the stern truth of life stands against them. However, now they will be gladdened by your letter.

They will repeat your words for several days, they will seize upon them, like a drowning man clutching at a straw, and they will fling into the faces of the honest and steadfast people of Russia the vile and offensive, the exultant and gloating words:

'Lev Tolstoy is not with you!'

M. Gorky

SOURCE: *SS* 28: 357–61.

[1] Gorky is responding to an article by Tolstoy which had just appeared in *The Times*. Entitled 'On the Social Movement in Russia' ['Ob obshchestvennom dvizhenii v Rossii'], and composed at the request of several foreign newspapers, it was highly critical of the radical movement and its aspirations. Gorky's letter was never sent to Tolstoy, nor was it published at the time.

[2] A settlement near Riga.

[3] In his article 'What Then are We to Do?' ['Tak chto zhe nam delat'?'], Tolstoy had identified these two peasants as the principal inspiration for his own ideas on morality.

[4] Religious sectarians were subjected to increasing official persecution during the 1890s. There was a protest by sectarians in Pavlovka, Kharkov province, in 1901, after which the ringleaders were exiled to Siberia.

41. To A. M. Remizov,[1] [22 July 1905]

[St Petersburg]

Mr A. Remizov,

I cannot answer your question for the time being. One needs to know a book if one is to publish it.

What I can say, however, is that your *Pond*, like your handwriting, is something artificial, fanciful, and affected.[2]

At times it is downright offensive to read, it's so coarse, sick, and ugly. Worst of all, it's deliberately ugly.

But it's obvious you're a talented man, and it really is a pity that you are making your entrance in literature as if you were entering the circus with a bag of tricks, and not as if you were mounting a tribune in order to accuse and avenge.

If you were to rework your excellent material in a calm epic tone, everyone would shudder with horror, shame, and indignation.

But you prefer to fool around like a schoolboy swatting flies with a Bible.

Excuse me for this unsolicited and perhaps impertinent response, but I love beauty and I love strength. It pains me when a man of taste makes boxes from birch-bark and foil when he's capable of creating something major and important.

All the best!

A. Peshkov

SOURCE: *SS* 28: 377.

[1] Aleksei Mikhailovich Remizov (1877–1957), major representative of Russian Modernism in prose.

[2] Remizov had submitted the manuscript of this novel for publication in Znanie. It was serialized during the year in the journal *Voprosy zhizni* [*Questions of Life*]. A revised version was published in 1908.

42. *To K. P. Piatnitsky, [10 December 1905]*

[Moscow]

My dear friend, I'm rushing to jot down a few words to you. I've just come in off the street. They're fighting at the Sandunov Baths, at the Nikol[aevskii] Station, at the Smolensk Market and at Kudrino.[1] It's a great battle! Cannons are roaring—they started yesterday at 2 o'clock in the afternoon, continued all night and they have been rumbling continuously all day today. The horse guard artillery is in action. There are no Cossacks on the streets, the infantry is mounting guard, but for some reason it isn't involved in the fighting at the moment—and it is very small in numbers.

There's an entire corps here but only the dragoons are on the streets. There are three regiments of them and they are cowards. They are magnificent at running away from the armed workers' detachment. They're on Pliushchikha now. We have been fighting them at Strastnaia, at Pliushchikha and Zemlianoi Rampart.

The Caucasians[2]—thirteen men—have just routed some forty dragoons at Okhotnyi. One officer and some four soldiers were killed, seven were seriously wounded. In some places bombs are being used. It's a huge success! Everywhere on the streets the gendarmes and the police are being disarmed. A twenty-man detachment has just been disarmed after it was driven into a cul-de-sac.

The workers are conducting themselves very well! Judge for yourself: overnight eight barricades and magnificent barbed-wire barriers have been constructed on Sadovaia-Karetnaia—the artillery was using shrapnel. Overnight, barricades were built on both Bronnaia Streets, on Neglinnyi, Sadovaia, and Smolensk. There are twenty barricades in the Georgian district! Obviously, there are not enough troops and the artillery is hopping from place to place. There are also either not enough machine-guns or no crews. Overall, the conduct of the defence forces is incomprehensible! Mind you, they fight without mercy! There are rumours about unrest among the troops; some patrols have surrendered their weapons—that's a fact. The Fidler High School was destroyed by the artillery—eleven salvoes completely destroyed the façade. In general, these days will result in many mutilated buildings. Buckshot is being fired indiscriminately, many houses are being damaged and a few people are too. In general, despite the cannons, machine-guns, and other such things, there are as yet few dead and wounded. Yesterday there were about 300, today there are probably four times as many. But the troops are incurring losses as well, in some cases even heavier ones. At the Fidler School seven civilians were killed and eleven were wounded; twenty-five soldiers and three officers were wounded; two bombs were thrown. The Samogitskii regiment was in action. The dragoons are suffering more than anyone else. The public is in an amazing mood! Honest to God, I had expected nothing like this! They are efficient and serious in action against the cavalry and in the construction of barricades, and they laugh and joke when they are at leisure. The mood is excellent!

I've just received some more information: the square at the Nikol[aevskii] Station is littered with corpses. Five cannons and two machine-guns are operating there, but the workers' detachments are still managing to inflict casualties on the troops. According to all the information, our detachments are suffering very little. It's the idlers and inquisitive people, of whom there are tens of thousands, who are suffering more.

Everyone has somehow got used to the shooting, the injuries, and the corpses straightaway. As soon as the shooting breaks out, people immediately flock in from everywhere, carefree and cheerful. All but the very lazy are throwing what they can lay their hands on at the dragoons. The dragoons have stopped fighting with sabres, it's too dangerous, they're being shot very successfully. They fire their rifles as they dismount from their horses. On the whole there is fighting all over Moscow! The window panes are rattling. I don't know what's going on in the outlying districts or in the factories, but the sound of gunfire resounds everywhere. Of course, the authorities will prevail, but they won't do so for long, and what an excellent lesson this is for the public! This will surely cost them dearly. Four officers—three wounded and one dead—were carried past our windows today.

Will the soldiers say anything? That is the question!

My friend, I send my warm regards!

Marusia [Andreeva] is well, she sends her best wishes, she's very busy. On the whole it's vanity of vanities here right now.

A.

SOURCE: *SS* 28: 399–401.

[1] The Moscow armed insurrection, the last pitched battle of the 1905 Revolution, began on 9 December.

[2] i.e. a group of the insurrectionists.

3

EXILE: AMERICA AND CAPRI
1906–1913

INTRODUCTION

The defeat of the Moscow armed insurrection signalled the end of the 1905 Revolution. Although sporadic disturbances continued in various parts of the Empire for another year or so, the government had effectively regained control. This turn of events placed Gorky in a dilemma. Should he remain in Russia to face inevitable retribution for his revolutionary activities, or should he make use of his now considerable celebrity by continuing the struggle from abroad? Time was short and, encouraged by his friends in the Bolshevik Party, the writer decided to cross the border into Finland, whence he began a journey which was to take him through Europe and on to the United States.

The purpose of this trip was twofold. First of all, Gorky was to work actively against the efforts of the Russian government to raise foreign capital, money desperately needed to consolidate its power after the combined disaster of war and revolution. In so doing, he was also to serve as a sort of ambassador for the Bolshevik cause, gathering support—both political and financial—for the Party as it sought to maintain the revolutionary battle against the tsarist regime.

Judged against these objectives, Gorky's mission was to prove a disappointment. The Russian government quickly succeeded in its bid to secure large loans from foreign banks; and the American campaign yielded only 10,000 of the million dollars that Gorky had set as his target when he left for New York from Cherbourg in April 1906. In retrospect, the entire project appeared naïvely optimistic, but at the time the signs were most auspicious. The writer's journey from Finland through Germany, Switzerland, and France had certainly provided ample evidence of his popular appeal as a fighter for freedom and democracy. But, hardly had he set foot on American soil than things began to go badly wrong.

Gorky's arrival in New York was a triumphal occasion. Large crowds turned out to see the man whose acts of defiance against the Russian government were already legendary. A banquet was arranged in his honour, at which Mark Twain and other illustrious figures pledged their support for the writer and his cause. However, public opinion swiftly turned against him following the revelation in the American newspapers that his companion, Mariia Andreeva, was not his legal wife (see Letters 43 and 44). The effect of this news was truly devastating. The doors which had been opened to the writer were just as rapidly closed, quite literally so in the case of a New York hotel from which the 'immoral' Russian couple were evicted without notice. Mark Twain washed his hands of Gorky with equally unseemly haste, and the public appearances which had been organized for him were now cancelled.

Gorky was both bemused and enraged by this extraordinary change in his fortunes, but he stuck to his propagandistic task. Nevertheless, by the end of May, after abortive visits to Boston and Philadelphia, he was obliged to accept defeat. Indeed, had he not been befriended by John and Prestonia Martin, a wealthy couple with socialist sympathies, he would probably have been obliged to make a somewhat ignominious departure from the United States without delay. The Martins invited Gorky and his party to their estate in the Adirondacks, and it was there that they spent the summer and autumn in seclusion, away from the immediate glare of publicity. It was a welcome break and one that afforded him the opportunity of meeting a number of interesting people (see Letter 46).

Despite these set-backs—or perhaps because of them—Gorky remained in pugnacious mood. He vented his anger in a series of sketches and articles, of which 'The City of the Yellow Devil' ['Gorod zheltogo d'iavola'] and 'La Belle France' ['Prekrasnaia Frantsiia'] were the most notorious. These pieces were obviously calculated to cause maximum offence, which they duly did, much to the writer's delight (see Letter 46). Gorky also used his time in upper New York State to compose two literary works which were later to be instrumental in the promotion of his image as the 'father of Socialist Realism'—the play *Enemies* and the novel *Mother*. Remarkable both for their explicitly revolutionary content— *Enemies* is about a workers' strike, whilst *Mother* concerns the underground activities of a group of socialists—these are also unashamed pieces of political writing, designed to bolster faith in the Russian revolutionary movement in its hour of crisis. Little wonder, then, that both works served only to get him deeper into trouble with the authorities in Russia.

By this time, however, Gorky was little concerned with his status in the eyes of Russian officialdom. He knew full well that there could be no question of his returning to Russia in the forseeable future. But he was also anxious to leave America so that he might be closer to events as they unfolded in his native land. Thus it was that he left New York on 13 October 1906 for Naples. After a brief sojourn in that city, he travelled by boat to the island of Capri, which was destined to be his permanent home for the next seven years.

The move to Capri brought Gorky far closer to his homeland, and not only in the geographical sense. During his time in America, he had been able to follow the course of events in Russia only in the most general way and at a considerable remove. Now, however, he was able to establish more direct contact with new developments in political and intellectual life more or less as they happened. He took out subscriptions to a large number of newspapers and journals which he read as avidly as the many books he also ordered from Russia. More importantly still, Gorky's island retreat immediately attracted a regular flow of visitors with whom the writer was anxious to resume contact. In this last respect, Capri was ideally located, being far enough away from the beaten track to discourage the attentions of casual acquaintances or those merely curious to meet the notorious writer.

If these activities served to mitigate Gorky's sense of isolation from Russia, they did little to improve his mood. On the contrary, he quickly became alarmed at the immensity of the change which had overtaken Russian society in the wake of the 1905 Revolution. This change was nowhere more obvious than in literary life. From the books and journals he read and the people he met, Gorky discovered that the 'civic' literature which had brought such initial success to the Znanie miscellanies (as well as aiding the growth of revolutionary sentiment) was being rapidly eclipsed by other trends. Russian Modernism, which had already made its mark in turn-of-the-century Russia, now began truly to flourish in all branches of the arts, often combining with new currents in religion and philosophy which were part of the same post-revolutionary 're-evaluation of values'. At the lower end of the scale, this shift of sensibility was manifested in a variety of escapist forms—historical romances, detective stories, even mild pornography—which began to dominate the domestic market.

Gorky viewed these developments with undisguised dismay. In his eyes, Russian literature was in danger of losing its moral authority as a force for political and social change. What disturbed him most of all, however, was the extent to which his fellow Znanie writers had been infected by this 'literary disintegration'. (The term later became (in)famous as the title of a collection of articles to which Gorky contributed.) A number of these writers came to visit him on Capri soon after his arrival there. Gorky recorded his impression of them in a humorous letter to Ladyzhnikov:

Many Russian writers are here at present—Veresaev, Aizman, Leonid [Andreev]—and gloomy people they are. They sit with knitted brows as they silently contemplate the vanity of all earthly things and the insignificance of man. And they talk of corpses, graveyards, toothache, and headaches, of the tactlessness of the socialists and other such things which lower the temperature of the air, and of body and soul. Flowers wither, flies expire, fish die, stones pull faces, as if they are about to be sick. Woe is me![1]

Despite the comic tone employed here, Gorky's concern was only too real. In fact, things had already reached something of a crisis point. Just as Gorky had already come to believe that he was being deserted by colleagues who had been seduced from the true path of democratic literature by the decadent ideas abroad in society, so his Znanie associates held

---

[1] *SS* 29: 18.

equally firmly to the view that Gorky himself had allowed his revolutionary sympathies to run away with him, to the detriment of his literary judgement. As Leonid Andreev put it in a letter to Serafimovich from Capri: 'Life here is not so good. The only real person is Gorky and even he is not quite right somehow. He has become extremely narrow, and his brains are well and truly scrambled. . .'[2]

It was not only the Znanie writers who felt this way, however. Gorky's business partner, Piatnitsky, was also experiencing doubts about the direction of the entire venture. The simple fact was that the firm could no longer function as it had before. With the change in the political climate, censorship had been tightened considerably, which meant that overtly 'revolutionary' works of the kind that Gorky favoured were now a real liability.[3] What is more, declining sales suggested that the public was no longer so interested in reading such 'committed' literature anyway. It is no surprise, therefore, that Piatnitsky should have been among the first to visit Gorky on Capri at the end of 1906. The two men evidently did some hard talking about the future of Znanie, the outcome of which was the decision, early in the new year, that Gorky should relinquish the editorship of the miscellanies to Andreev, with effect from the autumn.

Whilst it would appear that Gorky had bowed before the various pressures exerted upon him by Piatnitsky and others associated with the Znanie firm, his decision may have been no more than a tactical retreat. Whatever the case, it was already clear by the middle of the year that he was not prepared to leave editorial affairs completely in the hands of others. His letter to Andreev of July 1907 (Letter 50) was, in effect, a declaration of intent on his part. With its uncompromising definition of purpose ('The Znanie miscellanies are miscellanies of a literature which is democratic and for democracy') and its open opposition to the inclusion of the Modernists Blok and Sologub among the contributors, this was a gross infringement on Andreev's independence of action. As for Andreev himself, he reacted at once by handing back the job of editor to Gorky, a move which precipitated the exodus from the venture of most of the original Znanie writers.

Gorky's renewed belligerence may be attributed in part to his attendance that spring at the Fifth Congress of the Russian Social Democratic Party, which was held in London. He went to the British capital as the special guest of the Bolsheviks, having received an invitation from Lenin himself, which was delivered in person to Capri by Lenin's representative, Desnitsky. The trip had a most positive effect upon the writer's spirits, as can be seen from the letter he wrote to his wife on his return home (Letter 49). The Congress allowed him the opportunity both to become

    [2] *Moskovskii al'manakh*, kn. 1 (Moscow, 1926): 299.
    [3] Between 1906 and 1913, the firm was taken to court no less than twenty-three times.

better acquainted with Lenin and also to observe his main political opponents within the Social Democratic movement—the Mensheviks, led by the veteran campaigners Plekhanov and Akselrod. As always, however, Gorky's reaction to the conduct of these competing groups was decidedly mixed. Whilst the letter to Peshkova makes no secret of his preference for the Bolsheviks against the 'old men' of Menshevism, he was not inspired by the prospect of witnessing further confrontations of the same sort. When Lenin suggested that he join him at the Seventh International Socialist Congress in Stuttgart, he declined, pleading the pressure of other commitments.

As it turned out, Gorky's dealings with Lenin were already beginning to enter a critical phase. Although he liked the Bolshevik leader personally and had been particularly charmed by his kind attentions at the time of the London Congress, the writer was by now closely involved with a group of thinkers which were soon to be the cause of a major controversy within the Social Democratic movement. Known as the 'God-builders', this group comprised a number of prominent Bolsheviks, of whom Aleksandr Bogdanov and Anatolii Lunacharsky were the most important. Both men had written substantial theoretical works in which they argued for a fusion of Marxist ideas with a collective religious spirit, which combination they believed would best express the spirit of social-ist revolution in Russia. Such views held an enormous appeal for Gorky, who found in the works of Lunacharsky, Bogdanov, and their associate Bazarov an elaboration of notions about God towards which he had already been moving independently from the late 1890s onwards. To be sure, his enthusiasm for 'God-building' during the early years on Capri is almost impossible to exaggerate. Bogdanov was among the writer's earliest visitors on the island, as was Lunacharsky, and the three men obviously spent many hours talking over their views on socialism and religion. By the end of 1907, one might reasonably suggest that Gorky's involvement with these two men had become something of an obsession (see, in particular, Letters 51, 52, and 53).

In short, 'God-building' provided Gorky with a faith by which he could live and—much more importantly—by which he believed the Russian revolution might properly be achieved. His fervour is unmistakable, all the more so when viewed against his pessimism during the first months on Capri. 'Surely life is beautiful when it has a goal?'—these words to his wife (Letter 53) capture perfectly the utopian zeal which was to characterize Gorky's activities throughout 1908 and 1909. One manifestation of that new zeal was his suggestion to Piatnitsky that the Znanie firm be transformed, at least in part, into a publishing outlet for the 'God-builders' (Letter 52). Piatnitsky himself was evidently less than keen on this idea; he studiously ignored many of Gorky's proposals when replying to his letters, and he used every possible excuse not to visit the writer again, despite constant requests that he do so. Matters were only made worse when Piatnitsky took the decision to publish in the Znanie miscellanies works by Andreev and Skitalets in defiance of Gorky's own wishes (see Letter 58). Affairs had effectively reached the breaking-point, although it was to be some time before the final parting of the ways.

But if the showdown between Gorky and Piatnitsky was yet to come, the writer's relationship with Lenin was already entering one of its most delicate phases. The Bolshevik leader had identified 'God-building' as a dangerous heresy as early as 1904, and he looked upon Gorky's close involvement with Bogdanov and Lunacharsky with unconcealed displeasure. A resolute materialist and atheist, he wanted no part of any theory which sought to reinvent God. But he was also determined not to lose the support of Gorky, whose international fame was still so potentially useful to the cause. In March 1908, he visited Capri for discussions with Gorky, Bogdanov, and Lunacharsky. But there was no real question of any agreement or even compromise between them. As for Gorky, his own position was quite plain. He wrote to Piatnitsky:

> The argument which has blown up between Lenin-Plekhanov, on the one hand, and Bogdanov-Bazarov and Co., on the other, is very important and profound. Although they disagree over questions of tactics, the first two both believe in historical fatalism; the other side propounds a philosophy of activism. It is clear to me on which side is the greater truth.[4]

His own writings of the period, such as the article 'The Destruction of Personality' ['Razrushenie lichnosti'] and the novel *Confession*, also contained unmistakable signs of his new 'activist' faith. Lenin himself was equally resolute: in fact, he had already sent to press *before* his departure for Capri a major critique of the 'God-building' movement which appeared later that year under the title *Empiriomonism and Empiriocriticism*.

If the battle lines between Lenin and the 'God-builders' were already drawn by 1908, the real fighting took place the following year. The cause of the conflict was a political school for Russian workers, which was set up by Gorky and his new comrades on Capri (see Letter 59). Financed by Gorky and Andreeva, with additional support from Chaliapin and Amfiteatrov, the school was to offer introductory courses on philosophy and political economy taught from a Marxist perspective. Major figures from within the Russian Social Democratic Party, such as Plekhanov, Kautsky, and Trotsky, were invited to give lectures. In the end, however, the Capri school was boycotted by all but the 'God-builders' themselves. (Significantly enough, Lenin was not even invited to participate in its work.) The signs were already ominous. But things went well enough to begin with. The first group of workers was recruited in Russia and they duly arrived on Capri in the summer of 1909. There they heard lectures

---

[4] *Lenin*: 29.

by Bogdanov, Lunacharsky, and Gorky himself (he was responsible for a course on the history of Russian literature). But Lenin was already doing everything he could to undermine the authority of the Capri school, and his efforts were finally rewarded in November, when the venture collapsed after a walk-out by the students, some of whom went on to an alternative school set up by Lenin himself in Longjumeau, on the outskirts of Paris.

The impact of these events on Gorky was truly crushing. In many ways, the Capri school had offered him the perfect outlet for his type of utopian revolutionism. After all the frustrations associated with Znanie, here was a way he could once again feel that he was working practically for the socialist cause. But now he was obliged to accept the failure of a venture in which he had invested so much of his personal faith and energy. Dismayed by that failure, and appalled by the ruthless tactics employed by Lenin, Gorky fell into a depression which was to cast a pall over his remaining years on Capri. The effects were immediate. His personal association with Bogdanov and Lunacharsky failed to survive the pressure created by the Capri school fiasco. Although Lenin visited him in the summer of 1910 in an attempt to heal the breach between them, the meeting was at best only a partial success. A letter from Gorky to Elena Malinovskaia of November 1910 really says it all. Declaring his unwillingness to 'play at politics', he also complained of 'various people' who were distracting him from his work with their 'trivialities'.[5] Nevertheless, it would appear that Gorky had begun to learn the art of political pragmatism. Whilst he never really forsook 'God-building' as a personal philosophy of revolution (see Letter 84), he later dropped the term from his vocabulary so as to avoid further confrontations with the Leninist centre. By January 1913 he was even writing to the Bolshevik leader in terms designed both to dissociate himself from the 'Forward!' ['Vpered'] faction (as the Lunacharsky-Bogdanov group was now known) and to acknowledge Lenin's rightful position as the arbiter of Party ideology (Letter 76). Thus the tone was set for a somewhat tenuous association between the two men in the years leading up to the revolutions of 1917.

Gorky's gloomy mood was compounded by other factors, both professional and personal. On the professional side, his involvement with Znanie had dwindled to the point where he had effectively renounced all editorial responsibilities by the autumn of 1909. He continued to publish with the firm, however, mainly because he needed a ready outlet for his work at a time when his financial position had become extremely precarious.[6] As for his personal life, it is perhaps most appropriately

---

[5] N. A. Trifonov, 'A. V. Lunacharskii i M. Gor'kii (K istorii literaturnykh i lichnykh otnoshenii do Oktiabria)', *M. Gor'kii i ego sovremenniki*, ed. K. D. Muratova (Leningrad, 1968): 146.

[6] Piatnitsky finally assumed full legal control of Znanie in 1911.

described by the word the writer himself employed in a letter to his
wife—'abominable' (Letter 70). His liaison with Andreeva had actually
placed the writer in an awkward position. Although he continued to correspond with Peshkova (even sharing his most private thoughts with her),
she was understandably unwilling to visit Capri (see Letter 47), which
meant that he was denied the possibility of seeing his son except on the
rare occasions when he could leave the island for the Italian mainland.
What is more, his relationship with Andreeva had itself run into difficulties. From the end of 1909 there are growing signs that Gorky wished to
separate from her. In the event, she left Capri for Russia in November
1912 (see Letter 74). But despite Gorky's assurance that the separation
was permanent, the two soon resumed their association, which was to last
until after the Revolution.

Inevitably, these various pressures and disappointments took their toll
on Gorky's health. Andreeva had been expressing concern over his physical condition as early as December 1908.[7] The main problem was over-
work. Indeed, when one considers the full extent of the writer's
commitments over these years—literary, political, editorial—it is remarkable that he coped at all. He was certainly not exaggerating when he
wrote to Rozanov in the spring of 1912: 'I shall probably die soon' (Letter
72). Had it not been for an intensive period of medical treatment on the
Italian mainland, his gloomy prediction might well have been realized.

In short, Gorky's last years on Capri were characterized by an increasing sense of doom and foreboding. His involvement with both the
Bolsheviks and the Znanie firm had ended in virtual catastrophe. His
personal life was causing him considerable distress. His health was seriously undermined. His financial affairs were in disarray—hence the need
to work furiously on his major literary work of this period, *The Life of
Matvei Kozhemiakin*. Under such circumstances, almost every new event
seemed to compound Gorky's unhappy mood, be it the death of Tolstoy
(Letter 64), the theft of the *Mona Lisa*, or a spate of recent suicides (Letter
66). Appalled by what he described as 'the atmosphere of barbarism' in
the West (Letter 68), he was also disturbed by the evidence that the revolutionary movement in Russia was all but a spent force as the country
entered a new period of economic growth. Hence, the anguished confession to his wife that he feared he was losing his most precious item of
belief, a 'faith in Russia and her future' (Letter 70). In fact, Russia—des-
ignated by the highly emotive term *Rus'*—had become Gorky's central
preoccupation by the end of the Capri period. And, in traditionally
Russian fashion, that preoccupation is articulated, as often as not, in
terms of the difference between Europe and Russia, West and East,
action and passivity. 'What kind of attitude towards life predominates in

---

[7] See her telegram to Piatnitsky, *AG* 4: 386.

Russian literature—an active or a passive one?' (Letter 67). 'Is Russia to be or not to be?' (Letter 65). 'And will it not turn out, upon serious investigation of the matter, that the struggle "in the heart of man" between "God and the Devil" simply represents the struggle of the Aryan with the Turanian, [which constitutes] the psycho-physics of the Slav?' (Letter 69). Such concerns inform Gorky's major articles of the post-1905 years, such as 'On Cynicism' ['O tsinizme'] and 'The Destruction of Personality' as well as his artistic prose—*Okurov Town*, *The Life of Matvei Kozhemiakin*, and the autobiographical writings *Childhood* and *Through Russia* [*Po Rusi*] which brought the Capri period to a close. They were to occupy his mind with even greater urgency when eventually he returned to his native land at the end of 1913 in connection with the 300th anniversary of the Romanov dynasty.

43. To E. P. Peshkova, [between 1 and 4 April 1906]

[New York]

My friend!

This is what has happened: the Russian Embassy in New York has bribed *one* of the newspapers here which has a fair degree of influence, and this newspaper in turn has kicked up a fuss in the American *gutter* press *apropos of my bigamy. Bigamy is punishable by law over here and they are using this in an attempt to have me thrown out of America.* A certain part of the bourgeois press is against me. The most widely distributed papers—*The New American, The New York Herald, The Tribune,* and *The Times*—have taken my side.

M[ariia] F[edorovna] [Andreeva] has become ill from the persecution. All these things prevent me from doing what I came here to do. But I will not give up. They will have to send me away by force, or else I will leave here a victor, even if I have to spend a year here in the process.

This is not a question of pride but of fighting against the morality of the petty bourgeois. I don't really want to get involved in all this, even though it too is revolution, a revolution in people's heads. Would you like to alleviate my situation? Send a telegram to *The New York Herald.* Say that you are indignant at this invasion into the privacy *of a person who, although he is not your husband, is still your close friend none the less.* Say that the cause to which he is sacrificing his talent ought to be placed above personal relationships of a kind which are obviously still inaccessible to the psychology of the American people, who have managed to create widespread political freedom but have yet to free themselves from slavery to prejudices which have long since died out in Russia. In doing this you'll be rendering a service both to me and to the revolutionary cause.

Apart from the Russian Embassy, the Bund and the SRs are also against me. Chaikovsky is here; he arrived before me.[1] Don't say anything for the moment about this united action of the Russian political parties and the government.

Zina and one other comrade from Russia are here with me.[2] I'm working like an American typewriter. I have three meetings this week: in New York, Boston, and Philadelphia. I'm contributing to *The American.* It's not so easy! But never mind! I'll manage, no matter what. In spite of everything, it's interesting here, awfully interesting! What a life! It's sheer fantasy!

I understand that I'm asking a great deal of you, but you know that you have the right to refuse if you want to. But if you do agree, then your hand will deliver a wonderful slap in the face of the bourgeois! Goodbye for now! Regards, my dear friend!

Did Maksim receive the Indians?[3] Write to me at: New York, M. Gorky.

Love to everyone. Keep well!

A.

SOURCE: *AG* 5: 177.

[1] The Bund was a Jewish socialist movement; the Socialist Revolutionaries (SRs) were the largest of the revolutionary parties and opposed to the Social Democrats. Nikolai Chaikovsky (1850–1926) an SR, who later briefly headed a White government in Arkhangelsk before going into exile after the Civil War.

[2] Zina (sometimes Zinka) is Gorky's pet name for Zinovii Alekseevich Peshkov (real name Sverdlov, 1884–1966), his adopted son; the 'comrade' is Burenin (see Letter 39, n. 5).

[3] Gorky had sent his son picture postcards depicting American Indians with tattoos.

44. *To E. P. Peshkova, [14 or 15 April 1906]*

[New York]

I received your sad letter on my return from a meeting in Boston. I was awfully glad to hear that Maksim is learning to play—even with some success, from what you say.[1] This is splendid, truly! It would be a great pleasure to see you all. But the ocean lies between us, *although that is not the most important obstacle as far as you are concerned.*

By the way, if you haven't yet sent a telegram to *The Herald* as I requested, then don't bother. I was too hasty in asking you to do this. To hell with them! The Russian Embassy has an inexhaustible supply of 'authentic facts' about my life, and they're determined to wear me down one way or another. It doesn't matter! This old Tatar is strong, he won't break; he's all sinew, the dog, and he won't fall apart at the seams.

I must tell you that the energy and tempo of life in America are really quite amazing. Here's an incredible fact for you: San Francisco was utterly destroyed nine days ago.[2] Yet just today I received a photograph from there of a San Francisco *which has already been restored* in the main areas. In three days' time every trace of the earthquake will have disappeared. On the first day, New York gave 16 million dollars to the victims, that's 32 [million] of our roubles. In just five days a total of 139 million was collected. Isn't that great? The day before yesterday a three-storey building with eleven rooms was transported there by train, and today it's already fully assembled and people are moving into it. A twenty-six-storey building was built in sixty-three days! To believe it, you have to see how these devils work! By comparison with New York, European cities are just so-so. There are many beautiful old things over there, of course. Aesthetics are alive there. But once you've seen New

York, you can't help but say that there is something decrepit and tired, something sickly and highly strung about Europe. There is not much in the way of aesthetics here, perhaps none at all. Here one finds the crude cheerfulness of a young country, the healthy restlessness of political and social adolescence.

It is all awfully interesting.

My plans have become so disrupted that I won't be able to leave here for some time. I shall probably stay until the autumn. I'll take a holiday in the south of France in the winter and expect to see you there. You say that you don't understand my reasons for leaving. They're simple. If I were still in Russia, I'd be in prison. The order for my arrest was already in the hands of Salz, the chief of police in Helsingfors. Luckily for me, he refused to arrest me there so as not to incite unrest amongst the Finns, with whom I am very popular. We also needed some money. And here is the easiest place to raise it. Such are the motives behind my travels.

My friend! For some reason I've been thinking a great deal about you and the children lately. Is this a sign of old age? Surely not! But people are very bad. They're crude, stupid, and greedy. Am I getting tired? Yes. But this will soon pass.

How are you thinking of spending the summer? Please write and tell me. I would like to know where I can meet you.

But until then—goodbye! I'm going to Philadelphia tomorrow. I've got three meetings in one week. My friend, I'm becoming a public speaker. I'm studying the language. I can speak it a little.

Regards,

A.

Address:
America
M. Peshkoff
Stapleton N.Y.
'El Paradiso'

I'm sending this letter via Berlin, as I fear that otherwise it won't reach you.

SOURCE: *AG* 5: 178–9.

---

[1] Maksim was learning to play the piano.
[2] San Francisco was severely damaged by a major earthquake on 5–6 April 1906.

45. *To K. P. Piatnitsky, [August 1906]*

[The Adirondacks]

My dear friend!

My play *Enemies* has been sent to Ladyzhnikov[1] with a request that he send it on to you as soon as is convenient. I am finishing the tale *Mother*. I am not sending it to you directly, since I am afraid it won't get through. After all, you live such a tumultuous and stormy life that the authorities must surely be reading your correspondence.

There will be no revolution here soon, not unless it comes crashing down on the thick heads of the local multimillionaires in ten years or so. Oh, what an interesting country! What these devils accomplish, how they work, how filled they are with energy, ignorance, smugness, and barbarity! I am enraptured and I curse; I feel both sick and cheerful—it's devilishly amusing! Do you want to be a socialist? Then come here. The need for socialism is revealed here with fateful clarity.

Do you want to be an anarchist? You can become one in a month, I assure you.

In general, once people come here they turn into obtuse and greedy animals. As soon as they see the piles of riches, they bare their teeth and walk around like that until they become millionaires or drop dead from hunger.

Emigration! What a nightmare! Today's emigrant is not at all the same person who made America. He is simply Europe's garbage, its refuse, an idler, and a coward, a weak little man who lacks the energy without which nothing can be done here. The modern emigrant is incapable of making a life for himself; all he can do is look for a ready-made life of peace and abundance. The best thing would be to drown all emigrants of that sort in the ocean, and when I become a senator I will put such a bill to the vote.

Here's a strange fact: did you know that the English are dying out in America with striking rapidity? By the time they reach the third generation you already encounter nervous breakdowns, suicides, and spineless people. But the Jews are flourishing, and the Irish are holding their ground.

We are living in an area called the Adirondacks, about which I have already written to you, I believe, and have also yet to receive a reply. The mountains are covered with deciduous forest. The highest point is 1,500 metres. There is a view of a lake from up there. It's all right, quite decent. A school of philosophy is located a mile from us.[2] A number of professors live around here and they make use of their vacation to earn some money by giving lectures on all manner of subjects. You pay ten dollars a week and may attend six lectures; for that they also feed you, albeit primarily on greens. The audience sits in a small auditorium (boring!) and listens to little Professor Morris (boring!) giving a lecture on psychology (boring!). 'Metaphysics, ladies and gentlemen. What is metaphysics? Every word, no matter which you choose, is a symbol, ladies and gentlemen! When I say "metaphysics", I imagine a staircase which rises from the ground and leads away into space. When I say "psychology", a row of pillars appears before me.' Somebody should just hit him over the head with one of those pillars! I met James and Channing, *et al.* James is a wonderful old man, but he is also an American. Oh, to hell with them. They are funny people, especially when they call themselves socialists.

I've sold 'My Interviews' ['Moi interv'iu'] to the magazines for five thousand. Do you happen to need any money? I'll sell my play as well.[3]

Listen, write at least once!

Send the enclosed to Ekaterina Pavlovna; she has not written to me for sixty-four years either, and I don't know where she is, whether the children are alive, etc.

I hope you never get to see America; that's a kind wish, I assure you!

It's quite enjoyable on this earth for a frivolous fellow such as myself. And what about you? i.e. how are you feeling?

Again, all the very best!

I would like to talk to you. You are essentially the only person with whom I can talk about everything as I know it.

There are a great many individuals here. But deplorably few real people.

So long! The enclosed note is about a Finnish miscellany; hide it away somewhere.[4]

A.

SOURCE: *SS* 28: 429–31.

[1] Ivan Pavlovich Ladyzhnikov (1874–1945), publisher and active member of the Social Democratic movement. For many years he headed a Berlin publishing house for Russian authors.

[2] Glenmore, a camp and summer school for philosophy on East Hill, near Summerbrook, where Gorky was staying. John Dewey had a summer house nearby, and William James, whom Gorky mentions here, also spent summers in the area.

[3] *Enemies.*

[4] The note concerned an anthology for which Gorky was to supply the preface. The anthology did not appear.

46. To E. P. Peshkova, [end of August or beginning of September 1906]

[The Adirondacks]

I've sent you a letter and I also received yours with the photographs of the children. What good timing!

Maksim has interesting eyes and they are, no doubt, beautiful. Tell him that I will bring him back some genuine Indian bows and arrows if I can find any. And I'll bring him some American butterflies; they have some amazing ones here. Otherwise there's nothing here, everything beautiful comes from Europe. America itself is too young to understand the meaning of beauty. I live almost on the border of Canada and I'll probably go up there to see the Dukhobors and the Indians. The Indians and the Negroes are the most interesting things here. The Americans themselves arouse one's curiosity only in terms of their ignorance—which is amazing!—and their greed for money, which evokes disgust.

Now that I've received your letter, I feel quite well, for which I have you to thank. You've dispelled my bewilderment, which was serious but unnecessary, as it now transpires. And if it weren't for the loss of Katia, I would be happy.[1] But I won't talk about her. It's unnecessary. You can't say anything against death.

I ask you please to look after our son. I ask you not only as a father but also as a man. In the story which I am now writing—*Mother*—the heroine, a widow and the mother of a working-class revolutionary (I had Zalomov's mother in mind),[2] says: 'The children are out in the world. . . the children are going towards a new sun, the children are going towards a new life. . . Our children, who have condemned themselves to suffer *for all people*, are out in the world—don't abandon them, don't forsake your own flesh and blood without a care!'

Later on, she will be tried for her activities and she will give a speech in which she will sketch the entire world-process as the progress of *children* towards the truth. The progress of children, do you see? There is a dreadful escalation of the world's tragedy in this. I find it hard to explain such an important idea to you in a letter, it's too complicated, and it raises another idea, also very profound, concerning the fateful difference between a reformer and a revolutionary. This is a difference which we cannot perceive, yet it causes terrible confusion.

I should tell you that I've come to understand a great deal here, and one of the things I've understood is that up until now I have not been a revolutionary. I am only just becoming one. The people whom we have been accustomed to consider revolutionaries are really only reformers. The very concept of revolution must be made more profound. And that is possible!

It seems that you've been mixing a great deal with people of certain opinions and that you've already become accustomed in part to a certain discipline of thought, to certain views of the revolution, etc. I think, therefore, that you will find it strange to hear my words and that they will seem heretical to you.[3] When we see each other you may perhaps understand me, and if you don't sense the truth, then I hope that you will be able to explain it to yourself anyway.

I'll probably be involved in a court case here with a likely candidate for the presidency of the States.[4] I want to take him to court on a charge of fraud.

If only you knew and could see how I am living here! You would laugh till you dropped and be struck dumb with surprise. I am the most terrible person in the country. As one newspaper writes: 'This country has never experienced shame and humiliation such as that brought down upon it by this insane Russian anarchist who lacks all natural moral sense and who stuns everyone with his hatred for religion, law and order and ultimately for people themselves.' Another carried an appeal to the Senate with the proposal that I be deported. The yellow press is raging. On the gates of the house where I'm living people paste cuttings of the sharpest attacks against me. They even curse you!

And despite this—please note!—the papers solicit and request my articles. It's profitable for them and profit is everything here!

Did I write to tell you that my article about New York[5] provoked more than 1,200 objections? There were even some senators who objected. I can just imagine what will happen when my interviews and other articles about America appear!

By the way, Europe is not very courageous either. They refused to print the interview with Wilhelm—'The King who keeps his Flag flying high' ['Korol', kotoryi vysoko derzhit svoe znamia']—and not only in Germany and Austria. Even Jaurès[6] did not dare publish it in his *Humanité*! And in Rome *La Vita* printed it only with certain omissions. So much for freedom of the press! And for European culture too! What's more, in terms of content this is a most insignificant piece. I'm already convinced that the interview with the multimillionaire—'One of the Kings of the Republic' ['Odin iz korolei respubliki']—will bring down all manner of storms and disasters on my head.

I'm living in a forest in a very deserted area. It is eighteen miles to the nearest town, Elizabethtown, but Americans come here to look at me. They're afraid to come to the house: it's compromising to be acquainted with me. So they walk about in the forest, in anticipation of a chance meeting. Five of us are living here: myself, Zina, a Russian who came with me in the capacity of secretary,[7] and a physics professor, Miss Brooks, who is a charming old maid.[8] There are no servants, we cook and do everything ourselves. I wash the dishes, Zina rides into town for provisions, the professor makes tea, coffee, etc. Sometimes I do the cooking. I make *pelmeni*, cabbage soup, and so on. I get up at seven o'clock, by eight I'm already at work, which I do until twelve, dinner is at one, at four o'clock we have tea, eight o'clock is supper-time, then I work until twelve o'clock. Our Russian comrade is a graduate of the piano class at the conservatoire and plays extremely well. He gives concerts from six o'clock until half-past seven. We're studying Scandinavian music—Grieg, Olo [*sic*] Olsen, Schytte etc.[9]

I've sold and contracted all my works to American journals for 16 cents a word. This works out at about two thousand for one of our printer's sheets of 30,000 letters. Life goes by very quickly with all the work.

I live separately from everyone else in a large shed with an iron stove and no ceiling. Its walls on two sides are made of glass in huge sliding frames. I sleep with them open. My back aches because I sit a lot, I sometimes have difficulty breathing, I've lost a lot of weight, I've got a tan, and I've shaved my head. In general my health is passable.

There is a philosophy school near here which runs for just three months a year each summer.[10] It was founded by Professor Dewey. A variety of people give lectures there, although there are no systematic courses. James, the psychologist, gave a lecture recently. He is revered here as a star of the first magnitude. I met him—he's fine, a splendid old man. Gidding [*sic*], the sociologist, is very nice.[11] He and I are friends. *Zinka has been serving as my interpreter, although I can understand simple speech by myself now.

Zinka has become quite an interesting person. He doesn't write at all badly. I think that he will even come to write well. One of the things he has written will be published here quite soon, and he is also sending it to Russia. He has had a lot to bear here and has developed a wicked intelligence. In the autumn he will be going to Australia, Guinea, and other English-speaking countries.

He's taken on a fine task*—English culture is remarkably interesting. What strikes me about it is the way that political freedom exists alongside total slavery of the spirit. They live on the breath of the dead. The way they yield to authority is savage.

The day after tomorrow about a hundred people—Fabian socialists, apparently—will assemble here at the house of a certain John Martin.[12] I will go to watch. They're coming to my place for tea.

Such, in outline, are my life and thoughts. These are far from being all my thoughts, however! The mind functions most vigorously here. I live in a state of intense excitement all the time, and at least sixteen years of continuous work lie ahead of me!

It's time for me to get down to some serious work, that's what I feel! All these hurried writings of mine have little value.

Well, goodbye for now, my good friend. Once again I thank you for everything! From the bottom of my heart.

This letter will reach you in fifteen days. And it'll be fifteen more days until I receive your reply.

Do write. I'm leaving here at the beginning of October—that's decided. So you should write to this address: Bühnen- und Buchverlag russischer Autoren J. Ladyschnikow. Berlin W. 15. Uhlandstr. 145.

Ivan Pavlov[ich] [Ladyzhnikov] will forward any mail, he always knows where I am.

Well, goodbye for now! I'll be very glad to see you. Smother Maksim with kisses. Did he receive the postcards of the Indians? I've sent several lots.

All the very best! And remain firm of spirit. That is the best thing, the most precious.

Regards.

Give my regards to Elena [Malinovskaia], P[avel] P[etrovich] [Malinovsky] and to any of my old friends.

A.

SOURCE: *SS* 28: 434–7.

[1] Gorky's daughter, who died on 16 August.
[2] Petr Andreevich Zalomov (1877–1955), a worker from Sormovo, the prototype for Pavel Vlasov in Gorky's novel. Zalomov's mother, Anna Kirillovna (1849–1938), was a friend of Gorky's mother in her youth.
[3] Peshkova was close to SR groups at this time.
[4] Randolph Hearst, the newspaper magnate, had been publishing Gorky's works without authorization or payment.
[5] The notorious 'City of the Yellow Devil' ['Gorod zheltogo d'iavola'].
[6] Jean Jaurès (1859–1914), French socialist and co-founder of *L'Humanité*.
[7] N. E. Burenin. He is also the 'Russian comrade' mentioned below.
[8] Harriet Brooks was a professor of physics at Columbia University. The fifth person, whom Gorky omits to name, was M. F. Andreeva.
[9] Ole Olsen (1850–1927) and Ludvig Theodor Schytte (1848–1909), Danish composers.
[10] See Letter 45, n. 2. Thomas Davidson, not Dewey, was the founder of the school.
[11] Franklin H. Giddings (1855–1931).
[12] John Martin and his wife provided refuge for Gorky and his entourage, first at their Staten Island residence and later on their estate in the Adirondacks.

47. To E. P. Peshkova, [no earlier than 15 December 1906]

[Capri]

Could you come here, to Capri?[1] That's the question, and it's very important. The fact of the matter is that I am living under very strict surveillance by the press and I do not want to have a repetition of those sordid American tempests here in Europe—human stupidity and banality are most oppressive and irritating. The populace here is nice to me and there aren't any newspapers.

There are two reasons why I don't want to budge from here right now—I'm not in the best of health, and I have to work. There's an entire colony of us here: Leonid and Dimka,[2] Ivan Pavlovich [Ladyzhnikov], and Piatnitsky. It's a nice place. Later on we could all travel around Italy together.

If you did come, you would have to see a person who irritates you;[3] I know that, and I know it will probably be difficult both for you and for her. And for me too. People, even very nice ones, continue to be divided into men, women, wives, writers, gravediggers—that is the origin of all melodrama and foolishness.

But, you see, I don't want to force you into doing anything, and I will not go against your wishes. If I say all this, then it is on the following grounds: I do not live for my own pleasure by any means, and if I conserve my energy, if I don't want to waste it on melodramas, then that's because I want to put it to greater use and I am actually capable of doing so. Is that clear?

I want to see Maksim.

Bring me some pictures of Katia. How pretty she was! A really special girl. She has broken my heart.

What's Maksim like? From his letters and from Konstantin Petrovich [Piatnitsky]'s stories I imagine someone quite wonderfully endearing. But we'll see each other soon!

And for now, so long!

I'll be anxiously awaiting your reply. If you agree to come to Capri, send a telegram. I'll rent a villa for you — how many rooms will you need?

Al.

SOURCE: *AG* 9: 20–1.

[1] Gorky arrived in Naples on 13 October from America. He moved to Capri on 20 October.
[2] Andreev and his son, Vadim.
[3] M. F. Andreeva.

48. *To E. N. Chirikov, [March [?] 1907]*

[Capri]

You ask me, Evgenii Nikolaevich, if I like your *Legend*.[1] I don't like it at all. More than that, in fact, it grieves me. I was sad to read *Fires*[2] and just as sad to read your *Legend*. Then my sadness changed to a feeling of anger with you. It seems to me that you have taken on a task which is not your own, thereby placing yourself in a curious position in the eyes of the reader. I am talking of my personal impression, of course—I am not preaching or criticizing, but merely answering your question.

'Why?' Because one shouldn't write on such themes without some sense of the spirit of the times you are depicting or without seeing the people you describe. You write carelessly. Your servants speak the language of Russian provincials—'why have you ignored the heavens?', 'precisely', 'use your influence', and so on. But what's done is done. You will be roundly abused for this.

Don't take offence. Contemporary literature makes a strange impression upon me. Only Bunin is true to himself. All the others have fallen into a sort of wild rage and evidently take no responsibility for their actions. One can sense an alien influence, harmful and evil, which is perverting people. And sometimes it seems that this is quite consciously hostile to you all—to you, to Serafimovich, Iushkevich,[3] etc.

On the other hand, literature is under attack from various paranoiacs, sadists, pederasts, and psychopathic personalities of every kind, like Kamensky, Artsybashev & Co.[4] One can sense the spiritual chaos, the confusion of thought, the unhealthy, nervous haste. Language is losing its simplicity, and hence its power. The beautiful is being replaced at the very best by the pretty: instead of silver, we are given foil. This is all understandable, yet offensive.

Life is becoming grander, but people are becoming more petty. Literature is breaking away from heroic reality into the realm of fantasy and is becoming blind and deaf in the process. Sometimes this gives rise to the thought that these authors desire to sully with their dark, sick spittle the great displays of creative spirit, the brave efforts of people who are strong in heart and free of soul, and who seek to defeat and overcome the dark forces of life.

And when you see the cunning, cowardly work of this huge animal which needs nothing other than peace and quiet, it becomes impossible to understand the role of that group of writers which appealed to the minds of the democratic masses in difficult times, but now looks on calmly as those same minds are being poisoned, and fails, as it seems to me, to see clearly the task of the moment.

Forgive me. Don't take offence. Accept my sincere desire for the very best for you.

A. Peshkov

SOURCE: *SS* 29: 17–18.

---

[1] Chirikov's play, *The Legend of the Old Castle* [*Legenda starogo zamka*], appeared in the fifteenth Znanie miscellany (1907).

[2] Another of Chirikov's plays, *The Red Fires* [*Krasnye ogni*].

[3] Semen Solomonovich Iushkevich (1868–1927), writer, contributor to the Znanie miscellanies.
[4] Anatolii Pavlovich Kamensky (1876–1941), Mikhail Petrovich Artsybashev (1878–1927), and writers associated with the 'pornographic' trend in post-1905 Russian literature.

49. *To E. P. Peshkova, [20 May 1907]*

[Capri]

I returned from London yesterday. I was glad to get the letter from you and Maksim.[1] Tell Max that I'll send him some books about savages—no, never mind, I'll write and tell him myself.

I found the Congress awfully interesting; the three weeks flashed by without my noticing, and during that time I absorbed a great many sound and hearty impressions. I like the workers awfully, especially ours, the Bolsheviks. They are amazingly lively, varied, and intelligent people, with such a pure thirst for knowledge and such an avid, all-round interest in life. I set up a meeting with them in Hyde Park, where I spoke about contemporary literature, and was quite astonished at the keenness and acuity of their attention.

Our old men—Plekhanov, Akselrod, and others of their ilk[2]—left me with the sad impression of people who have been blinded and stunned by life. They are half-ill and become irritated for the slightest reason; they have a great deal of ambition but one can sense no sign of strength in them. Yes, they're a sad lot, but it's pleasant to see that life is already pushing such people aside, people who only yesterday were far in advance of so many others. This is pleasant, because it points to the speed with which life is developing and to the growing demands placed upon people by proletarian ideas.

I hardly got to see the city of London at all; I attended sessions of the Congress from morning till night. But it's clear to me none the less that this is a wondrous and monstrous city. Its pearl is the British Museum, which is amazingly rich and intelligently organized. I visited the picture galleries, which were interesting. I shall be writing an article about the city at the request of a magazine—or, to be precise, I shall be writing apropos of the city, about my external impressions.[3]

So you received my package—that's good. I'm sending you another: Miscellany XVI, the first part of *Mother*, and the illustrations for it.[4]

Also, in about two weeks' time I'm going to France for the entire summer.[5] The question of my return to Russia was decided in the negative. A charge of *lèse-majesté* was brought against me for my article on 1848 which appeared in Hungary.[6] A correspondence of some sort is going on with the Hungarians; I don't understand the meaning of it.

My article against the Russian loan from England will soon appear in the English newspapers; I don't think that will lead the authorities to look upon me any more kindly either.[7]

In general, my situation *vis-à-vis* my homeland remains as it was— uncertain. I don't know whether I regret that or not. I don't feel any longing for home; I don't have time for it.

If you are still in Nice two weeks from now, let me know. It hasn't been decided where I'll live, but it will be somewhere by the sea.

So long, goodbye for now! My very best.

A.

I didn't go to Rome because the Italians wanted to put me on display at the centre of a May-day parade and even invited 'the democratic sections of society' to a welcome meeting for me at the railway station. I know what these democratic elements are like! To parade oneself before them is no fun at all.

It's disappointing, very disappointing, that you didn't manage to see Sergei Ivanovich.[8] I have hopes for him, great hopes.

Why is it that you don't send me the protocols of the Socialist Revolutionaries' Second Congress? Do please try; I need them very much indeed.

Andreev left here without me after creating a fine scandal on the island. He got dead drunk, wanted to shoot himself as usual, fell down, smashed his forehead, pushed somebody into the water, etc. I have a hard time with him in general! All these writer fellows of today are mentally ill, pathetic, and perverted; to hell with them!

And I still can't get my story finished![9]

All the best!

SOURCE: AG 9: 28–9.

[1] Gorky had just returned from the Fifth Congress of the Social Democratic Party. See the Introduction to this section for further details.

[2] Georgii Valentinovich Plekhanov (1856–1918) and Pavel Borisovich Akselrod (1850–1928) were leaders of the Menshevik faction.

[3] The article was requested by the *Daily Mail* but it appeared in *Berliner Tageblatt* on 26 July.

[4] The American edition of *Mother* had illustrations by S. Ivanowski.

[5] This trip did not take place.

[6] The article 'Tyrants' ['Tirany'], which was highly critical of Nicholas II and Wilhelm II.

[7] *The Nation, 22* June 1907 (no. 17).

[8] Gusev-Orenburgsky (1867–1963), writer. Gorky had wanted to meet him on his way to London.

[9] *The Life of a Useless Man* [*Zhizn' nenuzhnogo cheloveka*].

50. *To L. N. Andreev, [26 to 30 July 1907]*

[Capri]

Konstantin Petrovich [Piatnitsky] is going to Finland soon and he will write to you or talk to you in person about the limits of your authority.[1] I will talk about literature.

As you know, my attitude towards Blok is a negative one.[2] This young man is simply remaking the bad half of Paul Verlaine in a Russian manner and he has infuriated me of late with his cold affectation. His petty talent is drying up completely under the burden of philosophical labours which are weakening a conceited boy who is too greedy for fame and whose soul is without trousers or heart. No, you should leave him in peace for about three years, perhaps he'll grow up a little in that time and learn to talk sincerely about simple things, as well as about those things which seem remarkably wise to him at present and which have already been said in France with far greater power and beauty than he is capable of.

Sologub[3] is an old coquette who is in love with death, the way that lackeys fall in love with their mistresses. He is always flirting with it in the fearful expectation that it will give him a crack on the skull. Sologub is inclined to sadism and he does not belong in the Znanie miscellanies. Please don't disturb him in his dotage and rest assured that he will never write another *Petty Demon* [*Melkii bes*]—the only work he has written with love, as a creative writer, and a work with a curious beauty of its own.

One cannot know what Auslender will say next, but I have nothing against him, just as I have nothing against Somov, for example.[4]

I would ask you to think a little about 'the liberation of man'—your own words in your letter to me—for this has a most profound significance and the people whom you have named are incapable of serving that 'liberation'. They are all old slaves, people who *cannot help but* confuse freedom with pederasty. For them 'the liberation of man', for example, has become confused in a strange way with the removal of man from one cesspit to another. At times it is even reduced to the freedom of the sexual organ, and nothing more.

The Znanie miscellanies are miscellanies of a literature which is democratic and for democracy. It is only through this literature and its power that man will become free. True individualism—one which is worthy of man and which alone is capable of liberating the individual from thrall and dependence on society and the state—will only be achieved through socialism, that is through democracy. This is what we must serve, and we must arm it with our audacity to think about everything without fear, to speak without dread.

You mentioned Sologub and Blok: these are men who are afraid of their own imagination, who kneel down before their fear. How could they possibly liberate man?

Zaitsev, Bashkin, Muizhel, Tsensky, Lansere, L. Semenov, and one or two other newcomers—these are the people with whom you could put together some fine miscellanies, in my opinion.[5]

Some of these people love literature sincerely and passionately; they don't just dress up in it so as to attract the reader's attention to the pettiness and beggary of their own 'I', which they always mentally pronounce with a capital letter, hoping by this means to increase its significance, for how else could they increase it?

Most unpleasant are those folk who are poor in spirit!

It's wonderful here. I bathe, fish, and write.

It's a pity you've undertaken the building work.[6] A year from now you will find it unbearably disagreeable. In two, you will burn the place down. Don't forget to have it insured, as people of experience do.

I'm reading a lot of 'new' literature—Kuzmin, *Severnye al'manakhi*, *Belye nochi*, *Vesy*, and such like.[7] I'm sure all this would have given me pleasure twenty-five years ago.

Regards. Do write.

A.

SOURCE: *LN* 72: 287–8.

[1] This concerns the transfer of the editorship of the Znanie miscellanies to Andreev. For further details, see the Introduction to this section.

[2] Aleksandr Aleksandrovich Blok (1880–1921), major poet and playwright of the Russian Symbolist movement.

[3] Pen-name of Fedor Kuzmich Teternikov (1863–1927), poet, prose writer, and dramatist associated with Symbolism.

[4] Sergei Abramovich Auslender (1881–1943), writer and dramatist; Konstantin Andreevich Somov (1869–1939), artist. Both moved in Symbolist circles.

[5] Boris Konstantinovich Zaitsev (1881–1972), Vasilii Vasilievich Bashkin (1880–1909), Viktor Vasilievich Muizhel (1880–1924), and Sergei Nikolaevich Sergeev-Tsensky (1875–1958) were all prose writers. Leonid Dmitrievich Semenov (1880–1917) was a poet, and Evgenii Evgenevich Lansere (1875–1946) an artist.

[6] Andreev was having an elaborate wooden house built at Vammelsuu in Finland.

[7] Like *Severnye tsvety*, *Belye nochi* [*White Nights*] and *Vesy* [*The Scales*] were both Symbolist publications. Mikhail Alekseevich Kuzmin (1872–1936), poet, dramatist, and translator, prominent Russian Modernist.

51. To A. V. Lunacharsky,[1] *[after 25 November 1907]*

[Rome]

Dear Anatolii Vasilievich!

Your notion about revolutionaries as a bridge, uniquely capable of uniting culture with the popular masses, and about the restraining role of the revolutionary is one that I hold close and dear; this notion has concerned me for a long time, and I am terribly glad that you have stated it so simply and powerfully.[2] In *Children of the Sun* I toyed with that notion but did not—indeed, could not—formulate it. For who among 'my' *Children of the Sun* is capable of perceiving that notion and that task?

It must arise in the hearts and minds of the proletariat, it must be uttered by their lips—isn't that so? And of course they will broaden that notion and deepen it.

I read the second part of your article on religion;[3] I liked it a lot, although you hurried it. It was as if you were on your way to a fire. The place where you objected to 'Cosmism', apropos of my comment on religion, seemed to me unclear—but this is probably my fault, not yours.[4]

I don't remember ever inviting people to 'wonder at the wise harmony of nature'; I think that this wonder must have appeared in the French translation.[5] But I do believe in that wisdom, and I am inclined to look upon nature's imperfections and its enmity towards me as imperfections in my own cognitive mechanism—i.e. as something which my descendants will overcome. The conviction that the enmity of nature is ineradicable would lead us again to dualism, in my opinion. Whilst the idea that 'everything is in mankind and everything is for mankind' still forms the basis of my belief, I cannot help believing in victory over *my own* nature.

I received Al. Alek.'s *Red Star* [*Krasnaia zvezda*] and I'm reading it.[6] I both like it and don't like it, nevertheless it's an intelligent work. If you don't have a copy, drop me a line and I'll send you mine when I've finished with it.

What struck me most of all in this book was the conjecture that there exist substances which are *repelled* and not attracted by the bodies which are known to us. I remember that when he was on Capri, Al. Al. mentioned this hypothesis in passing, but for some reason I did not pay attention to what he said at the time. But on this occasion my heart immediately stood still, as everything is possible for man and all his conjectures are being realized, just as his dream of the Philosophers' Stone has now been realized too. Isn't that so?

And if there is unity of matter and force, that means monism is the basic law of the universe; and that means harmony!

I'm saying all this in such a slipshod manner; please excuse me—I write more intelligibly about people than ideas.

I am glad that you liked the Zolotarev.[7] As soon as I get some money I'll send it to you with the humble request that you stuff it into the hands of Brzozowski![8] Please do! I would never manage to do it myself, whilst it's easy for you, now that you have become closer to him.

I walk around Rome, and my soul is on fire! There is so much that is touching, beautiful, and, alas, offensive! I will never forget a lecture I heard by an officer here. It was about labour and its significance, and he delivered it to half a company of soldiers at an exhibition mounted by the children's professional schools. An officer, soldiers, and an fervent respect for labour, how about that, eh? And on holidays here [. . .][9]

SOURCE: *AG* 14: 20–3.

[1] Anatolii Vasilievich Lunacharsky (1875–1933), writer and critic, member of the Bolshevik Party, later first Soviet Commissar of Education.
[2] Lunacharsky had suggested that the revolutionaries alone were capable of directing the energy of the masses, who would otherwise destroy culture.
[3] Lunacharsky's essay 'The Future of Religion' ['Budushchee religii'] reflected his interest in 'God-Building'. For further details, see the Introduction to this section.
[4] Lunacharsky considered 'cosmism' (the worship of the 'harmony' of natural forces) the highest form of naturalist religion, but he warned that it can also lead to resignation before fate.
[5] Gorky's comments on religion had appeared in the journal *Mercure de France*. Lunacharsky had indeed paraphrased from the French.
[6] Science fiction novel by Aleksandr Aleksandrovich Bogdanov (1873–1928), Marxist philosopher, writer, and prominent 'God-builder'.
[7] Aleksei Zolotarev (1878–1950), a writer who published in the Znanie anthologies.
[8] Stanisław Brzozowski (1876–1911), Polish philosopher, critic, and novelist who was seriously ill in Florence.
[9] The letter is unfinished.

52. *To K. P. Piatnitsky, [14 or 15 January 1908]*

[Capri]

Dear friend,

I received your letter and the money yesterday. Sincere thanks for both, but I'm obliged to ask you also to send at the first opportunity money for the discharge of a debt to Morgano,[1] to whom it seems you still owe 200 l[ira].

I was most disturbed by your very long silence. Even though I know how busy you are, it is essential that I have news from you, since I fear greatly for your health, and I sometimes imagine that you've already been put in the lock-up and so on. The content of your letter inspires no joy whatever in my heart, but, for all that, it's better to know than to remain in ignorance.

Although you reported your conversation with the 'comrade',[2] you didn't say anything about your writer-comrades, and I think that the latter are no better than the former. In this connection, I expect to hear various [. . .] anecdotes from you, even though I know that you are not much of an enthusiast for literature of that kind.

To move on to business.

In one of my letters I told you that Veresaev might perhaps be approaching you with a request to publish a miscellany for charity and that I would like this to happen; I can now inform you that this project has fallen through. I received a letter from Ver[esaev] in which he refused to have any dealings with Znanie, and he writes that he has lodged a complaint about this firm with a justice of the peace. Not the sweetest of surprises. The tone of the letter is 'comradely'.

Aizman[3] is very badly off, he's asking for money. So is Desnitsky, send him 300!

The 2,700 roubles received by the secretary of the commission for the publication etc.—would you be so good as to transfer this to my account and to inform Goldenberg[4] about it.

Now for the most important matter.

Tell me about your further plans concerning the miscellanies—how many are you thinking of publishing, how often and what is their content to be? I really need to know this. You'll remember that I spoke to you about the need for us to change the nature of the miscellanies by including literary criticism and social philosophy. I consider it essential to do this right now, while the hot air generated by the petty bourgeois is at its height and many people have talked themselves to the point of uttering the most terrible stupidities, baring their filthy souls to the core.

It would be easy for me to do this—I can organize a group of thoroughly valuable contributors, such as Lunacharsky, Voitolovsky,[5] Brzozowski, Bogdanov, Bazarov,[6] and a few others.

Lunacharsky is a very talented man, and in my opinion, he has a brilliant future as a publicist-philosopher.

Voitolovsky has written a very valuable study of social psychology—*In Defence of the Crowd*.[7] This is a most original work which is directed against the ideas of Tarde.[8] It abounds in the most interesting facts about crowd psychology observed by the author during the last war and over recent years generally in Russia and Europe. The study comes to about eight of our sheets.

All the others would work seriously, since they understand the importance of this enterprise. The editors would be Lenin, Lunachar[sky], and Bogdanov. I'm also counting on some translations from the Italian—certain authors here are offering their manuscripts on very favourable terms, about 50 roubles a sheet, and are prepared to wait until the books have appeared in Russian before publishing in any other languages.

We can make this a general stipulation, and it's essential that we do so. I myself also intend to write a series of articles about so-called 'contemporary psychology'. I've already written one which will appear in a miscellany to be published by a company headed by P. Iushkevich. The miscellany is directed against contemporary trends in literature.[9]

I didn't submit it for publication in our miscellanies because it would be out of place there alongside certain works, and also because I didn't want to appear alone in the role of publicist, even though my publicism is mostly lyrical. I'll only print articles of this nature in the company of the individuals I've named and to whom I'm bound by a community of views, mood, and intention.

All these people—and I too—understand that the present moment is most dangerous and yet most advantageous for democratic thought and literature. It's essential that this moment be seized in the sense of strengthening democratic trends. And it is also necessary to give a deserved rebuff to all the smart alecs and scoundrels, and to Sologubism of every kind. You will get more from my article than from any of my letters, and I ask you particularly to read it when the miscellany is published.

Has Andreev left altogether?[10] If so, I'd be glad. His 'Darkness' ['T'ma'] and *Tsar-Hunger* [*Tsar'-Golod*] are things which disturb me. Over-productiveness is no less harmful to him than the fame which has apparently poisoned the young man's weak stomach.

So let me know what you think of this plan for changing the miscellanies, and let me know as soon as possible, as I should not like to let any material slip through my fingers. I'll send the manuscripts of the articles to you from here. Tell me also what fee we could offer the authors.

I imagine that you will have some questions about this, and I also think that you might perhaps view the people I've named as 'comrades'. In the event of something barely human—or all-too-too human—presenting itself to us again (and I doubt that this will happen), it would make no difference to me in any event—my path lies with them, and that is the path I will take.[11] My fiction remains as it was, and if I can't find a place for my publicism in our miscellanies, then I'll have to print it in the same place as the others, although I don't want to do this.

In my opinion the task I have sketched here belongs with Znanie; there is no other publishing house which can fulfil that task to the extent that we can.

I also enclose a letter from Keltuiala, author of the book *A Course on the History of Russian Literature*.[12] I've read the first part of the course, and in my opinion it's a very valuable book. If we could help the author in his work, it would be a very good thing for the Russian public, which would obtain the first comprehensive *popular* work on the history of literature, a work written with love. I understand that there are no funds at present, but all the same I find it necessary to point out Keltuiala to you. His address is Sergievskaia, No. 60, flat 23.

Of the newspapers, I receive *Rech'* [*Speech*] and *Nash vek* [*Our Age*]. They come very irregularly, may God damn the post. I've received just two issues of *Russkoe znamia* [*The Russian Banner*]—the fifth and the seventh. How stupid.

Has *Nash vek* been shut down? If so, order another newspaper for me.

I can't work out if I've received all the books you sent. It seems that some have disappeared—the Droysen, for example.[13] I ask you earnestly to send me the books from my shelves as per the enclosed list, and to buy everything mentioned on the printed list.

Perhaps you could find someone who—for a small fee, of course—would get all these books for me. Some of them will have to be bought in second-hand bookshops. My dear friend, I ask you particularly to add to my list any valuable books on epic and folklore which aren't on it.

Ia. Grot has written works on the literature of the Scandinavian sagas.[14] I don't know who published them or where they were published. Do you know?

Is there a Russian translation or a summary of *Edda*?

Please help me with this. I'll be very grateful and send you my face cast in bronze in return.

At the moment I have two people doing sculptures of me at the same time—a German and an Italian.[15]

Warm regards, I truly wish you the spiritual courage which is so necessary when dealing frequently with intelligent people.

I send my best and wish you every happiness!

My story[16] is going well, it will come out at about five sheets.

I've asked Semen Pavlovich[17] to write to *Vesy* about delivery of the free offer they promised me. I selected two books: *Gold in Azure* [*Zoloto v lazuri*] by Andrei Bely, and *The Works and Days of Pushkin* [*Trudy i dni Pushkina*] by Lerner.[18]

You don't look a gift horse in the mouth.

SOURCE: *SS* 29: 47–51.

[1] Enrico Morgano organized lodgings for Gorky's Capri visitors.

[2] The reference is unclear, as Piatnitsky's preceding letter has been lost. Originally used to describe writers who were also Znanie shareholders, the term is now used ironically by Gorky.

[3] David Iakovlevich Aizman (1869–1922), writer and Znanie contributor.

[4] Iosif Petrovich Goldenberg (1873–1922), a Bolshevik.

[5] Lev Naumovich Voitolovsky (1876–1941), literary critic and publicist.

[6] Vladimir Aleksandrovich Bazarov (real name Rudnev) (1874–1939), political philosopher and economist, member of the breakaway group Vpered. See the Introduction to this section.

[7] The first part of Voitolovsky's *Sketches of Collective Psychology* [*Ocherki kollektivnoi psikhologii*] was called *Psychology of the Masses* [*Psikhologiia mass*].

[8] Gabriel Tarde (1843–1904), French sociologist and criminologist, whose views on social interaction were influential at the time.

[9] Gorky's article 'On Cynicism' ['O tsinizme'] was published in the first volume of *Literaturnyi raspad* [*Literary Disintegration*]. Pavel Solomonovich Iushkevich (1873–1945), Marxist philosopher and brother of Semen (Letter 43, n. 3).

[10] i.e had Andreev left Znanie.

[11] Gorky's Russian is very dense here. It is not clear what he means by 'something barely human' etc., although his prime commitment to his Bolshevik colleagues is evident.

[12] The first part of V. A. Keltuiala's *Kurs istorii russkoi literatury* appeared in 1906. Gorky's opinion of Keltuiala's work changed radically when the second volume of the course was published in 1912. See his letter to E. A. Liatsky of 9 April 1912 (*SS* 29: 236).

[13] *A History of Hellenism* [*Istoriia ellenizma*] in two volumes.

[14] Iakov Karlovich Grot (1812–93), linguist and scholar. The book in question is a study of the *Fridthjófs saga*.

¹⁵ The Italian was Italo Campagnoli.
¹⁶ *Confession.*
¹⁷ Bogoliubov (d. 1927), manager of the Znanie office.
¹⁸ The subscription to *Vesy* for 1908 came with a bonus of two free books from their list. Andrei Bely (pseudonym of Boris Nikolaevich Bugaev, 1880–1934), poet, novelist, and theoretician of the Russian Symbolist movement.

53. To E. P. Peshkova, [February 1908]

[Capri]

I'm sending you the almanac *Earth* and *Essays*.¹

It would be good if you were to study Bogdanov's article carefully. I'm ready to repeat a hundred times that he is the most original and sound philosopher of today and that great fame awaits him. Then there are the articles by Bazarov and Lunacharsky too.

I've just finished a rather large novella,² but I don't know what I'll call it yet. I'll start publishing it right away in Znanie. Ivan Pavlovich [Ladyzhnikov] is publishing *The Spy*³—write and ask him to send you a copy of it together with all the other books he has coming out.

Is Maksim receiving the magazines? And has he received *The Life of Fresh Water*⁴ and the other books ordered for him?

'The Destruction of the Personality' ['Razrushenie lichnosti'] is an article of mine which should appear in a German magazine.⁵ It is directed against individualists. It will be quite a major work in Russian, although I won't publish it for some time.

Get Maksim to send me the meerschaum cigarette-holder which he gave me in Genoa. All right?

Why arc you melancholy? Surely life is beautiful when it has a goal? Work, study: this is what brings enormous pleasure and calms the restlessness of the soul. My kind advice is not to place too much importance on this restlessness, and not to pay it too much attention.

In my new novella⁶ I have tried to illuminate the path towards a merger with the whole; it is in this merger, and nowhere else, that happiness and the source of the highest spiritual pleasures are to be found.

Every individual, if he is a spiritually sound being, ought to be striving towards the world and not away from it—that's the thesis of my novella. And I make so bold as to think that I have proved that thesis.

Never before have I written so readily and so easily as now; it is here that my entire life resides.

Everything personal is amazingly insignificant, of this I am convinced. It is not that I'm recommending a renunciation of the self, not at all. I am just talking about the need to find, to comprehend, and to cultivate the humane within one's self. There is little of the humane in the personal.

I very much want Maksim and you to lack nothing, and therefore I ask you to let me know what books you need, etc.

Has Piatnitsky sent any books? The man is amazingly slow, and at times it makes me as mad as hell. He is slow at everything. Something in his soul has rusted away, the springs are worn out, and he's not keeping pace with the times. That's a shame.

My best to Maksim. And warm regards to you. You shouldn't be sad! Look at what wonderfully interesting times we are living in—the earth is quivering and shaking everywhere.

All the best!

A.

SOURCE: *AG* 9: 46–7.

---

[1] The first issue of the almanac *Zemlia* [*Earth*] included stories by Andreev, Bunin, and Kuprin, and poems by Blok and Bunin. *Essays on the History of Marxist Philosophy* [*Ocherki po istorii filosofii marksizma*] (St Petersburg, 1908) contained articles by Bogdanov, Bazarov, Lunacharsky, and others.

[2] *Confession.*

[3] Working title for the novel *Life of a Useless Man.*

[4] The Russian version of a book by Konrad Keller (1848–1930).

[5] The article was eventually published in *Essays on the Philosophy of Collectivism* [*Ocherki filosofii kollektivizma*], 1909.

[6] *Confession.*

54. *To S. A. Vengerov,*[1] *[end of July 1908]*

[Capri]

My sincerely respected Semen Afanasievich!

As I have already informed you by telegram, I am refusing to participate in the committee organizing the celebration for Lev Nikolaevich.[2]

Please permit me not to mention the reasons for my refusal. I would like to avoid unnecessary arguments over this matter.

However, I will tell you personally that for me revolution is a phenomenon of life as rightful and blessed as the movement of a baby in its mother's womb, and that the *Russian* revolutionary—with all his shortcomings—is a person who has no equal, as far as I know, either in beauty of spirit or in the strength of his love for the world.

Count Lev Tolstoy is an artist of genius, our Shakespeare perhaps. He's the most amazing man I have ever had the pleasure to meet. I have listened to him a great deal, and even as I write these lines, he stands before me, wonderful, beyond comparison.

But although I am amazed by him, I don't like him. He is an insincere man who is excessively in love with himself. Other than himself, he sees and knows nothing. His humility is hypocritical and his desire to suffer is offensive. In general, such a desire is the desire of a sick, perverted spirit. In this case, the great egoist only wants to spend a little time in prison so as to strengthen his authority.[3] In my eyes, he degrades himself with his fear of death and his pitiable flirtation with it. He is an individualist for whom the assertion of authority is a kind of illusion of immortality. He already has his immortality, but that is not enough for him. Such greed is ridiculous. It's truly comical.

Finally, for a good twenty years now the chimes from this belfry have been hostile in every possible way to my faith. For twenty years the old man has kept on talking about how to convert splendid young Russia into a Chinese province, and the gifted young Russian into a slave.

No, despite his great beauty, he is alien to me.

My judgement will seem harsh to you, perhaps. It probably does, in fact. But I cannot think differently. I have paid dearly for my right to think precisely as I do.

I apologize for any awkwardness; in any case, it's not the words that are important, but their spirit.

Yours sincerely,

A. Peshkov

SOURCE: *SS* 29: 74–5.

[1] Semen Afanasievich Vengerov (1855–1920), critic and literary historian.
[2] Vengerov had invited Gorky to join a committee organizing the celebration of Tolstoy's eightieth birthday.
[3] An apparent reference to the furore which surrounded Tolstoy's anti-government pamphlet 'I cannot be silent!' ['Ia ne mogu molchat'!'].

55. *To E. P. Peshkova, [before 23 August 1908]*

[Capri]

My dear friend,

I probably won't be coming in August. I'll write and tell Maksim that I definitely won't be coming, since I don't want to raise his hopes. But I will say to you only that I *probably* won't be coming, since there is still the chance that I might snatch the time. Mind you, even if I were free right now I wouldn't come—my mood is so depressed and rotten.

As always, I'm being held up by a series of chance occurrences that have arisen unexpectedly—there was no way of foreseeing them! K[onstantin] P[etrovich] [Piatnitsky] should have come here back in July, yet he still hasn't made it. He's been held up because of illness. He and I have a mass of business and many serious issues to discuss. Of course, I could bring him with me on a visit to you, but I would have to ask two others, Bogdanov and Lunacharsky, to come with us as well, and that's impossible. I expect K[onstantin] P[etrovich] any day now. I have to edit a number of things, and it all needs to be done urgently, by September. We are putting together a small library of philosophy—three or four volumes are supposed to come out this very autumn. I am studying mathematics and Italian, and soon I'll begin to study English. I need to do all this, and I need to do it soon. And on top of all that there's this most abominable mood of mine, a mood which has a variety of causes, the chief of which is human folly. My life in general is not very pleasant. There are times when I want everyone and everything to go to hell, and I want to set off on foot, without money, without a definite tomorrow, etc. My mood is probably the result of fatigue. Right now I'm involved in editing a huge tetralogy, Weiser's *Jesus*, in five parts. I read it and become irritated, and I do the corrections.[1]

You do not write often or very clearly. For instance, whilst you let me know that the school will remain for the winter 'in the old place', you do not indicate which place you are talking about: Geneva or Paris?[2] Please let me know, so that I can arrange my affairs accordingly in case I don't make it to Alassio.

I'm sending you the silk. I forgot all about it, of course, and only remembered by chance. If I do come, I'll bring the chain for you with me, or else I'll send it.

Have you received the Strauss and the Haeckel?[3] They're good books. So long and goodbye for now, my friend.

Regards,

A.

SOURCE: *AG* 9: 53.

[1] A work by Karl Weiser (1848–1913). The book was never published in Russian.

[2] A reference to the Party school organized by Lenin and his supporters. See the Introduction to this section for further details.

[3] David Strauss, *The Life of Jesus*, and Ernst Haeckel, *The Riddle of the Universe*.

56. To O. O. Gruzenberg,[1] [8 September 1908]

[Capri]

Dear Oskar Osipovich!

I was surprised by your question—whether to defend Artsybashev or not.[2]

I think that on this matter there can be no question: in my opinion, the point is not that someone has written an apologia for the bestial element in man, but that those fools who rule over us consider that they have the right to judge a man for his opinion, to constrain his freedom of thought, to punish him—and for what?

What is a writer? He is this or that system of nerves organized in this way or that by the pressure of the surrounding psychological atmosphere. Man today is painfully defenceless against the influence of an environment which is so often hostile to him. He is defenceless because he is psychologically weak and impotent. The selection of impressions which imprint upon the mind—the receptacle of experience—does not depend on the will of an Artsybashev, a Timofeev, or an Ivanov.[3] Timofeev is perhaps a very chaste and pure fellow, but both the quantity and quality of his observations of reality will force him unwittingly to choose Diu-Liu for a hero.[4] And it's very possible that Artsybashev finds Sanin no less offensive than I do. Perhaps Sanin has been poorly depicted, but can we claim that he has been invented?

If you will excuse the crude comparison, a great deal of contemporary literature is like vomit. People have been poisoned with impressions of reality and they have fallen ill. The vast majority of those writing today have organisms in which the capacity to resist the social poisons that percolate through to them is insufficiently developed, and in many cases simply not developed at all. Their psyche is unstable and constantly vacillates alarmingly. In addition to this there is an impressionability which has increased to an almost unhealthy degree, and a complete absence of any sort of corrective, which might be able to execute from within—in the brain of the writer—the work of selecting impressions and organizing them. It seems to me that this corrective is a sense of the world as an active and dynamic process in which everything is temporary, and only motion is everlasting. I know that there are people who claim that this motion is meaningless, an insult to human pride, but I also know that the people who talk of that pride so loudly and so frequently are the ones who actually have least in the way of true human pride. But for me life is full of meaning, it is a most splendid process of accumulating psychic energy, a process which is manifest, undeniable, and perhaps even able to convert dead matter into matter which feels and thinks.[5]

But my opinions are irrelevant in this instance, and I apologize for going off at a tangent. I repeat that I was greatly surprised by your question, for I hear in it, far too loudly for my ear, the sad dissociation of people, the psychological breakdown and alienation which are destroying so many in these militant days of ours.

I apologize once again, but I must say that we would act more intelligently and beautifully if we were to unite in the defence of one of our people—whether it's Artsybashev, as in this case, or someone else, it makes no difference! Our enemy is the vulgarity into which we are sinking up to the knees, a vulgarity which is so zealously and cleverly cultivated in life by those who need it as a muddy ditch to protect the entrance to their fortress.

The trial against Artsybashev is vulgar and impudent, like all so-called 'literary' trials.

Thank you for the report about *Mother*.[6] It seemed very foolish to me: may those on the Committee for Stupidities in Press Affairs not take offence.

But there's something that annoys me in all this: by paying so much attention to me all these authorities of ours have greatly enhanced my 'popularity', and they continue to enhance it even now. This disrupts my life in the same way that, for example, fleas, mosquitoes, and other insects do. Please don't think that I'm striking a pose, but it's annoying when a person is written about in the newspapers. In my opinion, this is only acceptable in those cases when you have your leg broken by a tram, or if you commit suicide or kiss a strange lady in public without her permission.

Well, how I've prattled on! You did once complain that I don't write— so try this for size!

My sincere greetings to Roza Gavrilovna.[7] M[ariia] F[edorovna] [Andreeva] sends her best.

Regards. And I thank you very much.

Burenin was here the other day; we talked about you a lot.

All the best!

A. Peshkov

SOURCE: *LN* 95: 1000–1.

[1] Oskar Osipovich Gruzenberg (1866–1940), a lawyer who had acted for Gorky in 1905.

[2] Gruzenberg had informed Gorky that he had been approached to defend Artsybashev's notorious novel *Sanin* against pornography charges.

[3] Boris Aleksandrovich Timofeev, writer and doctor; Gorky apparently uses the name Ivanov in the way an English-speaker might use Jones to signify ordinariness.

[4] Diu-Liu was the defendant in a celebrated case involving the sexual violation of minors.

[5] The influence of Bogdanov's ideas is most evident in this paragraph. See the Introduction to this section for details.

[6] Gruzenberg had attached to his letter a copy of a lawsuit against Gorky's novel on the grounds of treason.

[7] Gruzenberg's wife.

57. To K. P. Piatnitsky, [28 September 1908]

[Capri]

My dear friend,

I know that my attitude towards you often assumes unforgivably rude forms, that I spoil hours, perhaps even days, of your life. I understand perfectly how busy you are. I can imagine the bog of vulgarity, quite terrifying in its depth, which our gentlemen writers have created all around you. I sense that your life is difficult and probably even detestable at times.

Despite all this, I sometimes feel an unbearable desire to abuse you. Why? Well, first of all because I really need to see you. You must excuse me: the more I get to know people, the higher you stand in my regard. I know you don't much take to such effusions—I'm not greatly disposed towards them myself, either—but at this accursed time one *must* sometimes speak *for oneself* and say that, despite everything, there is one man whom I respect with all my soul. For, you see, my patience is at an end. I seem to be developing a chronic nervousness, my skin is becoming painfully sensitive: when I touch the mail from Russia my fingers involuntarily clench into a fist, and I feel everything trembling within my chest with anger and contempt in anticipation of some inevitable obscenity. I'm not exaggerating.

What's the matter? The matter is that I love Russian literature, I love my country and I believe in its spiritual power. This is a great love.

But what I see is something mad, incomprehensible, and savage, something which causes me pain and envelops me in a cloud of fiery, agonizing rage. I see things which I didn't think were possible in Russia. The people have truly awakened, but the prophets have run off to taverns and brothels. I see that Kuprin and Andreev, talented men, walk side by side with hooligans who use the names of journalists as a cover and advertise the banking house 'Zakharii Zhdanov and Co'. I see the Chukovskys, the Pilskys, the Merezhkovskys, the Razumniks, the Izgoevs, and the Miliukovs[1]—for me they are all fantastic green faces, vague blotches like bruises on the corpse of a murdered man. They are something altogether distorted, confused, and sick. And they all tell lies the same way. It's impossible to fight this liquid, clinging filth—there's nothing to fight it with.

A German bacteriologist once said: cholera sets an examination for the stomach. Apparently the Russian revolution set an examinaton for the brain and nerves of the Russian intelligentsia. This 'classless group' is becoming ever more alien to me organically, it arouses my contempt, it fills me with rage. It is an incurable hysteric, a coward, a liar. Its spiritual make-up is quite beyond my comprehension now, because its mental instability beggars all comparisons. These are filthy streams, not people.

I feel that I don't have the strength to express my thoughts and feelings coherently in this regard. But understand this: every day brings me, a Russian writer who loves his country and his occupation, a dozen unwarranted insults. For example, Gruzenberg recently sent me a letter in which he explained his motives in refusing to defend Artsybashev.[2] Do you know, this affected me like a slap in the face? But Gruzenberg is right, he's right one hundred times over! To defend the author of *Sanin* means to defend vulgarity. And this vulgarity was adjudged an important literary event, a work of remarkable talent. But that is true too! There are some talented pages in *Sanin*.

They are writing incredible things in *Utro* [*Morning*].[3] They are hooligans and renegades, renegades and hooligans. Now and then so-called 'decent people' find themselves in their midst, but they are hysterics one and all. Veresaev is an example.

What the country needs—it is clear to me—are strong, healthy, working people, and an unpretentious, clear, healthy literature. I receive information from everywhere about self-education groups, about the voracious interest there is in natural science and philosophy. Who will satisfy this thirst?

My former comrades: the Andreevs, the Kuprins, and the Chirikovs are people of whom I'm ashamed to the point of despair. 'The Seven who were Hanged'! 'Sulamif'![4] The cats![5] And they all display a disgusting and degrading greed for money.

I am tormented by all this; it is tearing me to pieces. I've begun to write a series of strongly worded articles in the form of open letters to literary men. I wanted to point out to them the demands of the moment and their responsibilities. But where do I write? For whom? It is like throwing a stone into a quagmire—there is not a sound, not a ripple. These unhappy, sick, drunken people are cut off from life and will not understand anything or hear anything. Damn them.

I'm devilishly alone. Loneliness has never oppressed me, and it doesn't oppress me now as A. Peshkov. But you should understand that, speaking as a writer, things are hard for me! Very hard. I want to fight, to swear and shout.

And sometimes fragments of this mood fall on you. Believe me, I find it difficult knowing that this is happening, but it's hard to control myself. As far as my nerves are concerned, I should say that they're getting worse and worse. The worst thing of all is that at times one starts to think of one's entire native land as a creature incapable of life, a future Chinese province. Partly German too, to be precise.

To see you is a moral necessity, apart from various business reasons.

By the way, concerning business. Militsyna has sent a letter asking for an advance.[6] But the point is this, you see: her story, besides being inconvenient from the censorship point of view, is also superfluous as material for us, because I already have a more striking work on the same theme. For this reason I'll write and tell her that her story is not suitable. She'll take offence, of course.

You say Petrishchev is proposing a second edition of his book?[7] Allow me to decline this honour. You will, of course, remember that he published articles in *Russkoe bogatstvo* which we had paid for. And after that he published his articles all over the place and got himself into a polemic with that renegade Izgoev. In my opinion, that nonentity of ours, Izgoev, had truth on his side in that polemic. For these reasons I do not consider Petrishchev an author worthy of Znanie.

Ah, many are the people in this publishing house that I'd like to throw out on their ear! Miliukov is one of them! Not for his politics, but for his lack of talent and the obvious lies in his letters from Turkey.[8]

I've telegraphed about Skvortsov's proposal.[9] I'm setting it out on a separate sheet in the words of A. Bogdanov.

1. Send me or, better still, send Bogdanov the money for Stepanov, the translator of Verworn[10] *30 roubles a page.*

2. Send Bogdanov:

An honorarium for the preface to Verworn—100 roubles a page.

15 copies of Verworn's booklet.

50 of *The Adventures of a Philosophical School.*[11]

Pay him for editing Verworn's booklet. How much? I don't know.

Bogdanov's address is: Geneva. Rue de la Halle, 1, Genève, A. Malinovsky.

Please be quick!

3. I want—and I consider it very necessary—to publish translations of popular booklets:

Le Dantec. *Philosophy of Biology.* V. Bazarov is editing it and writing the preface.

Le Bon. *The Birth and Death of Matter*, which hasn't been translated yet.

Le Dantec. *Laughter*, which won't be translated for the time being.

Kenton. *The Beginning of Life.* Ditto.

These are all small books, 3 to 7 sheets in length, and with very valuable contents.

On the whole we should pay attention to this side of things. Look how the French operate: all serious scientific works are published there almost immediately in the form of popular booklets and, what is more, people read them!

We've had enough of fiction from writers who are expensive and dangerous for the publishers!

I feel very sorry for Andreev. But I can no longer maintain any dealings with him and I haven't answered his letters. He's stopped writing to me now.

Towards the spring we'll put together an interesting collection.[12] You'll see! Perhaps even two.

Warm regards.

Come soon!

I really do fear that you'll fall ill. Your letter with its description of the cholera vaccinations made me laugh and also made me angry. Good heavens! To think that it's necessary to vaccinate oneself against cholera as an example to people! And smallpox!

How many vaccinations do you still need to have?[13]

Do come.

I embrace you.

A.

1. Bogdanov and Stepanov are offering:

A Course on Political Economy [*Kurs politicheskoi ekonomii*]. *Forty* printer's sheets. The work will be completed by 1 October 1909. The honorarium is 80–100 roubles a page, depending on the cost of the book and the number of copies. They should be paid 250 roubles a month from the date of signing the contract. The manuscript will be delivered from January onwards. It will be printed after Easter. Talk with Stepanov about it.

Address: Iv. Iv. Skvortsov. Moscow. Bolshaia Presnia, Zdorovaia House, flat 8.

This work is an expansion of the Bogdanov book which you already know. As I understand it, this is a work of political economy illustrated by the history of culture. In my opinion, it is an important piece and we should publish it.

On the whole I think very highly of Bogdanov and his group. They are extremely valuable people.

2. Bogdanov is offering his book *From the Psychology of Society* [*Iz psikhologii obshchestva*], third edition. His terms with 'Pallada' were as follows: 4,250 copies, at 80 kopecks, an honorarium of 800 roubles. The book runs to about 15 sheets. It is supplemented by the article 'Towards a Characterization of the Philosophy of the Proletariat' ['K kharakteristike filosofii proletariata'], a new preface, and footnotes. 'Pallada' stipulates that publication should be no earlier than 1 February, so as to ensure that its remaining copies will be sold out, and that the price should not be less than 80 kopecks.

It's a good book, and very saleable, as you can see. I'd also like to publish the three books of *Empiriomonism*, for, as I've already said, I really value Bogdanov's works.

3. Lunacharsky is preparing a book *A History of Folk Art in Russia* [*Istoriia russkogo narodnogo tvorchestva*].[14] This is my idea, and I'm paying him a little bit at a time for the work. I've paid about 2,000 lira so far. The book won't be ready for some time.

Answer my first two questions as quickly as you can, and if you settle them in the affirmative, then:

In the first case, telegraph Stepanov to let him know that he should come to you for the negotiations, as it seems that he's in a big hurry and might offer his book to someone else.

In the second, write to Bogdanov and ask him to send the material.

Then ask dear Semen Pavlovich [Bogoliubov] to send the books and give him the enclosed note.

A.

Mariia Fedorovna [Andreeva] asks whether you received the letter which she wrote three months ago. She's angry, of course. But, as you know, all people are angry nowadays. It's a pointless business.

A.

SOURCE: *AG* 4: 260–4.

[1] Kornei Ivanovich Chukovsky (1882–1969), writer and critic, later famous as a writer for children; Petr Moiseevich Pilsky (1876–1942), writer and critic; Ivanov-Razumnik (real name Razumnik Vasilievich Ivanov) (1878–1946), critic and scholar; A. Izgoev (real name Aleksandr Solomonovich Lande) (1872–1935), publicist; Pavel Nikolaevich Miliukov (1859–1943), historian, leading figure in the Consitutional Democrat (Kádet) Party.

[2] See Letter 56, n. 2.

[3] A newspaper which dealt heavily in gossip about Russian writers.

[4] Stories by Andreev—'The Story of the Seven who were Hanged' ['Rasskaz o semi poveshennykh']—and Kuprin, respectively.

[5] On 18 August *Peterburgskii listok* [*The Petersburg Sheet*] reported that a number of prominent writers had been present at a tavern where cat-baiting had taken place.

[6] Elizaveta Mitrofanovna Militsyna (1869–1930), writer who published with Znanie.

[7] A. B. Petrishchev's *Notes of a Teacher* [*Zametki uchitelia*] was published by Znanie in 1905.

[8] Miliukov's 'Travel Letters' ['Pis'ma s dorogi'] appeared in *Rech'* in July 1908.

[9] I. I. Skvortsov-Stepanov (1870–1928), publicist, later active in the Soviet government. *Course on Political Economy A* by Bogdanov and Skvortsov was eventually published in 1910.

[10] Max Verworn, a German physiologist, whose work was published as *The Question of the Limits of Cognition* [*Vopros o granitsakh poznaniia*] by Znanie in 1909.

[11] *Prikliucheniia odnoi filosofskoi shkoly*, a pamphlet by Bogdanov.

[12] The 1909 *Essays on the Philosophy of Collectivism* [*Ocherki filosofii kollektivizma*].

[13] Piatnitsky's trip was delayed because of a cholera outbreak in St Petersburg.

[14] The book was never written.

58. *To E. P. Peshkova, [late December 1908]*

[Capri]

Don't be afraid, old friend, everything's over! I mean everything, and for tens of thousands of people. Military ships will bombard Messina so as to destroy it once and for all; they'll cover the corpses with lime. It's already impossible to work, for even now soldiers are swarming through the ruins, their mouths and noses covered with wadding—tens of thousands of people are decomposing and being cremated.[1]

As for me, there is also something like an earthquake in my head and in my heart: Piatnitsky has published Andreev's *A Student's Love* and an idiotic story by Skitalets against my wishes.[2] They'll hound me for this.

I keep on asking him to come here, but I get no answer. I'm so distressed and hurt that I can't sleep at night. Things are hard for me, damn it, and I would like to get some rest for once. This is what I've been wanting to do for some ten years now, but there just isn't ever any time.

I'm not losing my energy, of course, but there are times when I look around and it hurts.

These are such uncanny, important, and demanding times, and yet there's no one to work with!

There is something monstrous and barbarous going on in Russia; everyone is moaning, and loudest of all are the recent victors. There was a discussion of *Confession* at the Religious-Philosophical Society; what banality, what poverty of thought, what hypocrisy!

Everyone has become strangely stupid, as if they've lost half their brain, half their heart.

The second issue of *Literary Disintegration* has appeared, with good articles by Bazarov, Voitolovsky, and Lunacharsky. The articles by Bogdanov and by myself and other Znanie people will be out soon.[3]

Well, goodbye for now, so long. I'm waiting for Piatnitsky! This is so damn stupid. We'll probably fight like cat and dog, and there's even the possibility of my leaving Znanie.

My patience is gone!

Warm regards,

A.

I'm sending a letter I received from an eleven-year-old boy; get Maksim to read it if you think it won't upset him.[4]

SOURCE: *AG* 9: 58–9.

[1] On 28 December 1908 southern Italy was struck by an earthquake which resulted in some 100,000 deaths. Gorky raised funds to help the victims.

[2] 'Stages' ['Etapy'] by Skitalets and Andreev's play (under the title *Days of our Lives* [*Dni nashei zhizni*]) were published, respectively, in volumes 25 and 26 of Znanie.

[3] In the collection *Essays on the Philosophy of Collectivism*.

[4] On the Italian earthquake.

59. *To I. P. Ladyzhnikov, [end of March 1909]*

[Capri]

Dear Ivan Pavlovich!

As you know, complaints are pouring in from all over Russia about the lack of intellectual resources, and workers everywhere are taking party business into their own hands.

Such complaints have increased especially of late, and this can be explained by the growth of the organization. The workers write that they lack the personal resources to satisfy the requirements of the common man, requirements which are always increasing and expanding.

This situation obliges us to do everything that we can to increase the party's intellectual energy. We—that is, Al. Al. [Bogdanov], the worker from the Urals who is living here,[1] Lunacharsky, and myself—have agreed about the need to establish abroad a course for training organizers and propagandists.

This is how we're setting things up: organizations in Russia will be informed about the courses, and these organizations will select the most able workers from their midst and send them abroad for about three or four months. Only workers will be sent.

We calculate that the maximum upkeep here is 100 lira a month per person. Initially we propose that fifteen to twenty people be sent (including some weavers from the Moscow region and farmers from the 'Spilka' region).

We already have a certain amount of money. I've written a series of letters and I expect further success. Chaliapin has made a donation, and Amfiteatrov will too.

Now, as it is some time since I claimed any 'royalties' due to me, I was wondering if you could put them towards this cause, should the money be available.

It makes no difference what the royalties amount to. Even if it's just a hundred marks, it is still money. Think it over. But don't be at all afraid to refuse. Nevertheless, I consider this matter so important that I'll get the money, even if I have to mortgage wives and children for it!

I send my best! Regards.

Show this letter to N-ch[2] to see what he has to say. Get him to reply to me. Perhaps he could help too? A. A. said he might. Not out of his own 300 marks, of course, but from some other sources, provided he has them. Heavens above, how good it would be if we were to succeed in this! I'd go crazy with joy.

I send my best.

A.

SOURCE: *AG* 7: 190–1.

[1] Nikifor Efremovich Vilonov (1883–1910), also known by the Party name 'Mikhail'.
[2] Leonid Borisovich Krasin (1870–1926), Party name 'Nikitich'.

60. To F. I. Chaliapin, [no earlier than 1 September 1909]

[Capri]

My dear Fedor,

Konstantin Petrovich [Piatnitsky]—he is here, by the way—has told me that you want to write and publish your autobiography. This news makes me very excited and anxious! So let me quickly tell you the following, my friend.

You are undertaking a serious business which is of broad significance, i.e. of interest not only to us Russians but also to the entire cultured world, especially the artistic world! Do you understand?

This business demands a profound approach; it cannot be done 'just anyhow'.

I beg you most earnestly—you must trust me!—not to speak of your plan to anyone until you have talked to me.

It would be very sad if your material were to fall into the hands and teeth of a person incapable of comprehending the huge—national—importance of your life, a symbolic life, a life which provides indisputable testimony to the power and might of our motherland and to the living springs of pure blood which beat in the heart of a country under the yoke of its Tatar lords. Look, Fedor, you must not cast your soul into the hands of the word-traders!

You can believe me when I say that I am not pursuing my own interests in warning you of the mistakes you might make as a result of your goodness and disorderliness.

This is what I propose. Either come here for a month or so, and *I will write your life for you as you dictate it*, or else invite me to come to you abroad somewhere where we will work together on your autobiography for three or four hours a day.[1]

Of course, I would not constrain you in any way. I would simply point out what should be brought into the open and what should be left in the shade. I would supply the language if you wish, but if not, you could change it in any way you like.

I look at it like this: it is important that what needs to be written should be excellently written! Believe me, I do not wish to push myself forward in this business—far from it! It is necessary for *you* to speak about yourself and *you alone*!

Don't say anything to anyone about this letter and don't show it to anyone! I beg you!

Damn it all, I am terribly frightened that you might not understand the *national*, Russian significance of your autobiography! My dear friend, close your eyes for an hour and think about it! Look carefully and you will see the heroic figure of a peasant genius on a grey and empty plain!

How can I tell you what I feel and what fills my heart with fire?

Ask Kon[stantin] Petr[ovich] [Piatnitsky]—the best and most honourable man I know!—ask him how important your fine idea is, how dear it is to me, and he will tell you.

Our friendship gives me the right to beg you not to hurry, and not to begin anything until you have talked it over with me!

I would not spoil anything—trust me!—and you can rest assured that I would help you with many things!

Please reply, by telegram if you like.

Once more, I beg you earnestly to say nothing about this letter to anyone!

Aleksei

Dear K[onstantin] P[etrovich] sends his regards to you and M[ariia] V[alentinovna].[2] I send my regards to her too.

SOURCE: *SS* 29: 94–6.

---

[1] Gorky and Chaliapin eventually collaborated on this project in 1916.
[2] Mariia Piettsold, Chaliapin's second wife.

61. To O. O. Gruzenberg, [2 December 1909]

[Capri]

Dear Oskar Osipovich!

Please accept my hearty and most sincere thanks. I think that *Mother*, because of its tone, is a timely work and that a good few people will perhaps breathe a little easier for having read it. And, should they raise a smile, I would like such people to know of your kind assistance to them at such a difficult time, when everyone's life is sad. In short, my task is to buttress the declining spirit of opposition to the dark and hostile forces of life, and you have helped me to accomplish this. I value your assistance highly and send you my warm, grateful and amicable regards.

My greetings and compliments to your wife, all the best and, above all, good health.

A. Peshkov

SOURCE: *LN* 95: 1004.

62. To A. V. Amfiteatrov, [no earlier than 9 January 1910]

[Capri]

Your praise of *Okurov*[1] is premature: as evidence of this I am sending you the proofs of the conclusion to Part One.

The Sholem Asches owe a lot of money, that is why they're being published.[2] I'm fed up with them too. And—alas!—I can understand the mood which inspired A. Bely to take up the business of anti-Semitism.[3]

Just look at what a tactless and unruly lot they are, all these Meierholds, Chukovskys, Dymovs, Ol'd'Ors and others, their name is legion![4] When it comes to Russian literature, they just about manage to understand the words, but nothing more than the words: its spirit is completely alien to them. This is where such catch-phrases as 'down with everyday life!' come from.[5] And this is in Russia! They import the 'latest things' from Europe, they cause trouble, they make a lot of noise and behave like hooligans. And in the end all this fuss and bother serves only to play into the hands of the anti-Semites. That's a fact! This should have been identified as a source of anti-Semitism long ago.

Why are you always nagging me about 'Bolshevism'? You're supposed to be an attentive reader, after all! Bolshevism is dear to me to the extent that it is the work of monists, just as socialism is dear and important precisely because it's the only way by which a man can arrive as quickly as possible at the fullest and deepest consciousness of his *personal* human worth.

I do not see any other path. All other paths lead *away* from the world, this one alone leads *towards* the world. There comes a time when a man must say to himself: I am the creator of the world. Then and only then can the new man and the new history be born.

Keep your hands off my socialism.

What do you know about Stepan Razin, besides what's in Kostomarov, Soloviev, etc.?[6] Are there any specialist studies? Is there anything by the sectarians? Please help me, for this man, whom Pushkin called 'the only poetic figure in Russian history', is giving me no sleep. I will have to write about him, that much is plain. I may not publish it, but I will certainly write something!

I still haven't read Chekhov's letters.[7]

Regards and greetings. I would like to have the 'devils'.[8]

Will this come about soon?

A. Peshkov

SOURCE: *LN* 95: 183–4.

---

[1] *Okurov Town*, the first part of an intended trilogy about provincial life.

[2] Sholem Asch (1880–1957), prominent Yiddish novelist and dramatist. Amfiteatrov had complained to Gorky: 'Listen! We've had enough of all these Sholem Asches.'

[3] See his article 'Rubber-stamped Culture' ['Shtempelevannaia kul'tura'] (*Vesy*, no. 9, 1909).

[4] Vsevolod Emilievich Meierhold (1874–1940), theatrical director and leading figure in the artistic avant-garde; Osip Isidorovich Dymov (real name Perelman, 1878–1959), dramatist; Ol'd'Or (real name Osip Lvovich Orsher, 1879–1942), wrote for the right-wing *Novoe vremia* [*New Times*].

[5] Gorky has in mind the escapist trends in literature which he associated with the rise of Russian Symbolism.

[6] Stepan (or, more commonly, Stenka) Razin was the legendary leader of a popular rebellion. Kostomarov and Soloviev were the authors of well-known histories of Russia. Gorky wrote a film scenario, *Stenka Razin*, in 1919; it was published only posthumously.

[7] The first volume of Chekhov's collected letters had just been published in Moscow.

⁸ In his letter to Gorky, Amfiteatrov mentioned the possibility of commissioning a translation of Arturo Graf's book *Il Diavolo*.

63. To E. P. Peshkova, [late October 1910]

[Capri]

I'm sending you the miscellany.

Andreev is flirting with young people of both sexes, while I'm only paying court to your sister.

Artsybashev's *The Breaking-Point* [*U poslednei cherty*] is an abomination, a sick abomination. He's stupid, that Artsybashev. And destitute. In his novel you'll meet Tolstoy's Ivan Ilyich, Chekhov's Von Koren, and many familiar figures from Dostoevsky: Arbuzov is Rogozhin, without a doubt! Svidrigailov's there, you sense the presence of Kirillov, and every one of them is vulgarized.[1] The writing is even worse than in *Sanin*.

Some sad things have been going on here: the entire bay is covered with fragments of wood, furniture, household items, and all sorts of stuff! Hundreds of boats come daily from Sorrento and all the seaside villages—also from Capri—and pick up all this stuff: kerosene tins, mirrors, doors, boxes, tables, and chests of drawers. They pile these things on the shore and sell them to aid the victims.[2]

Would such a thing have been done in Russia?

As for the matter that caused me to break off the trip—the need to arrange a loan for Znanie—don't say a word! For a while, a year or two, I would like to publish nothing at all; I'm tired, and there are some tasks that require a lot of preparatory work. As K[onstantin] P[etrovich] [Piatnitsky] is trying to convince me, my dream of selling Znanie is impractical. He and I have gone through a great deal of difficulty and unpleasantness of late, but our relations are somewhat smoother now. He will apparently be leaving for Russia in December.

All the news from Russia is sad, in so far as writers and literature are concerned. Kuprin has drunk himself to the point of having hallucinations. Andreev is suffering from delusions of grandeur in a most pernicious form. I'm unbearably sorry for him. There are times when he understands the dramatic nature of his condition himself. People mock and abuse him: quite recently one woman called him a 'lout' to his face. It is evident that writers generally have completely lost their old charm and prestige in society.

People continue to slander me. This time they've linked my name with the expropriation in Mias,[3] while Stolypin[4] has written in *Novoe vremia* that I was teaching workers how to make bombs at the school on Capri. It's all stuff and nonsense, but it's annoying and wearisome.

I still haven't sent money for a bicycle—please apologize to my son for me; he appears to crave a vehicle very much. And I didn't send you the scarf that you were talking about in Alassio either. Just hold on! I'll remember!

I can pass on some news: Zinovii [Peshkov] is getting married. While he was at Amfiteatrov's place in Spezia, he met a girl who is the daughter of a Cossack colonel, and five days later they decided to marry. Mariia Fedorovna [Andreeva] has gone to see the bride. This makes me neither happy nor sad. It feels to me as if this is not happening to us at all, but to the neighbours. I very much like Zinovii—he's a wonderful fellow, unusually honest and straightforward—but I don't permit myself to meddle in affairs that I don't understand. The girl seems nice. And it may also be nice that all this occurred so hurriedly and so unexpectedly.

In general, 'worldly affairs' don't affect me much, except where they concern literature. I'm becoming more and more of a professional.

I'm sitting and writing *Kozhemiakin*;[5] I really want this to be a success! It's hard, though: the theme is complicated, and it requires too much knowledge. I have to read dozens of old books.

Thank you, my fine one, for your letters and for the way you treat me in general. You are dear and close to me. I live with you in my mind, and my thoughts about you are many, constant and good.

Keep well, and take care of yourself! Please don't be upset!

A.

From what I've seen of Amf[iteatrov]'s children, I can tell you that we have a nice son! Granted, he's older. But still! His is a different disposition, a different spiritual make-up. Tell him that I'm not answering his letter now because I'm very busy, but that his letter is extremely interesting and that I'm looking forward to receiving the history of aviation that he promised. Get him to write and get used to conversing with paper. One has to learn to do this, since ultimately, no matter how much you've lived, what remains before you is a blank sheet of paper and that's where it all is! Well, goodbye for now, my dear friend! All the best, be of good cheer and health.

A.

Have you by any chance come across the catalogue of a second-hand bookseller who deals in old editions of literary works? If you have, please send it to me.

And also, if on the bookstalls along the Seine you come across a book that discusses antique weapons—a 'History of Side-Arms'—do buy it! Or a 'Description of Medals'; that is, a description of someone's medal collection.

But these books must be illustrated—especially the one on weapons! Without illustrations they won't be any good to me.

I've taken quite a fancy to medals! I've already collected more than a hundred of them, and there are some extremely interesting items among them.

I'm getting old! Alas!

But it's time I did, you'll agree!

SOURCE: *AG* 9: 101–3.

[1] The works in question are Tolstoy's 'The Death of Ivan Ilyich' and Chekhov's 'The Duel'. The Dostoevsky characters are from *The Idiot, Crime and Punishment,* and *The Devils,* respectively.

[2] The Italian coast had just been ravaged by a violent storm.

[3] An item in *Novoe vremia* for 6 October 1910 suggested that Gorky was associated with the revolutionary terrorists who had committed a robbery at the station of Mias, near Ufa.

[4] Petr Arkadievich Stolypin (1862–1911), Minister of Internal Affairs.

[5] *The Life of Matvei Kozhemiakin,* the sequel to *Okurov Town.*

64. To E. P. Peshkova, [5–6 November 1910]

[Capri]

Lev Nikolaevich [Tolstoy]'s 'flight' from his home and family provoked an outburst of scepticism on my part and aroused a feeling akin to animosity towards him. Knowing that he has long yearned to 'suffer' for the sole purpose of magnifying the significance of his religious ideas and the force of his preaching, I felt that there was something contrived and artificial about his 'flight'.

You know how I hate this preaching of a passive attitude towards life; you should understand how pernicious Buddhist ideas are for a country steeped in fatalism.

Of course, to instil such ideas in our life with such stubborn consistency, and in an onslaught that comes to resemble coercion—this is something that I find anything but delightful, and this is not what causes me to bow in respect before Tolstoy.

He is the only person to whom the lofty title of national genius rightfully belongs. But as a national genius he has reflected all the bad qualities of the nation, all the deformities inflicted upon it by history. His teaching is the eructation of deep antiquity, the seething of that Tatar-Finnish blood which appears to be chemically hostile to the West, to its ideas and way of life; it has fought against the West since time immemorial and has found in Tolstoy's attitude towards the state, science, and art a form and expression of striking power and consistency.

Troubled by all these thoughts, I wrote about them to V. G. Korolenko.[1] Then, all of a sudden, I get a telegram from Rome about Lev Nikolaevich's death together with a request to write an article for *Nuova Antologia.*[2] For about five minutes, perhaps, I had a rather vague feeling and wondered what was going on. Yes, the inevitable had occurred. And then I began to howl. I locked myself in my room and cried inconsolably all day. Never in my life have I felt so forsaken as on that day; never have I felt such a fierce longing for another human being. I cried and wrote to Vladimir Galaktionovich about what had happened since he is the only person and writer who would be able to understand. Then, in the evening some reporters turned up with the news that Tolstoy was still alive!

But that did not cause me to rejoice. Yes, I did feel better, but the presentiment of his end still remained. Perhaps even at this very moment the end has already come.

It's very painful, my dear friend. The finest, mightiest, and greatest of men is leaving our poor and miserable life. Do you remember what he was like in Gaspra and how he would come to visit us at 'Niura'?[3] I just can't imagine him dead. It seems to me that he will lie in his coffin with that little smile of his hidden in his beard, and that he won't have anything in common with ordinary people who have died.

What you wrote about Sofiia does not move me.[4] She is a person whom I don't like; I have too many bad impressions of her, and these cannot be forgiven or forgotten. I'm also convinced that for him the 'flight' was not such a serious drama as it seems to you.

He doesn't like people; he treats them coldly and had long since prepared himself for this act. His flight was a mechanical act, so to speak, because all its inner causes had long been thought over and felt deeply.

It is not just one woman but the whole of Russian literature which is being widowed. Even though he has not been active as a writer for some time, he was active once! And it was probably the mere fact of his existence which restrained many people from doing many things of which they might otherwise have been capable. But once he is gone, there will be even more of a witches' sabbath, even more licentiousness in language and thought.

In his person an old paladin of truth is disappearing; the aristocratic traditions of literature are on the way out—at the very time when these traditions need to be revived, when we need austerity in thought and imagery, restraint, and modesty in language.

I know that what goes on nowadays does so outside the sphere of his interests and his attention.

Nevertheless, he would sometimes express an opinion about Andreev, Artsybashev, etc., and his words most probably had some effect on people's consciences, turning their thoughts away from the humdrum and the base, and towards the true, fundamental, and pure behests of literature.

A judge is leaving us. I also feel mortally sorry for the prophet, even though I don't like him.

My soul aches terribly.

Keep well. Have you really not received my cards and letters?

In this picture Maksim really reminds me of myself. I was actually like that once.

Goodbye for now,

A. Peshkov

SOURCE: *AG* 9: 105–6.

[1] This letter was never posted. Gorky later included it in his memoir of Tolstoy.

[2] On 4 November a false rumour that Tolstoy had died spread both in Russia and abroad. The editor of this Italian magazine asked Gorky to submit a piece for a Rome newspaper.

[3] The villa in the Crimea where Gorky and Peshkova lived in 1900.

[4] Sofiia Andreevna, Tolstoy's wife.

65. To I. A. Bunin, [beginning of December 1910]

[Capri]

I read the final part of *The Village* [*Derevnia*] with such excitement and joy for you, such great joy, because you have written a first-rate piece.[1] I am in no doubt about this myself. No one has dealt with the village so profoundly and with such a *historical sense* as you have. One could mention L[ev] N[ikolaevich] [Tolstoy], but his 'Morning of a Landowner' ['Utro pomeshchika'] and such like belong to a different era and are episodes from the life of Tolstoy. 'The Peasants' ['Muzhiki'] and 'In the Ravine' ['V ovrage']² are also mere episodes—you must forgive me for saying so!—from the life of a hypochondriac. I see nothing to compare with your piece. It has moved me most powerfully. This lament for our native land, so modestly clothed and so muted, is dear to me, as is its noble sorrow and agonizing fear. And all this is new. No one has written *this* way before. The death of the beggar is magnificent. Everyone here turned pale and sobbed when they read it. 'The shadow of a pagan' is a marvellous feature!³ You may not realize yourself just how profoundly and truly that is expressed.

'The train began to come later'—because the days were shorter—this is an example of the way the Slavs thought in the tenth century. And it is so true! Indeed, it is terribly true. Yes, you have written boldly, one could even say heroically. My God, what a great thing Russian literature is, and what agonizing love it inspires.

And you a nobleman too, Bunin, Ivan Alekseevich! Don't smile, I say this without envy or irony, it is simply a fact. A nobleman wouldn't write like this, and that's all there is to it. I read recently in a manuscript by a revolutionary who is living in emigration: 'There is no cautionary voice among our 300–year-old nobility, and that is why he is a provocateur.' I realize, of course, that this is not entirely and not always 'why' it is so, but 'cautionary voice' is a magnificent way of putting it! For it is the voice of culture, and one that is heard ever more faintly nowadays.

Please don't look upon what I have said about *The Village* as being inflated or exaggerated; it is not. I am almost convinced that the Moscow and Petersburg types of every party and stripe, those dolts without knowledge or memory who compose critical articles for the journals, will not appreciate *The Village*, nor will they understand its essence or its form. The threat concealed within it is as unacceptable tactically to those of the left as it is to those of the right. But no one will notice that threat.

However, I know that when the shock and confusion die down, when we are cured of our boorish dissoluteness—which must happen, or else we are lost!—then serious people will say: 'In addition to its first-rate artistic value, Bunin's *The Village* was the stimulus which impelled a broken and shattered Russian society to think seriously not just about the peasant or the people but also about the most serious question of all—is Russia to be, or not to be? We have yet to think about Russia—as an entity—and this work has indicated the necessity of thinking about the country as a whole, of thinking historically.'

This will be said—even if not in these exact words—or else I understand nothing. I offer my heartfelt congratulations, my dear friend. Yours is a good job well done. For art is a sacred undertaking.

The death of Lev Nikolaevich has depressed me greatly and I remain sorely upset by it. I live constantly in a colourful whirl of memories of him and I cannot rid myself of a sorrowful feeling of orphanhood, a feeling which is new to me and quite unexpected. It is probably the case that there were many more occasions on which I did not like him than those on which I did, and yet all these feelings of ours are somehow strangely beneath him and not applicable to him. When he left home, I fell into a great rage. That attempt to realize at last his old, and *despotic*, desire to 'suffer', so that 'the life of Count L. N. Tolstoy' might be transformed into the 'Life of Our Saintly Father, the Blessed Boyar Lev'—I couldn't overcome my hostility to all that. It was despotic because he wanted to 'suffer' a little, not simply for Christ's sake, but for the sake of imparting greater conviction to his sermons. 'If I were to suffer a bit, then my ideas would acquire a quite different significance,' he used to say. As I say, I fell into a rage, because I cannot bear violence, and that's what this is.

But then I got the telegram saying he'd died. And I sobbed as I have never sobbed before. Even now I cannot come to terms with this natural death, which has reminded us so many times of the proximity of our own.

Then there are the venomous newspapermen who poison the soul with scandal and filthy rubbish of all kinds.

My dear fellow, you should read Prishvin's 'The Black Arab' ['Chernyi arab'] in the latest issue of *Russkaia mysl'* [*Russian Thought*]—it's very well done![4]

As for Aleksei Tolstoy, he's a force to reckon with, no matter what you say. Just so long as they don't heap too much praise on him.[5]

The first offer by Prosveshchenie is offensive, the second is a trap for you.[6] After all, what they want to do in the second instance is to pay you thirty-one thousand for what they would have originally paid forty for. This is so, you may rest assured! By publishing 200,000 copies of your books they would still have you in their clutches for as long as it would take for you to capitulate completely. Don't deal with them, Ivan Alekseevich. If you hold out for a couple of years or so and publish another two or three novellas, this self-same Tsetlin [*sic*] will pay you double what he is offering now. Bear in mind that in the near future you will be a more valuable commodity than Andreev is today. Yes, indeed!

Forgive me for using the word 'commodity', but we are talking about a merchant, after all. And this is a greedy merchant, although he is not a very intelligent one, as you will soon be convinced. By the way, he knows that your books and Leonid's sell in almost equal quantities, with only a very small advantage in favour of Leonid. I refuse to talk to him.

I advise you most earnestly: wait a while, don't sell.

Would you like to give me great pleasure? If you would, then simply have *The Village* bound for me when it comes out as a separate volume and send it to me with your autograph. I ask for the binding because there is nowhere around here to get books bound, and they get so worn otherwise. It would be especially difficult to see yours all ragged and stained, with those disgusting threads on the spine all encrusted with that sort of dried-up jelly.

Is this a whim, perhaps? Well, I am an old man now, you know!

Do please visit us here! What magnificent quarters we will find for you, oh my! Facing south, sun all day, a covered balcony. Do come! Give my greetings to Vera Nikolaevna.[7]

I also have a plaintive request to make of Nikolai Alekseevich[8]—I need Tibullus and Martial! Please! I shall read all the Latin poets in Fetted form[9]—I have to do it.

This letter has been typed, and for a scandalous reason. After I had finished writing it, I spilt ink all over it, and my right hand is fit to wither even without copying it out again. I'm writing all the time.

Sovremennik [*The Contemporary*] is scarcely a serious business, and my 'permanent' collaboration in it is an invention, of course.[10] And one which I find unpleasant, to tell the truth.

Look after yourself, my friend. I don't believe that you have got old, but that you have grown thin—this I do believe! But then a fat man could never have written *The Village*; this was foretold by Julius Caesar.

With regards,

A. Pesh[kov]

SOURCE: *Chteniia*: 52–5.

¹ The last instalment of Bunin's novel appeared in *Sovremennyi mir* [*Contemporary World*], 1910, no. 11.
² Famous tales of peasant life by Chekhov.
³ These are references to scenes from the novel's third and final part.
⁴ Mikhail Mikhailovich Prishvin (1873–1954), writer of works on nature.
⁵ Aleksei Nikolaevich Tolstoy (1883–1945), later a prominent Soviet novelist, was making a name for himself with stories of Russian provincial life.
⁶ Gorky and Piatnitsky had approached N. Tseitlin's firm, Prosveshchenie, regarding the continued publication and sale of works by Znanie authors. Tseitlin's terms proved unacceptable.
⁷ Bunin's companion, later his wife.
⁸ Pusheshnikov (1882–1939), translator, Bunin's cousin.
⁹ The famous Russian poet Afanasii Fet had issued a series of annotated translations of the Latin poets.
¹⁰ On 9 November 1910 the newspaper *Rech'* carried a notice stating that Amfiteatrov's journal *Sovremennik* was to begin publication in 1911 with Gorky as one of its permanent contributors.

66. *To P. Kh. Maksimov,*¹ *[10 December 1910]*

[Capri]

My dear young man, there is in your letter a great deal that is superfluous, provocative, and unjust, but it seems to me that it's a good letter from an honest man. I will answer you because I am moved by a sincere desire for your well-being and I have faith that the divine spark of holy dissatisfaction with yourself and with life which burns in your soul will blaze up into a large, bright fire.

Everything you write about I have experienced myself at some time or another and it all remains firmly imprinted on my memory. While loud speeches were being made all around me, I used to sit, depressed, in a corner, asking myself, 'Who am I and what is my purpose?' But one must get through all this. The questions 'Who am I and what is my purpose?' are ones that you alone can answer. I advise you to study. Study persistently, stubbornly, and at all times. Read serious books. I really recommend Kliuchevsky's *History* and Miliukov's *Studies in the History of Russian Culture*. These books will tell you who you are historically, what you were in the past, in your forefathers' time, and perhaps they will even show you what you should be now.

'Work on yourself'—that is essential. You should also set limits for yourself, and then perhaps you will come to shine like a nugget or a precious stone. I've worked hard for a long time, I'm working now, and I'll continue to do so until my death. My journeys on foot through Russia were due not to a yearning for vagrancy, but to a desire to see where I was living and what kind of people were around me. Of course, I've never invited anyone to 'go to the tramps',[2] but I have always loved— and I continue to love—active, energetic people who value life and enrich it even if only a little, with anything at all, even if it is just the dream of a good life. In general, the Russian tramp is a phenomenon rather more frightening than what I managed to depict. He is frightening first of all and most importantly in his imperturbable despair, in the way that he denies himself and excludes himself from life. I knew that environment very well, I lived in it. My cousin died just recently.[3] He was a tramp for twenty-odd years and a fine fellow, although he was completely lacking in will. Among the tramps there are people for whom life is too small, but these are rare. One feels sorry for them, for these are the very people who could work and leave a good, bright mark on our poor life. Our country is very unfortunate, its people are passive, they work poorly, they don't love what they are doing—and one must love what one does. I have condemned—and I continue to condemn—the intelligentsia for always living off the ideas of others, for not knowing their own country well enough and also for being passive, for dreaming and debating rather than working. This is destructive; one must fight against it. But you should know that the Russian intelligentsia, considered as a historical force and not as this or that group of individuals, is an extraordinary, almost miraculous phenomenon, so there is still reason to love our intelligentsia and respect it. It often falls into scepticism and despair, but that is our national characteristic, it is the nihilism which is no less characteristic of the common folk than it is of our cultured people—like master like man!

The Russian writer—I'm not talking of myself here, believe me!—must be treated with redoubled respect for he is a person of almost heroic stature, a living vessel of amazing sincerity and great love. Read about Gleb Uspensky, Garshin, Saltykov, and Herzen, look at Korolenko, who is still living and is the best and most talented writer we have today. And in general, study, read, learn to respect people for their work, for all they've done for you in the past, for this is what you are living on now, unaware of how much labour went into everything you use, unaware of how it was made and how much blood it cost.

And don't think about villas and other such nonsense, because that's all rubbish.[4] By the way, I have no villa, and it's unlikely that I ever will have.

I repeat once again: do not extinguish the anxiety and dissatisfaction which are overwhelming you. Let them torment you, but let them burn, for this is what will help you to be the sort of person that our country needs. We Russians are always too calm, and this is bad for us, it's destroying us.

Take care, study, work, and read!

And thank you for sending your greetings to the girl.[5] This was a very good thing to do. Only she isn't called Korena, there isn't such a name, although there is Carmela. She's called Zhozefina, but she pronounces it 'Shushufina'. She's learning to speak Russian.

I don't think I've given you any bad advice.

A. Peshkov

SOURCE: *SS* 29: 147–9.

[1] Pavel Khrisanfovich Maksimov (1892–1977), office worker, later a Soviet writer.
[2] Gorky alludes to the 'tramp' figures in his early stories and to the Russian Populist movement and its ill-fated campaign of 'going to the people' in the 1870s.
[3] Aleksandr Mikhailovich Kashirin died of typhus in November 1909.
[4] Maksimov had read reports that Gorky was living a life of luxury in his own villa on Capri.
[5] Maksimov had seen a photograph of Gorky with a young Italian girl in a magazine.

67. To A. V. Lunacharsky, [before 15 January 1911]

[Capri]

Dear Anatolii Vasilievich!

I don't have any copies of my books; I've managed to find only two, and I'm sending you those. I've written to Petersburg and to Berlin asking them to send you whatever they have.[1]

Allow me to share with you a couple of notions which have some significance, I think, and may perhaps be correct.

As the apostle of a thoroughly active doctrine, it would be good for you to look at Russian literature from the following viewpoint: what kind of attitude towards life predominates in Russian literature—an active or a passive one?

Once you have weighed all the phenomena of Russian literature on these scales, you will probably see that a fatalistic world-view predominates among the best representatives of our literature and that such giants as Tolstoy, for example, are totally nationalistic in this sense. All Russian folklore is steeped in fatalism: take the teachings about destiny, the Fates, and *Woe-Misfortune* [*Gore-Zloschast'e*],[2] as well as the common conviction, expressed everywhere in folk-songs and tales, that the will of man is powerless in the struggle with the mysterious and invincible wills which surround it.

*Now, every time the Russian intelligentsia argues with the common people, it adopts their mood and operates with their ideas. On the one hand, 'non-resistance to evil'—a doctrine formulated during the reactionary era of the 1880s—the 'non-acceptance of the world' by the mystical anarchists,[3] and the pessimism of today; on the other, the '*beguny*', the '*dukhobors*', the 'red death' etc.[4] And between them there is a perfectly clear line uniting the intelligentsia ideologically with the common people, a relationship which coincides exactly with the years when the intelligentsia was becoming sick with disappointment in the creative power of the common people. The reverse is also true: the Russian intelligentsia is more energetic, more spiritually alert, when it lives in accordance with the vigorous ideas and moods of the West. It is like a struggle between two races—the Aryan, which is Slavic and works for a renaissance through union with the West, and the Mongolian, which is poisoned by a fatalism that strives only for peace.*

Note also the words of the tempestuous Lermontov: 'I would like to find oblivion and sleep.'[5] You will find the same in Khomiakov, Ogarev, Fet, Tiutchev, and Nekrasov[6]—everywhere you look. And as for the idea that Oblomov represents not just the Russian nobility but also a purely Mongolian desire for rest, take a look at how the talented A. N. Tolstoy depicts our contemporary Oblomovs.[7]

Recall, too, the inclination towards 'dreaming' even among such heroes as Sleptsov's Riabinin,[8] and especially among our contemporary writers, fatalists and pessimists.

All in all, this is a historical point of view from which the history of Russian literature has not as yet been examined. I have presented all this very hastily and haphazardly, but I think you will find it not without interest.

I am working on an article about 'self-taught writers', and when it's finished, I'll send send you a copy so that you can become familiar with the psychological rebirth of the peasant and worker, a rebirth which, I think, can now be taken as fact.[9] I believe this article may be of some use for your work, since it consists almost entirely of examples of writings by self-taught authors; you already know some of them, but when they are collected together they make a very serious impression.[10]

SOURCE: *AG* 14: 70–2.

[1] Lunacharsky had asked Gorky to send him a copy of his collected works for use by a group of Marxist critics writing a history of contemporary Russian literature.

[2] An anonymous seventeenth-century work in which a disobedient young man is pursued by the title-figure before taking refuge in a monastery.

[3] An intellectual group active in the aftermath of the 1905 Revolution. Georgii Chulkov was one of its central figures.

[4] Each of the groups named was active in Russia's religious 'underground'.

[5] A line from Lermontov's famous poem 'I come out alone on to the road' ['Vykhozhu odin ia na dorogu'].

[6] Nineteenth-century Russian poets, representing a broad range of styles and thematic concerns.

[7] The name of Oblomov, the title-character of the famous novel by Goncharov, is synonymous with apathy and lack of initiative. On Tolstoy, see Letter 65, n. 5.

⁸ Vasilii Sleptsov (1836–78), minor prose writer close to radical circles. Gorky is probably thinking of Riazanov, the protagonist of Sleptsov's *Hard Times* [*Trudnoe vremia*].

⁹ Gorky's article 'On Self-Taught Writers' ['O pisateliakh-samouchkakh'] appeared in the February issue of *Sovremennyi mir*.

¹⁰ The letter exists in a typed copy with no signature.

68. *To E. P. Peshkova, [18 August 1911]*

[Capri]

The loss of *La Gioconda* has affected me almost as painfully as Tolstoy's death, and perhaps even worse, even more painfully.[1] After all, death is a natural, unavoidable phenomenon. But I cannot call this event natural: it shows yet again just how delicate and fragile is the crust of culture, a culture on which we pride ourselves in vain, given the presence of the barbarians in our midst and within ourselves. Is this natural?

I dare say the painting was stolen by Americans; it is so like them. Those savages boast before Europeans of their superior energy and regard them with ever greater contempt. And yet the things that go on over there are beyond description. Recently one of their newspapers announced a contest to see who could kill the most flies in a week. Fifty-three thousand people took part in the contest, and the prize was won by a twelve-year-old girl who killed 83,000 flies in a week! Another instance: a policeman beat a black on the head with his stick, a club. The black man shot him and was admitted to hospital with a fractured skull. Since he was enormously strong, they chained him to a hospital bed. A lynch-mob broke into the hospital and, finding themselves unable to break the chains, they dragged the black man out on to the street along with the bed, and began to beat him up right there. He managed to fight them off and tried to run away. They caught him, built a bonfire, and began to burn him alive. Again, he broke away from the fire, imploring that he be given a legal trial. But the mob threw him on to the fire and roasted him alive, holding him down with pitchforks. Then they broke up his chains and distributed the links as keepsakes.

The New York papers tell this story with such relish that I wouldn't be surprised if they were to proclaim a person a hero if he were to blow up Notre Dame.

The atmosphere of barbarism is dreadfully dense, and for some reason it seems to me that in recent years it has become even denser and heavier—especially among my countrymen. The tourists here this year have behaved like pigs, and rabid ones to boot. What bizarre interests they have and what preposterous questions they ask! And the hooliganism! There was one old Russian fellow who wanted to photograph me inconspicuously, but when his Italian boatman told him that he shouldn't do this, and that he didn't like it, the Russian set about giving him a beating. And 'so much, so much of everything'.[2] *It's enough to make you want to hide from Russians.*

Dr Bykhovsky was here; he used to run a psychiatric colony in Nizhnii at one time—do you remember going to his place dressed as mummers? He came here with his wife and his seventeen-year-old son—they're all lifeless.

Mania Iartseva[3] is living here: she is lonely, pathetic, and bored.

I have just read in the papers that Eleonsky has thrown himself out of a window in a fit of insanity and killed himself.[4] Well, what can you say? Yesterday Gofman,[5] today Eleonsky. Our newspapers are filled to overflowing with reports of murders and suicides. And to accompany this, especially loud and tragic, there is this ever-increasing sermonizing on the triviality of life. This sermonizing corrupts even such seemingly strong natures as our friend Konstantin Petrovich [Piatnitsky], who has now become an ardent worshipper of trivialities, and in his clumsiness has chosen some rather sordid trivialities as his lot. Things will end badly between him and me.

Fedor [Chaliapin] will be here any day now, perhaps tomorrow. I feel unbearably sorry for him; the letters he writes are despairing, and I don't know how I can help him.

As you see, life is rather difficult. Such a painful time has come. Of course, I wouldn't even give a sigh if this weren't interfering with my work. It seems that *Kozhemiakin* will be the end of me. I had invested certain hopes in this novel; for its sake I have cut back a great deal on things that are personal and dear to me.

I'm sending you some clippings about the Nizhnii Novgorod fair; read them, they're interesting. The Mark Twain is for our son. Help him read *The American Claimant*. It's a useful and wholesome piece. Explain the character of the colonel to him thoroughly and contrast him with our Khlestakov.[6]

Goodbye for now, and keep well. This has turned out to be a sour letter, but I can surely be excused for that. There have been so very many negative impressions of late and so little that's joyful. *Sovremennik* depresses me with its 'manifestos'.[7] No, I'll set up another journal in the autumn; it's essential that I do so.

Warm greetings, and once again, keep well!

A.

SOURCE: *AG* 9: 116–17.

---

[1] The *Mona Lisa* had just been stolen from the Louvre; it was not recovered until 1913.

[2] A line from Lermontov's narrative poem *The Demon*.

[3] Mariia Grigorievna Iartseva-Rein (1884–19?). Gorky and his wife were friendly with her family when they were in Yalta.

⁴ Eleonsky (real name Sergei Nikolaevich Milovsky) (1861–1911), author of works depicting the life of the clergy.
⁵ Viktor V. Gofman (1884–1911), Symbolist critic.
⁶ The central character in Gogol's comedy *The Government Inspector.*
⁷ The journal published two different statements of its editorial policy in its January and July issues for 1911.

69. *To D. N. Ovsianiko-Kulikovsky,*¹ *[16 December [NS] 1911]*

[Capri]

Dear Dmitrii Nikolaevich!

Yesterday, 15 December, I received the issue of *Vestnik vospitaniia* [*Education Courier*] containing your articles devoted to my literary work. I feel compelled to thank you sincerely for your serious treatment of my work, and to share with you the joy which your articles have brought me and the thoughts which they have inspired.

You will know that in my day I have been treated with great kindness by the critics, but this has brought me nothing whatever apart from a few pleasant feelings. It didn't teach me anything. Allow me to tell you that for the first time in twenty years of literary activity I experienced a sense of deep moral satisfaction after reading your articles, which are instructive and absolutely timely.

Lest you think that I'm uttering pleasantries and that these statements result from the joy of an author who has been praised by the critic, I should explain that this is not so and that my joy is the result of other, more objective, factors.

On pages 22–4 of issue no. 6, you give for the first time in Russian literature an amazingly accurate and profound description of 'melancholy'—that mysterious quality of the Russian soul which we are in the habit of praising and which I too, in my time, have considered a creative force, but which is, in essence, nothing other than a *national disease* of the spirit, superbly described by you on page 12 of the same issue as 'Iaroslavtsev's disease'.²

What I'm saying is that this is the first time I have encountered in such an acute and precise form a sad, yet much-needed and amazingly timely indication of the innate inclination of the Great Russian towards an Oriental passivism which, in combination with the renowned 'breadth of the Russian soul'—or rather with the shapeless and chaotic nature of that soul—gives us that 'dashing nihilism' which is so typical of us, and yet is always so baneful and especially destructive in the present severe times.

It is right here, my dear Dmitrii Nikolaevich, that I am convinced one can find the roots of such unhealthy and ugly phenomena as

Karamazovism and Karataevism.[3] *And will it not turn out, upon serious investigation of the matter, that the struggle 'in the heart of man'
between 'God and the devil' simply represents the struggle of the Aryan
and the Turanian, [which constitutes] the psycho-physics of the Slav?*[4]

This is the source of all our 'superfluous men', of the pilgrims and
tramps, and also of the intelligentsia's 'anxiety and the desire for a
change of place' whether on earth or in the realm of ideas.

In my view, it is here too—in 'the weakness and inability of the individual to fight for his own and for the common cause, for a better future
in the heart of society itself'—that one is to discover the explanation of such
phenomena as our peasant anarchism which has found expression in
religious sects like the *beguny* and the *netovtsy*, and of the peasant pessimism
as expressed in the act of flight into the forests and deserts, in self-
immolation, in the story of the Ternovsky flatlands and the history of
northern Russia in general which, as we know, has always displayed a
tendency to 'scatter apart' in all directions.

'My idea is a corner'—this is what F. Dostoevsky said repeatedly,
Dostoevsky, the evil genius of cultured Russia, the man who described
with the greatest power and clarity the spiritual diseases grafted on to us
from the Mongols and the mutilations inflicted upon our soul by the ago-
nized history of Muscovy.

To provide a correct diagnosis of a patient who is hopelessly sick is to
go half-way towards conquering his illness. It seems to me, Dmitrii
Nikolaevich, that you have provided a diagnosis of Russia's national disease and that the entire history of Russian thought, literature, and public opinion should be reviewed from this new, fruitful, nationally
important point of view. By looking at things from this position, we
should finally be able to understand why our people constantly rush from
a social fanaticism which obliterates the personality to a passive anarchism which completely negates society.

These thoughts of yours are indescribably important right now, when
the ruling tribe in Russia is gradually yielding to the suggestions of zoological nationalism, when our cultured society is exhausted and inwardly
shaken, and evidently lacks the strength to resist the revival of despotic
Asiatic ideas, and when the doctrine of enslaving the tribes which consti-
tute the empire does not encounter either in literature or in the heart of
society a rebuff that is sufficiently well-founded, energetic, or necessary.

Some three days ago I sent a short note on this theme to *Zaprosy zhizni*
[*Issues of Life*],[5] and today, after reading your articles, I was, I repeat, profoundly excited by the coincidence of my thoughts with yours. I must also
thank you for noting with the necessary clarity my long-standing and
constant aspiration to advocate a purposeful and active attitude towards
life. I consider this idea essential for the nation and the sole means of our
salvation.

There is one more thing I should say to you. You southerners are apparently more sharp-sighted than people from northern Russia: hundreds of books have been written and are still being written about the Russian peasant, yet it was V. G. Korolenko who provided an exhaustive sketch of the soul of the Russian peasant, creating a peasant type which is historically true.

Dmitrii Nikolaevich, I hope you will not think that everything I have said has been said for any motive other than the desire to share with you ideas which your work has inspired so very powerfully and which have pained my soul for a long time.

How I would like to meet you personally and talk with you about things which are so important and timely and which could have marvellous results not just for us alone. Do you ever look in on this lovely stone set amid the sea? How good it would be if you did!

With all my heart I wish you good health and good spirits. Warm regards.

A. Peshkov

SOURCE: *MI* 3: 135–7.

---

[1] Dmitrii Nikolaevich Ovsianiko-Kulikovsky (1853–1920), literary scholar and linguist.

[2] Iaroslavtsev is one of the two main characters in Gorky's story 'A Mistake'. Ovsianiko-Kulikovsky described the 'disease' as 'tiredness, spiritual depression, intellectual fear, dread of Russian reality'. This leads to mental illness in Iaroslavtsev's case.

[3] Gorky is recapitulating the argument of his article 'The Destruction of Personality', in which he took Tolstoy and Dostoevsky to task as the spokesmen for 'passivism'. He refers specifically to characters in *The Brothers Karamazov* and *War and Peace*.

[4] In a famous passage in *The Brothers Karamazov* the human heart is described as the site of a struggle between God and the devil.

[5] The article, in the series 'From Afar' ['Izdaleka'], appeared in the November issue of the journal for 1911.

---

70. To E. P. Peshkova, [30 January 1912]

[Capri]

I'm very upset.

I haven't read *Solntse* and I don't know which article you're talking about; or perhaps I did read it but have forgotten about it.[1] They write so much nonsense of every sort. You didn't tell me what effect this discovery had on Maksim, and there's no need to do so yet; leave it until we meet in person. As I am telling Maksim in a letter, I shall be coming.

At the moment I have on hand a tale[2] for *Vestnik Evropy* [*The European Herald*]—you can see what things have come to! This is all thanks to Znanie, which has absolutely slaughtered me.

I'm having a hard time of it in general, Katia, and it keeps getting harder. I seem to be losing the main thing by which I have lived, the dearest thing of all to me—my faith in Russia and her future. Events are gathering into such a tight circle that their menacing nature should be sufficient to raise the dead, and yet with us everything remains placid. Nobody feels anything, except for that wretch Struve, who has designs on Katkov's role.[3] Such is the 'evolution' of the Russian soul—from Herzen to Katkov! It's all very painful and sinister.

My personal life is abominable. I never talk about this, you know, and if I've begun to talk about it now, that means things are really very bad!

I very much urge you to keep your distance from Stahl.[4] Don't believe any of his testimony and old wives' tales. It's useless to think of returning to Russia; *Stahl should know that* as well as I do. I know that you would be arrested just as soon as your acquaintances and connections became known—believe me. 'In a matter of two or three months all the old sins and blunders will be linked together and brought to light.' Bear in mind that these are not my words and so they cannot be an invention. Stahl has no entry to the places from which I receive my information; a member of the State Council is a very dubious source, even if it were *Kamensky*, to say nothing of Kovalevsky.[5]

There will be a general purge in the lead-up to the elections and the celebrations of 1912 and 1913; nothing will prevent this, not even the *possible* war.[6] Even now severe persecutions are taking place, and I beg you to abandon your dreams.

I've written an article 'On Contemporary Life' ['O sovremennosti'], but it appears that it won't be published anywhere yet, and if it is published I'll really catch it in the neck! It is quite probable that the article will appear—don't be surprised!—in *Russkoe slovo*, since this publication might take it on for the sake of the uproar which it is liable to create.[7]

Keep well then! I'm very tired; my heart is very heavy.

Regards,

A.

SOURCE: *AG* 9: 135–6.

[1] *Solntse Rossii* [*The Russian Sun*] had reported that Gorky was living with Andreeva.

[2] 'Three Days' ['Tri dnia'].

[3] Petr Struve had expressed strongly nationalistic sentiments in a recent article. Katkov (1818–87), the founder and publisher of *Russkii vestnik* [*The Russian Herald*], held similar views.

[4] Aleksei Stahl, an *émigré* lawyer consulted by Peshkova concerning the possibility of returning to Russia without risk of arrest.

[5] P. V. Kamensky, member of the Duma and State Council. M. M. Kovalevsky, historian, lawyer, editor of *Vestnik Evropy*, and founder of the Kadet Party.

[6] Elections to the Fourth Duma were held in 1912, which was also the centenary of the 1812 victory over Napoleon, whilst 1913 marked the tercentenary of the Romanov dynasty.

[7] The piece did in fact appear there on 2 and 3 March.

71. *To L. N. Andreev, [10 to 16 March 1912]*

[Capri]

You write: 'You have never allowed me to be open with you and you still don't allow me to.' I think this is untrue. Since the age of about sixteen right up to the present day I have been the recipient of other people's thoughts and secrets. It is as if some invisible finger had inscribed on my forehead: 'here is a rubbish dump.' Oh, how much I know and how difficult it is to forget!

I have never allowed anyone to touch upon my private life and I don't intend to start now. I am I, and it is no business of anyone else where I hurt, if indeed I do hurt. To reveal one's wounds to the world, to scratch them in public, to bathe in pus, to squirt one's bile into people's eyes, as many have done—the most disgusting being our evil genius Fedor Dostoevsky—is a vile occupation, and a harmful one, of course.

We will all die, the world will live on; it has revealed to me and foisted upon me a great deal that is filthy and bad, but I do not want its abominations, and I will not accept them. I have only taken the good things from the world and I shall continue to do so. I have no cause to avenge myself upon it and no reason to poison people with the disgraceful sight of my wounds and sores, or to deafen them with my screams.

'Brotherhood' is not at all a matter of revealing one's inner dirt and filth to a comrade—even though this is how we Russians understand it; it is a matter of at least maintaining a bashful silence about such things, if you are unable to destroy them.

The literary people of today have become particularly repulsive in recent times due to their habit of going about in public without their trousers, backsides first, dolefully revealing their pain to the world. And the reason they have this pain is that they don't know of a comfortable place to sit.

You write: 'Why have you undertaken to judge my life?' I have never judged your life, I have spoken about your writings—I have spoken but I have not judged. In general, I don't judge, although I do speak of my likes and dislikes.

For me a book is more harmful or more useful than a person, depending on what sort of book it is. A book lives in the world longer than a person does, and for me, as a man of this world, a book is more interesting than the head which created it. I speak of the head because nowadays no one knows how to write from the heart. The world stands upon deeds, and the longer it does so, the more real it becomes. I feel hostility towards any person, no matter who he may be, if he displays a passive attitude towards the world, because all my life I have asserted the necessity for an active attitude towards life and people. In this I am a fanatic. Many people, attracted by the depraved chatter of that Asiatic nihilist Ivan Karamazov, speak in the most vulgar manner of 'non-acceptance' of the world, because of its 'cruelty' and 'powerlessness'.[1] If I were a governor-general, it's not the revolutionaries I would hang, but those self-same 'non-accepters', for, verily, such language-fornicators are more dangerous for our country than plague rats.

I've read *Sashka*.[2] It is poorly written, pretentious, and boring. In my opinion, only Sashka's sister came out well. She was the only character you created without striving to be clever, and it worked wonderfully. But Sashka himself is a blockhead of the kind that has long been familiar; he is that self-same 'lamb'—read sheep—who has been chewed over by Russian literature, the lamb who sacrifices himself for 'the sins of the world'. He places an intolerable burden upon himself and sighs in many voices—but always in identical fashion, in the 1880s and the 1910s alike—under a yoke which he has loaded upon his shoulders supposedly of his own free will.

But this is actually nothing to do with his free will at all, and it is a task which will always lie beyond his powers; he never acts for himself, but invariably in the name of someone else.

In general, you've become too literary, in the sense that your ideas are invented and cold. You surely deceive yourself when you say that 'everything that I write, think, and feel is the result of my personal experience'. Let's leave thoughts and feelings out of it: they don't belong in that sentence at all. But you cannot even begin to assert that *Sashka* is the result of 'personal experience' either. For although this story is saturated with facts taken from Russian reality, the elucidation and interpretation of those facts are purely literary, that is—artificial and not alive. Now, if you had gone to see the lawyers who have worked on expropriation cases (those in the Urals, say) and if you had taken the indictments or—better still—the reports of the investigations, and read them, then you would have been able to talk about 'personal experience'. And you would have seen from these documents how unnatural you have made the entire set-up of Sashka's life and how unnecessary the Gnedykhs are.[3] At the moment I have someone living with me who knew Savitsky as a grammar-school boy and has been following his activities.[4] Of course, such isolated testimonies aren't worth that much because of their subjectivity, but all the same one should treat life rather more seriously than you do.

I'm even beginning to wish that you would be exiled to Viatka so that you might emerge from the 'ocean'[5] of your cold philosophizing and run up against the rocks of reality. Then you would at least howl and yell like a human being!

We have drifted apart, you and I, and we will drift further apart. This is not because no personal relations grew up between us but because they couldn't do so. We thought that they were possible, but we were mistaken. We are too different. I'm an outsider and I live to the side. I'm not an intellectual—God forbid! Yes, it's awfully sad that Lady Shura is no more.[6] What a wonderful creature, I still love her. To this day I can clearly see her eyes, her smile and behind that smile, her crooked teeth—it's awfully good that they were crooked.

But nowadays everything with you is strict and proper, everything is neatly ruled, and hence everything is boring.

Please don't think that I consider myself a moral surgeon or that I believe it possible to remove what a man has been born with. Of course I don't. If you happen to be snub-nosed, then snub-nosed you will die.

Each of us has to keep the nose with which nature has endowed us. But there's no need to assert so persistently, 'My olfactory organ is the most sensitive and beautiful in the world, for it smells decay everywhere'!

Take care, grow big and strong and don't be angry with me, there's no point. And, besides, there is no reason for you to do so. I think very well of you, this I know.

Goodbye for now,

A. Peshkov

SOURCE: *LN* 72: 327–8.

[1] In Book 5 of *The Brothers Karamazov*, Ivan Karamazov lists a series of atrocities committed by human beings in order to justify his refusal to 'accept' God's world.

[2] Andreev had sent Gorky a copy of *Sashka Zhegulev*, a novel about a revolutionary terrorist.

[3] Eremei and Ivan Gnedykh are two of Sashka Zhegulev's associates.

[4] Aleksandr Ivanovich Savitsky (1886–1909), a revolutionary terrorist.

[5] Andreev's drama of 1911 *The Ocean* [*Okean*] was one of a series of non-realistic plays he wrote in the post-1905 period.

[6] Andreev's first wife, who died of a post-natal blood infection in 1906.

72. To V. V. Rozanov, [about 10 April 1912]

[Capri]

I have just got back from Parizhsk,[1] a city where all the people have a talent for feigning joviality, and found your *Solitaria* [*Uedinennoe*] on my desk; I grabbed it, read it through once and then read it again. Vasilii Vasilievich, your book filled me with the most profound sorrow and pain on behalf of Russians, and I burst into tears; I am not ashamed to admit that I burst into the most bitter tears. Lord have mercy, how agonizingly hard it is to be a Russian. For there is no other people which feels so profoundly the pull of the earth, and there are no greater servants of God on earth than we, here in Russia.[2]

My favourite book is the Book of Job; I always get extremely agitated when I read it, especially Chapter 40, where God instructs man on how he can be God's equal and how he can *calmly* come to stand at God's side. Whenever I read this chapter, I mentally shout to my fellow Russians: 'May you stop being God's servants!'

And as I read your book, that is what I shouted to you, not out of spite but out of the great pain I felt on your behalf and indeed out of love for you. What a huge talent you have, what an avid, lively, and tenacious mind! I don't know whether you were born too soon or too late, but you are an amazingly untimely person. I can imagine how everyone will dislike this book and get angry about it. I rejoice in that, for everything that people do not like has to be vanquished by them, and it will be.

Your servitude to God will be vanquished as will that of Dostoevsky, Tolstoy, and Soloviev; for either we shall vanquish it or we shall perish 'like the Khazars'.

I have no desire to reply to your previous letter, in which you reduced all of Russian literature to Govorukha-Otrok, Strakhov, and Leontiev.[3] You were playing games there, and it was all terribly confused.

You are not a conservative at all, but a revolutionary in the best sense of the word—in the real Russian sense, like Vaska Buslaev.[4] Vaska and Job have a lot in common: after all, Job did not repent 'in ashes and dust'; that was attributed to him later, when the church slandered him.[5]

The one good thing that your Govorukha-Otrok has done is to write the first and best study of Korolenko, while Strakhov wrote well about Tolstoy. Leontiev was a true 'servant of God' even in his fiction; he was a most untalented and vicious person. How can he live on in your memory? I can't understand it. There is a lot about you that I can't understand, and a lot that I don't like; there are times—forgive me—when I am even disgusted to read certain lines of yours, when your articles do not seem like you at all. But what I do comprehend in your amazingly good, profound, and superhumanly intelligent soul gives rise to such an intense, vivid, and tender feeling towards you that my heart actually melts with joy.

If I were in Russia, I would come round to see you straightaway and we would talk for ten hours on end about everything that is important in the world. But the likelihood is that we won't see one another at all; I shall probably die soon. But perhaps I am mistaken—I am very tired and constantly expect something to happen that might shake the entire world. This is a very stressful feeling and I'm rather afraid that it might cause my heart to burst. If I outlive you, I'll send some beautiful flowers for your grave—they will be beautiful, like some of the sparks from your beautifully smouldering and burning soul.

But I wish you a long life and sharpness of mind until your final hour.

Why won't you send me 'When the Bosses Went Away' ['Kogda nachal'stvo ushlo]? Please send it!

Keep well and be happy—when you are happy, you are just like a child, and what can be better than that?

My warm regards.

SOURCE: *Kontekst*: 306–7.

¹ Gorky returned on 7 April from a visit to Peshkova in Paris.

² Here, as on many other occasions over the next few years, Gorky uses the archaic word *Rus'* for Russia.

³ Iurii Nikolaevich Govorukha-Otrok (1850–96), literary critic and writer; Nikolai Nikolaevich Strakhov (1828–96), philosopher and critic; Konstantin Nikolaevich Leontiev (1831–91), writer and critic associated with conservative circles.

⁴ Vaska Buslaev is a figure from the Russian epic song (*bylina*) admired by Gorky, an untamed mischief-maker and a heretic in his attitudes towards religion and tradition.

⁵ See Job 42: 5–6, which Gorky believed to be a later addition falsifying the true import of the story of Job.

73. To D. N. Ovsianiko-Kulikovsky, [10 or 11 September 1912]

[Capri]

Dear Dmitrii Nikolaevich!

I don't know what title to give the sketches which I have sent you. I had the bold intention of giving them the overall title *Russia. The Impressions of a Transient* [*Rus'. Vpechatleniia prokhodiashchego*], but that may perhaps be too bombastic.¹

I deliberately use the word 'transient', and not 'passer-by': it seems to me that a 'passer-by' doesn't leave any trace of himself, whereas a 'transient' is, to a certain extent, an active person who not only gleans impressions of life but also consciously creates something definite.

But perhaps you will agree to call it *The Impressions of a Transient*, simply dropping the word 'Russia', which is too broad and too demanding.

I have conceived a series of sketches similar to those I've already sent you. I would like to use them to outline some features of the Russian psyche and those attitudes of Russian people which are in my view the most characteristic.

I would like to know for sure whether you consider these sketches valuable and suitable for your journal.²

Keep well!

I very much regret that I didn't know how near you were or the dates when you were around Genoa. I was also between Genoa and Nice, in Alassio, where I spent about a month in June.

I wish you all the best!

A. Peshkov

Give my respectful regards to Konstantin Konstantinovich [Arseniev].

SOURCE: *SS* 29: 251–2.

[1] Gorky eventually chose the title *Through Russia* for the collection.
[2] *Vestnik Evropy*, for which Ovsianiko-Kulikovsky was a literary editor.

74. To E. P. Peshkova, [November 1912]

[Capri]

Mariia Fedorovna [Andreeva] left on Monday morning; we parted on friendly terms. She's taken all her things and won't be returning here again.

I have a bad cold; I'm coughing like an old dog, my head aches, and my temperature is scaling the heights. I don't go out of doors, of course; anyway, the weather is rotten—it's windy and rainy.

It would be difficult for me to come to Alassio now; I'm afraid of falling ill, and in any case the times are such that I can't get away from my desk.

Do I have to come to you? Wouldn't it be better if you were to come over here? Think about it. It doesn't seem to me that it would be all that awkward for you: I'm living alone, in a detached house; there are few Russians here, they've all gone their separate ways. Maksim would have a tutor in the person of Zolotarev—which would make me very happy.

Or perhaps you might find it convenient to send Maksim here on his own for the time being, and to wait a while before coming yourself? That is in case you find it awkward to come straightaway yourself, of course.

Well, you decide what's best. My nerves are so worn out that I can't think things over properly myself. My head aches so much. And I'm just generally worn out!

Boris Timofeev is here—he is a Russian doctor and an acquaintance of Aleksin's. He's stuffing me full of powders to stop me coughing.

Keep well; give our son a hug for me.

Pass on the enclosed letter to Miroliubov.[1] Please don't ask him to accompany Maksim if our son comes here before you do! Miroliubov is so crude and stupid that I consider his company absolutely undesirable for Maksim.

All the best!

A.

SOURCE: *AG* 9: 149.

[1] Possibly a letter expressing his refusal to contribute a story to the journal *Zavety* [*Behests*]. See Gorky's letter to Miroliubov of October or early November 1912 (*SS* 29: 283–4).

75. To F. K. Sologub, [23 December 1912]

[Capri]

To Mr Fedor Teternikov

Dear Sir,

I was very surprised by your letter. What foundation do you have for supposing that my *feuilleton* about Smertiashkin[1] was 'aimed' at you specifically?

Seeing that you consider me a 'sincere man', you must believe me when I say that if I had wanted to tell you: 'Yes, Smertiashkin is you, F. Sologub', I would have done so.

I have a negative attitude towards the ideas which you preach, but I have a certain feeling of respect for you as a poet. I consider your book *The Fiery Ring* [*Plamennyi krug*] quite exemplary in form and I often recommend it to beginning writers as a work which is profoundly instructive in that respect. This alone makes it impossible to place an equals sign between Smertiashkin and Sologub.

If you want to see the difference between my attitude towards you and Artsybashev, for example, you should look at my note about suicides in *Zaprosy zhizni* No. 27.[2]

If you had read my *feuilleton* more calmly, you would probably have realized that Smertiashkin is that nameless but terrible person who simplifies and sullies everything—including your ideas, even your words— bringing it down to the level of the street, a person to whom all things are equally alien in essence, apart from having a full stomach.

I hope that the above will permit me to pass over in silence your quite absurd charge that I have 'slandered a woman' and that I harbour some sort of animosity towards your wife.

I will add that I have not read any articles devoted to your books and did not even know that any such had been written.[3]

I am quite unable to understand how it is that a literate and self-respecting man such as yourself could have interpreted my *feuilleton* in such a strange and clumsy way.

But if you think about it calmly, what possible reason could I have had for making a personal attack on you?

I can find only one explanation for your letter. Evidently, certain 'shrewd commentators' made their presence felt and sprayed some of their filthy spittle in your direction.

If this really is what made you write such a savage letter, then you should publish the answer I have given you.

I find it hard to believe that you yourself, acting on your own, *without encouragement from others*, could have identified yourself with Smertiashkin.

A. Peshkov

I consider the tone of your letter to me unworthy of you and I can explain it only by the fact that life is really hard for you and that at times you get angry.

SOURCE: *SS* 29: 289–90.

[1] The third of Gorky's *Russian Fables* [*Russkie skazki*].

[2] 'From Afar' ['Izdaleka'], *Zaprosy zhizni*, no. 27, 6 July 1912.

[3] Sologub's wife, A. Chebotarevskaia, published a number of articles about his work. She also edited the collection *On Sologub. Criticism. Essays and Notes* [*O Sologube. Kritika. Stat'i i zametki*], St Petersburg, 1911.

76. To V. I. Lenin, [12 January 1913]

[Capri]

Dear Ilyich,

The other day I passed on to Tikhonov[1] and co. an excerpt from your letter concerning the 'Forwardites'.[2] So that you should know exactly how your words were reported, I enclose a copy of the excerpt for you.

I was impelled to pass on your views because of Lunacharsky's *feuilletons* in the newspaper *Den'* [*The Day*] and his *feuilleton* in *Kievskaia mysl'* [*Kiev Thought*], 'Between Fear and Hope' ['Mezhdu strakhom i nadezhdoi'], a semi-mystical piece of writing which justifies your cautious attitude towards one of the members of the group. It is as essential for Tikhonov to know of that attitude as it is for a proof-reader to know grammar.[3] I hope that you have nothing against this action of mine.

The other day several hundred roubles were collected for a Moscow newspaper; we'll get hold of some more money in February.[4] It is very likely that one of the St Petersburg publishing houses will undertake to publish miscellanies of contemporary literature, about 10–15 printer's sheets in length at a price of 25–35 kopecks, and we will offer them to *Pravda* as a supplement, a premium to go with the subscription. We need the subscriptions. The miscellanies will increase the circulation. We will submit good material. This is still just an idea, so we should keep quiet about it for the time being. We need to keep quiet because there will probably be an argument over the editorship of the miscellanies. Even though it is unpaid, this is still a position of some esteem, especially for those with a dubious political reputation because of their sins against democracy.

From all the plans and proposals put forward by the Russian intelligentsia, it appears absolutely certain that socialist thought has become overlaid with various tendencies which are fundamentally hostile to it, including mysticism, metaphysics, opportunism, reformism, and throwbacks to a worn-out Populism. These trends are all the more hostile as they are extremely vague, and because they have no platform of their own, they are unable to define themselves with sufficient clarity.

It is essential, as far as possible, to help them to go out into the open and then to lead them to fresh water. *Zavety* is taking on a definite form— it has gone out on to the street and is causing great surprise in its multi-coloured costume. In its wake, the Trudoviki[5] will probably define their position in *Krugozor* [*Horizon*], and then there is *Sever[nye] zapiski* [*Northern Notes*].

It's time that we had our own journal, but we don't have enough people who see eye-to-eye about things.

Tell me, what do you think of I. I. [Skvortsov-]Stepanov? And whom—in Russia—could you suggest for the role of organizer of the political-economic section of the journal?

SOURCE: *Lenin*: 104–5.

---

[1] Aleksandr Nikolaevich Tikhonov (pseudonym A. Serebrov, 1880–1956), writer and editor.

[2] Lenin's letter of January 1913 contained a lengthy critique of the revisionist 'Forward' ['Vpered'] group. For further details, see the Introduction to this section.

[3] Tikhonov was literary editor of the Bolshevik newspaper *Pravda*.

[4] The first issue of *Nash put'* [*Our Path*], appeared on 25 August 1913.

[5] The largest cohesive group within the Second Duma, made up of moderate Populist leaders and peasant deputies.

4
WAR AND REVOLUTION
1914–1921

INTRODUCTION

Gorky arrived at St Petersburg's Warsaw Station on the very last day of 1913. But he spent only a few hours in the Russian capital, leaving immediately for the settlement of Mustamäki in Finland, which was still part of the Russian Empire at that time. This was an act of prudence on his part. Despite the amnesty which had enabled his return, Gorky was still very much a political 'undesirable' and he obviously found it advisable to avoid public attention until he had taken stock of his situation. Once assured of his relative safety and freedom of action, he moved back to the city in March 1914, where he took up residence at No. 23 Kronverkskii Prospekt. Other than exchanging his apartment for a larger one within the same building, Gorky was to use this as a permanent base for the remainder of his stay in Russia.

Although it took him some time to get back into the swing of things, Gorky relished the opportunity once again to participate directly in the social and intellectual life of his country (see Letter 78). His apartment on Kronverkskii soon became a gathering place for St Petersburg's cultural élite. Rachmaninov and Scriabin played there, Chaliapin sang, and the house guests included such famous writers as Bunin and Kuprin. Almost every night Gorky played host to a veritable crowd of visitors, some of whom stayed for a meal or even ended up spending a night or two. It was truly an invigorating time. After the isolation and frustration of the Capri years, Gorky soon felt that he had reclaimed his place as the leader of 'progressive' literature in Russia. His elation was palpable—nowhere more so than in a letter to Malyshev of May 1915: 'Never before have I felt so necessary to Russian life, and it has been a long time since I have felt such courage. . .' (Letter 80).

A great deal of Gorky's energy during these early years was devoted to the establishment of new publishing ventures. The first of these was the firm Parus [The Sail], which Gorky founded together with A. N. Tikhonov and I. P. Ladyzhnikov in the summer of 1915 to serve the democratic cause by publishing books for children and for the so-called 'new readers' amongst the Russian proletariat. At the end of the same year, the first issue of a major new journal *Letopis'* also appeared under Gorky's editorship. As well as publishing literary works by many leading writers of the day—including Korolenko, Bunin, Blok, Esenin, and Maiakovsky—the journal had the aim of popularizing important developments in the world of science, in much the same way that a number of early ventures, including *Zhizn'* and the original Znanie had done. Gorky's letter to the venerable Russian scientist, Klimentii Timiriazev, typifies his didactic concern at this time (Letter 81), as does his request to H. G. Wells that he write a biography of Thomas Edison that would be suitable for children (Letter 84).

In the literary sphere, Gorky had by now effectively broken with the legacy of Znanie. Although he did occasionally see his old colleagues Kuprin and Andreev, there was none of the old comradeship left. Of the original Znanie writers only Bunin published his work in *Letopis'*. But if the ties were broken, there was still a considerable residue of bitterness, as Gorky's scathing reference to Skitalets in a letter of March 1916 makes clear (Letter 83). In the case of Andreev, that bitterness was even to reach the point of public dispute after the publication of Gorky's notorious article 'The Two Souls of the Russian People' ['Dve dushi russkogo naroda'] in 1915.

By this time, however, Gorky was already extending his contacts with an entire younger generation of Russian writers. Even during the years on Capri he had been ever alert to the signs of new literary talent in Russia, especially when the authors concerned were, like himself, of humble origin. Now that he was back in the capital, he was able to identify such individuals far more easily, even meeting them in person on occasion. Gorky was now well known for his willingness to read and comment on unsolicited manuscripts by unknown authors and he gave up a large amount of time to such work. Letter 86 to Vsevolod Ivanov—who was to achieve great success as a novelist and playwright in the 1920s—is typical of literally scores of similar missives from Gorky to Russia's beginning writers. With its mixture of praise and censure, its advice to attend closely to matters of language and technique, and—above all—its insistence on the need constantly to study the craft of writing by reading the works of its greatest practitioners, it rehearses themes which were to recur with almost monotonous regularity in his letters of this and the following decade.

If Gorky's editorial activities in the years up to 1917 reflect his continuing commitment to the cause of democratic literature, it is evident that his conception of the democratic was rather less narrow than it had been hitherto, especially during the early part of the Capri period. Perhaps his experience with Znanie had taught him to be more tolerant of diversity. The fact that he was prepared to publish works by writers as different as Maiakovsky, Esenin, and the young Isaak Babel speaks for his more liberal frame of mind at this time. Nevertheless, he still had his blind spots, especially when it came to works of non-fiction. Thus, Aleksandr Blok, with his inherently sophisticated and complex manner, found it impossible to produce a critical article capable of satisfying Gorky's demand for writing which would be comprehensible to the larger audience he had in mind.[1]

---

[1] K. Chukovskii, *Dnevnik 1901–1929* (Moscow, 1991): 142.

In politics too the indications were that Gorky wished to steer a more moderate line. Although he remained very much aligned to the left, he was determined none the less to retain a certain independence from all political parties. Needless to say, this did nothing to improve his already troubled relations with Lenin. The Bolshevik leader had, in fact, been one of those who had particularly urged the writer to take the risk of returning to Russia under the terms of the amnesty. Knowing of Gorky's organizational skills and his broad support for the Bolshevik cause, he no doubt hoped that the writer would once again serve as the Party's loyal aide in the battle against tsarism. Things worked out somewhat differently, however. In the first place, it was clear that, despite all Lenin's protestations, Gorky remained temperamentally close to the ideas of 'God-building' (see Letter 84). Even worse, it soon emerged that the two men had fundamentally different views on the major question of the day—Russia's involvement in the First World War. The Bolshevik position was typically uncompromising. Condemning the European conflict as a manifestation of bourgeois imperialism, they argued that the best thing would be for Russia to lose the war, thereby hastening the onset of a socialist revolution which would quickly sweep through the entire continent. It is easy to understand, therefore, why Lenin was so infuriated when he found out soon after the outbreak of war that Gorky had put his signature to a 'patriotic' open letter together with such dubious personalities as Struve, the leader of the liberal Kadet Party.[2] Even though the writer soon dissociated himself from those who supported the war effort, his position was still a long way from the militant defeatism promoted by Lenin and his followers. Moved by a humanistic concern for what was happening to Russia and the Russians as a result of the war, Gorky was perturbed by such things as the rise of anti-Semitism (Letter 80) and the suffering of children (Letter 84). Like his fellow socialist H. G. Wells, whose anti-war novel *Mr Britling Sees it Through* he admired thoroughly, the Russian writer stood for the principle of pacificism. Lenin was none too pleased either by developments within *Letopis'*, especially when he was told that an article he had submitted for publication there (under a *nom de plume*) had been deemed too radical by Gorky and his associates. But if relations between Gorky and the Bolsheviks were tense, they had not yet reached the point of open conflict. Such conflict was soon to come, however, as Russia entered a new period of revolution.

In order to understand Gorky's reaction to the events of 1917, it is useful to consider the views expressed in the article 'The Two Souls of the Russian People', which appeared in the first issue of *Letopis'* at the end of 1915. As the very title of this piece suggests, its argument was cast in the form of a simple opposition. Russia, Gorky wrote, was torn between

---

[2] V. Ia. Grechnev, *Gor'kii v Peterburge-Leningrade* (Leningrad, Lenizdat, 1968): 119.

two poles—the 'European', characterized by reason, progress, and an active attitude to life; and the 'Asiatic', which is brutal, obscurantist, and passive and associated above all with the Russian peasantry. Although Gorky's sympathies were obviously on the side of the 'European', he feared that the conditions of war might lead to the victory of Russia's 'Asiatic soul'. It was this same anxiety which was uppermost in his mind when the Russian monarchy fell in February 1917. Whilst many people—including his own son, Maksim—were prepared to rejoice at the collapse of the old regime, Gorky was decidedly sceptical. 'The events taking place may appear grandiose, even moving at times, but their meaning is not so profound and sublime as everyone imagines,' he wrote to his wife (Letter 87). And a week later he was warning Maksim that, the fall of the Romanovs notwithstanding, 'a counter-revolution is possible' (Letter 88).

Gorky's views on the Revolution were not confined to his private letters, however. In April 1917 he at last succeeded in his efforts to found a newspaper. Called *Novaia zhizn'*, it became the outlet for a remarkable series of articles which appeared under the general title *Untimely Thoughts*. In these articles, Gorky presented his readers with an extended political commentary on the events of the revolutionary year. Their tone was predominantly gloomy. Thus, the first of the series, entitled 'Revolution and Culture' ['Revoliutsiia i kul'tura'], bemoaned the backwardness which Gorky saw as the legacy of the Russian monarchy, and warned that the Revolution had not yet done anything to correct that state of affairs or to enrich the country spiritually.[3] As the year progressed, Gorky became more pessimistic still. Instead of ushering in a new age of culture and science, he believed that the Russian Revolution simply threatened to reduce the entire land to the condition of anarchy, which he associated with 'Asia' and the 'peasant'. As he was later to put it in a letter of 1919: 'The revolution has degenerated into a battle between village and city' (Letter 97).

Gorky defined *Novaia zhizn'* as a 'right-wing' newspaper (Letter 89), and so it was—in the eyes of the Bolsheviks at least. Indeed, once the Bolsheviks themselves had begun to make their presence felt on the domestic political scene, the writer was quick to identify their party with the very tendencies he most feared. In his eyes, the Bolshevik leaders—especially Lenin and Trotsky—were dangerous 'adventurers' and 'lunatics', people who appealed to the very worst instincts of the mob in order to promote their cause. He repeatedly likened the Bolsheviks to misguided scientists who were conducting an insane experiment on the Russian people. It was in these terms that he condemned the so-called 'July Days', Lenin's first (and unsuccessful) effort to foment a second rev-

---

[3] M. Gor'kii, *Nesvoevremennye mysli. Zametki o revoliutsii i kul'ture* (Moscow, 1990): 82

olution (see Letter 90). Little wonder, then, that when the Bolshevik coup finally did take place in October, Gorky was to write to his wife: 'Things are bad for Russia, bad!' (Letter 91).

The writer continued his attack against the Bolsheviks into the new year of 1918. He condemned the activities of the new security agency, the Cheka, with its policy of spreading the 'Red Terror' throughout the land. He was equally outspoken in his criticism of the Treaty of Brest-Litovsk, under the terms of which the country's new leaders withdrew from the war against Germany. As for the Bolsheviks themselves, Gorky's continual barbs were the source of considerable annoyance. They responded first of all by attacking him mercilessly in their own newspaper, *Pravda*. (On one memorable occasion, Trotsky compared the writer's attitude to that of a frightened 'museum curator'.) By the spring of 1918, however, they felt that it was necessary to take more practical measures: publication of the newspaper was temporarily suspended on two occasions. But when it became clear that Gorky was unlikely to change his ways, the decision was taken on 16 July, 1918 to close down *Novaia zhizn'* indefinitely.

The closure of the newspaper placed Gorky in a quandary. No longer able to broadcast his opposition to the Bolsheviks, he had to consider what other means he might employ to have some real effect on the course of events. By now, of course, Russia had been plunged into even greater chaos with the onset of civil war. Although the Bolsheviks still held power in the main centres, very few people believed that they would do so for long. So when Gorky performed what was undoubtedly the most spectacular volte-face of his political career, he may well have done so in the belief that it was merely a temporary expedient. Whatever the case, he now decided that the best course of action was to work in collaboration with the very Bolsheviks whom he had so recently castigated on the pages of *Novaia zhizn'*. It was an act for which he would never be forgiven by many Russian intellectuals, who were quick to brand him a turncoat and political opportunist.

Gorky's dealings with the Bolsheviks between mid-1918 and 1921 have been one of the Soviet Union's most closely guarded secrets. Only now are the documents beginning to emerge from the archives which will allow the full story to be told. The few letters assembled here nevertheless shed considerable light on the competing impulses behind Gorky's activities at this important time. Of these, pragmatism was certainly among the most powerful. When one reads a letter of early 1919, where the writer first offers Lenin advice on how best to conduct propaganda on behalf of the Bolsheviks, then enquires about the possibility of resuming the publication of *Novaia zhizn'* (Letter 94), it is easy to see why his enemies labelled him a hypocrite. But Gorky was a complex man, and although he was still resolutely opposed to many Bolshevik policies, that attitude was tempered by other considerations. As the Civil War progressed, it would appear that he came to view the Bolsheviks as the lesser evil and—more significantly still—the only power in the land capable of offering proper resistance to the dark 'peasant' force which he so feared (see Letter 97). Nor should we overlook the role of sentiment in all this. Although the telegram he and Andreeva sent to Lenin after Fanny Kaplan's attempted assassination has a rather perfunctory air about it (Letter 92), Gorky's sympathy was genuine, as was his grief when he learnt of the Bolshevik leader's death a few years later.

Gorky's involvement in Russian political life during the first years of Bolshevik rule took two main forms. Most immediately visible was his work in a number of enterprises designed to promote culture and science in the new Russia. One of the most grandiose ventures of this kind was the World Literature [Mirovaia literatura] publishing house. Gorky set up the firm together with his colleagues from Parus—Ladyzhnikov, Tikhonov, and Z. I. Grzhebin. Its aim was nothing less than to publish Russian translations of all the greatest literary works written in foreign languages since the middle of the eighteenth century. Although the task was obviously unrealizable in the conditions of the time, Gorky was undeterred. He worked hard to overcome many of the practical difficulties which hampered the firm's operation (see Letter 100), and it was largely because of his unflagging efforts that World Literature managed to achieve what it did: over 200 titles were issued before the firm closed down in 1924. The outstanding modern Russian tradition of literary translation undoubtedly owes much to this early initiative. At the time it also provided a most valuable source of practical support for a large number of scholars and writers who might otherwise have perished.

World Literature quickly became a meeting-place for Petrograd's writers. Literary studios were set up, where established writers could pass on the fruits of their experience to the younger generation of aspiring authors. Many of those who were to make important contributions to Soviet literature attended the studios and later attested to the important part they played in establishing their careers.

As always, Gorky's concerns at this time were both intellectual and practical. When the Civil War was at its height, he displayed enormous energy and resourcefulness in attending to the material needs of Russia's intellectuals, many of whom had literally no place to live and no means of obtaining the ration cards which were essential for survival in the Petrograd of 1919. Towards the end of that year, he helped set up the House of the Arts [Dom iskusstv]. It occupied a massive building on the city's central thoroughfare, Nevskii Prospekt. Many of those involved in the World Literature project found a temporary home there, as did many other writers, young and old. Even more important in many ways was the Scholars' House [Dom uchenykh], an institution which was established through the efforts of the Commission to Improve Scholars' Living Conditions (popularly known by its Russian acronym, KUBU), another of the bodies to which Gorky was devoting his energies (see Letters 98 and 100). Here many of Petrograd's intellectuals and scientists received the so-called 'academic ration' which enabled them to survive the dreadful deprivations caused by the Civil War.

Gorky's activities were not limited to the service of writers and scientists, however. He also worked on the so-called Expert Commission, a group which was charged with evaluating antiques, art works, and other items of value which had come into the hands of the Bolsheviks since the Revolution. And in 1921 he was enlisted to serve on the All-Russian Committee for Battling Hunger, which was set up in an attempt to ameliorate the effects of the disastrous famine which had added to the problems facing the new regime.

All the time, of course, Gorky was also working behind the scenes in order to help many people who had somehow run into trouble with the Bolsheviks (see Letter 95). We will probably never learn the full extent of his efforts in this area, but it has long been known that he was prepared to aid all manner of individuals, even those whom he had never met and whose political views were often quite inimical to his own. The writer's engagement in these cases was often passionate. Kornei Chukovsky recalls the time when he saw him weep with anger and frustration on learning that the scholar Sergei Oldenburg had been arrested.[4] Gorky intervened successfully in this case, but he was not always able to work to such good effect. His failures caused him great pain, and never more so than in the cases of two famous poets—Nikolai Gumilev, who was executed for counter-revolutionary activities in August 1921, and Aleksandr Blok, who died earlier that month at the age of forty. Blok's death was particularly aggravating, as permission for the poet to obtain medical attention abroad—for which Gorky had worked so hard—came through too late to save his life (see Letter 101).

The deaths of Blok and Gumilev contributed in no small way to Gorky's decision to leave his native land. By this time, he had become quite worn down both by the massive amount of work he had had undertaken and by the constant provocations to which he was being subjected by the Bolshevik leadership. Although Lenin himself was uncharacteristically tolerant of Gorky's maverick behaviour, his colleagues—especially Grigorii Zinoviev, head of the Petrograd branch of the Party—were far less charitably disposed towards him. In fact, Zinoviev was an implacable foe, who rarely missed an opportunity to undermine the writer's activities. He had Gorky placed under surveillance and authorized a police search of his apartment in 1920. He also approved the arrest of

[4] Chukovskii, *Dnevnik*: 114.

Gorky's fellow members on the All-Russian Committee for Battling Hunger, which placed the writer in the unfortunate position of appearing to be some sort of *agent provocateur* (see Letter 102). By now it would appear that Lenin too had lost patience with his erstwhile comrade. In the wake of the Kronstadt Rebellion, he had already issued his famous call for Party unity in the face of widespread public disaffection. Under such circumstances, the unpredictable Gorky posed too great a potential danger. He was also no doubt sincerely alarmed by reports of the writer's extremely poor state of health, hence his insistence that he go abroad for treatment without delay. Although Gorky was indeed very ill, his indisposition served as a most convenient excuse for his departure to Europe in October 1921. In this way the writer's second—and considerably more ambiguous—period of 'exile' from Russia began.

Gorky's extensive editorial, journalistic, and political commitments between 1914 and 1921 inevitably had a major impact on his own work as a writer. In a letter to V. Zazubrin of March 1928 he was to claim that 'between autumn 1916 and winter 1922 I did not write a line' (Letter 146). Although not strictly true—Gorky forgets that the magnificent memoir of Tolstoy was written during these years, for example—the comment nevertheless reflects accurately enough the extent to which his life was rapidly taken over by concerns other than his own literary compositions during these years. This was an enormous personal sacrifice, all the more so since his writing had by now achieved a new maturity. Gorky returned to Russia as the subject of considerable critical acclaim. His novels *Okurov Town* and *The Life of Matvei Kozhemiakin* had confirmed his stature as a fiction writer, whilst *Childhood*, the first volume of his autobiography, was immediately applauded as a masterpiece, even by those who had earlier been among his most vocal detractors. He continued to write autobiography after his return to Moscow, completing *Among People* and a number of shorter pieces later published in the collection *Through Russia*. Although these had somewhat less critical success, they still rank among Gorky's very best writing.

As for Gorky's personal life, the move from Capri inevitably entailed important changes. His son Maksim was growing up now, and his wife began to exert considerable pressure on Gorky to see him more often (see Letters 82, 83). With the benefit of hindsight, it is possible to discern that Maksim was already experiencing some difficulty with his unchosen role as the 'son of a famous man'. Interestingly enough, by the time of the October Revolution, father and son were fundamentally opposed on questions of politics, Maksim having become an ardent supporter of the Bolsheviks and their policies (see Letter 97). Gorky's relations with Mariia Andreeva are, perhaps, somewhat easier to judge. Andreeva had of course left Capri a year before Gorky did, and although they resumed their life together on his return to Russia, it would seem that they now lived more separate lives. Andreeva had resumed her career as an actress and spent quite a lot of time away from their Petrograd apartment in connection with her theatrical work. The couple eventually parted quite amicably after the Revolution. In 1919, Gorky met Mariia Ignatievna (or Moura, as she was affectionately known) Budberg, who had come to work at World Literature soon after ending an affair with the British diplomat Robert Bruce Lockhart. She soon moved into the crowded apartment at 23 Kronverkskii, thus beginning a liaison with Gorky which was to last until the early 1930s.

Given the intense turmoil of these years—not to mention their great historical significance—it is unfortunate that Gorky's letters tend to be less illuminating than for almost any other period of his life. Now that he was back in Russia, it would appear that his correspondence was no longer quite the 'life-line' that it had been during his exile. It is not that he was necessarily writing any fewer letters, but just that he revealed far less of himself in them. Even his correspondence with Peshkova—usually the place for his most intimate confessions—seems to have become less open as the Revolution approaches. It may well be that important letters from this period have yet to be released by the Gorky archive, yet one senses also that the writer himself had already become more wary about recording his personal life. Such concerns were to be even more evident in the years to come, as he became increasingly to understand that his 'biography' was passing into public property.

77. To E. P. Peshkova, [10 January 1914]

[Finland]

You will already know from reading the newspapers that I crossed the border absolutely safely, quietly, and without fuss. However, some of my fellow countrymen managed to find out about it and they followed me around for a while, scrutinizing my face with horror, as it seemed to me.[1]

I'm living in Finland, where letters take a desperately long time to arrive. I will probably stay in this country, which resembles a saucer of cream; I'll stay, only I'll move further out, beyond Vyborg. Any day now I shall receive my passport—that is, I hope to receive it. If I do, I'll come to Petersburg to buy some glasses; I left mine behind on Capri. I may also get to Moscow, but it's unlikely to be very soon—I just don't know, though.

You'll be getting a permanent passport; you can live 600 years on one of those, if you want to. I've already written to the Nizhnii Novgorod Trade Council to say that you should be issued with such a document.

Write to me care of Ivan Pavlovich [Ladyzhnikov], not here: the village is a long way from the station and letters come irregularly—they probably lose them.

How's Maksim?

Keep well, my children.

A.

Correspondents and reporters! They're like fleas!

My first welcome in my homeland has been from the Finns.

SOURCE: *AG* 9: 152–3.

[1] Gorky left Italy on 27 December 1913, arriving in St Petersburg on 31 December. He left there for Finland the same day.

78. To A. V. Amfiteatrov, [23 March 1914]

[St Petersburg]

My dear Aleksandr Valentinovich!

Don't be angry with me for leaving without seeing you, and also for not getting round to writing to you before today!

The fact is that I left, one might say, suddenly and unexpectedly even for myself; I had thought that from German Berlin I would make a 'zurück', but it turned out that Russia was closer. And now I'm in Russia! I have arrived and I live of course 'without sleep or rest'. What a fine fellow that Ivan Manukhin is![1] Were it not for him, you would now be writing your memoirs of a Gorky who died prematurely and had already become invulnerable even to the Petersburg climate! So much for your memoirs! They'll have to wait a while!

My impressions? I don't understand a thing, Aleksandr Valentinovich! Everything has become so muddled, and everyone is so crushed and devoid of God's image that you look at something in front of you and begin to wonder just what kind of being this creature is imitating.

Is this a bit too strong? Ah well, what can be done? I really don't want to start cursing, but 'circumstances oblige'.

Joking aside, I haven't yet become accustomed to my native land again and I'm almost surprised to hear everyone speaking Russian! They speak none too well and what they say is tedious, but it is still Russian! And certain literary people even mock each other with Russian words—both verbally and in writing—although they arrange these words in an unorthodox, foreign manner. Seriously!

Oh, I can't decide whether or not the smoke of the fatherland is sweet to me, and if so, to what extent. I still can't!

Democracy received me most affectionately and in a touching way— Moscow alone congratulated me more than seventy times. There were bakers and stocking-makers, plumbers and even 'the peasants of the Novotorzhskii district'. I was very moved by all this. But the intelligentsia still doesn't like me very much, you know! Every so often you catch an arrow-like glare which reduces you to ashes and asks: what do you want to do, you devil?

But I remain silent. And even if I'm asked point-blank, I still remain silent, i.e. I say, 'What am I to do? I need to get treatment!' 'But surely you've been cured, haven't you?' 'But I enjoyed it—so much so that I want to have some more treatment!' 'And how come you're still drinking wine and smoking?' 'But I've always liked doing those things too.'

Dear Aleksandr Valentinovich, I must tell you that Russia is a good country for all that. Why don't you come here too? Seriously.

Write if you wish: St P., Kronverkskii, 23, flat 10.

Give my best to your entire household. With warm regards.

A. Peshkov

SOURCE: *LN* 95: 450.

---

[1] Gorky's doctor, who had devised a method of using X-rays to treat tuberculosis.

79. To E. P. Peshkova, *[late July 1914]*

[St Petersburg]

I'm sorry to have taken so long to answer your letter—life has become hectic again; there are unexpected occurrences on all sides, 'marvellous adventures' that are possible only in Russia, and you have to take a firm hold on yourself just to keep your head from spinning. In recent days things have been especially turbulent, what with the workers' disturbances, the expectation of war, and along with that the attempt on Rasputin's life and the flight of Iliodor. They say that the latter is already abroad, presumably somewhere in Italy.[1]

His flight has aroused great interest among the authorities and in society at large. The former fear possible revelations, while the latter are looking forward to the same with great glee.

What a curious coincidence: it was a priest who was at the forefront of the Revolution in 1905,[2] and this time it's a monk. Let's hope that next time a bishop will come to play this part. O Lord, our Russian God! An ironical god Thou art. . .

I'll be able to answer your questions only at the end of July; Bonch has been arrested, and I'm sitting here with no money and a heap of worries.[3]

Don't forget to ask Plekhanov about the books. And do you really not intend to go and see Amfiteatrov? This letter is being sent to you via him, due to a certain special circumstance. Amf[iteatrov] should have an interesting fellow from Russia staying at his place at present;[4] you ought to go and see.

Chirikov has grown very old and is living here with his young family and his (still!) young wife. Iv[an] Metlin,[5] whom I haven't seen for twenty-two years, is also living here, as are many other members of the literary 'intelligentsia'. But much more interesting than them is 'Brother' Koloskov, a teetotaller, who's organized as many as 70,000 workers and artisans. Churikov and other brethren are of this order.[6]

The Petersburg factory workers are terribly interesting; the women are amazing—I imagine that the martyrs during the early years of Christianity were like this. Their children, kids aged from five to ten, are ghastly: they are totally neurotic, they have experienced a great deal and know everything. They convey the impression of being little old men and women; they are the sort who turn into hooligans. They live on the street from morning till night; there are no kindergartens and they have no supervision. These are sinister children.

How's Maksim? I'm very glad that he's in Italy again and that he likes it there. That's good; in time it will have a splendid effect on him.

Well, goodbye for now! I'll write soon. The extraordinary security measures are greatly hindering movement around Petersburg. And in general there are too many hindrances.

Regards,

A.

A hug for our son.

SOURCE: *AG* 9: 158–9.

[1] The monk Iliodor was accused of involvement in the attempt on Rasputin's life. Gorky actually knew that Iliodor had spent several days in the Finnish village where Gorky was staying before crossing the border into Sweden *en route* to America.

[2] Gapon. See Letter 37.

[3] Vladimir Dmitrievich Bonch-Bruevich (1873–1955), an active revolutionary and head of publishing house Zhizn' i znanie [Life and Knowledge], which was issuing Gorky's collected works.

[4] Possibly Iliodor.

[5] Ivan Ivanovich Metlin (1867–1945), Populist and Nizhnii acquaintance.

[6] Ivan Churikov, a peasant from Samara, founded a sect of teetotallers, a movement close to Tolstoyanism. Ivan Koloskov was one of its leaders.

80. To S. V. Malyshev,[1] [after 10 May 1915]

[Mustamäki]

Dear comrade, I thank you sincerely for your letter and for your friendly attitude towards me, but mainly, I thank you and those like you for the fact that you *are*, that you exist. What a great joy it is for me that you *are*! And, of course, when I tell the public: 'you have no business with me as a person', I am not thinking about you or the proletariat but about those to whom I am forever a stranger, who are forever antagonistic towards me. There are times when I pity everyone and I even pity, to the point of rage, those who are strangers to me. But one lives not by pity but by love towards those who are near and dear. And one should dance with strangers only to the extent that one expects to benefit one's own people by doing so. Quite often one wastes one's time on such dances. But what can you do about it? You won't get through to your own people, the road leading to them has been set with many traps and pitfalls. It's not that you should be frightened of falling into such traps, but time is precious, there's not much of it left, and there's endless work to be done. There's no time for sitting around. Well, enough of this. You understand me.

I'll tell you the news, starting with the good news. On 19 April Fedor Chaliapin gave a free performance for the workers at the Narodnyi house on Kamennyi island. As many as four thousand people turned up. They were doing *Boris Godunov*. The tickets were distributed through hosp[ital] cash desks. It was a triumph for Chaliapin both within the theatre and without. But don't get the idea that he wasn't reminded of what he had to be reminded about. The workers of eight factories wrote him a very good letter. It was so good that he cried when he read it. The letter said that it was not proper for him, Fedor, ever to kneel before anyone.[2] In the autumn he will give another performance for the workers—they will do *Faust*.

In the summer, concerts by Ziloti[3] will be organized in the working-class districts; one such concert has already taken place, on 3 May at the Putilov works. A theatre company has been formed and it will stage performances in various theatres in the working-class areas. There is a demand for all this, and this demand must be satisfied.

There is also a demand for a journal and a newspaper. But this demand cannot be satisfied. The m[ilitary] censorship is outrageously savage: it's impossible to write anything. It appears that they will soon shut down *Sovremennik*, which is the only journal that tries to speak in human language. I sent it to you.

You cannot imagine what is happening now to the Jewish people of Poland! Up to half a million people have already been deported, they have been deporting 15 to 20 thousand—the entire Jewish population of a town—in 24 hours! Sick children were loaded on to wagons like frozen cattle, like piglets. People walked in their thousands through the virgin snow, pregnant women gave birth on the way, old men and old women caught cold and died. It's awful!

It is said that the mass accusation of betrayal and treachery made against the Jews was provoked by a desire to explain our military failures and to conceal the real treachery of the Miasoedovs & Co.[4]

I see things differently. As I have already written to you, anti-Semitism is being propagandized with a view to smashing the opposition on the Jewish question. This propaganda is being conducted most successfully. I am ashamed to be alive, ashamed to meet Jews on the street.

In general, the atmosphere is stifling. Never before have I felt so necessary to Russian life, and it has been a long time since I have felt such courage, but I must confess, my dear friend, that there are times when I lose heart and everything goes dark before my eyes. It is very difficult. I am especially disappointed by our intelligentsia: how flabby, how lazy, careless, and inactive they are—it makes one quite desperate!

But there are several successes nevertheless. And this is mainly because the Petersburg proletariat has raised some very good people.

The Russian proletariat is confronted by tasks which are unknown in the West on the scale that we have them here. We are living with desperate contradictions. For example, many of the socialist-inclined public work in co-operatives, but these co-operatives are presently developing in such a form that they promote the growth of individualism and an instinct for private property. Isn't that so? But still, it is quite possible that spirits will rise after the war. However, it is necessary for these rising spirits to be conscious, and not spontaneous. Very little will be gained if the peasants just start burning the country estates again. The proletarian is obliged to instil his social consciousness in the peasant masses.

Ethnic issues are also being aggravated, and this is promoting a nationalistic chauvinism which threatens to poison socialism with imperialism. These are difficult times, comrade! Those who can remain calm in this tangle of events are worth a great deal now. But events are becoming ever more complicated. Italy has become involved in the war, and Romania will soon get drawn into it as well.[5]

There are dozens of crippled people in the streets here. It is expensive to live.

I received your gift, but—alas!—it had been smashed to pieces in the post. Keep well, dear comrade, and pass on my sincere regards to others who are with you in soul! Keep your spirits up!

A. Peshkov

The books have been sent off.

SOURCE: *SS* 29: 335–8.

[1] Sergei Vasilievich Malyshev (1877–1938), writer and Bolshevik activist.
[2] At the end of a performance of *Boris Godunov* at the Mariinskii Theatre in St Petersburg on 6 January 1911 Chaliapin and other members of the cast knelt down before Nicholas II, who was in the audience.
[3] A. I. Ziloti (1863–1945), pianist and conductor.
[4] In 1915 Colonel Miasoedov, who was close to ministerial circles, was exposed as a German spy. He was tried and executed.
[5] Italy declared war on Austro–Hungary and Germany on 23 May [NS] 1915; Romania did likewise on 27 August [NS] 1916.

81. To K. A. Timiriazev,[1] *[16 October 1915]*

[Petrograd]

Dear Klementii Arkadievich!

I am appealing to you as one who is much indebted to your thoughts and works for his own spiritual development. You have probably heard of me, I am M. Gorky, a literary man.

I am asking for your help in a cause which I've managed to organize, and I venture to hope that you will not refuse a good cause.

The essence of the matter is that from January 1916 a scientific, literary, and political journal—*Letopis'*—will be published in Petersburg.[2] The aim of the journal—which is somewhat Utopian perhaps—is to attempt to inject into the present chaos of emotions some sobering elements of intellectualism. The bloody events of our age have aroused too many sombre feelings, which they continue to do. I think it is time we tried to inject into this dismal storm the moderating element of a rational and critical attitude towards reality. People are living in fear, and because of that fear there is hatred of one another and savagery is on the increase, whilst respect for man and interest in the ideas of Western European culture are in constant decline. More and more frequently in Russia the cry rings out, summoning people to the East, to Asia, away from action and towards contemplation, away from study and towards fantasy, away from science and towards religion and mysticism.

The people who head the journal would like to revive in the memory of those who have been intimidated by recent events the global significance of the foundations of Western European culture and of science, in particular, as its principal foundation. I think that these intentions and their significance will be quite clear to you, a man who is a European at heart.

I don't wish to burden you with any further explanation of the aims of the journal, I'll move on to my humble request.

Would you be so good as to submit an article for our publication on the theme of the global significance of experimental science for all mankind? For us the natural sciences are an Archimedes' lever which is the only thing capable of turning the whole world to face the sun of reason.

If this theme doesn't appeal to you, my dear Klementii Arkadievich, perhaps you could choose another which is more agreeable and dear to you.

My comrades and I will be deeply grateful for anything that you might be kind enough to do for the journal.

In addition, would you possibly be able to recommend a science correspondent for the journal, a man of your cast of mind, a pupil of yours?

And could you indicate to us some themes which you consider it timely and necessary to develop?

I thank you sincerely in advance for any guidance you might offer.

Allow me to hope for your assistance both through your valuable work and through your advice, which is no less valuable.

Being an exceptionally good popularizer of scientific truths yourself, you will no doubt be familiar with popular literature in the West on questions of natural science: perhaps you could indicate some books which should be translated into Russian?

We would like to have a book on the theme of 'Scientific truths in everyday life'.

I apologize for this long letter. My respectful regards to you, Klementii Arkadievich!

A. Peshkov

Address: Aleksei Maksimovich Peshkov, Petersburg, Kronverkskii Prospekt, No. 23, flat 9.

SOURCE: *SS* 29: 341–3.

¹ Klimentii Arkadievich Timiriazev (1843–1920), distinguished physiologist and botanist.
² For details, see the Introduction to this section.

82. To E. P. Peshkova, [6 November 1915]

[Petrograd]

I'm very well aware that I deprive myself of great joy by seeing Maksim so rarely. But it has always turned out that I'm depriving myself of joy somehow, my friend. I know of no person who is able to appreciate the joy of life as much as I do. I am a man who has pursued the joys of existence most ardently. But I'll soon be turning fifty, and it's time to admit that my desire for joy has led to nothing but grief. It's a good thing that I know how to laugh at sorrow and that I don't like to 'suffer'; otherwise I would be in a bad way.

But that's by the by. We are not the issue; our song is nearly sung, and it hasn't been a bad one either. As for those who are to take our place—one fears for them. Harsh days and harsh years will greet our son. I've thought about this a lot. And when I consider the question of Maksim—which is something that happens more often than you might think—I say the following to myself.

It's good that you're pleased with the path you have taken and which you still follow; you have a firm belief in your own truth. That's good, but life is fluid, people are constantly changing, and along with them the truth is changing too. Look, is your truth suitable for your son? One's beliefs are not a coat; they adorn the soul and can greatly distort its shape. Nowadays I see many young poets and students, and young people in general. Among them I see few people I could like, very few indeed! They all seem terribly poor and wretched; they're all like house guests in this life. But perhaps I think such things simply because I'll soon be fifty? I don't much believe in myself or in my ability to live. I'm a good worker, but what kind of teacher am I? A very bad teacher, I think. And this is why I feel somewhat ill at ease with Maksim.

There's another thing which makes me deferential towards him too. I say this seriously; I really do regard him with deference, a feeling which I experience only rarely even towards adults. Maksim, a youth worthy of respect—does that sound ridiculous? No, it's true. You probably don't understand me completely, but you will do in due course.

I think that the woman who falls in love with Maksim will be most fortunate.

From everything I've said above you can come to one conclusion only: there are many things that I'm embarrassed to talk about with my son.

The frankness of an adult is almost always unhealthy, and when that adult is me, it's such a muddle—God forbid!

Such, then, are my thoughts. I've jotted them down very hurriedly and not entirely intelligibly. I've written to him asking him to come here, if it's essential that he does so. I myself cannot budge from this spot, there's no way I can! He could stay at a hotel. There's no one here whom he would find unpleasant. Iv[an] Pav[lovich] [Ladyzhnikov] is living with me at present. Well, then.

Things here are going full speed ahead. There's a possibility that they'll close *Letopis'* after the first issue. Some consolation that, isn't it?

All our consolations are more or less of this sort.

Goodbye for now, my friend! Keep well and grow up big and strong. Behave yourself, and don't eat a lot of sugar—it's too expensive.

And eat less in general; food is expensive right now.

I would very much like to shoot myself, but it would be shameful.

Your father and old friend,

M. Gorky, writer, eccentric despite himself, and romantic.

A.

No, not a romantic of Dr Aleksin's type.

The journal hasn't yet come into existence, but its enemies are already emerging. How pleasant!

In a few days I'll be sending you the questionnaires on the subject of 'Children and War'.[1] Help me with this!

SOURCE: *AG* 9: 172–3.

---

[1] Part of an unrealized project for *Children and War* [*Deti i voina*], a collection of anti-war pieces.

83. *To E. P. Peshkova, [8–13 March 1916]*

[Petrograd]

My friend, the point is not the 'Siberian students', the 'readings', and all that nonsense:[1] there are incomparably more substantial reasons which keep me from going to Moscow. The confusion which has been whipped up by our 'public' has seized me with all its might. I know very well that I have to see Maksim, and I'm dying to see him anyway; but today the 'Progressive Bloc'—that freak which has arisen from the Petersburg quagmire—made a botch of the Jewish inquiry, and that means we will be holding a meeting of the committee this evening. I'm the vice-chairman, Iv[an] Iv[anovich] Tolstoy is sick and can't go out, we had a general meeting scheduled for the 14th, the reports had been prepared, and now it is all going to hell. A Sisyphean task.[2]

Besides the society, I have the journal;[3] and besides the journal, the publishing house;[4] and besides all that, I am expected to be like a country magician and meet no fewer than a dozen different people every day. Yesterday I saw seven at home and sixteen at the editorial office. At 7 o'clock Chaliapin and I were present at a sumptuous dinner at one of the 'best houses'—I couldn't refuse as it was a business dinner. At 9 o'clock I was at the arts commission at the other end of town, and at 11 o'clock I took the chair in the porter's room beneath the staircase, where it was as hot as a bath-house and terribly smoky.[5] I'm not complaining, even though I could do so—I am just explaining. All these sessions put together were worth two kopecks, at a generous estimate. On top of it all I've come down with a cold, and I'm coughing like a camel.

Yesterday I saw Sofiia Izrailevich; she's a pleasant person, as I had expected her to be.[6] Her short story is not bad and will do. That fool Skitalets has written a play and wants to read it in a dark house, where Boris and Nastasia Suvorin will be among those in attendance.[7] That gives me real pleasure. To think how much money and effort I've wasted in the attempt to fashion that log into something resembling a human form!

My soul is very heavy, and this damned loneliness is terrible. I'm truly amazed at how much I can endure. I know that things aren't so sweet for you either; they're not easy—I'm well aware of that. But none the less we will play our part and we will do so until the end of our days, right? We'll cope. 'They'll do their bit and we'll do ours.'[8]

Goodbye for now, keep well, and take care of yourself! I'm not writing to our son; there's just no time, and besides, my mood is lyrical—in other words, sour. I fear for him. Does he draw? I need to know.

Warm regards,

A.

SOURCE: *AG* 9: 181.

[1] Gorky refers to obligations mentioned in a previous letter to his wife.

[2] The Russian Society for the Study of Jewish Life (chaired by Ivan Tolstoy) was active in fighting official anti-Semitism. The 'Progressive Bloc', formed the previous year within the Fourth Duma, turned out to be ineffective in leading the inquiry into government-sponsored anti-Semitic acts.

[3] *Letopis'*.

[4] *Parus*.

[5] i.e. he was taking part in an illegal meeting.

[6] A Nizhnii Novgorod teacher to whom Gorky had given financial support when she was a student.

[7] Boris Suvorin, a right-wing journalist, son of the prominent (and equally right-wing) journalist Aleksei Suvorin. Skitalets's play *The Free Men* [*Vol'nitsa*] was eventually published abroad after the Revolution.

[8] A favourite phrase of Gorky's at the time and one which appears in his story 'The Deceased' ['Pokoinik'] in the *Through Russia* collection.

84. To H. G. Wells, [end of December 1916]

[Petrograd]

Dear friend!

I've just finished proof-reading the Russian translation of your latest work *Mr Britling*, and I want to express my delight, because you have written an excellent book![1] Undoubtedly, it is the best, most daring, truthful, and humane book written in Europe during the course of this accursed war! I'm certain that in the future, when we have become more human again, England will pride herself on the fact that it was in England that the first voice of protest was heard—and such a vigorous protest too—against the cruelties of war. And all honest and intelligent people will utter your name with gratitude. Your book belongs among those which will live for a very long time. Wells, you are a great and fine man, and I'm so happy that I have seen you, that I can remember your face and your splendid eyes. Perhaps I'm expressing all this in a some- what primitive fashion, but I simply want to say to you that in these days of universal cruelty and barbarity your book is a great and truly humane work.

Of course I do not agree with the ending of your book.[2] I know of no God other than the God who inspired you to write of how Mr Britling drained to the dregs his cup of world sorrow mixed with blood. But this God lives only in your soul, in the human soul, he exists nowhere except in that soul. We—mankind—have created our own God for our sorrow and joy. We will not find God in the external world; all we will find there is other people who are as unhappy as we are and who are the creators of their own God—of goodness.

You have written an excellent book, Wells. I congratulate you warmly and I love you dearly.

And now I want to tell you the following. Two of my friends, Aleksandr Tikhonov and Ivan Ladyzhnikov, have organized a publishing house for children.[3] Today—more than ever, perhaps—children are the best and the most essential thing on earth. And Russian children, more than any others, need to learn about the world, about its great people and their labours for the happiness of humanity. We must cleanse chil- dren's hearts of the bloody mildew of this terrible and senseless war. We must restore in the hearts of children faith in humanity and respect for it. We must reawaken the social romanticism about which Mr Britling spoke so beautifully to Letty and about which he wrote to Heinrich's par- ents in Pomerania.[4]

Wells, I'm asking you to write a children's book about Edison, about his life and works. You will understand how essential it is to have a book which teaches one to love science and work. I will also ask Romain

Rolland to write a book about Beethoven, and Fridtjof Nansen to write about Columbus. I myself will write about Garibaldi. In this way, children will have a gallery of portraits depicting a series of great people. Can I ask you please to suggest which English authors could write about Charles Dickens, Byron, and Shelley? Would you also be so kind as to indicate a few good children's books, so that I can arrange for them to be translated into Russian?

I hope that you will not refuse to help me. Once again I must tell you that you have written a superb book, and I thank you with all my heart.

Yours sincerely,

M. Gorky

My address: Petrograd, Bolshaia Monetnaia, 18, 'Parus', for Maksim Gorky.

SOURCE: *SS* 29: 372–4.

---

[1] Wells's anti-war tale *Mr Britling Sees it Through* was serialized in *Letopis'* in the second half of 1916.
[2] Wells's novel ends with Mr Britling's discovery of a new faith in God.
[3] This was part of the Parus operation.
[4] Scenes from Book 3 of Wells's novel.

85. To E. P. Peshkova, [29 January 1917]

[Petrograd]

I very much advise against your coming here, Katia!

The fact of the matter is that yesterday, at a defence meeting in the Mariinskii Palace, the Minister of Railways reported that the Nikolaevskii line has only enough fuel for another four days, and that it's no better on the others—some lines have just two days' fuel left!

That's why freight transport is coming to a halt. There are 36,000 freight trucks loaded with all sorts of goods standing on various tracks, but there are no engines, and the majority of those they do have are broken down. In Vladivostok there are about 540,000 tons of military freight, but they are dispatching only 100 trucks a day—that's 100 tons!

The situation is critical. If transport stops for two weeks, famine will set in. There's already no flour here. The session of the Duma probably won't open on the 14th, although all manner of turmoil could occur on that day.

The working group of the Central Military-Industrial Committee[1] has been arrested. Amfiteatrov came to see me yesterday; he's being exiled from Petrograd.[2] Things here in general are alarming and grim, and there would be nothing for you to do.

I'm giving a reading on the first. It will be a success. Zinovii Peshkov has been promoted to lieutenant, he has been sent by the French to America and is getting forty dollars a day! He's having an affair with Countess Chernikh, wife of the Sarajevan consul, the one who aided the Austrian plot against Serbia. The countess, who is English by birth, asked her husband for a divorce when the war began, and now Zinovii's turned up!

Things are going badly with *Luch* [*The Ray*], and not so nicely with *Letopis'*, but well enough with Parus.[3] But could you ask Iurii Aleksandrovich anyway not to refuse to take part in Parus.[4] This will be a partnership, not a stock company; I wrote to him about that.

How's Maksim Peshkov getting on and how's his work going?[5] You didn't say a word about him.

Aleksei Peshkov is working like an ox. I've caught a cold, I've lost my voice, I'm sneezing, and I'm afraid that I won't get better by the first!

But that's nothing! Everything here is abominable. I say this to you not by way of consolation, but just because that's how it is.

Keep well!

A.

SOURCE: AG 9: 191–2.

---

[1] Set up to help mobilize the war effort, the committee was accused of subversive activity.

[2] Amfiteatrov was exiled to Irkutsk for writing a satirical poem and an article critical of the Interior Minister.

[3] Plans to establish the newspaper *Luch* eventually fell through; *Letopis'* was experiencing censorship difficulties.

[4] An industrialist, Iulii (not Iurii) Aleksandrovich Meller-Brezhnev had expressed an interest in Gorky's publishing ventures.

[5] Maksim was studying at the Moscow secondary school directed by N. G. Bazhanov.

---

86. *To V. V. Ivanov,*[1] *[about 3 February 1917]*

[Petrograd]

Vsevolod Ivanov,

Two of your stories will be published in *A Miscellany of Works by Proletarian Writers* [*Sbornik proizvedenii proletarskikh pisatelei*] and they've already gone to press.[2]

'On the Tugboat' ['Na buksire'] will not do.

The thing is, my dear sir, that you are undoubtedly a talented man; your literary ability is indisputable. But if you don't want to lose yourself, to fritter yourself away on trivialities to no purpose, you must get down to some serious self-education.

You are not very literate and make a lot of spelling mistakes. Your language is lively but your vocabulary is too small, and you often use words which are non-literary and local. These are all right for dialogues but inappropriate in descriptions. You're also short of ideas and images. This is all a 'matter of experience'. I advise you to take yourself in hand. Read, study the technique of such master-stylists as Chekhov, Turgenev, and Leskov. Leskov has a particularly rich vocabulary. Study grammar, read 'The Theory of Literature'. You should pay serious attention to yourself in general.

When *Luch* comes out, I'll send you a copy.

I can send you books if you need them.

And another thing: your stories display much daring, but it is a cheap and shallow sort of daring. Even calves are daring when they are young—do you understand? But you should look further than the cattle-yard and seek out what is human and good. Not all people are 'swine', far from it, even if they have been running wild of late.

Let me tell you that those of us who know life realize that there is nothing to believe in other than man. This means that you must believe in yourself; you need to know that you are not only a judge of people but also their blood-brother. You should not be too rude.

One can and one should be angry, but one must also know how to forgive.

There, then. Don't write too much.

Better less, but better.

A. Peshkov

I wish you all the best.

Thanks for the photograph!

SOURCE: *SS* 29: 378.

---

[1] Vsevolod Viacheslavovich Ivanov (1895–1963), a young writer who went on to become a major Soviet literary figure.

[2] The stories were 'Grandfather Anton' ['Ded Anton'] and 'On the Irtysh' ['Na Irtyshe'].

87. To E. P. Peshkova, [1 March 1917]

[Petrograd]

The events taking place may appear grandiose, even moving at times, but their meaning is not so profound and sublime as everyone imagines.[1] I am filled with scepticism, even though I am also moved to tears at the sight of soldiers marching to the State Duma to the sound of music. I don't believe in a revolutionary army; I think that many people are mistaking an absence of organization and discipline for revolutionary activity. All the forces in Petersburg have gone over to the Duma, that's true; so have the units coming from Oranienbaum, Pavlovsk, and Tsarskoe. But the officers will, of course, side with Rodzianko and Miliukov up to a certain point, and only the wildest dreamer would expect the army to stand together with the Soviet of Workers' Deputies.[2]

The police, ensconced in attics, spray the public and soldiers with machine-gun fire. Cars packed with soldiers and bearing red flags drive around the city in the search for policemen in disguise, and these are then placed under arrest. In some cases they are killed, but for the most part they are brought to the Duma, where about 200 policemen *out of 35,000* have already been rounded up.

There's a great deal of absurdity—more than there is of the grandiose. Looting has begun. What will happen next? I don't know. But I see clearly that the Kadets and the Octobrists are turning the revolution into a military coup.[3] Will they succeed? It seems they already have.

We won't turn back, but we won't go very far ahead either—perhaps only a sparrow's step. And of course, a lot of blood, an unprecedented amount, will be shed.

A.

SOURCE: *AG* 9: 194.

[1] In late February food riots broke out in Petrograd. A few days later part of the Petrograd garrison went over to the side of the rioters. By 28 February the Petrograd Soviet had seized effective control of the city. The day after this letter was written, the tsar abdicated and the Provisional Government was formed.

[2] Mikhail Vladimirovich Rodzianko (1859–1924), conservative leader of the Octobrist Party and president of the Duma at the time of the February Revolution.

[3] Like the Kadets, the Octobrist Party emerged after the 1905 Revolution. It had a moderate reformist platform and was on the right of the political spectrum by 1917.

88. To M. A. Peshkov, [10 March 1917]

[Petrograd]

My dear friend, my son,

You should bear in mind that the revolution has only just begun; it will last for years, a counter-revolution is possible, and the emergence of reactionary ideas and attitudes is inevitable. And if you want to be of use to your country, if you want to work for its rebirth—don't get too carried away by what is happening now.

We have triumphed not because we are strong but because the government was weak. *But this weak and rotten government has corrupted us as well. We are not a healthy people, we lack confidence in ourselves and are most tentative in our opinions.*

The events taking place here threaten us with grave danger. We have accomplished the political revolution and now we must consolidate our conquests—such is the meaning of what has occurred and such is the task of the hour. I am a Social Democrat, but what I'm saying and what I will continue to say is that the time for socialist reforms has not yet come. The new leadership has not taken over the state but only the ruins of the state. For the time being, it must make use of the confidence and co-operation of all the forces in the land. This is what matters.

And we must remember that Wilhelm Hohenzollern could still play the same role in the rebirth of reaction as was once played by our own Alexander Romanov I.[1] The Petersburg bourgeois is capable of greeting Wilhelm with the same applause with which he once greeted Alexander!

It is only when we have firmly consolidated what has been won that we will be able to count on the success of further conquests with confidence. Russia is now a free country and the German invasion is threatening that freedom. If Wilhelm were to win, the Romanovs would be restored to power.

Such are my thoughts, my dear boy. For this reason I am organizing a newspaper which will soon begin to appear.[2]

Goodbye for now, take care!

Greetings to your mother! It was a pity that I couldn't see her.

A.

SOURCE: *AG* 13: 163–4.

[1] A German invasion seemed a distinct possibility at the time. Alexander I, although he encouraged liberal hopes early in his reign, turned towards conservatism after Russia's victory over Napoleon in 1812.
[2] *Novaia zhizn'*.

89. To E. P. Peshkova, [11 March 1917]

[Petrograd]

I sent a letter to our son yesterday. Now I'm taking advantage of a free moment to write you.

Don't get too carried away, don't allow yourself to yield to foolish optimism; and caution others against this disease. The situation is very complicated and dangerous. The slogan 'Down with the war' is idiotic in the new circumstances.[1] A German victory is a victory for reaction. One shouldn't rely on the soldiers. They are shifty Russian peasants who have dressed up in greatcoats; they have no idea what's going on and they won't grasp its significance for a long time yet. They might come to understand one day, but it will be too late. I'm starting a Social Democratic newspaper; it will be large and *right-wing*.[2] It is necessary to build up the party and to organize strongly. The government is made up of yesterday's men. It has three gifted people: Lvov, Kerensky, and Nekrasov,[3] but you won't get very far with that troika. They need to be given support.

The security forces are going all out, creating anarchy and panic, mixing up the slogans, and intensifying the issues. There's no end to the security agents in our midst! So cleverly have they done their work around here that the security agency was informed the very same day of everything that had gone on at my place. Letters have been stolen from my desk: a letter I received on 25 February was lying on my desk; it disappeared on the 26th, and on 2 March it turned up with the security agency!

About forty 'secret employees' have been arrested; the names of fifteen of them were published today in the papers. But that's nothing! There are as many as 400 of them here and they are still active to this very day, skilfully working on behalf of the counter-revolution. Don't imagine that I am exaggerating. Look after our son; our country will need his talents yet. It will be some time before we get through this chaos of destruction and construction, this fever of passion and illusion.

Keep well, take everything calmly, and carry on working![4]

How many ridiculous things are happening all around us! There is so much stupidity and banality! But of course there is still more that is childlike and moving.

It is possible that the mutual incomprehension of soldiers and workers will increase. The soldier does not comprehend the eight-hour working day. 'We sit in the trenches for three days at a time'—this is what they say. In general, there are enormous grounds for misunderstanding. The soldiers will be SRs, of course.

Well, that's enough! Keep well, my friend.

A.

SOURCE: *AG* 9: 195.

---

[1] The Bolsheviks argued against Russia's continued participation in an 'imperialist' World War.

[2] *Novaia zhizn'*.

[3] Prince Georgii Evgenieveich Lvov (1861–1925), President of the Provisional Government from March to July 1917; Aleksandr Fedorovich Kerensky (1881–1970), Deputy Chairman of the Petrograd Soviet and Minister of Justice (later President) in the Provisional Government; Nikolai Vissarionovich Nekrasov (1879–1940), a Kadet who held several ministerial posts in the Provisional Government.

[4] Peshkova was active in various societies, including those offering aid to victims of the war and to former political prisoners.

90. To E. P. Peshkova, [4 July 1917]

[Petrograd]

I had wanted to give you a treat yesterday, and myself too. I bought a ticket and got ready to set off for Moscow, but at 6 o'clock I was overtaken by events and my money was wasted, my plans shattered![1]

I have a ticket for the fifth from Rybinsk along the Volga, and for the seventh from Nizhnii, but it's already clear that I won't manage to slip away from Petersburg on either the fifth or the seventh.

Matters are becoming more and more muddled, and it's becoming more and more obvious that a civil conflict is inevitable here. To judge by the mood, the fighting promises to be brutal. There are meetings on the streets at night and a wild fury has flared up. Counter-revolutionary forces are actively organizing themselves, while the revolutionaries just spout rhetoric. In general, things aren't too cheerful. They're even somewhat sinister.

Madame! If you want to be a healthy person, you should come here and have yourself X-rayed at Manukhin's.[2] Do you believe in his method? If you do, then you should come as soon as possible. I urge you to! Manukhin continues to work wonders.

Our son hasn't written me a thing, not a line! Oh, the charlatan!

Zinovii has left for the front, to join Kerensky.[3] An old Nizhnii Novgorodian, Akim Chekin, has turned up. Do you remember him?[4] He has become paralysed and is now living in Sarakamysh. The revolution is mobilizing everything it can, but there aren't enough people anywhere for anything. On the other hand, there are an awful lot of windbags and idlers around. So far I'm feeling tolerably well, which rather surprises me.

That fool Burtsev has announced in the newspapers that he will soon identify a *provocateur* and spy whose name will 'stun the whole world'.[5] The public has already started to speculate and has guessed that the person in question is M. Gorky. You think I'm joking? Not in the least. I'm already getting letters with salutations such as 'to the traitor Judas, chief German spy and *provocateur*'. *Rech'* is definitely hinting that I'm done for.

Oh, how hard it is to live in Russia! How foolish we all are, how fantastically foolish!

And what about you—so you won in Moscow, did you? I'm not going to congratulate you. I shall soon have to argue with you, and most sharply too, you SR.[6]

When will I come? I don't know. The one thing I can say is that it will be unexpectedly.

Do get well, it is so very worrying otherwise. Thank Anna Nikolaevna for her kind letter; it reassured me somewhat.

Regards,

A.

SOURCE: *AG* 9: 198–9.

[1] Between 3 and 5 July, there were mass demonstrations against the Provisional Government by workers and soldiers demanding the transfer of authority to the Soviets and an end to military operations.

[2] See Letter 78, n. 1.

[3] The French government had just appointed Zinovii Peshkov to liaise with Kerensky, who was then Minister of Defence.

[4] Akim Vasilievich Chekin (1859–1935), a teacher.

[5] Vladimir Lvovich Burtsev (1862–1936), journalist who later joined the White emigration. Burtsev disclosed in his memoirs (1928) that the *provocateur* was N. P. Starodvorsky.

[6] The SRs had just won a majority in the elections to the Moscow City Duma.

91. To E. P. Peshkova, [2 December 1917]

[Petrograd]

I was not exactly ill, although I was a little unwell. A little discomfort in the lungs is nothing; I've had two sessions of X-ray treatment already and I'm feeling better. But my nerves are completely shattered. Completely. I can't sleep and my mood is so miserable that it's simply awful. I'm trying to hide this from those around me, but how does one do that?

Things are bad for Russia, bad!

Get the money from Kondratiev. They used to live on Tverskaia, in the house of the Governor-General. As to where they are now, ask the people in the theatre.[1]

How are things with your Soviet's theatre? Has it collapsed?[2]

*Lanina has been arrested and now she is being slandered. The stupid beasts.

This is most distressing.*

Well, goodbye for now.

Greetings to Max. What's he hatching , I'd like to know?

Regards,

A.

My respects to A[leksei] N[ikolaevich].[3]

I hope you aren't going to the Crimea!

Wait a bit!

SOURCE: *AG* 9: 204–5.

[1] Ivan Kondratiev, secretary of the Moscow Society of Playwrights.

[2] The Moscow City Soviet's Cultural Education Committee, of which Peshkova was a member, was attempting to found its own theatre.

[3] Aleksei Nikolaevich Bakh (1857–1946), prominent chemist who was staying with Peshkova after his return from emigration.

92. To V. I. Lenin, [31 August 1918]

[Petrograd]

Telegram

We are terribly distressed, upset, sincerely wish quickest recovery, keep your spirits up.[1]

M. Gorky
Mariia Andreeva

SOURCE: *Lenin*: 134.

[1] Lenin had been wounded in an attempted assassination by Fanny Kaplan.

93. To V. I. Lenin, [5 December 1918]

[Petrograd]

Telegram

Moscow,
To Lenin

We are extremely disturbed by the danger to which the treasures of the Hermitage, the Russian Museum, and the Academy in the Kremlin Palace are being exposed in connection with the organization of an exhibition which will require boxes to be unpacked without an opportunity to ensure proper guarantees of security.[1] The Hermitage Soviet, at a meeting held in the house of Maksim Gorky, decided unanimously to ask you to block arrangements for the exhibition and do everything in your power to have the collections returned to Petrograd, which is their only salvation. The members of the Hermitage Soviet are Troinitsky, Argutinsky-Dolgorukov, Benois, Braz, Waldhauer, Kube, Liephardt, Markov, Weiner, Schmidt, and Iaremich. I give my full support to the Soviet's petition.

M. Gorky

SOURCE: *Lenin*: 135.

[1] In 1917 the Provisional Government had moved a number of major art collections to Moscow. The exhibition never took place.

94. To V. I. Lenin, [January 1919]

[Petrograd]

Dear Vladimir Ilyich!

Our Communist workers returning from the front complain that their propaganda campaign among the diverse masses of the Red Army is not having the success which they expected.

The complaints made by these propagandists are profoundly important, and I ask you to give them your attention. Personally, I believe that Communist propaganda would enjoy far greater success if the propagandists themselves were to set about their work armed not only with *pure theory* but also with *facts about Soviet power drawn from the sphere of its government activities*. It is such facts which make the theory vitally convincing.

I have long insisted on the need to publish an informational journal which would provide an account and an explanation of all the positive things that Soviet rule has achieved in the course of the year in various areas of social life. My voice remains that of one crying in the wilderness, a wilderness which is, alas, not uninhabited. But all the same, I shall continue doggedly in my attempts to persuade you all that it is essential to provide Communist propagandists with either an informational journal or a pamphlet outlining the activities of Soviet power over the year. This sketch should contain a brief and intelligible account of everything that has been achieved in 1918 by the Commissariat of Public Education and other commissariats, the Committee for State Works, etc.

There are many facts of which Soviet power can even afford to boast, especially in Lunacharsky's department.[1] These facts ought to be made known to the propagandists, and you would be performing a good deed if you were to suggest in the appropriate places that they should set about the composition of the aforementioned sketch immediately.

Finally, even if such a brief sketch should prove impracticable, you ought to supply propagandists with a sheet containing a concise enumeration of everything which has been achieved during the year through the work of the various commissariats. I hope you realize how essential this is.

Furthermore, would you not find this a convenient time for the resumption of *Novaia zhizn'*?[2] If the answer is yes, then it would be good if this newspaper were to appear at the same time as the Menshevik newspaper.[3] I am inspired to insist on simultaneous publication by considerations which are of anything but a material nature.

In a few days' time we will finish printing the list of books intended for publication by World Literature. It wouldn't be a bad idea, I think, to have these lists translated into all the European languages and distributed in Germany, England, France, the Scandinavian countries, etc, so that not only the Western proletariat but also the A. Frances, the Wells's, and the various Scheidemanns[4] can see for themselves not only that the Russian proletariat is not barbaric, but also that it understands internationalism far more extensively than they do, even if they are cultured people, and that even in the vilest conditions one could possibly imagine, our proletariat has been able to achieve in a single year what they should have got done long ago.

Keep well!

A. Peshkov

In the mean time the Communist comrades are a negligent, ineffectual and conceited lot. It is a difficult business working with them, believe me!

SOURCE: *Lenin*: 137–8.

[1] i.e. Education.
[2] The newspaper was closed down in July 1918. See the Introduction to this section for further details.
[3] The journal *Vsegda vpered* [*Always Forward*] was revived in January 1919 but it was closed down again the following month.
[4] P. Scheidemann, organizer of the workers' movement in Germany.

95. To V. I. Lenin, [5 April 1919]

[Petrograd]

Dear Vladimir Ilyich!

Natalia Shklovskaia, a very *high-spirited seventeen-year-old* poet and the niece of *Dioneo*, has been arrested here as a left Socialist Revolutionary.[1] I know her; she was secretary to the poet *A. A. Blok*,[2] and her participation in any left Socialist Revolutionary adventures is more than dubious. She was arrested on the street carrying a revolver, but for her a revolver is just a toy and in all probability she does not even know how to fire it. However, I am afraid that high spirits could be the ruin of this child, that her romanticism will cause her to slander herself in some way and that she will get herself killed. I beg you to release the girl, for I am absolutely convinced that she cannot be guilty of anything.

She is talented too.

Allow me to hope that you will fulfil this request.

Within a few days I will send you a stack of horrific documents relating to plunder and theft at the nationalized warehouses.

All the best!

A. Peshkov

This letter will be transmitted to you by comrade Ivan Ananievich Mukhanov.

SOURCE: *Lenin*: 141.

---

[1] Shklovskaia was only sixteen at this time. Dioneo, pseudonym of I. V. Shklovsky (1865–1935), writer, translator, and London correspondent for various Russian newspapers.

[2] Shklovskaia had not in fact worked as Blok's secretary.

96. To G. E. Zinoviev,[1] [1919]

[Petrograd]

Grigorii Evseevich!

Allow me to draw your attention to the enclosed memorandum from the Joint Council of Scientific Institutions.

In my opinion, the arrest of scholars cannot be justified by any political considerations, unless you suppose these to include crazed, animal fear for the safety of their own skin on the part of those persons who carry out the arrests.[2]

Today the entire committee of experts which I set up on the instructions of A. V. Lunacharsky to examine the property of the Danish citizen Erik Bloom was placed under arrest.[3]

As organizer and chairman of this group, I should also have been arrested along with the board, or I should at least have been informed of the planned arrest and told of the charges.

I humbly request that the arrested experts be released, for their arrest is either a piece of stupidity or something even worse.

The barbarous outrages which have been taking place recently in Petersburg are compromising the regime completely, provoking universal hatred and contempt for its cowardice.

SOURCE: *Izv Ts K* 1989 (1): 239–40.

---

[1] Zinoviev (1883–1936), one of the leading Bolsheviks, went on to head the Party in the Petrograd region.

[2] The Bolsheviks were arresting scholars who had belonged to the Kadet Party.

[3] The Board of Experts (or Expert Commission) was established by Gorky to gather and study antiques, art works, and other items of value nationalized by the Bolsheviks. In this instance, an entire committee of the Board was arrested.

97. To E. P. Peshkova, [end of 1919]

[Petrograd]

Maksim firmly believes that life can and should be reorganized in the same spirit and using the same methods that Soviet power is employing. I don't believe that myself, you know, but I do not consider that I have the right to destroy the beautiful illusions of youth. He believes with certain reservations, whereas I don't believe with certain reservations; this doesn't mean that we are in complete agreement, but I do understand him. At his age it is a great joy to sense that you are a participant in the process of creating a new life; this is a joy which neither you nor I have known, nor indeed our generation as a whole.

I know what you are afraid of, but we'll all perish anyway; we will be crushed by the village, it's inevitable. The Western proletariat has betrayed the Russian workers; the Western bourgeoisie will support the Russian peasants until they are victorious over the city. The Kolchak movement takes us back to the beginning of the seventeenth century, it is like the Minin movement—something resolutely inimical to the city and urban culture.[1] Other than the Bolsheviks there is no force capable of opposing this movement. The revolution has degenerated into a battle between village and city—that's what one has to understand. The problem of the moment is the unification of the intelligentsia and *the representatives of large-scale industry* with the Bolsheviks, despite all the great mistakes and sins of the latter.

That's my view. Maksim understands it. He's much less of a youth than you think, and he's no fool. His childishness is not a trait of character but just a mask adopted by an intelligent fellow. There are many issues which he has resolved for himself in one way or another.

I very much advise you not to enter into any polemic with him; allow him some freedom of thought. His feelings towards you are excellent, and he doesn't find it easy having disagreements with you, believe me. Anyway, you won't accomplish a thing. Any more than I would. He's happier than we are.

He told me that you're drinking oceans of coffee; that's bad for your heart, madam! But none the less I'm sending you a cup for your coffee; drink no more than three at a time. It's a nice cup.

Keep well! My legs hurt; I have varicose veins, on both legs. It's really lousy. I'm very tired and working beyond my strength. Do you have enough money?

Warm regards and all the best, my friend.

A.

SOURCE: *AG* 9: 209–10.

¹ Aleksandr Vasilievich Kolchak (1873–1920), admiral in the pre-revolutionary navy, who set up an anti-Bolshevik government in Siberia. On Minin, see Letter 18, n. 4.

98. To H. G. Wells, [end of April or May 1920]

[Moscow]

Dear Wells!

I received your letter and the beginning of the book.¹ I was very touched by your kindness and by the fact that you haven't forgotten me.

I have shown your letter to some experts and they spoke of your work in the most flattering terms. This made me very happy, and I am intending to commission a translation of the book as soon as I receive the next instalments. I hope that I will succeed in arranging the publication of Russian books abroad, in Sweden. In this way, the appearance of the books will be quite satisfactory. Please tell me your terms.

You ask how my life is. I'm doing a great deal of work in the sphere of public education, but I am not writing anything. I have organized the publication of all nineteenth-century European literature (only the exemplary works, of course).² This comes to about 3,000 volumes. I have also organized a publishing house for the natural sciences.³ This is very extensive and deals with everything from the most popular books to university textbooks and classic works on natural science. I am chairman of the Commission to Improve Scholars' Living Conditions,⁴ and I have also served on several occasions as chairman of various organizations of a cultural-educational kind.

Life is difficult. This is not because I am hungry, cold, and have a lot of work, but mainly because I am prevented from working. The defeat of Kolchak and Denikin⁵ raised people's hopes that it would be possible to work peacefully towards the restoration of Russia, a country which needs sustained, steadfast labour above all else.

But then came Poland, and those hopes have been dashed.⁶ Once again thousands of people will perish in the fighting, and, as always happens, dozens of the most valuable cultural workers will be among those who disappear. Our exhausted country will be weakened even further by the new effort which is being demanded of forces that are already fatigued. You cannot imagine how distressing and painful all this is.

Perhaps I am mistaken, but it seems to me that the capitalist classes in Europe have become completely brutalized in their feelings of revenge and greed. Sometimes one's spirits fall, and one regrets having lived to see such loathsome pictures of human stupidity and cruelty, but one still clearly sees and feels that the Russian working masses bear within themselves the seeds of highly valuable qualities, one sees the awakening of a thirst for knowledge. This is a comfort, it even stirs some enthusiasm. One starts to work again with eagerness and faith. And so the days pass. It seems that I may not have many left.

You know how much I like you. Accept my sincere greetings and my heartfelt desire for all the best for you.[7]

SOURCE: *SS* 29: 392–3.

[1] Wells had sent Gorky the first part of his *Outline of History* in February 1920. It was eventually published in 1924.
[2] The World Literature project.
[3] Apparently the Z. Grzhebin publishing house, which had been set up in 1919 and carried a large number of natural science titles. See also Letter 167, n. 3.
[4] KUBU. For further details, see the Introduction to this section.
[5] Anton Ivanovich Denikin (1872–1947) leader of the White army in southern Russia.
[6] The Polish campaign opened a new phase in the Civil War.
[7] This letter was sent in an English translation. The Russian version was left unsigned.

99. *To V. I. Lenin, [17 July 1920]*

[Petrograd]

Dear Vladimir Ilyich!

I enclose two applications, please submit them to the Malyi Council of the SNK.[1] I am doing this in accordance with your own instructions.

My situation is idiotic: either as a result of an act of caprice on someone's part or of some misunderstanding, the World Literature business, which has been established so magnificently and which the French are already taking as a model for a similar venture in Paris, is now falling apart. The manager Tikhonov and his technical assistant Kogan have already left for Leipzig in Germany where they are negotiating with Volkmar over the publication of Russian books abroad, which is in accordance with the resolution of Sovnarkom. The fifty thousand pounds authorized by Sovnarkom for the needs of the State Publishing House is sitting uselessly with Gukovsky[2] in Revel, because it has *nothing* to publish abroad.

For some obscure and apparently technical reasons, World Literature is being refused 10 million Duma banknotes, waste paper which in three months' time could be converted into several million good books.

The question of the publication of natural science books—through the Grzhebin publishing house[3]—is also being held up by virtue of an obvious misunderstanding. The contract with the State Publishing House gives Grzhebin the right to receive the next instalment of 10 million Soviet banknotes. That contract has not been annulled. In accordance with the SNK resolution, Grzhebin has gone abroad and is setting up the technical side of things. Here in Petrograd money is needed urgently in order to pay the contributors who are working so efficiently—these are the best people in Russian science. If they are not paid, they will scatter in all directions, which is natural enough.

Comrade Avanesov, with whom—on your instructions—I have spoken about this matter, can see no obstacle whatsoever to the disbursement of this money on the part of the W[orker]-P[easant] Control.[4]

So, what's my purpose?

I ask you most earnestly, Vladimir Ilyich, to reconsider both resolutions of the SNK and *in connection with the first*: either pay out the 10 million Duma banknotes, transferring them to Comrade Gukovsky in Revel, or else authorize Comrade Gukovsky to pay out a sum equivalent to 10 million Duma banknotes from the fifty thousand pounds which he was sent for the needs of the State Publishing House [Gosizdat].[5] This sum should be handed to the representative of World Literature, Comrade Aleksandr Tikhonov, in Revel.

In connection with the second:

As a matter of urgency, send to Petrograd, in the name of M. Gorky, 10 million Soviet banknotes as payment to the contributors and editors at the Grzhebin publishing house.

I make this request most earnestly! Don't allow such trivialities to destroy two ventures of which the Soviet regime will be able to boast in three or four months' time. And finally, do take into consideration the book famine which has actually already begun. Illiteracy is being eliminated, but there are no books! After all, you can't stuff pieces of political literature straight into the hands of a person who has only just mastered the alphabet.

Keep well and all the best.

A. Peshkov

SOURCE: *Lenin*: 185–6.

¹ The Sovnarkom or Soviet of People's Commissars was the highest executive body of the Soviet government from 1918 until 1946. Its Malyi branch had refused funds to both World Literature and the Grzhebin publishing house.

² Isidor Emmanuilovich Gukovsky (1871–1921), People's Commissar for Finance.

³ See Letter 98, n. 3.

⁴ The Worker-Peasant Control was the main agency for ensuring that government directives were being fulfilled. V. A. Avanesov (1884–1930) was Deputy Commissar within this organization.

⁵ A Bolshevik institution which sought to exert some political control over publishing.

100. *To V. I. Lenin, [after 12, no later than 24 July 1921]*

[Petrograd]

Dear Ilyich!

'Pay no attention to trivialities'—that is a very good rule, especially for those like yourself who have been obliged to operate with the masses, with states and nations, and have become accustomed to that. I do not belong to that class of people who consider this an act of 'burying one's head in the sand', as I know full well how these damned trivialities, so terrible and vile, can prevent a man from living peacefully and doing what he loves.

But although I am a man who does not forget that tubercular, cholera, and syphilitic bacilli are trivialities, I also do not forget what I see—that extremely valuable and complex organisms are perishing because of those self-same trivialities. I cannot, therefore, ignore the enormous significance of trivialities in life and I have decided to write you something about these very 'trivialities'.

In a social organism it is the scoundrels and swindlers who play the destructive role of pathogenic bacilli. You know that every enterprise has its swindlers and that they are especially numerous in the magnificent enterprise of our revolution, being as they are the completely natural legacy of an 'old world' which was in essence a complete swindle.

I have been convinced for some time that here in Soviet Russia a certain black, but invisible, swindling hand is at work in a crafty and cunning way. Its work can be detected wherever any serious business—no matter how small—is starting to develop successfully. For some two years now I have been observing this hand operating in the work of the Expert Commission.[1]

Sovnarkom has decreed that the work of this Commission be accelerated, that the number of workers be increased to two hundred, and that they be given a good ration. The decree was promulgated in October 1920; and yet, despite my persistent efforts, it has not been put into effect. And just the other day the Commission for Supplying the Workforce flatly refused to distribute the rations. The work of the Commission has been delayed and the employees are dispersing, whilst the swindlers celebrate and keep on plundering and plundering.

Turning to another matter: A. A. Blok, an honest writer incapable of abusing or slandering the Soviet government, is dying of scurvy and asthma. It is essential that he be permitted to go to a sanatorium in Finland. He is not being allowed to go, and yet, at the same time, three other writers have been allowed to leave, writers who can, and will, engage in such abuse and slander.[2] I know that Soviet power will come to no harm through this, and I would like all those wishing to go abroad to be allowed to do so. But I do not understand this strange policy: it seems suspicious and predetermined to me. I cannot help being reminded involuntarily of the incident involving Spitzberg,[3] the 'Communist' and the Cheka[4] investigator of clergy affairs. In [the days][5] of the tsarist regime this Spitzberg was a petty, vile little divorce lawyer. A shady individual, he aroused disdain even in ecclesiastical circles. After October he declared himself a 'theomachist', appearing at meetings with A. V. Lunacharsky and editing the journal *Tserkov' i revoliutsiia* [*Church and Revolution*] with Krasikov.[6] In the end, he penetrated the Cheka and, while working there as an investigator, he performed an infinite number of abominations of all kinds which were extremely damaging to the prestige of the Soviet government. I heard that he was eventually thrown out of the Cheka, and out of the Party too, by the way. That is good, but can we be sure there are no Spitzbergs left?

The Commission to Improve Scholars' Living Conditions [KUBU] has managed to use Soviet currency to buy thirty thousand tins of preserved food very cheaply in Lithuania. Five months ago I submitted an application to the Cheka for an exit visa for a certain Adolii Rodet[7] to go to Lithuania in order to inspect, sample, and receive the tinned goods which have been bought. I was promised that Rodet would be permitted to go and I authorized the payment of an advance to the vendors. But the other day I was informed that Rodet is not being permitted to go to Lithuania. Why not? 'Politically unreliable.' You must excuse me for saying so, but this is rubbish. When Rodet was arrested along with some other bourgeois individuals in October, Uritsky himself went to the prison and had him released.[8] Badaev, Bakaev, and Pakhiev know Rodet well.[9] In the past he was an innkeeper, but now he is an outstanding and unselfish worker for KUBU, a man who is extremely gratified by the fact that he has given up innkeeping for the company of scholars who think highly of his intelligent work. As he is a Lithuanian by birth, he could opt to leave if he wanted to. But if he were to exercise this option, he would not be allowed back into Russia and hence would lose a good position, whilst the Commission would lose an excellent worker. Why has this been done? After all, this prohibition will cause great annoyance to people who have nothing to eat and yet are still able to work well at such a difficult time.

In addition, the Grzhebin affair is gradually assuming the character of a miniature Beilis affair.[10] Grzhebin is being persecuted like a dog or— even worse—like a Jew. You know that it was with your permission that I organized the Grzhebin publishing house. I have put in two years of work organizing this publishing house, I have commissioned dozens of new popular books on natural science from our most prominent scholars, I have achieved rare success. Thanks to our persistent work we have liberated the Russian science book market from the domination of

German publishing houses and publications. And yet Gosizdat[11] persistently rejects the manuscripts I submit by our best scholars, whilst it continues to publish translations of old books which have already lost their scientific significance, for example, Roscoe's *Chemistry* and Geikie's *Physics*.[12] These books were first published in Russian way back in the 1870s. Gosizdat did not accept Zlatogorov's book *What is Cholera?* for publication, and it also turned down *Directions for Hospital Orderlies and Hygienists* and other fundamental textbooks.

Despite the fact that on 26 April the Commission of the C[entral] C[ommittee] of the R[ussian] C[ommunist] P[arty] confirmed Grzhebin's contract with Gosizdat, obliging the latter to draw up within a week a list of books, circulation figures, and costs, Gosizdat dragged this business out for several months, and has now refused to carry out the decree of the C[entral] C[ommittee] Plenum. The decree itself was not passed on to me and has been lost both by Gosizdat and by the C[entral] C[ommittee].

All this is strange, you must agree. Gosizdat is the talk of the town, everyone is proclaiming that this institution is in need of reform, that Weiss[13] should be dismissed and the board—which comprises people who understand nothing about the business and whom Weiss is leading by the nose—be replaced. But, despite the general protest, Gosizdat is following its own line, as before. I consider this line not only unintelligent but also harmful and bad. There is no paper? The enclosed cutting from *Pravda* provides evidence of where the paper is going. There are dozens of such examples.[14]

SOURCE: *Izv Ts K* 1991 (6): 154–5.

[1] See Letter 96, n. 3.

[2] The writers in question were Balmont, Sologub, and (possibly) Artsybashev.

[3] I. A. Spitzberg (1881–1933), active in the Commissariat of Justice between 1918 and 1922.

[4] The Soviet security agency, the All-Russian Extraordinary Commission to Battle Counter-Revolution and Sabotage, also referred to by the acronym VChK.

[5] Crossed out in the original.

[6] P. A. Krasikov (1870–1939), Deputy Commissar of Justice.

[7] A. S. Rodet (d. 1930), director of KUBU in Petrograd in 1920–1.

[8] M. S. Uritsky (1873–1918), head of the Petrograd Cheka from March 1918 until his assassination that August.

[9] A. E. Badaev (1883–1951), Commissar of Industry for the Petrograd region; I. P. Bakaev (1887–1936), head of the Cheka in Petrograd; Pavel Pakhiev, Manager of Sanatoria in the Crimea.

[10] A celebrated court case against M. Beilis, a Jew accused of the ritual murder of a Russian boy in 1913. Gorky was one of several prominent Russians who spoke out on behalf of Beilis.

[11] The State Publishing House, established by the Bolsheviks.

[12] Works by Henry E. Roscoe (1833–1915) and Archibald Geikie (1835–1925) published in numerous Russian editions from the late 1860s onwards.

[13] D. L. Weiss (1877–1940) was in charge of affairs at Gosizdat from 1920.

[14] This is a draft letter with no signature.

101. To A. V. Lunacharsky, [29 July 1921]

[Petrograd]

Telegram

Urgent
Moscow, the Kremlin
To Lunacharsky

Aleksandr Blok has acute endocarditis. Condition extremely serious. Must get to Finland immediately. Definitely needs to be accompanied. Please seek permission for Blok's wife to go. Am sending forms. Hurry, or he'll die.[1]

SOURCE: *AG* 14: 100.

---

[1] Lunacharsky soon succeeded in gaining this permission for Blok's wife, but by then Blok was too ill to travel. He died on 7 August.

102. To E. P. Peshkova, [24 August 1921]

[Petrograd]

I had intended to go to Moscow—and even had the railway carriage organized—but on Friday I felt so lousy, both physically and morally, that instead of going to Moscow I went to Beloostrov, where it's so nice. I spent three days there amidst silence and stunningly beautiful scenery. I saw many interesting and joyous things.

On Tuesday morning I returned to Piter and found out that the Petrograd Soviet—that is, Zinoviev—had ordered an 'immediate halt' to the activity of the District Committee for Battling Hunger. (Tuesday was yesterday.)

I stopped work and sent a statement to Moscow announcing my resignation from the All-Russian Committee.[1]

Today I was summoned to a meeting with Zinoviev—politely, with two escorts, Bakaev and Evdokimov—so as to 'liquidate the incident'. We talked for a while, and then I informed Karpinsky, Marr, and the presidium about our conversation. Marr and Karpinsky, as members both of the All-Russian Committee and of the founding group in Petrograd, refused to work within the framework of the conditions laid down by the Petrograd Soviet, and thus the Committee does not exist for the time being, 'pending'—what? I don't understand.[2]

I have to sort out a few matters here before I leave for Moscow, and that's what I'm doing at the moment.

I may leave tomorrow but, more likely, it will be on Tuesday, after the session. I'll be bringing my luggage in case I have to leave from Moscow for Europe, even though I feel less desire to go there with every day.

The arrests here are horrific. People are being arrested by the hundreds.

Last night the entire city was alive with Cheka vehicles [. . .]

So you're not going to Siberia? I'm very glad; I didn't like the idea of that journey of yours.

The three days in Beloostrov did wonders for my health; I got a tan, even burnt my nose, went about naked, ate mutton, and drank beer—it was marvellous!

Well, then, goodbye for now—we'll see each other soon!

A.

Our Molecule[3] swallowed a pin, even though they're in short supply and expensive.

She boasts greatly of this feat and wants to perform an operation on herself, using a magnet and passing it over her stomach.

SOURCE: *AG* 9: 211–12.

[1] The All-Russian Committee for Battling Hunger, set up on 21 July 1921 to deal with the famine of that summer.

[2] Gorky was a founder of the Petrograd branch of the All-Russian Committee for Battling Hunger, whose leaders were accused by the Communist Party of harbouring political ambitions. A week after this letter was written, the Committee and all its branches were abolished. Nikolai Iakovlevich Marr (1864–1934); orientalist, archaeologist, and linguist. Aleksandr Petrovich Karpinsky (1846–1936); prominent geologist and first elected president of the Academy of Sciences.

[3] Mariia Aleksandrovna Geintse (d. 1927), doctor, the daughter of a family Gorky had known in Nizhnii Novgorod.

5
EUROPE REVISITED
1921–1928

INTRODUCTION

When Gorky left Bolshevik Russia, he was in a state of near total physical collapse. Together with his entourage of family and friends, he immediately made his way to Berlin via Finland. His first priority was to set about repairing his health: indeed, he was to spend the best part of two years at various spas in Germany and Czechoslovakia in an attempt to undo the dire effects of his recent experiences in Russia. As time went on he tired of life in central Europe and decided—as he had done during his first period of exile—to make his home in Italy. But on this occasion he was not permitted to settle on Capri. The Italian government was suspicious of the writer's Bolshevik ties and feared that he might cause mischief if allowed to live on the island again. And so, in the spring of 1924, he arrived in Sorrento, just across the water from Capri, renting a villa which was to be his home until 1928, when he made the first of his much-publicized return visits to Russia just after the celebration of his sixtieth birthday.

Despite his chronic ill health, of which he complains constantly, although often humorously, in his letters of these years, Gorky continued to work indefatigably almost from the moment of his arrival in Europe. In marked contrast to his first period of exile, however, he was extremely circumspect when it came to matters involving politics. Although his attitude towards the Bolsheviks was, understandably, highly antagonistic at the time, he took great care to ensure that his views remained private, deliberately avoiding the reporters, foreign and *émigré*, who began to press him for interviews (see Letter 103). He was equally determined that Maksim should not commit the indiscretion of broadcasting his father's opinions when he visited Russia in November 1922 (Letter 108). This concern may well have been sharpened by the Soviet response to the one occasion when he *did* voice his protest against the government—the trial of the Left Socialist Revolutionaries, which Gorky quite rightly interpreted as a sign of a new resolve on the part of the Bolshevik regime to suppress its political opponents by any available means (see Letter 105). *Pravda* condemned Gorky's attack in a number of strongly worded articles. Even as late as December that same year (1922), the newspaper was prepared to publish a scurrilous poem by Demian Bedny, who declared the writer to be an old man sick beyond all hope of recovery. It would certainly appear that he was anxious not to antagonize the political leadership again, even when faced with the most striking evidence of further assaults on personal liberty by the Bolsheviks. Thus, even though he was quite outraged to learn, in November 1923, of the publication of *A*

Guide for the Removal of Anti-artistic and Counter-revolutionary Books from Libraries serving the General Reader, a pamphlet which openly recommended a policy of intellectual intolerance hitherto unknown in Soviet Russia (see Letter 111), Gorky chose not to speak out on the subject, despite his initial declaration to Khodasevich that he would renounce his Soviet citizenship in protest.

This latter episode demonstrates once again the extent to which Gorky had learnt the lesson of pragmatism. As we shall see below, he was deeply involved at this time in practical negotiations which would have allowed him to participate—albeit indirectly—in Soviet literary life, and he could ill afford to upset the authorities there at such a critical moment. But this was not the only, nor even necessarily the most important, consideration. As the letters in this section show, Gorky became very quickly disaffected with the Russian *émigré* community. No sooner had he settled in Germany than he came to see how far he stood from the vast majority of his fellow countrymen, whose implacable hatred of the Soviet regime had engendered an extremism no less reprehensible in Gorky's eyes than that of the Bolsheviks themselves. Ironically enough, the very hostility of these groups to the new Russian leadership served only to encourage the writer's pro-Soviet sympathies. This was particularly the case following the death of Lenin in January 1924. Despite his many differences with the Bolshevik leader, Gorky experienced genuine and profound grief when he heard of his death (see Letter 113). And, as the same letter makes abundantly clear, he was appalled by the crude and callous reaction to this news in the *émigré* press. It was a significant turning-point in his attitude to Soviet Russia.

Gorky's hostility towards the Russian community in Europe was gradually matched by his dissatisfaction with Europe itself. Despite the passion with which he had espoused the European idea in 'The Two Souls of the Russian People' and the *Untimely Thoughts* articles, Gorky soon found the actual experience of living in Europe less than satisfying. Although his first letter to his wife from Berlin does contain a characteristically positive opinion of Finland ('What those calm, stubborn Finns manage to accomplish!'—Letter 103), the writer is soon recording his disillusionment, first with Germany, then with Czechoslovakia and Italy. He was dismayed above all by the pervasiveness of the bourgeois attitudes he encountered in these countries, attitudes which indicated how naïve had been the hopes of a pan-European revolution at the end of the Great War. This antagonism to post-war Europe was reflected in a new style of thinking. Instead of the opposition of 'Europe' and 'Asia' which had so dominated his journalism between 1915 and 1921, Gorky—like so many left-wing intellectuals of the day—now begins to subscribe to an ideology which sets a tired and decadent Europe against the youthful energy of Bolshevik Russia (Letters 112, 116, 120). Most significant of all in this respect is his letter to Nikolai Bukharin of June 1925, in which he explains his gradual *rapprochement* with the Soviet government in precisely such terms (Letter 119).

Gorky's sense of kinship with the new Russia was further reinforced by political considerations. The period of his residence in Sorrento coincided with the rise of Italian Fascism. Although he refers to Mussolini in understandably scornful terms in a letter of January 1925 (Letter 115), the writer was obliged to observe the relentless progress of the Fascist movement as it consolidated its power. Under Mussolini's regime, relations between Italy and the USSR steadily worsened, with inevitable consequences for Gorky, who was of course a Soviet citizen. The police stepped up their surveillance of the writer and his entourage, as a result of which Moura Budberg was subjected to the indignity of having her room searched in September 1925.[1] Gorky was also alert to the growing isolation of the Soviet Union in the larger community of nations during the 1920s. He was particularly incensed when he heard the news in 1927 that England had broken off diplomatic relations with Russia (Letter 138).

If the rise of Fascism and the gradual turn against the USSR by many European governments help to explain why Gorky eventually bowed to the pressure being exerted upon him to return to his native land, there is plenty of evidence that he was well aware of the tyranny, both actual and potential, within the Soviet system. Although he was to write enthusiastically about the 'heroism' of socialist construction (Letter 141), he was obviously disturbed by the darker side of life in the new Russia. He certainly wanted to have nothing to do with the militant extremism of the proletarian movement (known by its Russian acronym RAPP) (Letter 131); and he was extremely concerned when he learned that Voronsky had been removed from his post as editor-in-chief of the prestigious monthly *Krasnaia nov'* [*Red Virgin Soil*]—one of the more ominous manifestations of the new political climate (Letter 136). It may be suggested, therefore, that Gorky's first return trip to Russia was the product of both utopianism and pragmatism. Moved by the desire to see the socialist dream realized and decadent Europe confounded, Gorky also hoped to use his influence to tame the excesses of totalitarianism in Russia, much as he had striven to do in the immediate post-revolutionary years.

Although it would appear that Gorky experienced a change of heart towards Soviet Russia as early as 1925, he made the first of his return trips there only in 1928. The delay can be attributed to two factors. As Gorky himself regularly pointed out in his letters to the sizeable number of correspondents who asked him—often quite bluntly—to explain his continued absence from socialist Russia, he had begun work on a major

---

[1] L. P. Bykovtseva, *Gor'kii v Italii* (Moscow, 1975): 290.

literary project which he knew he would be unable to complete if he were to return home. (He was right, in fact: the work in question, *The Life of Klim Samgin*, remained unfinished at the time of his death.) But this was really only part of the reason, if indeed it was not merely a convenient excuse. More importantly, Gorky was deterred from returning to the Soviet Union because of the failure of a publishing enterprise to which he had dedicated himself with his customary energy during the early part of his sojourn in Europe.

Shortly after his arrival in Germany, Gorky had set about the task of organizing a new journal. It was called *Beseda* [*Dialogue*]. The original idea had come from the Formalist critic and writer, Viktor Shklovsky, who had suggested the great potential value of a publication which would accept contributions from Russian writers both inside and outside the USSR, hence facilitating a 'dialogue' between the two communities. As well as publishing literary works, *Beseda* was to carry items on developments in world literature and science. The journal was set up under the editorship of Gorky and the poet Vladislav Khodasevich.[2] For Gorky, in particular, this was a labour of love. He saw the journal as a means of securing an outlet for the works of talented young writers who were finding it difficult to publish elsewhere. He also seemed sincerely to believe that it might really serve to bridge the ever-widening gulf between the Soviet government and the Russian emigration. Although the editors succeeded in attracting significant contributions from Russians living abroad, it was a much more difficult business getting manuscripts from writers in the USSR. But this was not the worst of it. The key to the whole venture was the promise that the journal would be made available for sale within the Soviet Union. In the end, however, this promise was never honoured. The Soviet authorities placed obstacles of every sort in the way of *Beseda*, which meant that it was denied the income from what would most certainly have been a substantial circulation in the USSR. As a result—and much to Gorky's personal chagrin—the journal came to differ very little from other *émigré* publications of the time. Five issues appeared between the spring of 1923 and June 1924; a further volume, bearing the ominous number 6/7, came out in March the following year, after which publication ceased entirely. Although Gorky was to insist for a time that the journal would resume, and that it would at last be circulated within the USSR (Letter 120), nothing ever came of this.[3] The collapse of *Beseda* led to a break in relations between Gorky and Khodasevich. It also served to remind the older writer—not that such a

---

[2] Khodasevich, together with his companion Nina Berberova, became part of Gorky's extended family at the time. Both later wrote illuminating memoirs of their experiences during these years.

[3] For further details, see Richard Sylvester's preface to Valentina Khodasevich and Olga Margolina-Khodasevich, *Unpublished Letters to Nina Berberova* (Berkeley, 1979): 35–43.

reminder was really necessary—that his power to influence developments within Russia was still extremely limited.

If this second European exile was a frustrating time for Gorky the editor, the very opposite was true for Gorky the writer. Despite his continuing poor health, the frequent moves, and the considerable other demands on his time, he managed to create, within three years of his departure from Russia, a magnificent body of new writing. For the most part, these were autobiographical works—*My Universities*, the sequel to *Childhood* and *Among People*; a series of pieces originally intended for inclusion in what would have been the fourth volume of an autobiographical tetralogy; and the remarkable sketches collected as *Fragments from My Diary. Reminiscences* [*Zametki iz dnevnika. Vospominaniia*]. He also returned to fiction, writing a number of short stories which appeared under the rather modest title *Stories of 1922–1924* [*Rasskazy 1922–1924 gg*] and again demonstrated new heights of mastery. It was a spectacular renaissance, somewhat grudgingly acknowledged in Russia itself and largely ignored by the emigration, many of whose members had never forgiven the writer for his collaboration with the Bolsheviks after the Revolution. Gorky also began writing novels again, writing *The Artamonov Business*, an absorbing account of life among the Russian merchants, between 1924 and 1925. Such was his creative energy that he immediately embarked on his most ambitious literary project of all—*The Life of Klim Samgin*, a massive epic of Russian life from the latter part of the nineteenth century to 1917. The work was to push both his writing skills and his powers of endurance to the limit. His letter to Stefan Zweig puts it well: 'I have become passionately absorbed in this painstaking and difficult work' (Letter 117). So as to ensure its historical authenticity, Gorky undertook a prodigious amount of reading. In the end, he completed two large volumes between 1925 and February 1928. But, as he himself had predicted, the work began to founder once he began his 'slow return' to the Soviet Union. It was never completed and, despite the efforts of Soviet scholars to proclaim it a masterpiece, it has failed to gain wide critical approval.

Gorky's personal life during this period conformed by and large to the pattern established during the first, especially after he had settled in Sorrento. Once again, he lived amongst an extended family and received a constant stream of Russian visitors. There were, nevertheless, certain important changes. Most interesting, perhaps, is that for the first time since separating from Ekaterina Peshkova, Gorky had his son come to live with him. Maksim had evidently been a considerable worry for both his parents during his adolescence, although the letters which passed between them supply little real information about the nature of their concern. During the 1920s, however, their correspondence became far more explicit. Thus, Letter 103, even though it is couched in a jocular tone, speaks directly of their anxiety for his health, even alluding to his problems with alcohol. (In fact, Gorky himself appears to have been a fairly heavy drinker.) Throughout the following years, the writer's letters reveal his fears for a young man whom he believes to be immensely talented, yet essentially feckless (see, in particular, Letter 130). Despite his hopes that Maksim would settle down after his marriage to Nadezhda Vvedenskaia, he was to be constantly disappointed in his son, whether it be for his careless attitude towards Nadezhda during her first pregnancy (Letter 118) or his frivolous obsession with motor cars (Letter 130). By 1928, Max had reached the age of thirty, yet he still had no real profession. He had some talent as an illustrator and caricaturist (which Gorky was prone to exaggerate), but he lacked the discipline to dedicate himself to this, or any other, task. Most of his time seems to have been spent in idleness, although he did turn his hand to secretarial chores for his father from time to time.

There was, however, a more sinister side to all this. During the Civil War period, Maksim had worked closely with the Bolsheviks, coming into contact with a number of prominent figures in the Cheka, as the Soviet security police agency was first known. One such individual was Petr Kriuchkov. He was apparently a police agent from the start, although he first became acquainted with Gorky through his work for the publishing firm Kniga, which had an office in Berlin. Kriuchkov began dealing with Gorky as early as 1922 (Letter 108). Over the following years, he gradually made his way into the inner circle, gaining the writer's confidence and finally becoming his personal secretary. Through his person, the dark net of Stalin was already beginning to close around Gorky, although no one suspected it as yet, just as no one could have imagined the tragic fate which lay ahead for Maksim.[4]

His concerns about Maksim notwithstanding, Gorky's personal life was probably never happier than during these years. This was due in no small part to the arrival in the world of two new Peshkovs—the writer's grandchildren, Marfa (b. 1925) and Dasha (b. 1927). There is no mistaking the natural delight he takes when relating their latest antics in his letters to his wife. There are other signs that his life was more relaxed than before. It is interesting to note, for example, that he writes quite openly and regularly to Peshkova about the activities of his companion, Moura Budberg (see Letters 108, 115, etc.)—a marked contrast indeed to his earlier reticence about Mariia Andreeva. One senses also something of the warm spirit of intimacy which prevailed in the household at the time in the pet-names which crop up in letter after letter—'Nightingale' (the artist

---

[4] The story of Gorky's family sheds fascinating light on the almost incestuous personal ties involved in the history of the secret police in early Soviet Russia. Peshkova was a close friend of Feliks Dzerzhinsky, the first head of the Cheka (see Letter 115, n. 5) and Kriuchkov knew Mariia Andreeva well.

Rakitsky); 'Timofei' or 'Timosha' (Maksim's wife, Nadezhda); 'Titka' (Moura Budberg); 'the merchant's wife' (Valentina Khodasevich, an artist and niece of the poet Vladislav); and 'Didi' (Valentina's husband, Dideriks). Gorky himself was known within the family as 'the Duke'.

If Gorky had always been intensely interested in the direction of Russian literature, that interest was never more obvious than during these years. His natural curiosity about developments in post-revolutionary literature soon became bound up in an almost Messianic fervour as he came to identify Russian culture not only with the task of building socialism in his native land but also with that of revivifying an intellectually moribund Europe. Gorky remained, as always, an avid reader of all the current literature. He followed all the main journals (and many of the minor ones too), eagerly on the look-out for signs of the new talent which would confirm his hopes for the future of the fledgling Soviet literature. He also continued to receive a large number of manuscripts from aspiring authors, on which he commented with unaffected candour (see Letter 134). Gorky's attitude to the rising generation was by now a paternalistic mixture of praise and censure. Typical in this respect are his letters to the self-styled 'Serapion Brothers, a group of highly talented young writers who rapidly rose to prominence in the early 1920s. Gorky had met several of the Serapions before leaving Russia, contributing in no small way to their material support at that difficult time. The group strove to maintain a neutral position with regard to politics: Trotsky dubbed them 'Fellow-Travellers', by which he meant that they consciously strove neither to promote the socialist cause nor to oppose it. They were also quite different from one another in terms of style and subject-matter. To take three of the most famous writers associated with the group, Vsevolod Ivanov wrote realistic tales of the Revolution and Civil War, Veniamin Kaverin displayed a penchant for the grotesque and the fantastic, whilst Mikhail Zoshchenko was a master of satire. In Konstantin Fedin and Leonid Leonov the Serapions also produced figures who were later to become stalwarts of the Soviet novel.

Gorky was impressed by the unmistakable talent of the Serapions and he also felt considerable sympathy for their defence of politically neutral writing in the conditions of early Soviet Russia. His letter to Slonimsky (a minor writer who failed to fulfil his early promise) is characteristically friendly in tone (Letter 116). Writing to Fedin (Letter 106) he offers brief and mainly positive comments on other members of the group, but those are preceded by stinging criticism of Boris Pilniak, author of the experimental novel *Naked Year* [*Golyi god*] and one of the most influential writers in Russia at the time. Pilniak was, in fact, a real *bête noire* for Gorky. As usual he did not shrink from making his views known to the writer himself. Thus he wrote to Pilniak of his tale *The Blizzard* [*Metelitsa*], describing it as 'an absolutely dead thing, despite all its verbal ostentation and other tricks of every kind' (Letter 107). He was no less critical of Evgenii Zamiatin, whose influence was every bit as great as Pilniak's and who also sought to promote experimentalism in the arts. Thus, he dismissed Zamiatin's 'Story of the Most Important Thing' ['Rasskaz o samom glavnom']—one of that writer's most self-consciously 'experimental' pieces—as a work which was 'no longer art, but just an attempt to illustrate a philosophical theory' (Letter 116). The same letter contains an equally damning reference to the work of the Russian Formalist critics, which was another significant manifestation of the Modernist sensibility in early Soviet Russia.

In short, then, even though Gorky's own writing of the early 1920s was hardly conventional by nineteenth-century standards—witness *Fragments from My Diary* and *Stories of 1922–1924*, for example—he nevertheless wanted no part of any literature which depended on formal or stylistic play for its effect. He sometimes justified this position by appealing to the difficulty that such works presented to foreign translators (see Letters 121 and 123), yet it would appear that this was in the end simply a case of deep-seated conservatism on his part. What was going on here, of course, was nothing less than a battle both for the Serapions and for the very future of Russian literature. But the full implications of all this were to become clear only towards the very end of the decade. In the mean time, Gorky had already returned in his own writing practice to realist fiction of the more traditional kind (*The Artamonov Business*, *The Life of Klim Samgin*) and, as he did so, his attitude towards other styles of writing began to harden. The 'father of Socialist Realism' was very much in the making.

Despite these signs of growing intolerance on his part, Gorky showed that he remained capable of acknowledging real talent during these years. He can still admire the brilliance of Andrei Bely, even if he doesn't really approve of the 'ornamental' prose for which that writer was famous (Letters 106 and 107). His reaction to the work of Boris Pasternak is similarly revealing. He praised the narrative poem *1905* for its relative clarity of image and idea—something which he had not found in Pasternak's earlier poetry—and he also held the prose piece 'The Childhood of Liuvers' ['Detstvo Liuvers'] in high regard (Letter 140). More instructive still is his attitude towards Fedor Gladkov, the author of the novel *Cement*, one of the most overtly 'Soviet' novels of the 1920s and long cherished by critics as a model of Socialist Realism in literature. Gorky himself praised the novel as a 'first attempt among us Russians to poeticize creative labour' (Letter 126). His admiration for Gladkov was, however, qualified in two important ways. In a very interesting letter of November 1926, he expressed real concern at his younger colleague's poverty of imagination and his reliance on a poetics of 'verisimilitude' (Letter 131). Even more important for the light it sheds on Gorky's political position at the time is his refusal in the same letter to endorse the militant 'proletarianism' espoused by Gladkov at this time: 'You ask if I am "completely" with you. I cannot be "completely" with people who convert class psychology into a caste psychology.'

But which writers of this period does Gorky really admire? Oddly enough, they are for the most part authors who have long since fallen from view, even among experts on Russian literature. They include Viacheslav Shishkov, who is best known for his writings about Siberian life (Letter 122), and Olga Forsh, with whom Gorky (perhaps surprisingly) shares an interest in the semi-mystical philosophy of Nikolai Fedorov (Letter 129). But the three names which feature most regularly in these letters are Aleksei Chapygin, Sergei Sergeev-Tsensky, and Mikhail Prishvin. (Prishvin alone is still widely read today.) Gorky names this triumvirate as the great hope for Soviet literature in a letter to Prishvin himself (Letter 128). It would appear that his admiration for these writers was based on a number of factors. To Chapygin and Sergeev-Tsensky (and Forsh too) he was attracted because of their willingness to tackle historical themes on the largest scale. Prishvin (and Shishkov), on the other hand, dealt in minute detail with the *realia* of Russian life outside the main urban centres. But most significant of all, perhaps, was his explanation to Prishvin—the writer for whom Gorky reserves some of his most confessional moments—that he looked upon him as 'the affirmation of a geo-optimism [. . .] which humanity will have to adopt as its religion sooner or later' (Letter 128). (Once again, Gorky the God-builder has put in a return appearance.) It is also interesting to remark that not one of the writers named above was noted at the time for works dealing with post-revolutionary Russia. In his literary preferences—as in his own writing—Gorky was tending increasingly to look to the past, rather than the present. This is a somewhat curious attitude for a man who was soon to stand at the head of the Stalinist literary establishment.

Despite the unfeigned delight with which he writes of Prishvin, Chapygin, Sergeev-Tsensky, and their like, Gorky was by no means blind to the insufficiencies of the new Russian literature. The letters in this section contain all manner of hints and even direct statements which point to his serious doubts about the shape of contemporary literary life. Not only was he disturbed by the rise of an extremist group like RAPP, he was also depressed by the poor quality of much that he read. Thus, he was prepared openly to admit to Shishkov: 'I will not conceal my concern over the monotony of the subject-matter of stories and their overall tone, which is rather depressingly grey' (Letter 122). And to Prishvin he confessed in similar vein: 'I read a lot, all the "current literature"—but, alas, the current is flowing in the wrong direction' (Letter 135).

But if it is difficult to know which is the 'real' Gorky speaking—the enthusiast who looks upon Prishvin and the others as those who will deliver Russian culture into the new age, or the sceptic who regards with dismay the dull uniformity of so much post-revolutionary writing—there are certain themes here which will already be familiar enough. One such motif is his antagonism to the 'passive' tradition of the old Russia, which—as in earlier days—he associates with the writings of Tolstoy and Dostoevsky (see Letter 124). His preference for the 'enlightened' culture of the modern city over the darkness of the Russian countryside is another (see Letter 126). But, in the end, it is Gorky's fundamental ambivalence about the new Russia which is most striking here. 'The world is becoming better—witness the fact that ever more young eagles like your husband are being born': this is from a letter of May 1926, to A. N. Furmanova, the widow of the writer Dmitrii Furmanov (Letter 127). 'Good people disappear so quickly, and you don't see their equal again': this is Gorky again, writing to his wife the same December on the death of his old friend, Leonid Krasin (Letter 132). Although this contradiction may be explained in part by the writer's relationship to the correspondent—he had never met Furmanova, whilst Peshkova was his most intimate friend—this is only part of the story. One thing is certain: by the latter part of the 1920s the problem of understanding Gorky's innately contradictory nature is further complicated by the need to distinguish between his 'public' and 'private' selves. This will prove an even greater difficulty in the years to come, especially after the writer returned to stay in Stalin's Russia.

103. To E. P. Peshkova, [8 November 1921]

Most respected mother!

After many adventures on land and on sea, I have arrived in the little German town of Berlin, a town heavily populated with various representatives of the Russian people. And at the railway station I saw a being of the greatest interest to you—your very own son. We greeted each other with mutual respect and joy, and then we left by car to drink various alcoholic fluids on a street which is called Friedrichsdamenstrasse, which in Russian means the street of Friedrich's ladies.

In refutation of the completely accurate information which you have received from honourable people who claim authoritative knowledge about all manner of intimate details concerning the lives of those close to them, I can attest that M. A. Peshkov is quite modest—even more than modest—in his consumption of spiritous liquor. Those who live under the same roof as Maksim—and who are also people of the most sober habits—have confirmed this observation of mine under oath. Surmising that the young man was not in a proper state of health and hence lacked a capacity for spirits, I undertook a careful investigation of the state of his body and soul.

It turns out that he is completely fit in body, although his external appearance is gaunt. The professor who examined him expressed himself *literally* as follows: 'Your organism enjoys virginal health.' His mental attitude is in need of some repair, and I'll get to work on that straight away, probably even tomorrow.

The constant rushing back and forth between Berlin and Rome under the stressful circumstances of his work as diplomatic courier has strained his nerves, leaving him very tired.[1] Then again, the 'new economic policy'[2] and V. I. Lenin's speeches have made him confused and bewildered, as they have many others, causing the young man to ask a number of serious questions. I'll take him to a good doctor and ask where I should send the fellow for a vacation. We'll probably choose a sanatorium in the Black Forest and go there for a month or two. Once he's had a vacation, he'll take up some sort of study, but I imagine that he will do some painting, for which he has an indisputable and original talent. Ivan Nikolaevich[3] confirms that there is also a real possibility of Maksim becoming a distinctive and interesting illustrator and cartoonist.

He and Nadia appear to have a very good and amicable relationship; they are living in a decent boarding house where they have two rooms.[4] Rakitsky has a third room; he's on excellent terms with Maksim and Nadia. So in this respect things are going better than I had expected. Although he hasn't lost his good spirits and sense of humour, Maksim has somehow become more serious and attentive to life and to people. Overall, he's a very nice and very interesting person, as all those who know him say. When I reproached him for not writing to you, he produced totally convincing proof to the contrary. Letters make their way to Russia with great reluctance; M[ariia] I[gnatievna] B[udberg]⁵ wrote me seventeen letters, of which I received only six. A dismal proportion.

So don't worry about our son. In the most disturbing area there have been no changes for the worse, despite his nervous exhaustion. The specialist who examined M[aksim] was quite surprised by the general state of his organism and was even mistrustful of this fact, as though he suspected a mistake in the diagnosis.

To write about myself is very tedious. Of course, our friends the journalists like to gnaw and bite; they hunt me down in every possible way. They lie in wait on streets and on stairways, they click their Kodak cameras and humbly ask me to share my senile wisdom with them. This all began in Helsingfors, continued in Stockholm, and it's still going on here. It's agonizing and silly. Apart from the journalists, there are also the spies, Finnish, Swedish, and German, *but it is the Russian ones—both of the right and the left—who are the most numerous and impudent.* Boris Morkovin—do you remember him from Nizhnii (he was known as the Suitcase)?—well, he got a bullet in the back from the rightists for publishing *Smena vekh* [*Changing Landmarks*]; so now he's walking around with the bullet inside him.⁶

It was with envy and sadness that I read in the reputable press of our emigrants that 'M. Gorky has sold his valuables: antique silver, miniatures etc'.

The foreign press is most benevolent towards M. Gorky, but the ministers of foreign affairs are especially interested in this 'adventurer', to use A. I. Kuprin's *bon mot.*⁷ The Finnish minister displayed a delicate politeness, the Swedish one was courteously refined, whilst the German—three days before my arrival in Berlin—sent me flowers and then phoned to ask them to trim the roots and not to forget to change the water, lest my flowers should lose their freshness before I arrived.⁸ That's the way to do things! Grandmother⁹ would enjoy widespread popularity here in Germany with her phenomenal thriftiness, don't you think?

I'll stay here for a week or two, then I'll go to Bad Nauheim or some other place to get treatment. My heart is so-so, yet when our ship was tossed about dreadfully in the Gulf of Bothnia, only three of us could stand the hellish rocking without getting sick: the Swedish General Lind, one of the stewardesses, and yours truly, poor sinner that I am. Which must mean that my heart is not as bad as all that.

Well, I've written enough! Now, then: give my sincerest regards to my dear friend Aleksin and tell him that I was terribly touched by his concern for me during my illness, and that there is no one I love and respect as much as him, the Vologda devil—I know this well! And sincere regards to his wife, Liudmila, and to the Nikolaev brothers as well.[10] Etc.

None the less, my dear, this Europe is a force to be reckoned with! It begins in Finland, which is an amazing country: the more you see of it, the more you come to like and respect it. What those calm, stubborn Finns manage to accomplish! They have undertaken to construct a city of 150,000 people under the Saarinen project, and they've already begun building it. And what a city—it's simply a marvel! Sweden is also working with all its might and, as for the Germans, there is nothing one can say.

Well, goodbye for now! You should come over here. It's time you were a grandmother, time you stopped not being worth good Soviet salt. Yes, indeed. Regards.

A.

SOURCE: *AG* 9: 213–15.

[1] Maksim had been attached to the Russian embassy staff in Italy, a position he gained through the assistance of Lenin.

[2] The New Economic Policy (NEP) represented a sharp turn away from the extremism of 'War Communism' and a partial return to private enterprise, hence the 'confusion' felt by some of the Revolution's supporters.

[3] Ivan Rakitsky ('Nightingale'), artist and close friend of the family, a permanent member of Gorky's entourage in the European years.

[4] Maksim married Nadezhda Vvedenskaia in 1921.

[5] Budberg (*née* Zakrevskaia, 1892–1974) was personal secretary to Gorky until his return to Russia in 1932.

[6] The title *Changing Landmarks* harks back to the famous *Landmarks* [*Vekhi*] volume of 1909. The newer work, published in 1921, contained essays by six Russians living abroad who urged their fellow *émigrés* to rethink their opposition to the Soviet Union.

[7] Kuprin had recently published a vitriolic critique of Gorky. Gorky presumably quotes from that article.

[8] 'Upon investigation he turned out to be not quite a minister, but a bit below that. I'm chagrined.' [Gorky's note.]

[9] i.e. Peshkova's mother.

[10] Mikhail Konstantinovich Nikolaev (1882–1947), head of Mezhdunarodnaia Kniga, which ran the book trade between Russia and other countries. Fedor Konstantinovich (d. 1932) was Mikhail's brother.

104. To N. I. Bukharin,[1] *[1 June 1922]*

[Berlin]

My dear Nikolai Ivanovich!

Thank you for your fine, comradely letter. Over such letters one does not become angry, one simply wants to shake the writer by the hand.

I am sending you the original article. You are acquainted with it through excerpts which have been distorted by two translations: from Russian into Dutch and from Dutch back into Russian.[2]

I did not appreciate the tactlessness of publishing it while the Genoa business was going on, and I did not think it would be published so quickly either.[3]

However, it did convince some people—such as J. M. Keynes, judging by his letter to me—that the Sov[iet] regime is a regime which has historical justification. I am told that the most decent of the emigrants say that my article has helped reconcile them with the Soviet regime, and indeed that Bolshevism alone is capable of reviving the peasantry.

The question of cruelty is the most agonizing question for me; I am unable to dismiss it. Everywhere I observe meaningless brutality—why, right here in Germany they are hounding Aleksei Tolstoy.[4] They are probably organizing a public scandal for him right now. *Rul'* [*The Rudder*] and *Golos* write about him with savage malice.[5] And the man's only crime is that of being a sincere person and a splendid artist.

My body is falling apart at the seams. I shall soon leave for Heringsdorf, which is by the sea; I'll stay there until the end of July, then I'll go back to Russia.

I am afraid of missing today's airmail, so I close this letter; I'll write again soon.

A sincere hello to V[ladimir] Ilyich, Rykov[6] and Trotsky.

Warmest regards to you, my good man, my marvellous comrade.

I wish you all the best.

A. Peshkov

SOURCE: *Izv TsK* 1989(1): 242–3.

---

[1] Nikolai Ivanovich Bukharin (1888–1938), one of Lenin's closest associates at the time of the 1917 Revolution and a key architect of NEP during the 1920s, was then editor of *Pravda*. He fell from grace during the Stalin period and was executed in the purges.

[2] Presumably, 'On the Russian Peasantry' ['O russkom krest'ianstve'] an article emphasizing the cruelty of the peasants who fought against the Bolsheviks during the Russian Civil War.

[3] An international conference on economic issues, attended by a Soviet delegation, had been held in Genoa from 10 April to 19 May 1922.

[4] Tolstoy emigrated in 1918, living in France and Germany until 1923, when he returned to the Soviet Union. His generally pro-Bolshevik views earned him the enmity of many *émigrés*.

[5] *Rul'* and *Golos Rossii* [*The Voice of Russia*] were strongly anti-Bolshevik *émigré* newspapers.

[6] Aleksei Rykov (1881–1938), a prominent member of the Politburo. During the mid-1920s his influence waned, and in the purges he was tried and executed with Bukharin.

105. To A. I. Rykov, [1 July 1922]

[Berlin]

Aleksei Ivanovich!

If the trial of the Socialist Revolutionaries results in murder, then that murder will be premeditated and vile.[1]

I ask you to inform L. D. Trotsky and the others that this is my opinion. I hope that this will come as no surprise to you, for you know well enough that throughout the entire period of the revolution I pointed out to the Soviet regime a thousand times how senseless and criminal it is to exterminate the intelligentsia in our illiterate and uncultured country.

Now I am convinced that if the SRs are killed, this crime will lead to a moral blockade of Russia on the part of Socialist Europe.

M. Gorky

SOURCE: *Izv Ts K* 1989 (1): 243–4.

---

[1] Nearly three dozen SRs were on trial for counter-revolutionary activity and terrorism. A dozen defendants received the death sentence, which was to be carried out if their party did not cease its armed struggle against the Bolsheviks.

106. To K. A. Fedin,[1] [early September 1922]

[Heringsdorf]

I am most heartened by everything you write—and by the way you write—about yourself and the spiritual bond which unites the Serapions. This friendship of yours is truly an original, valuable, and unprecedented literary phenomenon. Your talents are so diverse and so sharply distinct; you are linked neither by the 'spirit of the era', nor by a common philosophy, nor even in the end by a 'school', but apparently by a powerful feeling of friendship which is all the more profound—as I would like to think and as probably is indeed the case—due to the serious and loving regard for the sacred cause of art which you all share. Don't break that tie: this is the most sensible advice you will receive from anyone who might examine your work attentively and honestly assess its enormous significance. Friendship is a feeling but poorly developed in Russia, and if you can manage to preserve it for a long time, it will be of benefit to you all even as it reveals something unusual to other people. Hold firm!

The question that troubles you personally—how should one write?—is resolved only by time and by a love for the business of writing. Tolstoy? As you know, his 'simplicity' was achieved through strenuous and persistent effort. The plasticity and sculptured quality of his writing are far from 'simple'. 'Simpler' yet is another great martyr of the word—Flaubert.

Yes, Pilniak does write 'ingeniously', but I strongly advise against paying him any attention. All his work comes straight out of Bely, and in part out of Remizov. Of Pilniak as such there is no sign as yet. Having read his 'Blizzard'—an utterly lifeless piece which is full of tricks—I cherish no hope of ever seeing the real Pilniak. Bely is a man of refined culture and broad education. He has his own original theme, a theme which could not, perhaps, have been developed using any other language: it demands precisely that language and those fanciful constructions which are available and appropriate to Bely alone. Remizov is a man who has been totally corrupted by Russian words; he perceives each word as an image, and hence his word-painting is ugly—this is precisely what he does, not painting, but word-painting. He writes psalms and hymns, not stories.

Pilniak—how strange it is to speak of him in this company—Pilniak is as yet a mere imitator, and not a very skilful one at that. He imitates rather crudely, since he is not very cultured and fails to comprehend the full profundity and complexity of his models. He tends to fabricate rather than feel. Bely does at least feel something, something which is difficult to express even with all the luxuriousness of his words and the serpentine suppleness of his language. No, stay away from Pilniak; you are no less a writer than he—believe me!

But don't go thinking that I am recommending either Bely or Remizov to you as a teacher—far from it! Yes, they have an amazingly rich lexicon, and they are of course worthy of attention, as is a third writer who possesses the treasure of a pure Russian language—N. S. Leskov. But you should try to find yourself. That is interesting too, and important, even the most significant thing for you, perhaps.

'Writing is very difficult.' There's an excellent, wise maxim for you. Do not deviate from it, and everything will go well. That maxim is the one true path towards perfection. And allow me to give you all a blunt but kind piece of advice: do not defer too much to your literary 'fathers' and 'elders'. It is better that you make your own mistakes rather than repeat the mistakes of others, even though such mistakes are always instructive. The history of mankind is the history of its multiform mistakes, and it would be best for us all if they remained unrepeated on the pages of literary history. But in life itself you can make other mistakes, mistakes which are more fun and less stupid and bloody.

On the subject of Zilber.[2] He is a miracle-worker who will go far, you'll see; his fantasy writing is already more interesting and subtle than Gogol's imitations of Hoffmann.

I am looking forward to Zoshchenko's book with anxious impatience.

I received your two works: 'The Garden' ['Sad'] and *Bakunin;*[3] my sincere thanks for the kind and flattering inscriptions.

I have received no letters from you other than the one I am replying to. Life abroad is lousy, as it is slowly but steadily decaying; but by the same token it is very good, because over here one gets to think about the 'big' questions. For everything is naked here, everything is bared so shamelessly and pathetically. I wish you well, and send my sincere regards to everyone.

A. Peshkov

SOURCE: *LN* 70: 469–70.

[1] Konstantin Aleksandrovich Fedin (1892–1977) had first met Gorky in 1920. One of the Serapion Brothers, he later wrote a popular memoir of Gorky. Other prominent members of this group were Vsevolod Ivanov, Lev Natanovich Lunts (1901–24), Mikhail Mikhailovich Zoshchenko (1895–1958), Veniamin Aleksandrovich Kaverin (real name Zilber, 1902–89), Mikhail Leonidovich Slonimsky (1897–1972), and Nikolai Nikolaevich Nikitin (1895–1963).

[2] i.e. Kaverin.

[3] Zoshchenko had two collections of stories in press. The first of the two works by Fedin is a short story; the second, *Bakunin in Dresden* [*Bakunin v Dreszdene*], a play which carried a dedication to Gorky.

107. To B. A. Pilniak, [10 September 1922]

[Heringsdorf]

I have no reason to be angry with you, B[oris] A[ndreevich], but I am very annoyed to see that you write more and more poorly, sloppily and coldly.[1] *The Blizzard* is an absolutely dead thing, despite all its verbal ostentation and other tricks of every kind. I shall say nothing about 'creativity', for even your craftsmanship is sinking gradually and steadily into mere 'craftiness', and that is very bad!

Bely is clearly an embarrassment to you. Quite recently a certain philologist demonstrated to me that you—in a manner which is perhaps unwittingly servile—employ his architectonics, his rhythm and his lexicon. I also spoke to you about your dependence on Bely back in Moscow. Bely is a man of subtle and very refined culture who writes on an exceptional theme—in essence his is a philosophizing sensibility. Bely cannot be imitated without accepting him totally, with all his attributes—like a distinct world, like a planet which has its own distinct plant, animal, and spiritual realms. I have no doubt that he is just as alien and incomprehensible to you as he is to me, even though I am always enchanted by the intensity and originality of his creativity.

The path you have taken is a dangerous one, and it could make a clown of you. The form you have so persistently adopted demands scepticism, irony, or at least some humour. Such qualities are not evident in your works.

Believe me, I am not trying to instruct you, but I am writing out of respect and love for your unquestionable talent, and I fear that you will either drown that talent in a murky foppery of words or shatter it with tricks.

It is still too early for you to look upon yourself as a mature writer, far too early! A certain degree of doubt in your powers, a certain lack of self-confidence would be extremely helpful to you.

You're receiving praise, you say? That means nothing. Look, I have received both praise and abuse for thirty years now, but every time I sit down to work I look upon myself as a beginning writer, and to this day I have not managed to write a single thing that has completely satisfied me. I mention this because I consider such an attitude to be more proper than any other.

Just recently a Siberian writer said to me: 'I don't give a damn about the near future or the distant future for that matter, but I want to do the very best that's possible for man right now.' That too is right and proper.

Keep well, and rest assured that what's written here does not contain anything insulting or even uncomplimentary about you.

Regards,

A. Peshkov

Excuse me for not writing myself, but I have a sore hand.[2]

A.P.

SOURCE: *LN* 70: 311–12.

---

[1] Gorky is responding to a letter of 18 August, in which Pilniak had written: 'You must be angry with me for something.'
[2] Gorky dictated this letter to Maksim.

108. To E. P. Peshkova, [15 November 1922]

[Saarow]

Everything is all right, mother!

Timofei has proved to have a real talent for painting;[1] she has surrounded herself with paints and bought herself a smock which looks like a nurse's, and is succeeding in daubing some still-lifes.

Inspired by her success, the 'Soviet Prince'[2] has also begun to draw more skilfully and amusingly. M[ariia] I[gnatievna] [Budberg] encourages him greatly in this, and it seems that things will go well. He could turn into a most original illustrator, and I intend to offer him paid work before too long.

There is nothing wrong with his health; his nerves are better. He recently saw a neuropathologist, who examined him thoroughly and found nothing except a slight neurasthenia, and had him stay for dinner. Given the high cost of living here, this has to be seen as something of a heroic act on the part of the German, but it can also be explained by the personal charm of our son. He can be charming when he wants to.

I'm sending you five 'Aera';[3] give one to Aleksin. I enclose a power-of-attorney to receive money from *Krasnaia nov'*.

The English lessons have come to a temporary halt since the teacher is busy translating my book into English;[4] this is very urgent work and M[ariia] I[gnatievna] spends all day at her desk. She and Mak[sim] get on very well together. She is also a very good influence on Timosha. The girl is growing visibly, she is becoming more intelligent, and indeed promises to be an interesting artist. I'm working a lot too.

Thanks for the cigarette-holder and cigarette-case.

The weather has been magnificent. There has still been no snow. It's sunny.

Regards to Aleksin and to all yours.

By the way: are there some folders with my letters somewhere at grandmother's?[5] There ought to be letters from Korolenko, Rozanov, and Andreev. Could you have a look? I'd be most grateful. You can send them over with Kriuchkov.[6]

Be well and grow up big and strong. All my people have gone off to Berlin, and I'm sitting here all alone, if you don't count Nightingale.[7]

All the best!

A.

Of course, everyone sends their regards, and when our son gets back, I'll make him write.

Our honourable son has unexpectedly set off for Russia. You should not detain him there. And since he looks upon me as a lost sheep, tell him that he should not talk too much about me while he is there.

SOURCE: *AG* 9: 221–2.

[1] Timofei and Timosha are variants of the family nickname for Maksim's wife, Nadezhda.
[2] i.e. Maksim.
[3] Bronze Roman coins.
[4] *The Old Man* [*Starik*], published in 1924 in New York.
[5] Ekaterina Peshkova was living with her mother in a Moscow apartment, where she had many of Gorky's letters. She brought them to him the following year.
[6] Petr Petrovich Kriuchkov (1889–1938) liaised between the Soviet government and the Kniga publishing firm in Berlin. He subsequently became personal secretary to Gorky.
[7] See Letter 103, n. 3.

109. To R. Rolland, [27 July 1923]

[Freiburg]

My dear Romain Rolland,

I have just finished reading Zweig's marvellous book devoted to your heroic life,[1] and I shall start on *Annette and Silvio*[2] tomorrow, so I thought I would drop you a line again just to remind you of me and give me the opportunity to shake your hand, the hand of a determined and indefatigable fighter for humanity.

I do not dare write very much because I am disturbed by your long silence, which leads me to gloomy thoughts. I have the impression that your amicable feelings for me have changed. I have many enemies who will stop at nothing, just so long as they can turn my friends against me. Even though this is a matter of profound indifference to me, it distresses me when it happens with people like you.

Life has made me excessively sensitive, as you can see.

I will be most obliged if you reply to this letter.[3]

Friendly regards,

M. Gorky

P.S. My address is: Hotel Kyburg, Güntherstahl, Freiburg im Breisgau. I shall be staying here for some time.

SOURCE: *SS* 29: 413–14.

[1] Stefan Zweig (1881–1942), Austrian prose writer, dramatist, biographer, and translator. His book *Romain Rolland: His Life and Work*, appeared in Russian translation in 1923.
[2] The first volume of Rolland's *The Enchanted Soul*.
[3] In his reply of 3 August, Rolland assured Gorky of his continuing friendship.

110. To V. F. Khodasevich,[1] [28 August 1923]

[Günterstahl]

I am still living in the same place, Kyburg; the address is on the envelope. I've told you already that in order to find accommodation here you have to be capable of performing deeds which neither my taste nor the state of my health permit me to perform. I cannot marry a German woman and one who is a doctor of philosophy to boot; I don't like German philosophy etc. Besides, last night my temperature was 38° and my head is aching. And Stepun was sitting here, justifiably accusing Shklovsky of using history only as material for constructing an interesting personal biography, and stating that this is nihilism.[2] And so it is. Or perhaps it isn't? My head is aching, and since my head is close to my soul, that is aching too.

Allow me, dear friend, to ask you to read the enclosed manuscript; if you find it sufficiently interesting, please have it typeset for the third issue.

Not a word from [Sergeev-]Tsensky. And in general I have had no mail from Russia for a long time, perhaps a month or so. This is new, although hardly original. I have here an enquiry by telegraph: have you received the article on Dostoevsky and Fedorov?[3] I haven't received it either. Life is most dreary.

My body is falling apart at the seams: my lungs rattle, my bowels are upset, and my liver is emulating them. A real orchestra! Braun doesn't write.[4] The Americans are closing in on all sides. So are the Chinese. In my opinion, the Chinese are a useless nation; they do nothing but occupy apartments everywhere. At least the American has the dollar! He shows you a coin and makes an honest offer: 'Write what you think about something nobody knows anything about, and I'll give you a dollar!' As for your Chinaman, what can you say? All he has is the permanent revolution and a passion for tennis, nothing more.

As far as Stepun is concerned, he belongs to that 'glorious mob' of true Muscovite Russian intellectuals, those righteous people of the Russian land whom nobody has any need for these days, other than to delight in their form, colour, and the scent of their souls, as if they were flowers. But people don't need flowers these days, they need boots, and if you will permit the 'witticism', that's why there are so many cobblers in literature today. But Stepun is intelligent. He even seems to be a good man.

M. M. Prishvin's piece in *Krasnaia nov'* is extremely good, you know. And I even liked the Sokolov-Mikitov.[5] Verily I say, this is real literature, of the Remizov school, 'languagey' and very Russian—'brains askew' and all that. Very good!

Regards,

A. Peshkov

The temperature is 37° and the date probably the 28th. There is no calendar here and the newspapers aren't getting through.

SOURCE: *N Zh* 30: 192–3.

[1] On Khodasevich (1886–1939), see the Introduction to this section.

[2] Fedor Avgustovich Stepun (1884–1965), philosopher who also wrote fiction and criticism. Exiled in 1922, he then taught in German universities. Viktor Borisovich Shklovsky (1893–1984), critic, novelist, essayist and leading figure in the Russian Formalist movement (see Letter 116, n. 1). Stepun may have been referring to Shklovsky's novel *Zoo, or Letters not about Love* [*Zoo, ili pis'ma ne o liubvi*].

[3] Nikolai Fedorovich Fedorov (1828–1903), highly influential philosopher. The major part of his work was collected and published only after his death, as *The Philosophy of the Common Cause* [*Filosofiia obshchego dela*] vol. 1 (Verny, 1906) and vol. 2 (Moscow, 1913). His vision of a unified and harmonious world was based in part on a belief in the unlimited possibilities of science, which he felt should work towards the physical resurrection of the dead.

[4] Fedor Aleksandrovich Braun (1862–1942), literary critic and Germanist, emigrated after the Revolution.

[5] Ivan Sergeevich Sokolov-Mikitov (1892–1975), writer known for his travel sketches. *Krasnaia nov'*

contained the first three 'links' of what was to become Prishvin's *The Chain of Kashchei* [*Kashcheeva tsep'*], and Sokolov-Mikitov's story 'In the Forest' ['V lesu'].

111. To V. F. Khodasevich, [8 November 1923]

[Günterstahl]

Dear friends,

The question of our move to Prague has been resolved once and for all in the affirmative.

According to absolutely precise information received through the interrogation of Frau Pharoahnen Budberg, today is Wednesday, the eighth day of the eleventh month of the twenty-third year, and in a week's time—that is, evidently on the fifteenth day of the current month—we are setting off *tutta familia* [*sic*] for Berlin complete with books, kittens, dogs, and papers. And with great satisfaction, since, oh, how sick we are of this place!

Any day now I also expect the arrival of the Roman Straumian, who has informed me by telegram that it is possible to obtain Italian visas.[1] At the moment the aforementioned Roman Janus is in Switzerland where he is attending Konradi's trial, and upon the conclusion of that wretched trial he will visit us.[2] For this reason, might I suggest that it would be better for you to wait and see what comes of Straumian's visit? Should the outcome be favourable, we could go together—that is, in one or two sleeping compartments of the same train.

For mind-shattering news I can report that in *Nakanune* [*On the Eve*] one reads: '*La Gioconda*, a painting by Michelangelo', and that in Russia Nadezhda Krupskaia[3] and a certain M. Speransky have forbidden the reading of Plato, Kant, Schopenhauer, Vladimir Soloviev, Taine, Ruskin, Nietzsche, L. Tolstoy, Leskov, Iasinsky (!), and a large number of other similar heretics.[4] And it has been decreed that 'the section on religion should contain only anti-religious books'. All this is apparently[5] not a joke but has been published in a book entitled:

A Guide for the Removal of Anti-artistic and Counter-revolutionary Books from Libraries Serving the General Reader.

I have inserted the word 'apparently', since I still cannot bring myself to believe in this spiritual vampirism, and I will not believe it until I have seen the *Guide*.

My first impression was such that I began to write a declaration to Moscow renouncing my Russian citizenship. What else can I do if this atrocity turns out to be true?

If only you knew, dear V. F., how desperately difficult and distressing this is for me!

We'll see each other soon, and that makes me very happy. Very. Regards, heartfelt regards, to N. N.[6]

A. Peshkov

Best wishes from Frau faroanen[7] and all the others.

SOURCE: *N Zh* 30: 197–8.

[1] An employee of the Soviet embassy in Rome.

[2] Mavrikii Konradi was on trial for the murder of V. Vorovsky, the Soviet representative at the 1923 Lausanne Conference. Konradi had confessed, but the trial ended with his acquittal.

[3] Nadezhda Konstantinovna Krupskaia (1869–1939), wife of Lenin.

[4] Ieronim Iasinsky (1850–1931), a minor Russian writer very much out of place in this list of luminaries.

[5] This word was written in above the line.

[6] Nina Nikolaevna Berberova (1901–93). See the Introduction to this section for further details.

[7] Gorky used the Roman alphabet here.

112. *To M. M. Prishvin, [15 January 1924]*

[Marienbad]

Did you receive my letter, my dear Mikhail Mikhailovich?

It's a long time now since I sent it to you, and I've been waiting so long for the manuscript and proofs of *The Chain of Kashchei* that I have decided to write again.[1] However, I am not writing in an attempt to persuade you to accept the Teutonic working conditions at *Beseda*,[2] conditions which would obviously be disadvantageous for you. I just want to exchange a word or two with you.

We are waiting for them to allow *Beseda* into Russia, which would mean that the publishing house could increase the honoraria three or four times. But it seems that we are waiting for what is not to be.

How are you? And how are people and writers getting on in Russia generally? Judging by your essays, life is interesting but hard.[3] Am I right?

As for myself, I have moved from 'hungry' Germany to 'stuffed' Czechoslovakia, and I find that sated people lead more boring lives than hungry ones do. But do not take this to mean that I would like to see the entire world hungry.

Here I detect none of the spiritual hunger that I have seen everywhere else I have been. 'The People' continue to place their hopes on 'heroes' and miracles, but true heroism is being displayed by men of science and the arts, those Don Quixotes who strive indefatigably to arouse people who are tired and falling asleep from exhaustion and from the fruitlessness of their attempts to make life better. Life is hardest of all for the intelligentsia; these are the dray horses of history and yet, at the same time, its Arabian thoroughbreds. They do not expect miracles, for they realize that the expectation of a miracle is essentially an expression of secret disbelief, and that this expectation contains the glimmer of a hope that it might somehow be possible in some extraordinary way to restore a connection which has already been severed.

Everywhere—in Germany, in France, in England, here, and among the Scandinavians—the intelligentsia is becoming more and more active, and it is understanding its role better and better. And—to our honour—Russian literature is playing a prominent part in this process of regeneration among the Western intelligentsia, as they themselves acknowledge. Russian books are being translated all over the place, as they have never been translated before—in immeasurably greater numbers and with even greater attention than was the case previously.

I don't know what interests you. If you write, I will respond!

If, in spite of the low honorarium—two English pounds a page—you could offer *Beseda* a small essay or story, we would be very grateful. By we, I mean Khodasevich and myself.

I wish you all the best. Do you know where S[ergeev]-Tsensky is? Tell him that Stepun has written an ecstatic review of *Transfiguration* [*Preobrazhenie Rossii*] which will appear in *Sovremennye zapiski* [*Contemporary Notes*].[4]

Regards,

A. Peshkov

SOURCE: *LN* 70: 326–7.

---

[1] An autobiographical novel that appeared in sections between 1923 and 1954.
[2] On *Beseda* see the Introduction to this section.
[3] These essays were eventually collected under the title *From the Land and the Cities* [*Ot zemli i gorodov*].
[4] A leading literary journal for *émigré* writers; Stepun edited its critical section.

---

113. To M. F. Andreeva, [4 February 1924]

[Marienbad]

I received your very fine letter about Lenin.[1] I have written a memoir about him; people have said it's not bad. I'll send it off *to P[etr] P[etrovich] [Kriuchkov]* to be typed up in a day or two; I'm asking them to get it finished as quickly as possible because it has to be published in America, France, and Russia.[2]

I wrote it in a flood of tears. I didn't even grieve so much when Tolstoy died. And even as I write, my hand is trembling. Everyone has been shaken by this premature death, everyone. Ekat[erina] Pavlovna sent two letters describing the emotion in Moscow—apparently it is something unprecedented. Rozhkov and Desnitsky are going to publish a miscellany of memoirs about Ilyich, I received a telegram from them.[3] And letters full of the most intense and sincere grief are arriving from everywhere.

The only thing is that the vile emigration is pouring out its putrid poison against this Man, even though it is a poison incapable of infecting healthy blood. I do not like these scheming *émigrés*—in fact, I despise them—but it is still terrifying when one sees how Russian people have run wild and become brutal and stupid now that they are cut off from their native land. Those degenerates Aldanov and Aikhenvald are especially offensive.[4] It's a pity they're both Jews.

My heart is heavy. The helmsman has left the ship. I know that the rest of the crew are brave people and that Ilyich has trained them well. I know that they will not get lost in a violent storm. But they must not get sucked into the slime, nor must they become fatigued in the calm— that is where the danger lies.

But for all that, Russia is a talented land. It is as extraordinarily talented as it is unfortunate.

Ilyich's departure is Russia's greatest misfortune in a hundred years. Yes, the greatest.

If you see N. N. Krestinsky,[5] pass on my greetings to him.

All the best to you, Mariia, old friend. *Warm regards to P[etr] P[etrovich].*

A. P.

SOURCE: *SS* 29: 420–1.

[1] Lenin died on 21 January 1924.

[2] Gorky's memoir of Lenin was published in *Russkii sovremennik* [*The Russian Contemporary*], no. 1, 1924. A revised version, presenting a more 'canonical' view, appeared in 1931.

[3] Nikolai Aleksandrovich Rozhkov (1868–1927), historian and essayist. The volume was never published.

[4] Mark Aleksandrovich Aldanov (real name Landau, 1886–1957), *émigré* writer and critic, author of historical novels. Iulii Isaevich Aikhenvald (1872–1928), literary critic, exiled from Russia in 1922.

[5] Nikolai Nikolaevich Krestinsky (1883–1938), Russian ambassador to Berlin, later a victim of the Stalin purges.

114. To P. P. Kriuchkov, [5 May 1924]

[Sorrento]

Dear Petr Petrovich,

I received the books—my sincere thanks for your constant concern on behalf of an accursed old man! I sent number four of *Vostok* [*The East*] back to you; I have already received that issue from Russia. Please send me two other books, the titles of which are on the enclosed note.

I am not receiving any newspapers; I've received only the Easter issue of *Dni* [*Days*].[1] The Russian ones arrive punctually.

Would you happen to know where the Baroness Budberg, Mariia, is?[2] It is very strange; there has been no word from her.

We are living quite tolerably here; they treat us with affection and care, and give us food and drink—but they do still take money for it all the same. And I had thought. . .

We have rented a house on a bluff overlooking the sea; if an earthquake should occur, we would be the first to tumble into the water. The house is old but comfortable, with some fourteen rooms—yes! There is of course a room for you; we are expecting you. And what a garden! Palm trees, grapes, and oranges. They've taken about 500 dollars from us for all this until 15 November. A pretty penny! But we have complete isolation and even our own beach! We haven't moved yet. The move won't affect the address; it remains Sorrento, M. Gorki.

Excellent weather has set in; the sea is calm, and the sun and other heavenly bodies are toiling honestly, albeit without pay. I am hardly coughing at all, but I am beginning to suspect that the germs have switched apartments, moving from my lungs to my bowels. Well, never mind that! Germs want to live too. I am feeding myself on fish. Now and then I go for walks and boat trips. But there is an awful amount of work; manuscripts and more manuscripts! I have finished a story, begun another, and will soon submit the material for the new book. It will be a big one.[3]

I know that you have no time to write, but do so anyway: how are you, and when are you thinking of coming here for a vacation?

Keep well! And thanks again!

Pass on the [enclosed] letter to Mariia Fedorovna [Andreeva].

A. Peshkov

SOURCE: *AG* 14: 455–6.

---

[1] Gorky is talking of *émigré* papers (such as *Dni*) here.

[2] She was visiting her two children and a niece, who lived with a governess in Estonia.

[3] Gorky apparently has in mind the stories 'A Sky-Blue Life' ['Golubaia zhizn''] and 'The Dream' ['Son'], and the novel *The Artamonov Business*.

115. To E. P. Peshkova, [17 January 1925]

[Sorrento]

I received your letter today.

The weather here is wonderful; it's hot and everything is fine. Max is well, of course; the day before yesterday he, Timosha, Valentina

Khodasevich, and Dideriks[1] went over to Capri, spent the night there and returned yesterday, after having a good look round. Maksim said that 'it felt like home' to him and he would apparently like to live there; but as he himself points out, there is a horde of Milanese innkeepers who are rapidly turning Capri into a resort, so that the local populace, the fishermen, have been driven to the point of contemplating a move to Calabria. It's true.

You are right: I don't listen to music here because I am tied to my desk. However, I'll finish my work in a few days and go to Naples for a vacation. There's a good opera in San Carlo, and I'll also go to the Symphony once or twice.

Mariia Ignatievna [Budberg] will be back either today or tomorrow evening.

The books which were ordered for Maksim have not yet arrived; nor have the ones for me. He has done some marvellous illustrations for my tale *Mother*.

Everyone is working, a situation to which Valentina Khodasevich's arrival has greatly contributed. She's doing a painting of Berberova. After that she'll do Timosha and Maksim.

I enclose a note to Kiakhst about the transfer of the Persian paintings to your 'representative'.[2]

Max has already written to you two or three times. Has Ionov really 'expelled' Tikhonov from World Literature? I'm sad about that. My telegram to Ionov about this matter obviously had no effect.[3]

I've heard nothing from *Russkii sovremennik* [*The Russian Contemporary*]. Do you know if it will be coming out, or will it be shut down too?

Things are sombre here. There will probably be some fighting soon. Mussolini is no genius, certainly not! I think they will get stuck into each other as soon as the bad weather comes; it's uncomfortable fighting when it's hot.[4]

Keep well, and greetings to all the inhabitants of your ark.

That ark is firmly anchored!

Regards to your 'friend', and also to Avel.[5]

All the best,

A.

SOURCE: *AG* 9: 238–9.

[1] Valentina Mikhailovna Khodasevich (1894–1970), artist, niece of the poet Vladislav and close family friend of Gorky. Andrei Romanovich Dideriks (1884–1942), artist, husband of Valentina Khodasevich.

[2] Gorky had three ancient Persian paintings in his Petrograd apartment. Evgenii Kiakhst, Mariia Andreeva's nephew, was to organize their transfer to Peshkova's safekeeping in Moscow.

[3] Ilia Ionovich Ionov (1887–1942), director of Gosizdat, had removed Tikhonov from the governing board of World Literature.

[4] On 3 January Mussolini publicly accepted responsibility for the murder of the opposition Socialist Party leader the previous year. The expected disorders did not eventuate.

⁵ The 'friend' is Feliks Edmundovich Dzerzhinsky (1877–1926), founder of the Cheka. Peshkova had many dealings with him through her activities on behalf of the political Red Cross. Avel Safronovich Enukidze (1877–1937), prominent Party official who served on the Presidium and as a secretary of the Central Committee.

116. To M. L. Slonimsky, [8 May 1925]

[Sorrento]

I think, my dear M[ikhail] L[eonidovich], that the failing which you detect and which you call being 'tongue-tied', cannot be explained at all by an 'incomplete mastery of the material', as you put it, but rather by a certain timidity and intimidation when confronted with the formal method.¹ It seems to me that you are not the only one to feel such intimidation, but that Fedin and certain others do too. The point would seem to be that when an author works on his material, he is troubled—once in a while, let's say—by the thought that he must not make a mistake or commit a sin against that method. In so doing, he forgets that literary ideas, forms, schools, and trends are created not by the Shklovskys and Eikhenbaums² of this world, but by the artists themselves—by the Flauberts, Chekhovs, and so forth. *And he forgets the most important thing of all, which is the complete and absolute freedom of the artist.* Let the scholarly philologists create their science of literature, as they are promising and threatening to do, but just grant yourself the freedom not to be associated with them. A story written *à la* Einstein—as Zamiatin's is, for example—this is no longer art, but just an attempt to illustrate a philosophical theory or hypothesis which even a man of such profound learning as O. D. Khvolson finds difficult to comprehend.³ And Khvolson is not the only one; I am told that amongst all Italian scientists there are only two who understand Einstein. 'The Formal Method' is also not easy to understand, witness the fact, as F. A. Braun tells me, that the Germans have devoted a 35–page article to it in their *Journal of Slavic Philology*.⁴ This method is still only a project, an attempt at creating a method—this is how it seems to me when I read these 'Formalists'.

We can expect much from Leonov;⁵ he is talented but he has yet to find his path. I haven't read *The Badgers* [*Barsuki*]. Has it come out in book form yet? Babel?⁶ He is also a major talent; he is most cunning and shrewd in the way he deals with his experiences, he does not spare his 'imagination' and has the ability to be almost epic. But his brevity has a double-edged quality: it could either prove instructive to him or else be his undoing.

I like Bulgakov a lot, but the ending of his story is weak.⁷ He didn't make good use of the reptiles' march on Moscow—just imagine what a monstrously interesting picture that could have been! Kaverin has headed off in a bold new direction—I rate him very highly! He should produce something exceptional. The Zoshchenko is good—give him my sincere regards.[8] I do not know Lavrenev.[9]

Lunts's play *Outside the Law* [*Vne zakona*] was recently published in a nice Italian edition. It will soon be performed in Rome. The latest volume of *Russia* contains 'In the Desert' ['V pustyne'] and 'To the West!' ['Na zapad!'] in Lo Gatto's [Italian] translation together with 'Viktoriia Kazimirovna' in what everyone says is a magnificent version.[10] In general, Russian literature is held in high regard here in the West, and there are even people who understand it. Italy itself has no one other than G. Papini[11] and old man Pirandello. It's the same all over—pretty poor stuff. Everything is 'medium scale'. You Russians[12] are more interesting, more brilliant and better in every way. This is not just patriotism speaking here.

Be sure to send me the second *Kovsh* [*The Ladle*]! And in general, I beg of you, keep me informed of everything interesting in literature. Keep well, my dear man! Please ask Gruzdev to send me his book.[13] All best wishes!

A. Peshkov

SOURCE: *LN* 70: 388–9.

[1] The 'Formal Method' was the name given to an influential movement in Russian literary criticism. Reacting against subjective and eclectic approaches, the Formalists strove to establish the study of literature as a precise science. The main emphasis was placed on the analysis of the formal devices employed in literary works, rather than on the artist or the social milieu.

[2] Boris Mikhailovich Eikhenbaum (1886–1959), literary critic and prominent figure in the Russian Formalist school.

[3] Evgenii Ivanovich Zamiatin (1884–1937), prose writer and playwright, renowned for his interest in experimental styles of writing. Gorky has in mind Zamiatin's 'Story of the Most Important Thing'; Orest Danilovich Khvolson (1852–1934), prominent Russian physicist.

[4] The article 'Formprobleme in der russischen Literaturwissenschaft' by the Russian scholar Viktor Zhirmunsky appeared in *Zeitschrift für slavische Philologie*.

[5] Leonid Maksimovich Leonov (1899–1994), prose writer, later a major figure in Soviet literary life.

[6] Isaak Emmanuilovich Babel (1894–1940), prose writer and dramatist who later died in the Stalin purges.

[7] Mikhail Afanasievich Bulgakov (1891–1940), prose writer and dramatist, best known for his novel, *The Master and Margarita*. The story is 'The Fatal Eggs' ['Rokovye iaitsa'].

[8] Kaverin's 'The End of a Gang' ['Konets khazy'] and Zoshchenko's 'A Terrible Night' ['Strashnaia noch''] were both published in the anthology *Kovsh*, no. 1, 1925.

[9] Boris Andreevich Lavrenev (1891–1959), writer who often dealt with the Revolution and Civil War.

[10] The Italian journal *Russia* was edited by Professor Ettore Lo Gatto (1890–1983) of the University of Rome, a prolific translator of Russian literature. The first two works mentioned are by Lunts; the third by Zoshchenko.

[11] Giovanni Papini (1881–1956), Italian essayist, whose autobiographical work, *The Failure* [*Un uomo finito*, 1912] was translated into Russian during the 1920s.

[12] Gorky again uses the emotive word *Rus'*.

[13] Ilia Aleksandrovich Gruzdev (1892–1960), scholar and critic, Gorky's official biographer. His

Maksim Gorky: A Biographical Sketch (Based on New Materials) [*Maksim Gor'kii: Biograficheskii ocherk (po novym materialam)*] was published in 1925.

117. To S. Zweig, [14 May 1925]

[Sorrento]

My dear Zweig, I was deeply moved by your letter.

I did not answer you immediately since I was somewhat unwell, somewhat overwhelmed by letters from Russian writers living in Russia, and totally absorbed in my work on the novel I'm writing, a novel in which I wish to depict thirty years in the life of the Russian intelligentsia.[1] It seems to me that it will be something quite Asiatic in the variety of its hues, yet it will also be saturated with European influences as they are reflected in a psychology and frame of mind which are totally Russian and rich in suffering, both real and imaginary. I have become passionately absorbed in this painstaking and difficult work.

The book which I dedicated to Rolland will soon be published in Russian in Germany.[2] I have had no news of Rolland for a long time now—I think that my article on Anatole France must have created an unfavourable impression on him.[3] But I could not look upon France, the artist, any differently than I did, because I do not know France, the man, and therefore cannot judge him. I like the play of his mind, so elegant, easy, and sharp, although his epicureanism is alien to me. I find the sceptical smile of the French something which would be very useful to us Russians, since we are always in too much of a hurry to believe and we always believe blindly. This is why I envy a people which can count Montaigne, Renan, and France amongst its number. You must admit that it is somewhat difficult to live with Tolstoy and Dostoevsky. Our greatest genius, A. Pushkin, was killed ninety years ago, and only now are people starting to read him, to understand his great breadth, the profundity of his talent, and to admire his spiritual power.

Once again, thank you for your kind letter. I want you to know that it would be a great pleasure for me to meet you. I'll probably be here in the autumn—do come! I would be very glad to see you. Warm regards.

M. Gorky

SOURCE: *SS* 29: 429.

[1] *The Life of Klim Samgin.*
[2] *The Artamonov Business.*
[3] Gorky's 'On Anatole France' ['Ob Anatole Franse'], inspired by the French writer's death, appeared in French in the *Revue Européene* on 1 December 1924.

118. *To E. P. Peshkova, [2 June 1925]*

[Sorrento]

It's a shame that you can't come here now, mother, but it would be very good if you could come by September, for a month or six weeks. You must do this without fail, no matter what. A first birth is no joking matter: I well remember what it cost you.[1] And Timosha has a nervous disposition. She's feeling good at the moment, even somewhat blissful, it seems, but I'm afraid that when the pregnancy becomes difficult, she will be scared. She's on very good terms with Mariia Ignatievna [Budberg], who is most knowledgeable about medicine, and she is also on good terms with me. But Max, in his egotism, is not sufficiently attentive towards her, and it would be good if you could write and tell him (only, please, without mentioning me!) that a pregnant wife, and not a bad one either, needs his affection and care. Do write. He nearly went off on a trip in his car to Sicily recently, but I managed to dissuade him. I would also have been worried if he had gone alone: gangsters are on the loose in Calabria, and the Fascists are not always so considerate in their treatment of foreigners either. He has no time for anything except his automobile at the moment: he goes off driving somewhere every day. Early this morning he took off for Naples. He's become much stronger and has put on weight, which everyone remarks upon.

Mariia Ignatievna has brought back balalaikas for Nightingale and him from Berlin, and they do an excellent rendition of 'Barynia' accompanied by an Italian guitarist.[2]

Do you need any money? Just let me know, and it will be sent at once. Before you leave for here I'll send you 150 dollars or so to buy a gift for the new mother and baby. Please buy her something—only no furs, which she doesn't need.

I had never thought, mother, that I would live to attain the rank of grandfather, and I must admit that I'm enjoying it! It lifts the spirit. The Peshkovs are not a superfluous tribe; they've got talent, the devils! Oh, how richly endowed that damned Maksim is: he amazes artists with his talent even though he has never studied anywhere. But he doesn't want to do anything, no matter what you say! It's offensive. He's as egotistical as a pretty woman. All right, I'll stop.

Keep well.

A.

M[ariia] I[gnatievna] sends her best wishes and says thank you. Send grandmother some Mamin,[3] Korolenko, and Boborykin,[4] but don't give her any Gorky. And don't try to tempt me with mushrooms, I won't succumb. I have been immersed for a year or more in a novel, the largest book that I have ever written in terms of size. It is large in terms of its theme too.[5] I sit here like a prisoner.

Regards to all. Especially to I[van] P[avlovich] [Ladyzhnikov] , that dear man.

A.

Could you please get hold of the seventeenth volume of Gorky from Kniga and send it to Konstantin Fedin, Leningrad, Flat 3, 33 Liteinyi.[6] Please!

SOURCE: *AG* 9: 244–5.

---

[1] Gorky's first granddaughter, Marfa, was born on 17 August 1925.

[2] Literally, 'Lady of the Manor', the title of a Russian folk dance tune. The 'Italian' was actually Fedor Ramsha, a Russian guitarist and accordionist who lived in Italy during the 1910s and visited Gorky in Sorrento.

[3] Dmitrii Narkisovich Mamin-Sibiriak (1852–1912), writer best known for his stories of Siberian life.

[4] Petr Dmitrievich Boborykin (1836–1921), prolific writer of popular fiction.

[5] *The Life of Klim Samgin.*

[6] The seventeenth volume of Gorky's collected works contained *Fragments from My Diary. Reminiscences.*

119. To N. I. Bukharin, [23 June 1925]

[Sorrento]

No, my dear Nikolai Ivanovich, I do not fear that 'the peasant will devour us'. But when you consider the full immensity of the world's Russian-Chinese-Indian countryside and the small Russian Communist who stands before it, armed though he is with the discovery of Archimedes' screw,[1] then you must invariably experience a certain alarm on inspecting the alignment of forces. After all, the countryside is also to some extent a 'church', and people are always most willing to believe in something tranquil and comfortable. Tranquil beliefs cause people to plumpen—I create the verb 'plumpen' from 'plump', not 'plum'.[2] And when I see them—again!—writing about the countryside in dithyrambic hexameters, glorifying it in the manner of Zlatovratsky, I am not too thrilled.[3] Much closer to my mind and spirit are the spicy stories of village life by my old acquaintance, Panteleimon Romanov.[4] I realize, of course, that the perfidy of history imperiously dictates the need to turn one's face (not the back of one's head) towards the countryside. I also realize that there is nothing in the world which might free the Russian Communist from having to worry about the safety of the back of his head, not even the Russian 'emigration', despite its ever-increasing vileness and lack of talent, of which those new 'saviours' of the Russian countryside, Struve, Pilenko, and Shulgin, write with such conviction. Mind you, all those other 'reborn' people—in Prague, Berlin, Paris, and New York—are no less idiotic.[5] What is to be done? People want to believe that someone needs them for something.

But concern, my dear Nikolai Ivanovich, is by no means the same thing as fear. It's certainly true that the countryside is huge and that the anaemic European proletariat has been shaken apart. But what has been done by the leaders of the Russian proletariat cannot be eradicated; it will last forever. I say this of the leaders not in order to pay them any compliments, but with the intention of reminding them that I remain a bad Marxist. This is an organic failing and it is the source of my optimism. For even though I see at the helm of the world ship a numerically insignificant handful of my countrymen, who, etc.—I cannot deny myself the satisfaction of entertaining certain pleasant thoughts about alchemy, which has, after all, taught people today how to turn mercury into gold, and about those paltry atoms of radium, which Rutherford tells us could free the world from a great deal of useless labour.

I also doubt that the European civilizers will 'leave us in peace for some two or three years', as you hope. They will hardly do that. It is more likely that they will again dream up an intervention of some sort.[6] Because. . . well, put yourself in their situation! What else can they do? All those goings-on in China and Morocco oblige them to defend themselves.[7] I dare say that the USSR will have to live through a good many difficult days yet, although the proletarians of Europe will surely stir themselves in the end, won't they? Events in the colonies will, of course, increase unemployment.

But I am afraid that with regard to foreigners I am beginning to experience something resembling xenophobia and that I am becoming a 'patriot'. I am particularly bothered by the Germans. You know, of course, that Hindenburg's first decree was one which allowed Berlin dogs to wander about the streets without muzzles? The Germans love freedom. One can't help but prefer that 'sturdy people', of which P. Romanov writes in *Prozhektor* [*The Searchlight*].[8]

I am enthralled by our younger writers. The attitude of the 'Onguardists' towards them is foolish. All those Rodovs, Leleviches, and Vardins are, above all, lacking in talent.[9] They also appear to be only semi-literate. One shouldn't force beginning writers into a corner, even if it is a Marxist one. They are already sufficiently revolutionary in their innate hatred of everyday life [*byt*]. They must be allowed to unburden themselves of that hatred, to 'not write' about it, and then they will arrive of their own accord at a revolutionary, heroic spirit, a spirit calm in word and deed but merciless towards all the 'old ways'. And that will have an unprecedented educative significance. Besides, there is no path other than this. As I observe the efforts being made to create a 'positive' figure, I can of course see that these efforts are crude and unsuccessful, but this is a hellishly difficult problem after all! None the less, many of them—for instance, K. Fedin in his *Cities*[10]—have managed to achieve something profoundly significant in this respect. It's just a shame that some of them have become confused by a poorly understood 'Formal Method', all the more so since this method is expounded by a dilettante like Viktor Shklovsky.

This doesn't contradict what I said earlier about dithyrambs to the countryside. The contradiction between the psychology of the city and that of the countryside is a theme which is both inevitable and as natural as can be. There will be two lines in our literature: that of the peasants and that of the workers. These two lines have already been marked out. It won't be long before we'll be reading about a hero who is a rural correspondent. I have already had the satisfaction of reading the manuscript of a story where a Communist worker-correspondent who is ill and has overworked himself to the point of delirium and madness reduces a village to the same state of madness, to the extent that they even experience terror before him. They destroy him, of course, but his seed produces some unexpected offshoots. I'm not acquainted with the author. He's from Riazan and twenty-three years old. He's not very literate, but he has talent.[11]

When I think about Russian literature, I want to return home. But I am still only learning to write. I've begun work on a huge novel; it starts in the 1880s, I want it to close with 1918.[12] I'm excited, all a-tremble, and now my hand has taken to aching, damn it. I've been working eight hours and more a day. I've written a novella about three generations of factory owners, in which I have depicted a Platon Karataev type for which I would have been cursed by Lev Tolstoy.[13]

As for Italy, there's nothing to be said. Nature here is pretty, as everyone knows well enough. The people could be better, but they don't give much sign of striving particularly boldly towards that end. Well, let me wish you good health. Warmest greetings. My sincere regards to A. I. Rykov, F. E. Dzerzhinsky, L. B. Kamenev,[14] and anyone else to whom you might deem it necessary to pass on such regards.

I'll be writing my novel throughout the summer, autumn, and winter; I'll go to Russia in the spring, visiting villages, the Volga, the Urals, and travelling all over the place!

Goodbye for now,

A. Peshkov

SOURCE: *Izv Ts K* 1989 (3): 181–3.

[1] Presumably a reference to Marxist ideology.
[2] Gorky plays on the Russian words *salo* ['lard'] and *sol'* ['salt'].
[3] Nikolai Zlatovratsky (1845–1911), Populist writer who wrote primarily about peasants and the Russian countryside.

⁴ Romanov (1884–1938) wrote satirical, often ribald prose works about the NEP period; he later fell victim to Stalin's purges.

⁵ The 'Reborns' were members of the 'Union for the Rebirth of Russia' ['Soiuz vozrozhdeniia Rossii'] formed in 1918 by various political opponents of the Bolsheviks. V. V. Shulgin (1878–1976), a Russian nationalist who emigrated after the revolution and settled in Yugoslavia. Arrested at the end of the Second World War and sent back to the Soviet Union, where he was gaoled until 1956.

⁶ After the Bolsheviks had agreed to cease hostilities against Germany in 1917, British, French, and American troops occupied some areas of the former Russian Empire, giving mainly material support to anti-Bolshevik forces.

⁷ Liberation movements were active in both these countries.

⁸ Satirical magazine published in Moscow from 1923 to 1935; the 'sturdy people' were the Russians.

⁹ 'Onguardists' was the name given to the editors of the proletarian journal *Na postu* [*On Guard*], three of whom Gorky names here.

¹⁰ *Cities and Years* [*Goroda i gody*], published in 1924.

¹¹ The writer is Vasilii Riakhovsky (1897–1951), author of *The Scent of Lindens* [*Lipovyi dukh*], a collection of stories.

¹² *The Life of Klim Samgin.*

¹³ Gorky appears to be comparing Platon Karataev from *War and Peace* with Tikhon Vialov, a character in *The Artamonov Business.*

¹⁴ Lev Borisovich Kamenev (real name Rosenfeld, 1883–1936), high-ranking Bolshevik, executed during the Stalin purges.

120. To V. F. Khodasevich, [13 August 1925]

[Sorrento]

My dear Vladislav Felitsianovich, I cannot agree, of course, that in Russia today there is no 'will to work', as you maintain. We have a greater will to work than can be found anywhere in contemporary Europe; there can be no talk or argument here about the presence of a will to work, only of an ability to work. The reference to 'Windbag' is not appropriate; you don't know the text of that joke.¹ I don't think you should be condemning people for lacking the 'will to work', for that will is creative, it is 'progress', and you are, on your own admission, not to be counted among the 'lovers of progress'.

Beseda will apparently be a journal devoted to issues of contemporary science and art, without poetry or fiction.² It will be published in Russia because it is significantly cheaper to do so. It would be cheaper still to produce it here in Italy, but there aren't any Russian publishing houses here.

Fiction and poetry will have a place in *Russkii sovremennik*, which is being revived with the old editorial staff. As I understand it, just two expanded issues will come out this year, but from the beginning of 1926 there will be twelve issues a year.³

Tikhonov has had 'all rights restored'; his sentence has been quashed.⁴ He has taken on editorial work at Voronsky's⁵ publishing house, Krug. He is in the Crimea on holiday at the moment.

Zoia Lody was here and sang marveliously. Meierhold came; he is taking his theatre to Germany for the winter. We've had quite a few other interesting people here too. In general, this summer has seen a rich harvest of guests. Apparently, the wife of the artist Shaumian is staying with Kupchikha.[6] The artist himself is supposed to turn up soon.

Chapygin, Aleksei Pavlovich,[7] is publishing a novel about Razin's time in the supplement to *Byloe* [*The Past*]; his language is very interesting, as is his writing generally. Collections of stories by Leonov, Bulgakov, Chapygin, and Ognev have appeared, as has an amusing 'adventure' story by Kozyrev, called 'Mister Bridge'.[8]

Pasternak's 'Childhood of Liuvers'[9] is a beautiful thing. And nicely produced too.

There is quite a lot of pleasant news. But there is also some that is unpleasant: Suter has discovered a recurrence of Valentina Mikhailovna [Khodasevich]'s tuberculosis. She has gone to Naples, where she will enter his—Suter's—hospital for a couple of days to undergo tests. Thanks for *Sovremennye zapiski*. I didn't like the conclusion of 'Mitia's Love' ['Mit'ina liubov''']; it was a boring issue.[10]

Give my regards to Nina Nikolaevna [Berberova] and keep well. I am not in very good health myself. I've lost a lot of weight and grown weak. It must be because of the accursed heat. All July, right up until today, there has not been a drop of rain. But it has been very good for the grapes; they are amazingly sweet.

M[ariia] I[gnatievna] [Budberg] is in Estonia; she has gone there to see her children off. They are very charming—especially the youngest, Tania.

All the best,

A. Peshkov

I don't have the clipping from *Izvestiia*; I've lost it.

SOURCE: *N Zh* 31: 204–5.

---

[1] *Windbag the Drudge* [*Rabotiaga Slovotekov*], a short play of 1920 satirizing Soviet bureaucracy.

[2] On *Beseda*, see the Introduction to this section.

[3] *Russkii sovremennik* had been published within Russia, but, like *Beseda*, it never reappeared.

[4] Tikhonov was arrested early in 1925. He was soon released as a result of Gorky's indirect intercession (via Peshkova) with Dzerzhinsky. See Letter 115, n. 3.

[5] Aleksandr Konstantinovich Voronsky (1884–1943), literary critic, editor of *Krasnaia nov'* between 1921 and 1927.

[6] The artist was actually called Shiltian. Kupchikha (literally, 'merchant woman'), nickname of Valentina Khodasevich.

[7] Chapygin (1870–1937). His novel was entitled *Razin Stepan*.

[8] Nikolai Ognev (real name Mikhail Grigorievich Rozanov, 1888–1938) became well known for his stories of student life; Mikhail Iakovlevich Kozyrev (1892–1942), writer of satirical stories.

[9] Boris Leonidovich Pasternak (1890–1960), major poet and prose writer, best known for his novel *Doctor Zhivago*. 'The Childhood of Liuvers' was a short story first published in 1925.

[10] A novella by Ivan Bunin.

121. To L. M. Leonov, [8 September 1925]

[Sorrento]

Leonid Leonov,

I thank you sincerely for *The Badgers*. It's a very good book. It is profoundly moving. On not one of its 300 pages did I detect or sense that
plaintive, prettified, and deceptive 'inventiveness' which has so long been
customary in our writing about peasant life and the village. And at the
same time you have managed to saturate your terrible, pitiful tale with
that genuine artistic inventiveness which permits the reader to penetrate
to the very heart of the environment which you have depicted. This book
will last. I send my heartfelt congratulations.

I have just one regret: the story is not written simply enough. It will
be difficult to translate into foreign languages. Even skilful translators
have little success with the 'skaz' style.[1] And contemporary Russian literature needs to concern itself particularly with gaining the attention and
understanding of Europe, of those people over there who sincerely want
'to know Russia'. Honest Europeans are beginning to feel that we are living on the tragic eve of our Renaissance and that they need to learn a
great deal from us. It will be some time yet before they have the means
to achieve a renaissance of their own. Their interest in our art is growing and deepening all the time. This means that we should also take the
foreign reader into consideration when we write. Excuse me for all this
grumbling.

Warm regards. All the best and once again—thank you.

A. Peshkov

SOURCE: *SS* 29: 441–2.

[1] A vernacular narrative style very popular in the 1920s.

122. To V. Ia. Shishkov,[1] [20 December 1925]

[Naples]

I received your letter, my dear Shishkov. Please forgive me for calling
you by your surname, but I don't recall your patronymic.

Over the years I have read with great gratitude your sketches of
Russian life in a variety of journals and I have always thought how stimulating and reliable—and hence good and necessary—your work is.

And I find that same stimulating, intelligent note in your letter to me.
'I am attracted to humour, because I want reading to be enjoyment,' you

say. This slogan of yours gives me great joy, because in my view this is precisely what we have needed for a long time. Intelligent laughter is a magnificent source of energy.

As one who follows contemporary literature in Russia most attentively, and who takes a sincere delight in the abundance of gifted young people around nowadays, I place firm hope in the growth and development of great talents in this domain. However, I will not conceal my concern over the monotony of the subject-matter of stories and their overall tone, which is rather depressingly grey.

I am not forgetting, of course, that external factors play an important role in this—those 'circumstances' which are 'beyond the author's control' and which have always weighed heavily on our literature and continue to do so today.[2] And yet it was under the yoke of precisely those same 'circumstances' that G. Uspensky, Korolenko—even L. Tolstoy himself—lived and worked. However, they were magnificent at doing their job.

I don't mean to say that the job is being done much less magnificently nowadays. No, that would be untrue. I am talking only about the monotony of subject-matter and its depressing tone.

I am a long way from Russia, yet I sense that there are things there which give cause for joy. You are yourself confirmation of that. You are not the only one, of course. But you have given a very good formulation of what is needed.

Laughter is a good thing, a healthy thing. Just look at our *émigré* gentlemen—they have forgotten how to laugh, and yet they really ought to be able to laugh a little at themselves! However, they are completely incapable of doing so. They just agonize.

People have forgotten how to laugh here in Italy too. That is very bad. What is going on here is the condensation of hatred, a process which promises many dark days for the future.

When will I return to Russia? When I finish writing the huge novel which I have begun.[3] I will probably have to sit over it for at least another year yet. I wouldn't even try to get any work done in Russia, because I would be running all over the place like you do.[4] I envy you. Overall, such sketches of the contemporary village as the ones you write are remarkably timely and provide a good picture of present-day life.

M. M. Prishvin pleased me greatly with his *Shoes*.[5] It's a cunning piece of work. Akulshin is interesting.[6] But Klychkov's *The Saccharine German* [*Sakharnyi nemets*] only reminds me of N. N. Zlatovratsky.[7]

Well, look after yourself! I thank you for kindly thinking of me. I think of you too with warmth.

My best regards and greetings,

A. Peshkov

I have come here for the winter and to have medical treatment.

SOURCE: *SS* 29: 450–2.

[1] Viacheslav Iakovlevich Shishkov (1873–1945), novelist, short-story writer, and essayist, noted for his works set in Siberia.

[2] A reference to the censorship of literature.

[3] *The Life of Klim Samgin.*

[4] Shishkov spent the years 1921–5 tramping large areas of Russia on foot.

[5] *Shoes* [*Bashmaki*]: a book of sketches published in 1925.

[6] Rodion Mikhailovich Akulshin (1896–1988), peasant poet associated with the Pereval [Pass] movement. He later emigrated to the United States.

[7] Sergei Antonovich Klychkov (1889–1940), peasant poet and prose writer whose works contained a Gogolian mixture of the real and the fantastic.

123. *To I. A. Gruzdev, [9 January 1926]*

[Naples]

Ilia Gruzdev,

I am most depressed by Esenin's death, even though I have long had the presentiment, perhaps even the conviction, that this boy would come to a bad end.[1] I first had this presentiment when I met him in 1914. This was when he appeared before literary Petersburg in the company of the ever-resourceful Kliuev.[2] He was like one of Elizaveta Merkurievna Bem's pictures come to life: curly fair hair, blue silk shirt, patent leather boots, and the happy, yet perplexed smile of a birthday boy on his cherubic face.[3] I heard him read his fine, simple, naïve poems and I remember that I fell to thinking: how and where is this cherub going to live? At that time the terrifying, vile days of the European carnage had already begun. The second time I saw him was in Berlin, at A. N. Tolstoy's place. Isadora Duncan was with him, old and drunk.[4] He gave a magnificent reading of Khlopusha's monologue,[5] then he kicked Duncan in her international posterior and said to her: 'You shit'. I am a sentimental man, and I cried quite shamelessly at the sight of such a lethal combination of genuine Russian poetry and illustrious European vulgarity. And once again I had that gloomy thought: how and where is Esenin to live? Just imagine the insanely crooked path which led him from Kliuev to Duncan! That evening Esenin was violently and hysterically drunk, but he stood firmly on his feet. It was just that his eyes were somewhat strangely clouded and he kept disappearing into dark corners. And it seemed that it was not the wine that had made him drunk, but the inescapable melancholy of a man who has come into our world either far too late or else before his time. And it occurred to me then that this could serve as amazingly valuable material for a story about the disastrous life of a Russian poet! Precisely so: for all his hooliganism, Sergei Esenin is himself an outstanding work of art, and one which has been created cynically, for a joke, by our accursed Russian reality. He has a poem about a dog: the dog's puppies are drowned, she sees this happen, and then she runs about, howling as she goes, for it seems to her that the moon in the sky is her puppy. This is one of Esenin's best poems and in my opinion it has something autobiographical about it.

Thinking about him, one thinks of many other young people, and one's soul is troubled. We have lost a certain Blomquist, and it appears that he was not without talent.[6] Of course, 'bounteous is our land', and all that,[7] but how dreadfully cheaply do we value man here, and man is what we need plenty of right now!

I have read the third issue of *Kovsh*. It is interesting. Slonimsky has turned up something new for it; I was surprised by the 'memoir-like' quality of Kaverin's story; Forsh's 'Fifth Beast' is good[8]—and very wisely dedicated to Tikhonov; the Larionov is only 'so-so'; I would, of course, much prefer Zoshchenko to Shishkov; Barshev is very interesting—is he a young man? Is he from Nizhnii Novgorod? 'The Wolves' and 'The Mirage' don't appeal to me.[9]

In general, it would be almost impossible to translate any of these stories into any European language, and yet what we need right now is to write in a way that Europeans will understand. Never has interest in Russian literature been as serious and profound as it is now. But we all keep playing tricks, 'we put on the style', like Slonimsky, 'we show our style', like Andreev. Actually, Slonimsky and Andreev 'put on the style' considerably less and rather more cautiously than the authors of 'The Wolves' and 'The Mirage'. All the same, we are creating a literature which exists 'for its own sake', which is very much a 'family affair', an act of 'abdication'. This pursuit of new words, this fornication with language and excessive use of regional lexicons, I personally find most depressing. You must excuse me, but in this desire to decorate fiction with *non-literary* words one senses—apart from the littering of language with rubbish—a bourgeois aesthetic at work: the desire to decorate an icon with foil, paper flowers, and 'grapes'. This is bad. In *Cement*, by Gladkov[10]—an old writer—the dialogues are written in a language which I don't understand. In *The Third Capital* [*Tret'ia stolitsa*] Pilniak writes, 'The train contained a wagon-load of childrens' nipples,' apparently due to his inability to distinguish between the words 'nipple' and 'dummy'.[11] Fedin writes 'she is terrified by the shaggy head borne by the snowy shrouds', thereby creating the possible confusion of 'borne' and 'born'.[12] But best of all is Shaginian[13] in 'The Change' ['Peremena']: 'The renowned warrior Iskaev made a quail-like noise with his tongue.'[14] 'They suck with their rotten teeth.' 'Long-necked bottle.' This also derives from the desire to be 'aesthetic'. Our gentlemen critics should thrash our gentlemen writers for such things of beauty.

The monotony of themes provides no cause for joy either. I am sick of lightning outbursts of passion, I am sick of spur-of-the-minute marriages, I am even sick of the contrived way in which people who have become accustomed to fighting and have become neither willing nor able to do anything else, are raised to the level of 'heroes'. As yet no one has even touched on the poetry of labour, a theme which is quite new for us and very interesting. Doesn't such poetry exist in reality? One has only to invent it and it will exist. The Russian intellectual has been sullied and misrepresented, being depicted as one who is poor of spirit, a blot on the face of history. It has been forgotten that he is that very hero who brought the revolution to life and organized the forces which created it. There are a great many themes, large and new. There is a bootmaker in Tikhonov's story who displays the 'scars' he received in heroic battles. Ah, those scars! Was there ever a time when people didn't boast of them?

Well, I've cursed everyone and everything, now I'm giving you the opportunity to curse me. I enclose the manuscript of a story, 'On Cockroaches' ['O tarakanakh'], for the fourth issue of *Kovsh*. Publish it if you like it. I have already given this story to the old poet Viatkin for a journal which will be published in Siberia, in the town of Nikolaevsk.[15] Since I'll be getting an honorarium from Viatkin, there's no need for *Kovsh* to pay me anything. If you decide to publish it, have the manu- script knocked out on the typewriter and return it to me.

I have the fifth issue of *Krug* [*The Circle*]. The Bely is difficult to read, I can't stand Chulkov, Klychkov reminds me of the late N. N. Zlatovratsky, I don't read Pilniak at all, as he stands outside the realm of artistic prose.[16]

Does Gosizdat intend to publish a collection of Esenin's poetry? Has the fourth volume of *The Fall of the Tsarist Regime* [*Padenie tsarskogo rezhima*] been published? I have yet to read *Kiukhlia*. Apparently Tynianov has also published a brochure in which he ascertains that Dostoevsky's Foma Opiskin is a lampoon on Gogol.[17] If this is true, please ask him to send me a copy of this brochure!

Thank you for your kind letter. Take care.

A. Peshkov

Romain Rolland will be sixty years old in January. Comrades, we must congratulate him! He is a worthy man.

SOURCE: *AG* 11: 29–31.

[1] Sergei Aleksandrovich Esenin (1895–1925), Russia's best-known peasant poet, committed suicide on 28 December 1925.

[2] Nikolai Alekseevich Kliuev (1887–1937), peasant poet.

[3] Bem (née Endaurova) (1843–1914) was well known for her water-colours.

[4] Isadora Duncan (1877–1927), American dancer who enjoyed a *succès de scandale* in Russia. She married Esenin in 1922, but the marriage was a turbulent one.

[5] From his narrative poem *Pugachev* (1922).

[6] Georgii Karlovich Blomquist (1898–1925). Three of his stories were published posthumously in the *Kovsh* miscellany.

[7] An inexact quotation from A. K. Tolstoy's *History of the Russian State*.

[8] Olga Dmitrievna Forsh (1873–1961), writer renowned for her historical novels of the 1920s and 1930s.

⁹ The works referred to are: Kaverin, 'Nine-tenths of Fate' ['Deviat' desiatykh sud'by']; Forsh, 'Around Moscow' ['Po Moskve']; Larionov, 'Silence' ['Tishina']; Viacheslav Shishkov, 'A Wondrous Marvel' ['Divo divnoe']; Vasilii Andreev, 'Wolves' ['Volki']; and Petr Demin, 'The Mirage' ['Marevo']. Nikolai Valerianovich Barshev (1888–1939) published several collections of stories in the 1920s. V. M. Andreev (1899–1941), writer of novellas and autobiographical works.

¹⁰ Fedor Vasilievich Gladkov (1883–1958), writer associated with the proletarian movement. His best-known novel, *Cement*, was subsequently celebrated as a classic of Socialist Realism.

¹¹ In Russian the words are very similar. Nipple is *sosok*; dummy is *soska*.

¹² The problem which Gorky detects in the Russian is also a phonetic one. The words *ot nosiashcheisia* could be picked up as the single word *otnosiashcheisia*.

¹³ Marietta Sergeevna Shaginian (1888–1982), poet and prose writer.

¹⁴ Gorky is concerned by what he sees as the inappropriate use of modern colloquial Russian here.

¹⁵ Georgii Andreevich Viatkin (1885–1938) was associated with the journal *Sibir'* [*Siberia*]. Gorky's story did not appear in the journal.

¹⁶ The works in question are an excerpt from Bely's *Moscow* [*Moskva*], Chulkov's 'The Dagger' ['Kinzhal'], Klychkov's 'Two Brothers' ['Dva brata'], and Pilniak's 'Zavolochie'.

¹⁷ Iurii Nikolaevich Tynianov (1894–1943), writer and critic. *Kiukhlia* is a historical novel about the poet Kiukhelbeker. The 'brochure' is the 1921 study *Dostoevsky and Gogol (Towards a Theory of Parody)* [*Dostoevskii i Gogol': k teorii parodii*].

124. *To K. A. Fedin, [3 March 1926]*

[Naples]

My dear Fedin,

In true Russian fashion, we managed to turn our discussion of art towards questions of morality. Your taste for 'worthless nags' and your 'anger at the trotter' is really something from the realm of morality, and I fear that this is a path which will lead to the confirmation of the need for tendentiousness in art and will thus be a concession to the demands of the age.¹ Akakii Akakievich, the 'station-master', Mumu, and all the others who make up the 'insulted and the injured'—they are all a chronic disease in Russian literature, of which it might be said in the vast majority of cases that what it has taught people above all is the art of being unhappy.² We have learnt this lesson diligently and well. Nowhere do people suffer with such pleasure as they do in Holy Russia. Our physical maladies are being treated—and with ever greater success—by the doctors; but our moral maladies are being treated by the Tolstoys, the Dostoevskys, and others whom I would term village 'witch-doctors' in this respect. They are sometimes talented and wise too, but more often than not they simply aggravate the malady rather than cure it.

I have a long-standing hatred for suffering, both physical and moral. Each of them, considered both subjectively and objectively, arouses my indignation, disgust, and even rage. It is essential to hate suffering; this is the only way it will be destroyed. It is demeaning to Man, that great and tragic being. The 'nags' often parade their suffering, as beggars do their sores. The 'nags' very often confuse and destroy the lives of the 'trotters' like Lomonosov, Pushkin, Tolstoy, etc. Mercy is fine, yes indeed! But show me some examples of mercy displayed by the 'nags'! It is the mercy and love shown towards people by the 'trotters' which have cre-ated—and continue to create—everything that brings us joy, everything of which we can be proud.

Humanism in the form we have acquired it from the gospels and from the scriptures created by our writers about life and the Russian people—humanism of this sort is a poor thing. A. A. Blok is the only one who had any inkling of this, it seems to me.[3]

No, my dear friend, I find it hard to agree with you. In my view, it is necessary to tear the verbal rags from those who suffer. What one often discovers underneath is the healthy body of a sluggard or an actor play-ing for compassion, or something even worse.

It seems to me it is not that the 'nags' are 'moving you to tears' as an artist, but that you yourself are upset by the absence of meaning in the lives of the 'nags'. This absence is something you have understood only insufficiently. Don't get me wrong—I am examining this muddle not in terms of social confusion but through the eyes of instinct, a biological force which instils in me a hatred of all suffering.[4]

My best regards. Keep well.

A. Peshkov

SOURCE: *SS* 29: 456–8.

---

[1] Fedin later explained that he had always felt drawn to the 'poor person of everyday life, of inconspicuous labour—the innocent nag which carts the crude burden of history from epoch to epoch'. He also spoke of his dislike for the 'self-satisfied person, who considers himself a model of creation, spoiled by the grace of the fates, like a trotter which has become accustomed to winning races and looks down on the nag'.

[2] The references are to Gogol's *The Overcoat*, 'The Station Master' from Pushkin's *Tales of Belkin*, and 'Mumu' by Turgenev. *The Insulted and the Injured*, the title of a short novel by Dostoevsky, quickly became a generic term for that style of writing which encouraged sympathy for the suffering of the underprivileged.

[3] An allusion to Blok's article of 1919 'The Collapse of Humanism' ['Krushenie gumanizma'].

[4] Gorky's Russian is extremely obscure here.

---

125. To I. A. Gruzdev, [10 March 1926]

[Naples]

Your report about Esenin surprised me and painted him as an even more colourful figure in my eyes. His is one of those rare cases of that calm fury which sometimes enables a person's will for self-destruction to bat-tle against the instinct to live and overcome it.

Whilst I have never suffered, nor indeed do I suffer now, from 'suicidomania', as Dr I. B. Galant maintains in *Klinicheskii arkhiv* (*Clinical Archive*)[1] there was a time when I was extremely interested in the question of suicide and used to collect accounts of the most characteristic cases. In 1897 there was a tailor in Lyons who built himself a guillotine in the basement of his house with a mirror attached, so as to watch the blade cut off his head. The doctors concluded that he really would have seen this happen. In 1894, Kromulin, a student at Novorossiisk University, removed the mattress from his bed, placed three lighted candles beneath it and worked on a complex mathematical calculation as the flames burned his vertebrae and roasted his spinal cord. After twenty-seven minutes he was no longer able to work on the calculation, and then he died. There is no shortage of such incidents, but, in my opinion, they all have an 'experimental' character about them, as if they were a parody of 'scientific curiosity'. I don't recall any case similar to Esenin's. There's nothing easier than killing oneself 'straight off', nor is it at all difficult to starve oneself to death, but to destroy oneself in the way you say Esenin did is something which requires a fierce determination and an indomitable will.[2]

It's an easy matter to turn from this to the question which you raised concerning 'heroes'. I talked with V. G. Korolenko in Moscow, back in 1903 or 1904, about the world's need for 'psychological wholeness', and I became convinced that he took the 'psychologically whole' to involve a simplification of man, something roughly similar to N. Kliuev's 'angel of simple human affairs'.[3] I have a different 'joint of view'.[4] Man should make himself more complex, not more simple. Heroism doesn't simply mean the 'conquest of zoological individualism'. As a result of that conquest, along with other good things, there arise certain 'ennobled social instincts' which, in Tikhonov's view, make people into 'nails' with the strength of will to lead man 'onward and upward'.[5] As you know, this is an old idea of mine, perhaps the only one I have ever had. You also know that 'you'll never jump higher than your head'. But this is not what we need. After all, the world itself is contained in a person's head, the world is nothing other than a complex made up of his opinions, hypotheses, and theories about the essence of phenomena outside his head. The truth value of this mixture is extremely dubious, but it serves to adorn our life and, to a certain extent, even makes it easier in the practical sense of the word.

It would be wrong to dismiss this opinion of mine as individualism and anarchism. It's not that at all. I would put it like this: man is an organ of nature created by nature herself—albeit not entirely successfully—so as to enable her to understand her own strange, ridiculous, and repulsive mysteries and phenomena. Man is a light which has been lit in the darkness of chaos, perhaps even against the will of 'nature'. He is a chance creation of her creative madness, a creation which has already developed and continues to develop further the ability to employ the forces of nature, but which is also obsessed by the aspiration to under-stand—or rather to impart its own meaning to—the senseless play of those forces. As proof of this, witness the fantastically rapid development of scientific thought and scientific creation. Science is now more con-tentious than ever. It is divided into two schools with which we have long been familiar. The first strives towards 'mechanization', i.e. the simplifi-cation of all life's phenomena and its 'psychological essence'; the second finds this mechanization of the 'soul' offensive to its own soul. Standing against both these conflicting schools in all the majesty of his folly and with all the power of his influence over people is our collective Mr Bryan, author of 'the monkey trial' and the plan to expel all non-Christians from the USA.[6] Bryan, Mussolini, etc., these men are heroes, and it is as heroes that they should be perceived by the artist, for each one of them is an embodiment of 'psychological wholeness'. For me personally, there-fore, the hero who investigates, the hero who seeks, is far more valuable than the hero who is already confirmed in his faith and has thereby sim-plified himself. By this I mean that for me the hero is a vessel for all the anxieties and storms, for all the doubts and tragedies of a life which appears to merit love and hatred in equal measure. And it seems to me that the 'psychologically whole' person has become an impossibility in the face of the ever more rapid flow of life's phenomena. When Dostoevsky attempted to create a sort of Christ-figure in the person of Prince Myshkin, he prudently chose first to call him 'The Idiot'. And later, when he confronted him with reality in the form of 'The Grand Inquisitor', he convincingly demonstrated that there is no place for Christ in the world. Blok made the mistake of a lyric poet who is only a half-believer when he put Christ at the head of 'The Twelve'.[7]

The dream of a 'positive character' is impracticable, and any attempt to realize that dream is unlikely to get any further than 'Bazarov'.[8] I am also very pleased to say that the hero of Zoshchenko's story 'On Nightingales'[9]—a character who was once the hero of 'The Overcoat', or at least a close relative of Akakii[10]—manages to stir my hatred thanks to the author's clever irony. On the whole I hold Fedin, Zoshchenko, and Slonimsky in high regard for their ironical attitude towards those who are 'princes for an hour', and towards everything else in our life. I regret that I failed to understand Tikhonov, as Fedin has pointed out to me, but this is partly the fault of the poet himself, as I find it most difficult to make sense of verses written in the manner of Pasternak. But two old lines of his—about people from whom one could make good nails—have captivated me precisely because of their sad irony.[11] But perhaps I am wrong, and the author really does accept the idea of people as mere material? I have shown these verses to an archimandrite and he was most delighted with them. This troubled me.

I fear that this letter is insufficiently clear. I blame this on the enormity of its theme.

I received the fourth volume of *The Fall of the Tsar[ist] Regime*. I read one of Lavrenev's stories and liked something in it, but I don't remember what exactly. A bad sign.

I don't have Blok's 'unpublished' verses.[12]

Please give Fedin my photograph and the cutting from *Les nouvelles litteraire* [*sic*]. I also enclose a clipping about Shklovsky for its curiosity value.[13] Do you happen to know whether Ionov is going to publish the second edition of my books and when *The Artamonov Business* will appear?

And another thing: I've heard that Esenin wrote some erotic verses addressed to I. Duncan. Could you send me a list of them? Did Esen[in] customarily write erot[ic] poems? I'm collecting everything that is being written about him and I may perhaps write something myself, taking him and several others of his ilk as my subject. I very much want to depict the tragic life of the *Russian* poet.

There is a certain German author who has written a curious book about Dostoevsky, in which he argues that F. M. was morally an accessory to his father's murder.[14] The same idea occurred to me about fifteen years ago when I was rereading the Karamazovs on Capri. The idea has its source in two of the Karamazovs: Dmitrii and Smerdiakov.

Look how much I have written. I have had to take a few days' rest from working on the novel, so I'm writing letters in every direction.

Did you congratulate Romain Rolland on his sixtieth birthday? If you didn't, that is most sad.

Look after yourself,

A. Peshkov

SOURCE: *AG* 11: 40–3.

[1] Galant, a Freudian psychoanalyst, wrote several such articles about Gorky at this time.

[2] In his letter of 27 February, Gruzdev had described Esenin's suicide as follows: 'And do you know how he hanged himself? He wrapped the rope around his neck and took the other end in his hand. He then caught hold of the heating pipe with the other hand. The slightest weakness, and he would have let the rope slip out of his hand and fallen down. But he held on and *strangled himself*.'

[3] A refrain from the narrative poem 'Mother Sabbath' ['Mat'-subbota'] of 1922.

[4] Gorky playfully writes *kochka zreniia* (literally 'tussock of view') instead of *tochka zreniia*.

[5] A reference to 'A Ballad about Nails' ['Ballada o gvozdiakh'] by Nikolai Semenovich Tikhonov (1896–1979).

[6] William Jennings Bryan (1860–1925), three times nominated for the presidency of the United States. In later years he became known for his fundamentalist religious beliefs and aided the prosecution during the notorious Scopes trial, in which a schoolteacher was found 'guilty' of teaching evolutionary theory.

[7] At the end of Blok's famous poem about the October Revolution, the twelve soldiers see the figure of Christ ahead of them in the snowstorm.

[8] The main character in Turgenev's *Fathers and Sons* [*Ottsy i deti*].

[9] i.e. 'What the Nightingale Sang' ['O chem pel solovei'].

[10] Akakii Akakievich, the main character of Gogol's story.

[11] Fedin wrote to Gorky in a letter of 11 February 1926 that he had failed to appreciate the irony of Tikhonov's poem 'Searching for a Hero' ['Poiski geroia'].

[12] This book was published in 1926 and edited by P. N. Medvedev.
[13] The cuttings were from the issue of 6 March 1926.
[14] Johann Neufeld's Freudian study was published in Russian in 1925.

126. To A. K. Voronsky, [17 April 1926]

[Sorrento]

Dear Comrade Voronsky,

I have read your article.[1] I am very happy that you are the first to emphasize so precisely my 'man'-omania. I am even prepared to thank you for doing so, should you feel any need for my thanks. My warm congratulations. I am, however, a long way from thinking that I deserve your overly flattering evaluation of my *artistic* gifts. No, I am not a great artist; I am still only learning to write.

Let me put this another way. For me, the greatest and most wonderful literary work is very short and reads like this.

In deep antiquity, a shapeless and powerless living thing rises out of the mire, after which, transformed into the shape of man, it gradually and painfully overcomes all resistance by the blind and meaningless forces of the cosmos. Subjugating such resistance ever more quickly through the exercise of its will, it creates on this earth its own 'second nature'. This artistic creation is both wonderful and perfect. It bears the name 'Man'. Other than this miracle, there have not been, there are not, nor will there ever be any further miracles on earth; but it is to this one miracle that it has been given to grow over thousands of centuries. On this basis, it clearly goes without saying that I do not agree with you when you equate work in the village with work in the city. Not only do I consider this view to be mistaken, it is also harmful. It is particularly harmful for us Russians at the present time. These two forms of work cannot be compared in their essence, their difficulty, or in their end results. In the one instance a purely physical energy is being expended, in the other the energy expended is psychophysical. The peasant *did not create* rye, wheat, vegetables, and all the fruits of the earth; he discovered them, and now he simply gathers them. But the Diesel engine did not exist in nature; it was *created* by the imagination and reason of the city-dweller. Beets were discovered by the peasant, but it was not the peasant who worked out that sugar could be obtained from them. Nor was it his idea which led to the extraction of creosote from tar. His backbreaking labour is being eased not through the exercise of his will, but due to the will of those who invent harvesters, tractors, etc. It is one thing to catch a hare; to create electricity is another matter entirely. If the peasant and his grain were to disappear, the city-dweller would learn how to obtain grain in the laboratory. Creative labour is revolutionary; the labour of gathering is essentially conservative. Finally, just recall the brilliant work of the recently deceased Burbanks [*sic*], our own zoologist Ivanov, Voronov's experiments with sheep, etc., etc., and you will be convinced that city man is *creating* new types of fruit, new cereal grains, new species of animals, etc.[2]

I am aware that all this is very close to the dangerous idea that the majority is exploiting the creative energy of the minority. It seems to me, however, that it will do us no harm to pay a little more attention to this 'untimely thought',[3] since it is already becoming timely for us. As you well know, the things that are being written about the countryside at present are not always a cause for joy.

I think it would be particularly timely for you critics to note the presence in contemporary literature of two contradictory attitudes towards the countryside, attitudes which are already quite clearly defined: a poeticization of the countryside, which harks back to the works of Zlatovratsky and those of his ilk; and a sceptical attitude towards the countryside, which is reminiscent of Sleptsov.[4] I am not talking of tendencies—these cannot be discerned as yet—but about moods which already exist. Make of this what you will. Nevertheless, man revolts in order to achieve peace and quiet. There is no need to encourage him in this. Let the dear fellow revolt, but never let him forget that this work goes on forever, for millennia.

I rejoiced over Gladkov's *Cement*—a work that is *non*-literary in the usual sense of the word, but also not purely 'propagandistic'. I rejoiced because this is the first attempt among us Russians to poeticize creative labour. Even though it is most uneven and the dialogues are unreadable, you should just compare it to Zlatovratsky's hexameters depicting the hay-making in *Foundations* [*Ustoi*], or to Radimov's hexameters, or Klychkov's *The Saccharine German* and other works in the same vein.[5]

You won't be cross with me for all these instructions, will you? You shouldn't be. We both serve the same cause, which we love and hold dear. We can, and should, disagree over the particulars, for we are not striving to create a 'harmonious personality', which is of no use to anybody and which is impossible anyway, and will always remain so, I think. But in general terms we both want the same main thing—a life which is active through and through, a creative explosion of all the reserves of psychophysical energy, a tragic celebration of all human powers. Am I right? There, then.

I very much like A. P. Chapygin's *Razin*. He writes well, this workman of ours. After all, until the age of seventeen our Aleksei Pavlov was a 'painter of signs'. And now this quiet and crafty fellow is one of the most educated Russian writers, a superb talent.

A. Tolstoy's *Hyperboloid* is a much lesser work than Nikulin's *Not a Matter of Chance* [*Nikakie sluchainosti*].[6] That is a book fit for an Englishman.

In the area of 'plot-oriented' literature, A. Grin is becoming ever more interesting. There are some very good pieces in his book *The Gladiators* [*Gladiatory*].[7]

Pay attention to Iurezansky.[8] Pravdukhin was right to praise him. He is still young. His real name is funny: it's Nose [Nos].

By the way, what is your first name? Aleksei? Aleksandr? And your patronymic? Do write.

All the best!

A. Peshkov

Who is editing Esenin?

Khodasevich wrote an abominable piece about him.[9] [. . .]

SOURCE: *AG* 10/2: 31–3.

[1] Voronsky had published an article about Gorky in the April 1926 issue of *Krasnaia nov'*.

[2] Luther Burbank (1849–1926), American horticulturalist who developed many new species of flowers, fruit, and vegetables. Leonid Ivanov was a Russian botanist, and Sergei Voronov an endocrinologist.

[3] Allusion to *Untimely Thoughts*.

[4] Unlike the Populist Zlatovratsky, Vasilii Sleptsov (1836–78) wrote stories about rural Russia which stressed its desolation.

[5] Probably a reference to *The Village* [*Derevnia*] by the poet and artist Pavel Radimov.

[6] Aleksei Tolstoy's *Engineer Garin's Hyperboloid* [*Giperboloid inzhenera Garina*] was a work of science fiction; Lev Veniaminovich Nikulin (real name Lev Vladimirovich Olkonitsky, 1891–1967) was eventually best known for his Socialist Realist novels.

[7] A collection of stories by Aleksandr Grin (1880–1932), whose frequently fantastic works were often criticized in the 1920s.

[8] Vladimir Iurezansky (1888–1957), whose book of stories *Heat* [*Znoi*] had just been reviewed in *Krasnaia nov'*.

[9] It appeared in *Sovremennye zapiski*, vol. 27, 1926.

127. To A. N. Furmanova, [23 May 1926]

[Sorrento]

To Furmanova,

I was shaken by the tone of your letter. I cannot offer you any consolation—indeed, what consolation can one offer a person who has just lost her best friend?[1] Thoughts do not help on such occasions. The only thing that might help is that biological force which is sometimes capable of healing even fatal wounds. The other thing that might help is rage against that same biological force which is so often incapable of preventing a premature and *unwilling* death. But I think that the thing which might help you most of all is rage against those conditions in which we are all placed so tragically and pitilessly by history. For it is those very conditions which explain the death of many people, like Pushkin and Lermontov, who—had they lived—might have survived almost to our own day, almost to the age of Esenin, another sad sacrifice of the times.

This rage is a force capable not only of giving man strength in this world but also of inspiring him to work against everything which stands in the way of his life. You know this. Your husband was fully charged with this very force. There is no doubt that it is in your soul too.

Listen, my dear woman comrade, haven't you been somewhat hasty in deciding to bury yourself alive? You write: 'I do not wish to live.' But have you not tried to overcome your grief? Do try. We do not have many good people. I believe you to be a good person and, by that very token, one who is needed by others. Allow me to talk of my own personal experience. There was a time when my life was so hard that I was unable to bear it any longer and I wished to kill myself. Forty years have passed since that time, but even now I am ashamed of my faintheartedness then. My life is still not happy; I find it very difficult. Nevertheless, I live *with pleasure*—there's a contradiction for you! And I explain it like this: although things might be bad for me, the world is becoming better—witness the fact that ever more young eagles like your husband are being born, dozens of his kind, men like Zharov, Aleksandrovsky, Utkin, and others.[2]

Woman is the mother of the world. And she is the mother not just because she gives birth to children, but because—and this is the important thing—she is the one who brings up a man and provides the greatest joys in his life. Just remember how much you gave to Furmanov. It surely cannot be that the force which you shared has withered within you. I don't believe that it can have withered entirely.

You should think of the collective Man, for whom your life is as essential as fire and light, as essential as happiness itself. Don't get me wrong—I'm not talking about kisses, even though I don't deny their importance too. I am talking of woman as the agent of culture and its mother.

You must forgive me, I am unable to write more: my shoulder is desperately painful.

With my best regards,

A. Peshkov

SOURCE: *SS* 29: 466–8.

---

[1] Furmanova's husband, the writer Dmitrii Andreevich Furmanov (1891–1926), died of meningitis on 15 March.

[2] A. A. Zharov (1904–84), V. D. Aleksandrovsky (1897–1934), and I. P. Utkin (1903–44), Soviet poets.

128. To M. M. Prishvin, [22 September 1926]

[Sorrento]

I do not believe that our literature has ever known such a nature-lover, such a perspicacious connoisseur and pure poet of nature as you, M. M. I began to suspect this even when you had only written 'The Black Arab', *Small Round Loaf* [*Kolobka*] and *The Land of Unfrightened Birds* [*Krai nepugannykh ptits*]. I was finally convinced when I read your quite amazing *Springs* [*Rodniki*].[1] Aksakov's *Notes of a Hunter* [*Zapiski ruzheinogo okhotnika*] and *About Fishing* [*Ob uzhen'i ryby*][2] are magnificently done, Menzbir managed to write some excellent pages in his book about birds, and Kaigorodov and many others occasionally have some heartfelt words inspired by nature.[3] But these are all men of parts, in none of them have I discovered such all-embracing, such perspicacious and triumphant love of our land and all the living and—seemingly—dead things upon it as I have found in your works. You are truly 'father and master of all you see'. In your every word and feeling I detect something ancient, prophetic, a pagan beauty—in other words, something truly human which comes from the heart of the Son of the Earth, and of the Great Mother, whom you so revere. And as I read your 'phenological' conjectures and thoughts, I smile and laugh with joy, so wonderful and charming is everything you write![4] I am not exaggerating. I truly experience the most exceptional beauty, by virtue of which your radiant soul illuminates everything in life, endowing all creatures—birds, grasses, hares, 'impious' peasant women, the ludicrous 'glass-blower', and Palkin—with unusual significance and justification. All things in your works merge into a single 'living' current, everything is given meaning by your intelligent heart and filled with a touching, moving spirit of friendship towards man and towards yourself as poet and sage. For you are a sage. Who else would venture to say: 'and so by killing they become more just', and 'somehow or other they are even learning to respect man more'? You have many such great and unusual thoughts. But you have an even greater number of the most marvellous subtleties: 'Where did the little rascal come from?'; 'A mouse ran by!' (p. 15). You magnificent devil, you! 'And when I came, the world began'—that is so good that I want to shout out loud: hurrah, this is real Russian art for you! It's true, quite true!

One day some critic of a philosophical bent will write something about your 'Pantheism' or 'Panpsychism' or 'Hylozoism', and in so doing he will sully your human face with treacly praise or spicy homilies. In my eyes, however, right now, *at this very moment*, you are the affirmation of a geo-optimism which is fully justified and which you yourself have firmly established. It is this very same geo-optimism which humanity will have to adopt as its religion sooner or later. For if people are fated to live in love and friendship with one another and with their nature, if man is destined to be 'master and father of all he sees', and not its slave—as he is at present—then he will only achieve that happy state by following your path. You are performing a great deed, although it will not be understood or felt for some time. I am in no way so arrogant as to say that I understand you completely, but I am convinced that I understand unerringly the huge significance of the wisdom which you possess and preach so amazingly. This is what I wanted to say to you even when I read on the pages of *Krasnaia nov'* almost everything that was later to appear in *Springs*. I wish you strength and perseverance and good spirits, my dear man.

I am now going to write to a seventeen-year-old girl, who has described her 'boyfriend' to me in these terms: 'a thief, a drunkard, and a robber, but a fine lad'. I wrote her a letter asking, how could this be, my dear? Today I received her reply: 'Sometimes even bad people have one big good thing about them which makes up for all the bad, and you cannot help but forgive them for everything.' There's the wisdom of a seventeen-year-old for you. It's not new, however. But it's not bad, is it?

Will *The Youth of Alpatov* [*Iunost' Alpatova*] soon be published in book form?[5]

I am very pleased that Gosizdat has published *Valia*, the first volume of Sergeev-Tsensky's novel; I like the book a lot.[6]

I am also delighted by A. P. Chapygin's *Razin*. What a powerful piece!

Sergei Grigoriev-Patrashkin is living in Sergiev. He's an interesting man.[7]

I send my warmest regards, dear M. M.

Keep well.

A. Peshkov

Greetings to your wife and children!

What a charming family you must have.

There are three great writers in Russia today, and all three are unusual in a novel way. The three are you, the creator of a completely new outlook on life, S.-Tsensky, who is singing a requiem mass for the dear, absurd, old Russian intelligentsia with such amazing tenderness and love, and Chapygin, who is creating the first truly historical Russian novel and displays amazing insight into the very spirit and flesh of the epoch he is depicting.

I admit that out of a feeling of friendship or from kindness you might say that there's Gorky as well. I have my own opinion of him, and I would not place him alongside you three. I say this not out of false modesty, but because I know that he is a considerably lesser artist than any of you three. That is so.

All the best, my dear M. M.

A. Peshkov

SOURCE: *SS* 29: 476–8.

¹ *The Springs of Berendei*, published by the State Publishing House in 1926. Prishvin had just sent a copy of this book to Gorky.
² Sergei Timofeevich Aksakov (1791–1859), author famous for his nature books and semi-fictionalized accounts of his family.
³ Menzbir, *The Birds of Russia* (1893–95); D. N. Kaigorodov was professor at the Forest Institute in St Petersburg and author of many popular books on natural history.
⁴ Phenology is the branch of science concerned with the relationship between climate and periodic biological phenomena, such as bird migration. *The Springs of Berendei* bore the sub-title 'Notes of a Phenologist'.
⁵ Autobiographical novel by Prishvin.
⁶ The first volume of Sergeev-Tsensky's *Transfiguration*.
⁷ Sergei Timofeevich Grigoriev-Patrashkin (1875–1953), writer noted for his childrens' adventure stories.

129. To O. D. Forsh, [27 September 1926]

[Sorrento]

I enjoyed your letter, Olga Dmitrievna, and I would be very grateful if you could find a free hour to share your thoughts about Fedorov with me. His first book of articles is a rarity; it was published some twenty years ago in the city of Verny.¹ A third volume is being prepared for publication in Harbin by Fedorov's admirers; a certain N. A. Setnitsky is in charge. This group has published an anonymous 80–page booklet with the title *Deification of the Dead* [*Smertobozhnichestvo*]. The work aims at the reform of Orthodoxy in the spirit of 'participation'. The line of the argument displays the obvious influence of Fedorov; it also has something of the pagan from V. V. Rozanov, in my opinion. The critical section of the pamphlet contains many interesting things, but unfortunately the 'new faith' concludes with a fivefold anathema upon dissenters. It goes like this:

1. May anyone who restricts man's participation in the work of God be anathematized.
2. May anyone submitting before death itself and seeing no shame in it be anathematized.
3. May anyone who turns away from the task and the fight for the transformation of the flesh be anathematized.
4. May anyone justifying death and not opposing it be anathematized.
5. May those not fighting for the active cause also be cursed.

There is something of the archpriest Avvakum² and of a *rational* fanaticism in all this, and that is why it is unacceptable to me. But in general, as the expression of an inextinguishable, *heartfelt* idea, it is very interesting and a great deal more valuable than the anaemic meditations of Prince Trubetskoi on 'Eurasianism'—meditations that have also been borrowed from Fedorov, even though the prince and his comrades-in-arms remain silent about that.³

There are some big themes in your work, O[lga] D[mitrievna]; the Novikov theme is especially valuable. *Contemporaries* [*Sovremenniki*] allows one to expect with confidence that Novikov will prove a success, for you have an extremely finely developed intuition for comprehending the past—so it seems to me.[4] We have never had a historical novel in the true sense of the term, and now one appears at just the right moment. That's wonderful.

I do not remember whether I told you that I hold Tynianov's book *Kiukhlia* in high regard and that I am in total ecstasy over Chapygin's *Razin*. What do you think of these works? Don't be lazy—write! I have a tendency sometimes to exaggerate out of my love for literature, but that is natural enough for one in love.

I was sincerely touched by your words: 'We have met now.' You know, I have admired your soul from afar for a long time; I won't say that I understand it, but it somehow brings me joy. I wish you all the best. But how did you injure your foot? Was it a tram? With warm regards.

A. Peshkov

SOURCE: *LN* 70: 588–90.

[1] See Letter 110, n. 3.
[2] Avvakum (1621–82), archpriest and leader of the Old Believers, a breakaway sect from the Russian Orthodox church. He was burned at the stake for his uncompromising religious views.
[3] A reference to ideas expounded by Nikolai Trubetskoi in the volumes *Europe and Mankind* [*Evropa i chelovechestvo*] (1920) and *Exodus to the East* [*Iskhod k vostoku*] (1921).
[4] In a letter to Gorky, Forsh had talked of writing a novel about the eighteenth-century literary figure Nikolai Novikov, but the project was never realized. Her historical novel *Contemporaries*, on Gogol and the painter Aleksandr Ivanov, came out in 1926.

130. To E. P. Peshkova, [14 October 1926]

[Sorrento]

It's most amusing to watch Marfa running about and to hear her squeals of joy as she says 'I can do it myself', which she accompanies with a theatrical laugh and a toss of her head. She's rather capricious and nervous, although the nurse is trying to cure her of her caprices, and not without success. She's an amusing little lass.

Maksim is well. He is buying a car, and often goes to Naples. He went off there today with Fedor Chaliapin junior.[1] He and his wife have been living here for more than a month now and they have been dining with us. A. N. Benois's son was here too; he is also an artist, and not a bad one at that.[2] He's only twenty-two years old, but he's already done the designs for *Boris* [*Godunov*] at La Scala, for which he received 50,000 lira, and *Crime and Punishment*—30,000.

Fedor Chaliapin is also gifted but lazy. Both he and Benois have become great friends with Maksim.

Now here's a thing, mother: for my sixtieth birthday the Germans are preparing a book dedicated to that event. The book will give an account of my life. The Germans would very much like to have some 'illustrative material'. You don't happen to have any of my old photographs or other such things, do you? I seem to recall that there was a drawing of my cell in the Nizhnii Novgorod prison and a photograph of the house in Arzamas, wasn't there? Are there any writers' 'groups' or other rubbish of that sort?

If you do find anything, please send it. I need family photos—of Maksim, and Katia.

I'm very worried that the books Iola handed over to you won't get through to me here.[3] I need them desperately.

You should be receiving 500 roubles from Viatkin in Novosibirsk.

It's not right for you to be ailing. Why, you've even been to Italy.

My right shoulder is unbearably painful.

Keep well.

A.

I called Boris 'Fedor' by mistake. He paints decent studies. He is a most ignorant fellow, but he's talented. He drinks. And he's spoilt. Nightingale has begun to paint well. And a lot. Timosha has become lazy.

Maksim has not been himself, so distracted has he become by the purchase of the car.

SOURCE: *AG* 9: 256–7.

---

[1] Chaliapin's son was actually called Boris; Gorky recognizes his mistake in the postscript to this letter.
[2] Aleksandr Nikolaevich Benois (1870–1960), painter, theatre and ballet designer, art historian, and central figure in the 'World of Art' movement. Nikolai Aleksandrovich (1901–88) was his son; he emigrated to Italy. He was, of course, older than twenty-two.
[3] Iola Chaliapin, Italian ballerina, Chaliapin's first wife.

131. To F. V. Gladkov, [30 November 1926]

[Sorrento]

In your last letter, F[edor] V[asilievich], you wrote something very important about yourself. 'I appear to be disabling myself,' you wrote, 'through a lack of faith in my creative ability.' You are absolutely right. You have become disabled, and in my opinion this very lack of faith is your major shortcoming, and perhaps a fundamental one too. Because you lack faith in your powers of representation, in the solidity—I mean this in the corporeal sense—of your writing, and in your experience of life, you rely on verbose and sometimes feeble narration and description in places where proper artistic representation is needed and where, with your gifts, you could easily write with supple precision. Reading your works, one often feels that you are trying stubbornly to persuade yourself that 'these are the words that need to be used so that the story will be more "true to life" '. But instead, the opposite is often the result. You use superfluous words to 'record' an image or a character, in the same way that some painters 'record' a portrait or landscape, thereby achieving a photographic likeness and hence depriving that likeness of any 'spirit'. And yet your every idea is 'spiritual', that is, it represents the crystallization of your feelings, your thoughts and your spiritual energy. That is the main thing. You ask: 'Isn't verisimilitude one of the most important indications of artistic value, which even the most avid formalist would be unable to deny?' The formalists are quite 'beside the point' here; this has nothing to do with why they are bad—this is not their subject at all. But verisimilitude is a dangerous thing for artists. Zola, the Goncourts, our own Pisemsky—they are all true to life, that is so. However, Defoe (*Robinson Crusoe*) and Cervantes (*Don Quixote*) are far closer to the truth about man than the 'naturalists' or photographers are. Gogol is not very true to life in his treatment of the epoch depicted in *Dead Souls*, for in his day, as well as the Sobakeviches and Korobochkas,[1] there were also highly cultured landowners—the Aksakovs, the Khomiakovs, the Kireevskys, the Bakunins, and so forth. The image created by an artist's words is true to life when it seems almost physically tangible and three-dimensional—like Lev Tolstoy's Uncle Eroshka and his 'Polikushka',[2] or Flaubert's Madame Bovary. If you are to achieve this kind of tangibility, your writing should be spare, rich, and bold; you must believe *that what you know is known to nobody but yourself.* Don't be afraid of being naïve; many people have given this advice, and very good advice it is too.

You ask if I am 'completely' with you. I cannot be 'completely' with people who convert class psychology into a caste psychology; I will never be 'completely' with people who say: 'We, the proletarians' with the same sort of emotion as others in the past when they said: 'We, the nobility'. I still do not see any 'proletarians' in Russia, but what I do see, in the persons of the workers, are the true masters of the Russian land and the teachers of all its other inhabitants. It is time we understood the first part of this and were proud of it. As for the second, this calls for the careful treatment of each person, so that 'each person' should have no rightful cause to say of the worker that he is not the organizer and teacher of the new life, but just the same kind of tyrant as any other dictator, and one who is just as stupid. In particular, the position occupied by the workers does not require at all that they should steal, act like hooligans, rape girls, and beat up doctors.

But I *am* 'completely' with those who, despite the hellish difficulty of their lives, despite their personal torments, are carrying out the great task of organizing Russia as a country from which creative energy should be—and already is—pouring out over all *our man-made earth*. I am with those who, in the space of just five years, have already learned to establish enterprises which could not have been created even in twenty years under the old regime. I am with those who sense the poetry of free labour and understand its significance. When I receive *Rabochaia gazeta* [*The Worker's Paper*] and *Krest'ianskaia gazeta* [*The Peasant's Paper*], with their countless intelligent supplements, I am proud: there is no other country where such a phenomenon would be possible, where the interests of the people could be so comprehensively served. What is being done in Russia today is more evident from here, from afar, and it is amazing work. It is of course painful to see how quickly our best people are dying out, one after another; it is painful to lose the likes of Krasin. I knew him for twenty-three years; he was a great man. But what can you do? Others like him will come along, they must.

I live in Italy because, were I to live in Russia, I would never get any work done; I would simply travel from city to city, go from house to house and—chat. And—certainly, inevitably—I would quarrel bitterly with many different people, especially with the literary critics, who in their intellectual blindness and spiritual illiteracy still cannot understand what a wonderful phenomenon our contemporary literature is and how necessary it is to love and protect our men of letters, young men who already have the experience of old men who have lived half a century.

There, my dear F. V., is my answer to your wonderful, friendly letter. With warm regards,

A. Peshkov

SOURCE: *SS* 29: 483–5.

---

[1] Characters from Gogol's novel who represent negative traits of the Russian gentry in a caricatured form.

[2] Uncle Eroshka, a central character in Tolstoy's novella *The Cossacks*. Polikushka appears in a story of the same title.

132. To E. P. Peshkova, [14 December 1926]

[Sorrento]

So Andrei Iurievich has left us.[1] And so soon. Although he was, as you say, sixty-two years old, in my memory this wonderful man remains the same lively and spirited person I knew back in 1921. However, five years have gone by since then. Time flies incredibly quickly.

I feel dreadfully sad about Leonid [Krasin]. He worked himself to death well before his time. Good people disappear so quickly, and you don't see their equal again. I don't feel like talking about this.

Everything's all right at home. The number one person, Marfa, is of course becoming more amusing with each new day. She says German words: bitte, Porree, etc. If you make a face at her and say: 'Here comes terrible old granddad', she runs away squealing and laughs out loud. Nightingale dances with her to music on the record-player; she stamps her little feet and twists her head and arms in the funniest way. She has a good appetite. She's very wilful and capricious. Her father spoils her, of course. A wonderful little lass. What we lack is a boy as well, but the parents, damn it, are both such egoists!

Now, then: will you be going to Kharkov? If you do go, please visit the Gorky colony in Pesochin, have a good look around and write to me about it.[2] All right?

On the occasion of my thirty-fifth jubilee I would like the authorities to give me something for the benefit of the colony.[3]

It seems that Ukrainian nationalism is on the rise. That's all we needed!

For the holidays, could you possibly send me some mushrooms marinated in vodka? A number of people will probably be coming to Italy soon as replacements for Kerzhentsev.[4] Or else you could ask them to send me a parcel via diplomatic courier, since they come here often.

Downstairs is carefully preparing the Christmas tree. Marfushka is getting a wonderful pair of shoes, red ones. The rascal loves pretty footwear. What a girl!

Well, all the best. I hope your holiday is a merry one. It would be better, of course, if you were to celebrate it with us.

M[ariia] I[gnatievna] [Budberg] has gone to see her children.

Maksim has an abscess on the finger of his right hand. This is the result of his fussing about with his car and not taking care of himself. He goes around with dirty hands.

Goodbye for now,

　　　　　　　　　　　　　　　　　　　　　　　　　　　　　　A.

SOURCE: *AG* 9: 259–60.

[1] A. Iu. Feit, Russian doctor whom Peshkova knew through her involvement with the SRs.

[2] The famous educationalist and writer Anton Semenovich Makarenko (1888–1939) had set up a youth colony in Ukraine.

[3] The year 1927 marked the thirty-fifth anniversary of the publication of Gorky's first story, 'Makar Chudra'.

[4] Platon Kerzhentsev had just been relieved of his duties as ambassador to Italy.

133. To the Editors of Izvestiia, *[before 15 January 1927]*

[Sorrento]

Dear Comrade Editor!

Be so kind as to publish the following letter in *Izvestiia*:

For some time now people have been publishing in the newspapers my private letters to writers.

I recall that in the old days writers waited more or less patiently until a correspondent was dead and buried before they printed his letters.

I would ask my brethren of the pen to wait just a little in my case too, so as not to put me in the ridiculous and awkward position of a person who seems to be dispensing 'licences', 'attestations', etc. while he is still alive.

I think my fellow writers may themselves feel a little awkward, perhaps, about the haste with which they are publishing my letters.

It seems to me that they have been misled by A. Lunacharsky and N. Piksanov, who have mistakenly placed me in the ranks of writers who are deceased.

This is the only way I can explain the fact that, having decided to publish a volume of 'selected works' by M. Gorky, Lunacharsky and Piksanov have not asked the author whether he wants such an edition to appear and which of his works he himself would 'select' for it.[1]

Incidentally, the works of Leskov, G. Uspensky, V. G. Korolenko, and others already 'selected' by Lunacharsky and Piksanov have been chosen most arbitrarily and fail completely, in my opinion, to fulfil the task the editors set themselves, which was to provide 'rich social content together with a high level of artistry'.

M. Gorky

SOURCE: *SS* 30: 7.

[1] Lunacharsky and Piksanov responded lamely that the oversight was due to a change in the publisher's schedule.

134. To N. N. Narvekov,[1] *[13 April 1927]*

[Sorrento]

I think, N. N., that you yourself sense that your poetry and prose are 'imperfect', or to put the matter simply, rather bad. You are as yet unable to express your personality and soul in your own words, and you write almost exactly like hundreds of our rural correspondents these days. But note that I use the word *almost*. This is because it seems to me that you have a literary gift and a personality of your own, but it is just that you lack the words. However, a great many recognized writers publishing in journals today suffer from this same shortcoming.

I will not, of course, even begin to answer your question for you—literature or public service?—you are the only one who can make that decision. I will say, however, that in my opinion literature is also public service, and a very difficult service it is too. I have been writing for thirty-five years now, and I have probably not been satisfied with myself even fifteen times.

All the same I would give you this advice: learn to write, learn to observe, read, and keep on learning all things always.

You were wrong to call yourself (jokingly or scathingly?) a 'lousy rural-correspondent'; rural correspondents and workers' correspondents are an extraordinarily important phenomenon in our life, and the person who brought them into being is a real genius. You rural correspondents are the future rural intelligentsia, a force 'of the earth' which should reform the entire way of life and the entire economic system of the countryside down to its very roots, thereby forging the countryside and the cities both spiritually and psychologically into a unified and truly revolutionary force. I know very well that life is difficult for you and that you are not understood; I know how many of your fellow workers have been maimed and killed. That is of little importance: they will not destroy everyone. The old power, hostile to innovation, is becoming weaker and dying out, whilst your army is constantly growing.

What you all need is one thing, which is to have a proper understanding of the important work that awaits you, of the great task that you, the Communists of the countryside, can accomplish. And it is necessary for all of you to study persistently, to keep studying everything, always. That's the thing. Finally, let me say to you personally: if you love literary work, if you love to write, don't give it up! The work of a writer is bitter work, but it is necessary. And it is especially important now that it has been taken up by hundreds of people such as yourself.

I wish you all the best.

A. Peshkov

I am returning your poetry.

SOURCE: *SS* 30: 18–19.

---

[1] As this letter makes clear, Narvekov worked as a village correspondent for the local press.

135. To M. M. Prishvin, [middle of April 1927]

[Sorrento]

Dear Mikhail Mikhailovich,

Of course I have no objection to the footnote to the article, although I cannot for the life of me recollect what I wrote about Kant, whom I don't like.[1] I tend to have such a careless attitude to all my thoughts about things I don't like, and I forget them quickly. But I do like women, especially mothers. I am always thinking of them, and I peck about all over the place with my snub nose for thoughts which might compliment them. Quite recently I read in Bogdanov's book *The Struggle for Viability* [*Bor'ba za zhiznesposobnost'*]: 'in their initial composition, the cells of the male body are less complex than those of the woman's, and this means that one may assume them to be biologically inferior.' I have known Bogdanov well for a long time; I esteem him highly, for he is a heretic, and what is better than a heretic among men? I also love you for your heresy.

I still have not finished my novel,[2] nor do I know when I shall, but I am almost certain already that it will be a difficult and unsuccessful book. I cannot depict women, and my female characters will probably be like that painting of the Pope by a Catholic-Chinese artist (there was such a painting in the Missionary Exhibition at the Vatican during the *anno santo*), in which the Pope turned out to have slant eyes and yellow skin. Yes indeed. Generally speaking, I am a smart lad, but I have little talent. It's true.

Returning to the subject of women: I am certain that the twentieth century will be the century of a gynaecocratic movement. Men have worked themselves to a standstill. Their only talent is for counting: the distance to Mars is 10 miles, a nerve cell weighs 0.000? microns, the distance between one human soul and another is 249 billion light years, and so forth.

I read *The Republic of Shkid* [*Respublika Shkid*],[3] and I am corresponding with the authors. Have you met them? Judging from their letters, they are fine, modest, intelligent people. I enjoyed their book and I was terribly affected by it. But how did they manage to portray Vikniksor, the school director, so monumentally? That's Panteleev's doing; he is more talented than Belykh, who is inclined to use words to create photographs.

If you could send me Albanov, Arseniev, and *Man's Friend* [*Drug cheloveka*] I would be very grateful.[4]

I have *The Chain of Kashchei*, but I have yet to reread it. I read a lot, all the 'current literature'—but, alas, the current is flowing in the wrong direction. I take a rest from it with the *Notes* of the malicious Vigel, *The Paterikon of the Cave Monastery* [*Paterik Pecherskii*], the prophets, and a variety of old things.[5] My eyes hurt, my asthma is choking me, and I'm besieged by foreigners—woe is me!

Say hello to S. T. Grigoriev[-Patrashkin] and give him my regards. He is a man of good calibre.

Sergeev-Tsensky is publishing with Mysl'; I am afraid they will treat him badly. He should have been with Lengiz, but they were too slow to offer him their services.[6] Would you like to read a good book? Get *Belarmino and Apolonio* by Pérez de Ayala, Kubuch Publishing House, 1925.[7]

With warm regards,

A. Peshkov

SOURCE: *LN* 70: 344–5.

[1] In a letter to Gorky of 2 April, Prishvin explained that he had sent Gorky's last letter to Gruzdev. The passage in question read: 'I do not like Kant, for he is the one who places man beyond "heaven and earth", whilst I am a geocentrist, anthropocentrist, and anthropomorphist' (*LN* 70: 342). Prishvin also mentioned that Olga Forsh had told him that Gorky was writing about women.

[2] *The Life of Klim Samgin.*

[3] *The Republic of Shkid*, children's novel by L. Panteleev and Grigorii Belykh, both of whom had attended the Dostoevsky School for children made homeless by the Revolution and the Civil War.

[4] V. Albanov, *Between Life and Death. Diary of a Participant in the Brusilov Expedition* [*Mezhdu zhizn'iu i smert'iu. Dnevnik uchastnika ekspeditsii Brusilova*] (1926); V. K. Arseniev, *In the Jungles of the Ussuri Region* [*V debriakh Ussuriiskogo kraia*] (1926); Iu. M. Smelnitsky, *Man's Friend* (1925).

[5] *The Notes of Filipp Filippovich Vigel* [*Zapiski Filippa Filippovicha Vigelia*—1891–3]. Vigel (1786–1856), government official and writer who denounced the Russian philosopher Petr Chaadaev. The thirteenth-century *Paterikon* is a major work of Old Russian literature.

[6] Mysl' [Thought], private publishing house in Leningrad; Lengiz, Leningrad branch of the official State Publishing House.

[7] *Belarmino y Apolonio* (1921) by Ramon Pérez de Ayala (1880–1962).

136. *To A. K. Voronsky, [29 April 1927]*

[Sorrento]

To my regret, I did *not* receive your detailed letter about matters at *Krasnaia nov'*.[1]

I hasten to warn you of a possible mistake in your evaluation of Klim Samgin. For he too is an 'invented' person, although one invented more by others than by himself.[2] So it seemed to you that he observes life 'through simple eyes'? Yes, he would like to see it simplified, and to the greatest extent possible; but that is only because he is organically anti-revolutionary and—in particular!—anti-socialist. He will be a 'revolutionary despite himself' up until 1906; he will greet the failure of the first revolution with secret joy; he will live through to 1916 striving for a 'simplification of reality'; in 1917 he will again have to 'make revolution'; and the events of October will ultimately expose and overthrow him, destroying him in the end. His is that sort of nature which is typically represented by Melgunov, for example.³ In any case, he is not a mouthpiece for the author's sympathies (to the extent that one can talk at all of such sympathies in a work in which the author has intended to be completely objective).

'Perhaps there wasn't any boy' is not Samgin's only leitmotif; there is another—'But why are you making mischief?'⁴ You know, of course, that nowadays this is the leitmotif of all *émigré* thought, not only among the 'liberal democrats' but also among part of the 'socialist' emigration. And once this has been revealed in such a naked, unattractive, and—to put it plainly—such a cynical and embittered form, I take that to mean that the disease was chronic and has now 'come out into the open'. There you are, then.

Apropos of *Krasnaia nov'*, I have written to Mariia Ilyinichna Ulianova, pointing out that Bukharin should have paid greater attention to *Novyi mir* [*New World*] in his 'Angry Notes' ['Zlye zametki']. Surely the mistakes of that journal are more significant than the mistakes of *Krasnaia nov'*, even if one does admit that Danilin's poems were a mistake?⁵

N. Tikhonov—that's the poet, isn't it?—displays great talent in his *Venturesome Man* [*Riskovannyi chelovek*]. I also liked Bezymensky's *Feliks*; even though I am no great admirer of that particular versifier.⁶ But Tikhonov has a most original and very clearly defined talent. You should rope him in for *Krasnaia nov'*.

But what do they think they are writing in *Molodaia gvardiia* [*Young Guard*]? See issue 3, p. 194, the article by Kuzmin: '*the person . . . was transformed into a sedentary log of the pig-headed kind.*'⁷ What sterling stuff!

You should start a section in *Krasnaia nov'* in which such 'slips of the pen' would receive the emphasis they deserve. The sickly condition of grammar reflects upon the health of ideology.

Thanks for your comments on the first volume. I will shorten it for separate publication. I hope that the second volume will be richer and more colourful.

Keep well. Will you be going to see Sergeev-Tsensky in Alushta? The second volume of his *Transfiguration* is remarkably good. He has undertaken a grand task. So Krug has published Iavich—that's too bad! They obviously didn't read the manuscript. Had they read it, they would doubtless have suggested to the author that he edit it.⁸

SOURCE: *AG* 10/2: 54–5.

---

¹ Voronsky had just been forced off the editorial board of the journal.

² In a letter of 20 April, Voronsky had written: 'As far as I see it, *the novel depicts people who are inventing themselves*, whilst Klim observes the world through simple eyes' (*AG* 10/2: 53).

³ Sergei Melgunov (1879–1956), editor and member of the Kadet Party; he became noted for his anti-Bolshevik views in later years.

⁴ The first of these phrases is perhaps the most frequently repeated passage in the novel. Out of

concern for himself, Klim Samgin does not assist a drowning friend, and afterwards he comes to question in his mind whether that friend even existed.

⁵ Bukharin was still a powerful member of the Politburo, and Mariia Ulianova, as Lenin's sister and a member of *Pravda*'s editorial board, could exert some influence. The poet's name was actually Pavel Druzhinin.

⁶ *Feliks*, narrative poem about Feliks Dzerzhinsky.

⁷ Gorky quotes from an article by Vladimir Kuzmin, 'Culturalism and Politics' ['Kul'turnichestvo i politika'].

⁸ *The Way* [*Put'*], by Avgust Iavich (1900–79).

137. *To M. M. Prishvin, [15 May 1927]*

[Sorrento]

You were so right, Mikhail Mikhailovich, in what you said about Rozanov—that, like the cat in the bag, he is bound to get out. He was a most interesting person, a genius almost. I never met him, but we did correspond at one time, and I very much enjoyed reading his 'anti-incendiary' writings. It used to surprise me that such a furious enemy of Christ and Christian humanism could have been regarded for some time by the 'neo-Christians' of the Religious-Philosophical Society as one of their own!¹ He was the first Russian herald of the crisis of humanism. In this regard Blok owed much to him,² as did Gershenzon with his denial of culture, which was expressed with particular sharpness in 'A Correspondence from Two Corners' ['Perepiska iz dvukh uglov'].³ In this sense and in this domain—the battle against Christ—Rozanov was, in my opinion, one of our 'spiritual' revolutionaries, and although his shyness made him thick of speech, he was no worse than Konstantin Leontiev or Mikhail Bakunin in the directness of his thinking.

Yes, they removed humanism from our life. And like a potato, the best part of it is in the ground. When I look at what remains, I see that our humanistic intelligentsia, in its state of 'diffusion' throughout Europe, has lost its features with amazing rapidity. So now we have Professor Ilyin, who draws on the canonical gospels, the church fathers, the theologians and his own putrid, but sharp, intellect in order to concoct his own Gospel of Vengeance, in which he argues that one must not kill people except when they are Communists.⁴ And that God-loving neo-Christian Zinaida Gippius proclaims to her associates that there is no need to shout about the Bolsheviks—'let us just hang them in silence'. In this she is joined by the 'God-man' N. V. Chaikovsky, a man who gave his blessing to the intervention, and by Anton Kartashev, a professor at the Theo[logical] Academy and a God-fearing man but one who is as malicious as a fox.⁵

You must forgive me, for perhaps you won't find much of interest in any of this, but I cast my eye over two or three *émigré* newspapers every day, and it is difficult, you know, to look upon Russian people who have uprooted themselves from Russia to such an extent that they are insensitive to it and do not wish—or is it that they are no longer able?—to understand the pangs of its rebirth. Instead, they try to persuade each other, day after day, ever more tediously and in semi-literate fashion, that these are its death-throes. I do not speak of semi-literacy for nothing: even the old people here are forgetting the Russian language.

I was visited recently by a Moscow woman who was passing through here on her way back from Constantinople, where she had gone to take pictures of Byzantine art. She sang me some *chastushki*.[6] I was amazed by what they can do with the Russian language in Russia! And how witty they are!:

> Well, I'll get up and look around —
> To see how well I'm lying down.

I am reading your *Stories of a Hunter* [*Rasskazy egeria*]. They are excellent! You have such a wonderful knowledge of the language, such wise simplicity and resonance!

With warm regards,

A. Peshkov

In America they are writing good things, and with great understanding, concerning S[ergeev]-Tsensky and his book *Transfiguration*. I sent him some reviews yesterday.

SOURCE: *LN* 70: 346–8.

---

[1] Founded by Merezhkovsky, Gippius, and Filosofov, this society became a focal point for the religious renaissance in early twentieth-century Russia.

[2] In 'The Collapse of Humanism'.

[3] Mikhail Osipovich Gershenzon (1869–1925), literary critic and philosopher whose 1921 'Correspondence' with the Symbolist poet Viacheslav Ivanovich Ivanov (1866–1949) expressed his joy at being liberated from 'the imprisonment of culture' and his desire to forget all religion, philosophy, and art, in order to 'come on to the shore naked, like the first man'.

[4] Ivan Aleksandrovich Ilyin (1882–1954), prominent neo-Hegelian philosopher, exiled from the Soviet Union in 1922.

[5] On Chaikovsky, see Letter 43, n. 1. Kartashev (1875–1960), professor of theology and member of the Religious-Philosophical Society, later Minister of Religion in the Kerensky government.

[6] The *chastushka* is a brief folk lyric, generally two or four lines long, which is usually sung. Gorky's visitor was Olga Nikolaevna Bubnova, an art historian.

---

138. To E. P. Peshkova, [9 June 1927]

[Sorrento]

I will write to you about Marfa, but in return you must send me some books by Jerome K. Jerome, who is dying, despite the fact that he was a good humorist.[1] In general, I have noticed that everyone is dying. Children need Jerome; they're complaining that there's nothing to read. I understand them.

Marfa is growing hugely. She speaks Italo–Russo–German: Giduka is grandfather, aphisin is orange, fifi—bird, fifiauto—aeroplane, etc.

She does not suffer from respect for her elders. She likes to powder them; she has just powdered my nose and eyebrows. She likes to go for rides in her father's car. She's very popular with the local people; everyone around here knows her. She has learnt to squeal deafeningly from Titka.[2] She sings 'Tipperary' with her. Not a bad woman at all. She'll probably grow up to be an anarchist.

Timosha is feeling quite good. Maksim is planning to go with Benois to the Adriatic coast. He is well and has put on weight. He goes swimming.

The events in London have made me so upset that I felt like going to Russia just so that I could enter into a swearing match with Europe from there.[3] I can't do it from here: they would throw me out, and then I would never get my book finished.[4] I think that this will be my last book, after which I'll occupy myself with journalism.

Well, that's everything about Marfa and all the others. I don't know who published Jerome—probably Mezhdunarodnaia kniga.

Oh, yes, please send me Panaeva-Golovacheva's *Memoirs* as well.[5] I need them very badly.

Ask Petr Petrovich [Kriuchkov] why Gosizdat isn't sending any money. Pass on my regards—although not to Gosizdat, of course.

I sent a letter requesting that Dalmat Aleksandrovich Lutokhin be allowed to return to Russia.[6] Please find out whether the letter has been received. And what will the 'resolution' be, I wonder?

E. M. Lanina has written, asking me for money.[7] I'll send her some.

Zubakin and Tsvetaeva are a most interesting couple and you should be nice to them.[8] I'll take up the matter of getting a visa for Zubakin. Semenov has written to me. I'm waiting for the manuscripts from Khodia [Khodasevich]. Elena hasn't answered.

Do you happen to know the address of Pinkevich, Adam?[9]

Goodbye. Will you be here in September perhaps? For the birth?[10]

A.—father and grandparent, and I wish the same to you. Greetings to the great-grandmother. She ought to be ashamed of herself, living to such an age![11] If you look after yourself, the same thing could happen to you.

You see how gloomy my jokes are. It's all because of those Englishmen!

SOURCE: *AG* 9: 266–7.

[1] Jerome K. Jerome (1859–1927) was very popular in Russia at the time.
[2] Moura Budberg.

[3] After an incident in London involving the Soviet trade mission, England broke off diplomatic relations with the Soviet Union.

[4] *The Life of Klim Samgin.*

[5] A. Ia. Panaeva-Golovacheva (1819–93). Her *Vospominaniia*, published in 1927, contain valuable information about the literary milieu of her day.

[6] Lutokhin (1885–1942), economist and literary critic. He returned to the Soviet Union from Czechoslovakia in November 1927.

[7] Widow of the lawyer for whom Gorky had worked in Nizhnii Novgorod.

[8] Boris Mikhailovich Zubakin (1894–1937), archaeologist and improvisational poet. Anastasiia Tsvetaeva (1894–1993), sister of the poet Marina.

[9] Albert [not Adam] Pinkevich (1883–1939), a professor who had worked at KUBU.

[10] Gorky's second granddaughter, Daria, was born on 12 October 1927.

[11] Peshkova's mother, Mariia Volzhina, was seventy-nine in 1927.

139. To S. N. Sergeev-Tsensky, [15 July 1927]

[Sorrento]

Dear Sergei Nikolaevich!

Are you absolutely certain that your books 'will not appear'? I have heard that Gosizdat wants to 'buy up' your books from Mysl' so that it can publish them itself, just as it is doing with Prishvin and somebody else as well. Perhaps you will allow me to find out what's going on over there with your books?

My novel will most likely be a 'chronicle'. It will be factually interesting, and if they say that it was not written by an artist, then I will accept that as a valid judgement.[1] You remarked that I 'do not age'. That's bad. I think I belong to that category of people for whom ageing is a necessity .

It seems to me that you were wrong when you said of L. N. Tolstoy that he 'aged suddenly'. I think he was born with the intellect of an old man, a ponderous and somewhat dull intellect which was quite laughably insignificant when compared to his monstrous talent. Tolstoy became aware of the tragic disparity between these two qualities early on, and that is why he had no love of the intellect, why he reviled it and *struggled* against it all his life. Yet it was this very intellect that turned him into a preacher; hence the coldness of his preaching, its lack of talent. It was this very intellect that 'seized the artist by the throat', as L. N.'s letters and diaries of the 1840s and 1850s attest. By 1855 he had already decided to 'dedicate his entire life to the creation of a new religion', having just finished *The Cossacks* and a series of excellent works. His 'new religion' is really nothing other than a desperate and completely unsuccessful attempt by a misanthropically inclined rationalist to free himself from the narrow rationalism which constrained his talent. Everything which has been written about Tolstoy to date has been false and stupid, because it has been written from too *close* a viewpoint. After all, if you look at an enormous building from close up, you see only the details, not the entire edifice. People began to see Pushkin only seventy years after his death, they have been examining him in amazement for twenty years, and they still don't have a complete picture of him. Tolstoy was a lesser figure than Pushkin, of course, but he was an enormous one, none the less, and it will be some time before people succeed in making him out properly. In his figure and with his work he brought an entire epoch of our history to a remarkable conclusion.

So you complain that 'preachers seize artists by the throat'? But that has always been the case, my dear S. N. This world is not for artists; they have always found it too uncomfortable and small, and their role has been the more venerable and heroic for that.

A Kazan Tatar poet, dying from consumption and hunger, once said very aptly: 'My young soul is flying away, flying away from the iron cage of the world.'[2]

In that repetition of 'flying away' I hear joy. Personally, of course, I prefer the joy of living; it is *terribly* interesting to live.

Well, the heat here is no worse than yours over there; it hasn't rained once since May. The grapes will be excellent. I wish you good health, my dear S. N.!

A. Peshkov

SOURCE: *SS* 30: 29–31.

---

[1] *The Life of Klim Samgin.*
[2] From the poem 'Shattered Hope' by Gabdulla Tukai (1886–1913).

140. To B. L. Pasternak, [18 October 1927]

[Sorrento]

My dear Boris Leonidovich,

I said nothing about your book of poetry because I do not consider myself a sufficiently subtle connoisseur of poetry and also because I am convinced that you must be tired of praise.[1] But now that you have the idea that my silence signifies an unwillingness to tell you that the book is a failure, I shall tell you that is not the case. You are mistaken. The book is excellent; it is one of those books whose value is not immediately appreciated but which are destined to have a long life. I will be honest with you: until I read this book, I had always found reading your poetry something of a strain because its imagery was too dense, quite excessively so. And those images were not always clear to me; my *imagination* found it difficult to accommodate the wilful complexity of your images, their frequent lack of clarity. You yourself know well enough that you are a highly original creator of images; you probably know too that the rich-ness of those images often forces you to speak—to depict things—too sketchily. Your *1905* is more spare and simple; you are more classical in this book, a book saturated with a pathos which infects me, the reader, quickly, easily, and powerfully. No, this is an excellent book, of course; this is the voice of a real poet, a social poet, social in the best and most profound sense of the word. I will say nothing of the individual chapters, like the burial of Bauman and 'Moscow in December', for example, nor will I mention the numerous individual lines and words which pierce the reader's heart like red-hot needles.

'The Childhood of Liuvers' will come out in America in the spring, along with Olga Forsh's *Dressed in Stone* [*Odety kamnem*].[2]

What are you writing now? How are you?

An acquaintance of yours, Zubakin, stayed here with me for a couple of months. Judging from his letters, I had thought he was an interesting and talented person, but on making his personal acquaintance I was very disappointed and even annoyed by him. He is a man with good instincts, but he is quite incapable of doing anything, and he is amoral.

Once again, thank you for the book.

Warm regards,

A. Peshkov

SOURCE: *LN* 70: 300–01.

[1] Pasternak had sent Gorky a copy of his narrative poem *1905*.
[2] Moura Budberg translated both works into English and Gorky wrote introductions for them, but the book did not appear.

141. *To L. S. Danovsky*,[1] [*first half of November 1927*]

[Sorrento]

Yes, ten years ago I did not think as I do now. At that time I felt that Lenin was overestimating the might of a mobilized proletariat and that the Bolsheviks could not overcome the anarchy caused by the war and that they would simply be overwhelmed by that anarchy. In 1918, imme-diately after the attempt on Vladimir Ilyich's life, I rejected such notions, for the universal outrage of the workers at this infamous deed showed me that Lenin's idea, *and that of Bolshevism,* had become more deeply embedded in the consciousness of the masses than I had imagined. *Then followed the three years during which the proletariat heroically defended its freedom and attained victory.*

I observed the growth of those forces and their heroic deeds; and I have continued to observe the same from here over the last six years. I now think that the only people who cannot admit the significance of the great deeds accomplished by the Worker and Peasant State over the past decade are those who are blinded by malice towards the Bolsheviks because of their own personal failures, those who would want to return to that dubious 'cultural' life of the pre-war era, the petty bourgeois of various shades, small-minded men of ambition, and those who have had their day and are generally unfit for life.

*For your information, all of my articles from *Novaia zhizn'* have been published twice in book form, so there is probably no point in your threatening to publish one of them.*[2]

M. Gorky

SOURCE: *SS* 30: 45.

[1] Leonid Stepanovich Danovsky (1906–71), Leningrad worker.
[2] i.e the articles in the series *Untimely Thoughts*.

142. To E. P. Peshkova, [27 November 1927]

[Sorrento]

Now that you have had medals pinned on you by bourgeois governments inimical to the Russian people, you have begun to write this kind of Russian: 'drinks tea from the cup *which was dispatched by Maksim*'.[1] Shame on you; you went to a gymnasium, and you have been personally acquainted for thirty years now with one of the loftiest Russian writers,[2] a writer upon whom they have pinned every imaginable sin, and will continue to do so until the end of his days, and even beyond.

And another thing: you promised, you swore you would send me some books, but they haven't come. Shame on you again.

So please send:

Publisher: Zemlia i fabrika
Joseph Conrad, *Lord Jim*.
idem., Under Western Eyes

Be quick about it. By way of an advance, I'll tell you some stories about the girls. Dashka is a huge girl, she's already wearing the clothes that Marfa wore when she was six months old. Dashka has a calm disposition. When her mother finishes nursing her, she rumbles and belches. She smiles toothlessly at her grandfather and at the sun; the former finds this flattering, while the latter gets embarrassed and hides behind clouds. None the less Odarka remains a rather vague sort; that's probably because she is not yet two months old.

Marfa will probably be a lawyer and a café *chanteuse*. She is terribly talkative in three languages and her singing reveals that she has a good ear and also a penchant for a lively repertoire. She says, 'Ganpa, les sang' and 'Lo, ganpa'. She calls her mother 'Timosa'. She's becoming clever and wilful. And less nervous. She scratches the pimples on her face, looks at herself in the mirror and grimaces. She likes listening to music more and more, but when she does so, she gets coy and embarrassed for some unknown reason. In general, she's an excellent woman.

Olga Forsh is also excellent. Of all good women—yourself included— she is the very best. Everyone has fallen in love with her instantly: men, women, girls, the maid, dogs, and duchesses, to say nothing of the dukes, who are simply stunned. I've fallen in love with her too, of course, and she and I are going through a drama. In five acts. It's wonderful! Europe will gasp. Maksim has taken her to Rome, where he went to fetch Mariia Ignatievna [Budberg]. She has taken her sister there together with the body of her sister's husband; he poisoned himself in Naples and died as a result. He did it on purpose and left a note.

Everyone is healthy. Maksim is working most diligently, so please, don't you go inviting him anywhere.

Can you find out whether there is any truth in the report in *Rul'* that Khalatov[3] and [Skvortsov-]Stepanov have cobbled together a committee to organize a Gorky jubilee? I must have precise information about this, as I will be lodging an objection if it turns out to be true. And keep well— that you must also do.

Marfa has learned how to pull a fierce face. She also has the habit of running over to Nightingale and whispering nonsensical words in his ear most seriously. He does the same to her, and Marfushka then laughs out loud most charmingly.

A.

There's no time for me to write, damn it!

Send the books!

The Posse![4]

SOURCE: *AG* 9: 271–2.

[1] Peshkova had been awarded a medal by the Polish Red Cross in 1925.
[2] Gorky is joking here: he was a tall man.
[3] Artemii Bagratovich Khalatov (1896–1938) chaired the board at Gosizdat at this time.
[4] In a previous letter Gorky had asked for Vladimir Posse's book of memoirs, *My Life's Path* [*Moi zhiznennyi put'*].

143. To B. L. Pasternak,[1] [30 November 1927]

[Sorrento]

Should I wish you 'all the best', Boris Leonidovich? I am afraid that you might take offence. For, knowing how much of the best there is in your poetry, I can only wish it to have greater simplicity. It often seems to me that the connection between impression and image in your verse is too subtle, almost imperceptible. To imagine means to impose form and shape upon chaos. Sometimes I have the sad feeling that the chaos of the world is overwhelming the force of your creativity and is reflected in it only as chaos itself, disharmony. But perhaps I am mistaken? If so, you must excuse my mistake.

Sincerely wishing you *all* the best,

A. Peshkov

SOURCE: *SS* 30: 48.

---

[1] Although this was published as a letter in *SS*, the editors of *LN* 70 note that this message was written on a piece of notepaper which Gorky enclosed with a copy of *The Life of Klim Samgin*, part one. The first three parts appeared serially, 1927–31; the fourth, unfinished part was published posthumously.

144. To I. A. Gruzdev, [23 December 1927]

[Sorrento]

Dear I[lia] A[leksandrovich],

P. P. Kriuchkov has informed me that you are intending to include my correspondence with Timiriazev and Korolenko in the 'jubilee' miscellany. In my view, this should not be done.[1] Save such material for the 'posthumous' publications, it would be far more 'proper' that way. I will be sure to notify the public in advance of the day of my death.

I am also protesting—I believe I've already protested?—against the publication of a separate volume of 'early works' which are decidedly of no interest to anyone other than literary historians, of course, and I am sure that the latter will not all pass away before I do.

But I will tell you what would, perhaps, be both interesting and necessary to the *reader*, and that is a miscellany of articles about Gorky: by the Marxists—Plekhanov, V. V. Vorovsky, and others; the Populists—Redko, Mikhailovsky, etc; the literary 'modernists', e.g. Innokentii Annensky on *The Lower Depths* from his *Book of Reflections* [*Kniga otrazhenii*], D. Merezhkovsky's 'Unholy Russia' ['Nesviataia Rus''] about *Childhood*, Filosofov's 'The End of Gorky' ['Konets Gor'kogo']; I would even recommend Gippius's angry posturings and perhaps the crude pieces by Artsybashev and Kuprin.

Such a book would give the reader an extremely broad 'picture of opinions', it would also reflect the confusion of the era and probably help the reader to assess Gorky both as an 'artist' and—as I am bold enough to think—a typical Russian writer of the twentieth century.

Let me explain. When I call myself 'typical', I confer the same title upon my former comrades: Andreev, Artsybashev, Bunin, Kuprin, and many others.[2] It is time for it to be pointed out that we all had, and still have, something in common—not ideologically, of course, but emotionally. I leave it to the critics to surmise what exactly this might be. The writers named here have yet to be judged on their merits, and it is time for this to be done for the benefit and edification of our contemporary young writers.

So there's the plan, and it's not a bad one really. What do you think?

Kriuchkov wrote to me about Pribludny quoting your words.[3] If I'm not mistaken, this fellow has written some poems *of his own*. How might one help him? Do you have any thoughts on the subject?

Thank you for the book of 'Speeches'. It was my own 'speech' specifically that I needed. It turned out to be rubbish.[4]

All the best. Get treatment for your wife, and don't spare the money.

Regards,

A. Peshkov

SOURCE: *AG* 11: 158.

[1] Gorky's wish was heeded. However, his letters to Timiriazev were eventually published near the end of his life, in 1935.

[2] 'I exclude V. V. Veresaev, for he alone of all of us adhered most resolutely to the position of a "pure" literary man.' [Gorky's note.]

[3] Ivan Pribludny (real name Iakov Petrovich Ovcharenko, 1905–37), poet. Gruzdev had remarked on Pribludny's ability to recite Esenin's poetry almost exactly as Esenin himself had done.

[4] *The Free Association for the Development and Propagation of the Positive Sciences. Speeches and Welcoming Statements at Three Public Meetings in 1917, on 9 and 16 April in Petrograd and 11 May in Moscow* [*Svobodnaia assotsiatsiia dlia razvitiia i rasprostraneniia polozhitel'nykh nauk. Rechi i privetstviia na trekh publichnykh sobraniiakh, sostoiavshikhsia v 1917 godu 9–go i 16–go aprelia v Petrograde i 11–go maia v Moskve*].

145. To S. N. Sergeev-Tsensky, [30 December 1927]

[Sorrento]

Dear Sergei Nikolaevich,

I shall write at once to Glavlit about your books; I am almost sure there must be some misunderstanding. This is a sign, perhaps, that the battle against the 'private businessman' for good books has begun.[1]

I received *Cruelty* [*Zhestokost'*] and thanked you for the gift at the time. I am now sending you a copy of my book along with this letter.

Yes, I receive quite a few letters from Russia. Of course, they write a lot of nonsense, but on the whole that does not bother me, since the majority of my correspondents, are 'ordinary' folk: workers' correspondents, rural correspondents and 'beginning writers' from that same milieu; it seems to me that they write 'from the heart', which is quite touching, even when they scold me for my 'optimism'. Not long ago I even received a letter which went like this: 'I am a professional thief and I bear a name which has been very well known to the detectives of three countries for a long time.' He goes on to ask why I don't write about thieves and then criticizes Leonov's novel with the utmost scorn.[2] In general, I have an interesting correspondence, and my future biographer should thank me for it.

I am extremely embarrassed by the 'whirlwind of honours'. I have written to the 'jubilee committee' to put an end to the fuss if they want me to come in May.

I am going with the intention of visiting familiar places, and I do not want to be prevented from seeing what I have to see. If it is deemed necessary to 'honour' me, then let them postpone that business until September. In all probability, I will have taken to my bed by then from exhaustion and the 'climbat'.[3] I will certainly visit you. We will no doubt argue, although I'm not really a great one for that.

Yes, Sologub has died; he was a wonderful poet. His *Fiery Circle* is an astonishing book and one which will stand the test of time. As a man, he was antipathetic to me; he was an unbearable and arrogant egotist, and as quick to take offence as an old maid. What particularly bothered me about him was that in his writing, in his books, he pretended to be a voluptuary, even a sadist, demonic in nature; yet he lived the life of a prudent art master. He adored jam and, do you know, he used to eat it sitting on a couch, simply bobbing up and down with delight.

We have had an earthquake here. Rome was shaken, but not very badly; the little towns in the surrounding area suffered more. This came as no surprise to the Italians, but then, in the latter part of the month, there was a fall of snow, which settled on Vesuvius and the mountains around the Bay of Naples for three days without melting—now, that was a sensation! It was eight below zero in Naples; old men and women were freezing to death.

I'll begin publishing *Samgin* in *Novyi mir* in January. I seem to have dragged it out, so it's ten miles long. No, I am a not one for large books. I'm a poor architect.

You and I differ in our attitude towards man. I do not find man 'pitiful', not at all. I know that man's place on earth is precarious and that a lot of the things he should know about himself and the world will remain hidden from him forever, and that 'agonizing sores, sores especially agonizing in old age, rend his flesh', as L. Tolstoy confessed—but he is surely not the only one to know that? This is all quite true, even profoundly insulting, if you like. But this is also, perhaps, the very reason why I—just a small man myself—have such an amicable feeling for him, for Man. I like him even 'in his sins most foul, and when, for the sake of love and in the service of his own soul, he doth cast out, like filth and dust, his neighbour and the temptations of this world'. Even in his moments of joy, he is such a tender, clumsy, mischievous, and sad child, as you realize well enough. I take particular delight in his daring—not the daring which has taught him to fly like a bird and to do other things in that spirit—but in the daring of his tireless striving. 'And fruitless striving it is too.' So be it. As an old sectarian once told me in my youth—he was a stern fellow who felt a cold and even criminal hatred towards me—'We do not live for paradise, but only by the dream of paradise.' He put it well. I especially love dreamers, eccentrics, and 'homeless loners'.

I can accept your sorrowful words about 'pitiful' man only as words. This does not mean that I am inclined to deny their sincerity. Alas, you moralists! At any given moment man is sincere and his own equal. Does he ever pretend? Why, of course he does! But, after all, that is only so that he can become the equal of something higher than himself. And I have often observed that when he does pretend like this, he begins to open himself up to the world. This is not a play on words.[4] Sometimes this is a game, and, not infrequently, a fateful game which he plays with himself.

'Man' is a huge subject. And you, Sergei Nikolaevich, are a wonderful artist who is supremely aware of the importance, complexity, and profound fascination of this subject.

Keep well, and goodbye for now!

A. Peshkov

SOURCE: *SS* 30: 56–8.

[1] Glavlit, acronym of the Chief Administration for Matters Relating to Literature and Publishing Houses, the body responsible for censorship.

[2] Leonov's novel *The Thief* [*Vor*] was published earlier in the year.

[3] Gorky creates a playful combination of the Russian words for 'climate' and 'brand' or 'stamp' [*kleimo*]. The Russian climate was, of course, not good for the writer's health.

[4] Gorky uses two verbs of very similar form—*pritvoriaetsia* [pretends] and *priotvoriaetsia* [opens himself up].

146. To V. Ia. Zazubrin,[1] [25 March 1928]

[Sorrento]

I shall write to you before the writers' congress in April and send you something for it. This congress is a matter of great importance, and its initiators are fine, clever fellows.[2] I have informed Romain Rolland of the congress and he too should welcome it as part of his duties as advocate for the brotherhood of peoples.

Apropos of the 'Dostoevskian beard' that you and others have been sticking on me, I have the following to say.[3] You can, of course, see from my portraits that I shave my beard meticulously. *Stories of 1922–1924* is my attempt to shave off a certain amount of Gorky's inner shagginess. At the same time, it is a series of efforts to find a different form and tone for *Klim Samgin*, a very difficult and crucial work. I consider these efforts to have been useful for me personally, especially when it is borne in mind that between autumn 1916 and winter 1922 I did not write a line.

For many people—and apparently you are one of their number—all the *Stories* are coloured by one, 'Karamora'. That is not correct. My conception of 'The Story of a Novel' ['Rasskaz o romane'], 'An Enigma' ['O neobyknovennom'], and 'The Rehearsal' ['Repetitsiia'] does not coincide with that of 'Karamora'. You can see from the epigraphs to this story that Dostoevsky was not the only one to discern 'Karamazovism' in the Russian people. It is extremely characteristic and striking that this trait of the Russian psyche was also known both to one of our great scientists, Pirogov, and to the worker Mikhailov, one of the genuine heroes of the revolution.[4] As I have made my way gradually through all the 'classes' of society, I have observed this same characteristic in the representatives of each of them. Dostoevsky is the best and, of course, the most brilliant at depicting that weird mental state of 'Karamazovism', which is present not only in the *Brothers* but in all his other books too: recall Svidrigailov, Rogozhin, Lebiadkin, Ippolit, Verkhovensky, etc.[5] That other colossal artist of ours, L. Tolstoy, was no less brilliant in his depiction of the other highly characteristic trait of native Russians: 'Karataevism'. I consider both of these 'psyches' to be 'national', in the sense that they have been brought into being and nourished by the social history of the Great Russian nation. Or one could view this rather more narrowly, as a product of the psyche of people of the Moscow region. Let me say, by the way, that from my point of view there still has not been a real Russian literature; only now is it beginning to assume the same proportions as the literatures of England, Scandinavia, etc. It needs to be remembered that the mightiest creators of our verbal art are people of the Moscow region, people from Tula and Orel. Amongst the general mass of Russian writers it would be hard to find even a dozen like Gogol and Korolenko—

that is, writers who would be able to look at Russians from the side and not be blinded by love, as Turgenev, Grigorovich, and others, including the 'Populists', have been.

What is 'Karamazovism'? Possibly, it is the revolt of the 'ordinary' person, of the Russian plainsman who has confined himself within the city and, in so doing, has poisoned his plainsman's, God-fearing, 'Karataev' soul with the blandishments of the city and the irreconcilable contradictions of its social structure, contradictions which have a power and clarity quite unknown to the countryside. 'Karamazovism' can be understood as a revolt by man against himself, and for the sake of Christ, i.e. for the sake of an abstract notion of justice which is unrealizable in practice under existing circumstances. In other words, 'Karamazovism' is an active anarchism, and 'Karataevism' a passive one. I am opposed to both the one and the other, organically as well as intellectually.

There's my answer for you. If you find anything unclear, write to me and I'll try to explain it. For your own work you would find it helpful to acquaint yourself with B. Nikolaevsky's book *The End of Azef* [*Konets Azefa*], and also with the memoirs of the worker Okladsky, a friend of Zheliabov, who betrayed the entire executive committee of the People's Will to the police.[6]

Don't send me the manuscript; I'll probably pay you a visit in July to eat *pelmeni*. We can read the manuscript together and discuss it then.

Who is it over there who dares to disbelieve that I am an old man? I have sixty-four false teeth and hair growing on my nose.

I know of your work as 'mentor' to Siberian literature: this has made me feel a sincere sympathy towards you.

And did you know that one of your pieces has been translated into French and published in the *Revue Européenne*?

Warm greetings to you, and my sincere regards to those heretics who do not believe in my decrepitude.

A. Peshkov

SOURCE: *AG* 10/2: 351–3.

[1] Real name Vladimir Iakovlevich Zubtsov (1895–1938), Siberian writer and journalist who corresponded regularly with Gorky from 1928.

[2] Zazubrin was helping to organize a congress of Siberian writers. It did not take place, however.

[3] During the mid-1920s a number of critics had spoken disparagingly of the 'Dostoevskian' motifs in Gorky's recent work.

[4] The epigraphs to the story were taken from a letter written by the Russian surgeon N. I. Pirogov and from the testimony made before a 1917 committee of inquiry by Zakhar Mikhailov, a worker who turned out to be a *provocateur*.

[5] Characters from *Crime and Punishment*, *The Idiot*, and *The Devils*.

[6] Boris Nikolaevsky (1887–1966), political activist and historian, who emigrated after the Revolution. Evno Fishelevich Azef (1869–1918), infamous *agent provocateur*. Ivan Okladsky (1859–?) was a member of the radical political group, the People's Will, which planned and carried out the assassination of Tsar Alexander II. For his role in that plot, Andrei Zheliabov (1851–81), one of the group's leaders, was executed.

6

THE SLOW RETURN

1928–1936

INTRODUCTION

No period of Gorky's life has provoked greater controversy and speculation than his last years. Inevitably, both the controversy and the speculation have concerned the writer's involvement with the Stalin regime as modern Russia entered its darkest age. Why did Gorky go back to the USSR? How much did he know about what was going on? Why did he appear willing to take on the role of apologist for a government whose record on human rights was already being seriously questioned abroad? Where did he stand with regard to the great literary developments of the 1930s—the formation of the Union of Soviet Writers, and the formulation of Socialist Realism as the sole approved artistic method? Finally, how did he die: was it of natural causes, or was the writer murdered on Stalin's instructions? These are difficult questions and it would be unwise to suggest definitive answers to them. Although important new documents are now emerging from the archives, it is far from certain that the full story will ever be known. Nevertheless, the letters contained in this section will shed considerable light on the tragedy of Gorky's final years. Just how one describes that tragedy—as a case of a man who willingly and knowingly abetted a corrupt regime, or who was the innocent dupe of Stalin and his henchmen, or who strove in vain to serve as a force for moderation—will, inevitably, remain a matter for individual judgement.

The most certain thing that can be said about Gorky's return to Russia is that it was a very slow business. He made his first trip there in the spring of 1928, returning to Sorrento in the autumn so as to avoid the severity of the Russian winter, which he feared for health reasons. In 1929, he followed the same procedure. The following year he made no visit to Russia at all, ostensibly because of further problems with his health. But in 1931 and 1932 he again spent lengthy periods in the Soviet Union before leaving Italy for good, which he did in 1933.

Gorky's repeated peregrinations during these years might be seen as a metaphor of his indecision: was he a now part of Stalin's society, with everything that implied, or was he still a reluctant *émigré*? More importantly, the period of his divided residence marks a distinct 'period' in his life. As the letters here show quite clearly, in the years to 1933 Gorky speaks more often than not with optimism and confidence about the prospects for Stalin's Russia. By contrast, the final years in Russia witnessed his gradual decline into a condition of depression bordering on despair.

Given the fact that the Soviet Union was already well down the path towards Stalin's personal dictatorship—and this was something that

Gorky knew only too well—why did he return there at such a dangerous time? Clearly, there were all manner of motives at work here. On the one hand, there was considerable pressure from the regime itself. Stalin evidently wanted Gorky to return home, so that he could both ensure his silence on sensitive subjects (the memory of *Untimely Thoughts* would still have been fresh enough in his mind) and also harness the writer's unique authority to the cause of his new cultural policies. The pressure was probably exerted as much by indirect as by direct means: witness Gorky's letter to Popov (Letter 158), which was written in reponse to a criticism he had heard from many quarters—how can a man who considers himself a true defender of socialism continue to live in the bourgeois West? We can be sure that Gorky himself was vulnerable to such arguments. From quite early in his second emigration he had come to look upon Russia as the only potential bastion of socialism, a view which inevitably hardened as Hitler and Mussolini consolidated their hold on power, thereby adding to fears of a new world war. Khodasevich—who knew the writer as well as anybody did during those years—later suggested that the real choice had effectively been made by the mid-1920s and that, after a brief respite in Germany and Czechoslovakia, Gorky was ready once again to adopt his favoured role as bard of the proletarian revolution.[1]

Khodasevich may well be right. Certainly, the need to *serve* Russian literature and thereby guide Russia itself towards a better future had been essential to Gorky's make-up from the turn of the century. But there were other factors which pressed upon him with increasing urgency. For one thing, life in Italy was becoming increasingly difficult for him as international relations deteriorated. Then there was the problem of Maksim. Much to his father's concern, he still had no proper profession and appeared destined for a rather aimless existence. Even worse—and despite Gorky's attempts to convince himself to the contrary—his son was in very poor physical condition. Letter 147, with its jocular reference to Maksim's struggle to give up tobacco, suggests that he was again receiving close medical attention. (Gorky was writing to Maksim's wife, Nadezhda: hence he would have taken care not to alarm her unduly.) Letter 161, written in February 1932 to Ekaterina Peshkova, is much more direct. By this stage, things had evidently reached something of a crisis: Gorky now refers openly to Max's problems with alcohol and voices his belief that he needs to return to Russia for proper medical treatment.

There is also evidence that Gorky was experiencing increasing financial difficulties by the end of the 1920s. His income from publishing his works in the West was not what it once had been and public interest in him had also declined considerably. A return to the USSR thus offered

---

[1] V. F. Khodasevich, *Izbrannaia proza v dvukh tomakh* (New York, 1982), vol. 1: 246–7.

him a considerable practical benefit. Not only would he be guaranteed a substantial income from the publication of his works, there were other perquisites as well. Although the writer's detractors were rather too eager to explain his return to Russia solely in terms of his own pursuit of luxury, it would seem that the Soviet government *did* deliberately place such lures in his path. In 1931 the magnificent Riabushinsky house in Moscow was put at his disposal.[2] Later on he also had the use of a dacha in Gorki, the same Moscow suburb where Lenin had once had a retreat. And from the winter of 1933 onwards, he had a winter home at Tesseli, on the southern shore of the Crimea, within walking distance of the building in Foros where he had ghostwritten Chaliapin's autobiography two decades before.

Although such blandishments may have had rather more of an appeal to Gorky than he was prepared to admit, there was another side of life in the Soviet Union which was probably more seductive still. By the 1930s Gorky had come to see that only by living there was he likely to have any real possibility of influencing the destiny of his native land. In the event, of course, all of these pressures—personal, financial, and political—were pushing him in the same direction. It is difficult to know when exactly he finally decided to go back. His letter to Popov suggests that the choice had already been made by January 1931 (Letter 158). Whatever the case, he could not have suspected what actually awaited him on his return.

The impact of these events on Gorky's personal life was as obvious as it was profound. The periods he spent in Sorrento after his first return trip to the Soviet Union became increasingly unlike what had gone before. Although things appeared to be the same on the surface— Gorky's villa continued to be a place of pilgrimage for many of his countrymen and women, for example—his Italian existence had now acquired a new quality of impermanence. What is more, the writer's letters now show a degree of preoccupation with Russian affairs altogether different from what had passed in his earlier correspondence. In short, he was now much more a *part* of Soviet life than he had ever been before. One of the first people to detect the change was Moura Budberg. Indeed, the issue of returning to the Soviet Union was something which stood between her and Gorky. So when the writer announced in a letter to Kriuchkov of December 1931, that 'Mariia Ignatievna has left for London', he was effectively reporting the end of their relationship. Although she did eventually make a brief visit to Russia when Gorky was on his death-bed, by this time England had already become her permanent home.

---

[2] It became a museum in the 1960s. The staff of the museum have published an account of the writer's life there: *V dome na Maloi Nikitskoi* (Moscow, 1968).

From the very beginning of his first visit to Russia, Gorky was already aware that his life there was to be altogether different from what he had known in the past. In Letter 147 he complains of the ceremonial welcome which had been laid on for him in Moscow, and describes the extraordinary lengths to which he went in order to avoid public attention. Rather more sinister, however, is his comment in a letter he wrote to Kaliuzhny on his return to Sorrento, which suggests that his movements were already being carefully managed for him: 'Things turned out so strangely: I met hardly any of my old personal friends' (Letter 148). But it was only after his final return to Russia that the situation rapidly deteriorated to the point where Gorky's freedom to travel, receive guests, and even to correspond were severely curtailed. As Gorky's friends and acquaintances soon came to understand, control was firmly in the hands of the writer's 'secretary' Petr Kriuchkov. Kriuchkov it was who denied many of them access to Gorky during his last years. Konstantin Trenev, a prominent playwright who had known Gorky since before the Revolution, talks of an occasion in Tesseli in 1936: 'Getting to Gorky in those days was almost impossible [. . .] I made enquiries, and it turned out that his secretary, who impeded meetings with Aleksei Maksimovich, was then in Moscow.'[3] More moving still is a memoir by Mikhail Slonimsky, only recently published, which describes Gorky's existence during his last year in Moscow as that of virtual house-arrest and tells of a chance meeting with the ageing writer—now a tired old man with shaky hands and the 'face of a tiger'—on the staircase in his apartment.[4]

The constant indignities of Gorky's final years were further aggravated by a truly devastating blow—the death of Maksim. The writer refers to this sad event in a letter to Rolland of May 1934. Remarkable first of all for the way in which the writer turns from such painful personal news to comments on miscellaneous developments in the worlds of scholarship, education, and science, it is all the more interesting in that it says nothing at all of the circumstances surrounding his son's death. There has been considerable speculation over the years that Maksim did not die entirely of natural causes. Nina Berberova relates that Genrikh Iagoda, then head of the secret police, had become attracted to Maksim's wife Nadezhda and arranged for his associates to get Maksim drunk, after which he was left out in the cold, which so weakened his constitution that he died. As Berberova puts it: 'In the matter of Maksim's death there cannot be any doubt that he died violently.'[5] The story is not improbable, but it has yet to be confirmed by proper evidence. Given Maksim's frail health and his predilection for alcohol, it is quite possible he died

[3] K. A. Trenev, 'Moi vstrechi s Gor'kim', *Maksim Gor'kii v vospominaniiakh sovremennikov v dvukh tomakh*, comp. A. A. Krundysheva (Moscow, 1981), vol. 2: 334–5.

[4] M. Slonimsky, 'Dnevnikovye zapisi, zametki, sluchai', *Neva*, no. 12, 1987: 171.

[5] Nina Berberova, *Zheleznaia zhenshchina*, 2nd edn. (New York, 1982): 299.

without felonious interference. As with Gorky's own death, this is likely to remain a subject for debate among biographers for some time to come. There is no doubt, however, that the writer's state of mind was permanently altered as a result.

Throughout the entire period of his 'slow return' to Soviet Russia, Gorky was constantly engaged in all manner of new publishing and editorial activities. Despite the enormous pressure of this work, he continued to devote what time he could to his own writing. As he feared all along, progress on his *magnum opus*, *The Life of Klim Samgin*, began to slow. His occasional references to the novel (see Letter 164, for example) show that he was still absorbed by the book, but that the intensive research it required was proving too much for him. As it turned out, the concern expressed in a late letter to Rolland—'I am afraid of only one thing: that my heart will stop beating before I manage to finish the novel' (Letter 176)—proved well founded. The final part of the work was never completed.

One of the reasons why *The Life of Klim Samgin* remained unfinished was because Gorky had again become interested in the drama. Although he had many plays to his name, he had not written a major piece for the theatre since well before the Revolution. And, despite his confession to Babel—'I do not consider myself a "dramatist" ' (Letter 167)—he took time off from his work on *Klim Samgin* to write three new plays, *Dostigaev and Others*, *Somov and Others*, and *Egor Bulychev and Others*, and to produce a completely new version of his 1910 drama *Vassa Zheleznova*. This renewed activity as a dramatist can be seen as part of a more general interest in the development of the theatre in Stalin's Russia, which is reflected in several of the letters contained in this section. Writing to Tikhonov in January 1932, he expresses his conviction that the theatre needs more than ever to perform a pedagogical function, serving the promotion of properly socialist attitudes among the Russian masses (Letter 160). In the same place, he goes on to sketch an ideal repertoire for the contemporary theatre. And in a letter to Stalin, written shortly before his death, Gorky complains about the relative lack of theatres in Moscow and allows himself the pleasure of taking a side-swipe at the theatrical avant-garde, as represented by the well-known directors, Meierhold and Tairov (Letter 175). His interests were not confined to matters of repertoire and style of direction, however. A letter to Voroshilov records his concern about the architectural design of a proposed new theatre for the Red Army (Letter 171).

For the most part, however, Gorky's endeavours during the last years of his life were concerned with the organization of new publishing ventures. His activities in this domain were as all-encompassing as they had been in the years from 1918 to 1921, and for much the same reason. Once again, Gorky was driven by the desire to shape intellectual life in

Russia in accordance with his own vision of the ideal future. Although a number of the letters here do touch on his editorial work (see Letters 149, 165, and 170, for example), they represent only the smallest fraction of a huge volume of such correspondence. Almost without exception, these are prosaic exchanges about manuscripts and would-be contributors to the various publications with which Gorky was involved at the time. Although their contents are of interest only to the specialist, the sheer bulk of these letters attests to the writer's quite extraordinary willingness to take on the most onerous practical duties, even though this was to the detriment of his own writing and, ultimately, his health. Despite everything, he was in this respect indefatigable to the end, as can be seen from the very last letter in this collection, which contains a detailed response to a proposal for an *Anthology of Twenty Years of Soviet Poetry* (Letter 177).

A complete list of all the projects with which Gorky was involved between 1929 and 1936 would run to many pages. But each one of these ventures was inspired by the same general idea, which is set out clearly in a letter to Stalin of November 1929—the urgent need to propagandize the *good* things being done in Soviet Russia (Letter 151). This was not the first time that Gorky had addressed a Party leader in this way of course (see Letter 94 to Lenin), but the result on this occasion was far more spectacular. Within a few years, the writer had literally dozens of enterprises under way. One of the most important was the journal *Nashi dostizheniia* [*Our Achievements*]—the very title tells it all—of which he was the founder and the nominal editor-in-chief (see Letter 149). He was also the inspiration behind several other new periodicals, ranging from *Za rubezhom* [*Abroad*] to *Kolkhoznik* [*The Collective Farmer*]. Another important venture of this period was *Literaturnaia ucheba* [*Literary Study*], a journal which Gorky hoped would contribute actively to the development of serious literary discussion in Soviet Russia. In every case, the writer paid scrupulous attention to questions of editorial policy and direction. (The letter to Efim Dobin of April 1933 (Letter 165), is typical in this respect.)

Many of these new projects were as massive in their own way as World Literature had been. *The History of the Civil War* [*Istoriia grazhdanskoi voiny*], which is first mentioned in a letter of 1929 to Stalin (Letter 151), involved an enormous collective effort by scholars and writers. Its first volume took five years to produce, as Gorky explained in a letter to Kirov, a letter which, incidentally, would have reached the Leningrad Party leader only days before his assassination (Letter 170). As in earlier years, the writer's interests also ranged into the realm of science. His letter to I. A. Sokoliansky, who did pioneering work with handicapped patients, is again reminiscent of earlier approaches to scientists for contributions that would help educate the broad public (Letter 166). The same letter also demonstrates the degree to which he retained his utopian faith in the possibilities of socialism for harnessing the powers of nature, and perhaps even contains an echo of 'God-building'.

Several of the publications founded by Gorky were to last well into the post-Stalin era. *The Poet's Library* [*Biblioteka poeta*], which produced important editions of virtually every significant Russian poet, was one; *Lives of Remarkable People* [*Zhizn' zamechatel'nykh liudei*], an extensive series of popular biographies, was another. But it is perhaps more significant to note the number of publications which soon foundered after the writer's death. *Nashi dostizheniia* and *Kolkhoznik* closed down very quickly. *The History of the Civil War*—which had, of course, become an extremely sensitive subject in Stalin's Russia—proved another early casualty. *Literaturnaia ucheba* lasted until Russia's entry into the Second World War, although it never really lived up to Gorky's hopes of it anyway.[6]

In all these activities, Gorky was very much the loyal servant of the Stalin regime, constantly promoting a positive message about contemporary life and reinforcing the revolutionary utopianism which had always been synonymous with the Bolshevik cause. In his letters too Gorky often emerges as an apparently naïve apologist of the Stalin regime. This is particularly the case in his letters to Rolland. It was to Rolland that he wrote in 1932: 'We are living in a terrible time, my dear friend, and great tragedies await us, but what a joy it is to observe at the same time the pride of the young people in my country . . .' (Letter 162). Whilst it is clear that Gorky writes here from the perspective of one who sets 'socialist' Russia against the 'bourgeois' West, it is still painful to read in the same letter his *praise* of the notorious labour camp at Solovki for its humane treatment of the inmates there.[7] Equally disturbing is a letter to the same correspondent which had been sent from Sorrento the previous year, and in which Gorky defends the show trials and explains that the arrest of the prominent septuaginarian historian Sergei Platonov was quite justified (Letter 159). This was also one of several private occasions on which he spoke in support of Stalin's ruthless campaign for the collectivization of Soviet agriculture. Whilst it may be true that Gorky did not know the full cost of this particular policy in terms of human lives, it is difficult to avoid the conclusion that in all these cases he was guilty of turning a blind eye to the criminal excesses of Stalin's dictatorship. He had, of course, long considered the Russian peasantry a hindrance to the achievement of socialism. But, as several recent commentators have suggested, he appears also to have been seduced by the rhetoric of the age, which stressed the need to destroy those 'enemies' of the Soviet Union,

---

[6] It was revived during the Brezhnev period.

[7] Gorky had publicly defended the labour camps in what was undoubtedly his most notorious act of all—his leadership of the delegation of Soviet writers which visited the infamous White Sea Canal project. Conditions for the prisoners who worked on this project were quite inhuman, and many died as a result, yet it was later described in uniformly glowing terms in a collection of articles, edited by Gorky (*Belomorsko-Baltiiskii kanal imeni Stalina: Istoriia stroitel'stva* (Moscow, 1934)).

both inside and outside the country, who were supposedly bent on undoing the great socialist experiment.

But if Gorky certainly did serve, both publicly and privately, as an apologist for Stalin's policies, he was far from being the venal figure painted by his many detractors. In this connection, it is instructive to compare his letters to Rolland with those he was writing to the Soviet leaders at the same time. The letters to Stalin are of particular interest in this regard. Gorky clearly felt none of the personal attraction to the new Party leader that he had to Lenin. (Is it reading too much into the congratulatory telegram he sent to Stalin on the occasion of his fiftieth birthday (Letter 152) to suggest that its extreme brevity implies a considerable degree of coolness on the writer's part?) And although the writer obviously adopted a style in his letters to the General Secretary which was calculated to appeal to his ear—hence the frequency of terms like 'bourgeois' and other catch-phrases of the time—this surface compliance does little to mask the fact that he is mounting a serious critique of many features of Stalin's rule. To take the letter of 1929 again, Gorky's suggestions concerning the journals *Za rubezhom* and *Voina* [*War*] are of interest above all as a means by which the writer is seeking to intervene on behalf of Karl Radek and Aleksandr Voronsky, both of whom had fallen out of favour with the Party leader (Letter 151). It is also obvious here that Gorky had become seriously concerned by the first signs of Stalin's assault against the so-called 'Old Bolsheviks' and his policy of having them replaced by lesser men of his own choosing. Nor is there any mistaking his genuine dismay, in a letter of January 1930, on learning that he had been implicated (albeit quite unwittingly) in a case where individuals were punished for writing about him in a critical spirit (Letter 154).

Predictably enough, Gorky's most trenchant criticisms were reserved for developments in literary life. His activities during these years—in particular, his involvement in the establishment of the Union of Soviet Writers—have, of course, been the subject of many discussions, most of them unfavourable to the writer. However, as the letters in this section make abundantly clear, Gorky was no real supporter of Stalinist cultural policy. To put it another way, the Writers' Union which was actually created bore little resemblance to the Writers' Union to which he believed he was committing his energies.

By the late 1920s, Gorky occupied the middle ground on cultural matters. Whilst he was convinced that literature, like all the arts, had an important part to play both in the building of socialism and—increasingly—in the fight against Fascism, he was appalled by the extreme militance of groups like RAPP, which sought to impose controls over artistic life so rigid that there would be no room for healthy debate or alternative views. Indeed, the main reason he was prepared to work so hard for the creation of the Writers' Union was his belief that this would rid Soviet literary life of the RAPP-ite threat. As he learned to his immense consternation, he could hardly have been more wrong. Individuals such as Fadeev, Vishnevsky, and Panferov—all of whom had shown their ultra-proletarian colours during the campaigns against Babel, Bulgakov, Zamiatin, Pilniak, and others deemed 'anti-Soviet' writers—now rose to prominence within the new literary body. Despite Gorky's repeated protestations, these men came to form the core of a Writers' Union which was already threatening to embody his worst fears about the shape of things to come. Here was the clearest evidence—if such were needed—of the limits of his influence in Stalin's Russia.

Gorky's letters chart his growing disillusionment with the Writers' Union. Writing to Stalin in August 1934, he begins (rather interestingly) by conceding to the Party leader the right to amend the draft of his report to the first Congress of the Writers' Union as he sees fit, but then goes on to speak quite openly of the 'petty personal struggles' which were already impeding the proper work of the Union in his view (Letter 169). His declaration, in the same letter, of his wish not to stand for chairmanship of the Union may not have been altogether serious, but it is surely a mark of his growing desperation at the turn of events. His letter to Shcherbakov (Letter 172) reflects an even greater pessimism, particularly with regard to the possibility of open debate within the new body. By November 1935 he was writing to A. A. Andreev of the 'almost complete absence among the writing fraternity of any consciousness of corporate and collective responsibility for their work', a charge which was followed by some truly alarming tales of funds mismanaged, plans unfulfilled, and institutions failing to operate effectively (Letter 173). As he put it to Molotov shortly afterwards: 'It seems to me that these are the days of the spoilt, the sated, and the indifferent' (Letter 174).

But whilst he was quite appalled by the condition of Soviet letters by 1935, Gorky was no supporter of artistic pluralism, properly understood. His comments on Maiakovsky (Letter 155) and Blok (Letter 157) reveal the degree to which his attitudes had hardened by this stage. Although it is true that his comment on the final act of Babel's play *Mariia*—that it gives the appearance of being 'a "concession" to some external demand' (Letter 167)—suggests his disapproval of the pressures now being placed upon Soviet writers, he seems to accept that some government censorship of literature is inevitable. His letter to Platonov of September 1929 is particularly instructive in this respect, not only because it contains the blunt statement that he believes that author's *Chevengur* to be unpublishable in the Soviet Union, but also because he does not seem unduly bothered by that prospect (Letter 150). More revealing still is his letter to Grossman of October 1932, in which he returns to a theme he had broached back in 1926, when writing to

Gladkov—the question of 'verisimilitude' in art (Letter 131). This time, Gorky distinguishes between two 'truths': the first being the truth about what exists now and has existed in the past, a truth which is often 'base and sordid'; whilst the second is a 'truth' which does not yet exist, but must be created so that the socialist dream can be fulfilled (Letter 163). The naturalistic depiction of the 'first truth' (which Gorky discerns in Grossman's work) is something which obviously meets with his disapproval, even if he is not (quite) prepared to describe it as 'counter-revolutionary'. He takes up the same point early in 1935, when he suggests to Shcherbakov the need for a 'firmly-prescribed "working-class truth" ', which would, no doubt, be in line with his own conception of what Socialist Realism should be about (Letter 172). But he puts this view only to add: 'It stands to reason that within the limits of this "working-class truth" certain contradictions are both permissible and unavoidable.' Gorky's dilemma regarding Soviet literary policy is nowhere more clearly expressed than in these two statements. In the end, of course, the dilemma was only too effectively resolved by the brutally prescriptive practices of successive generations of literary bureaucrats.

It is, perhaps, fortunate that Gorky never lived to see what sins were to be committed by the Writers' Union in the name of Socialist Realism. By 1936, he was already a very sick man. The years of almost uninterrupted ill health, the massive workload, the increasing burden of stress and disillusionment eventually resulted in the irreversible collapse that his friends and family had feared on many occasions in the past. Gorky was first taken ill while in the south. He was rushed to Moscow on 26 May, where he was placed under the care of a team of doctors. On 1 June his illness was publicly announced; the writer died in Gorki seventeen days later, the cause of his death being described as influenza, complicated by inflammation of the lungs and chronic heart disease. The state funeral which followed on 20 June was a huge ceremony at which the Party leadership was finally able to launch its preferred image of Gorky as the great proletarian writer, the friend and supporter of Lenin and Stalin.

But did the writer really die of natural causes? Rumours to the contrary began to circulate quite shortly after his ceremonial funeral. In 1938, Iagoda, Kriuchkov, and the doctors responsible for treating Gorky during his last illness were among a number of people brought to trial for their part in what was described as a Trotskyite conspiracy to murder the writer (and his son Maksim). The accused confessed to the charges and were duly executed. This 'conspiracy' was, of course, as farfetched as any of those investigated in the notorious show trials of the late 1930s. Yet the rumours have persisted that Gorky *was* killed, although not by Troskyites, but on the instructions of Stalin himself. Over the years, many Western scholars have put forward arguments to support this claim. Quite recently, Viacheslav Ivanov, son of the famous writer Vsevolod—who was closely acquainted with Gorky during his last years—has published a memoir which leads to the same conclusion.[8] However, the Russian scholars who have examined the documentary evidence remain sceptical, although they are careful not to rule out entirely the possibility of foul play.[9] On this, as on so many matters to do with the life of this most remarkable man, we can only wait to see what the future may still hold in store.

[8] Entitled 'Why Did Stalin Kill Gorky?', it leaves little doubt about the author's position. 'Pochemu Stalin ubil Gor'kogo?', *Voprosy literatury*, no. 1, 1993: 91–134.

[9] This is the conclusion of L. Spiridonova in *Dialog s istoriei* (Moscow, 1994): 295. Hers is the most careful evaluation of the documentary and circumstantial evidence to date.

147. To N. A. Peshkova, [26 June 1928]

[Morozovka]

My dear, kind Timosha,

Here is the letter I promised you. Don't get the idea that it is obligatory over here to use red ink; I do so only because the black ink we managed to find is no good. I am writing to you from the country, some thirty miles from Moscow. People noticed that I had become worn out by the excesses of the ceremonial welcome, so the comrades have sent me away to have a rest. Max and Kriuchkov are with me, of course. We are living in a magnificent house, where we stuff ourselves with remarkably tasty food and don't drink too much. I am eating as I have never eaten before and I'm putting on weight.

Maksim, my second secretary, has been sorting through countless letters and manuscripts. He is in agony: he has been forbidden to smoke. You know what a frightful amount of tobacco he used to devour. So I put the doctors on to him, although he doesn't know that himself. He is behaving himself, and obviously misses Marfa and Daria, much as he tries to hide the fact. He is taking pictures of the house and will soon send you some photographs; I think that once you have seen them, you will be envious of us.

In general, everything is going well, although the weather is appallingly bad: rain and more rain every day. However, it appears that tomorrow will be our first nice day.

It goes without saying that I am working like a maniac. Last Sunday I walked the streets in disguise, wearing a false beard. That is the only way I can manage to have a look at anything without being surrounded by onlookers who stare straight at me. I saw a lot of interesting things, and it's most likely that I'll employ the same method of totally unhindered observation again in the future.

Maksim and Kriuchkov also went out with me, making certain changes to their appearance as well. Max took a photograph of me in my disguise.

It is quite interesting and pleasant here. The country—or, more precisely, Moscow—looks much younger. The city is cleaner; there are more people about; the traffic—trams, buses, and cars—is frantic; there is a multitude of beautiful shops and new buildings, whilst the old ones have been excellently restored. The people are not very expensively dressed, but there is equality: you don't see any sharp distinctions, just as you don't see any beggars. Everything is curious, new, and lively. There are loudspeakers in the squares and music in the public gardens. They ring the bells. I'll soon be off on a trip to Kursk, Kharkov, and the Don.

Kiss my sweet grandchildren for me, and tell Marfa I'll bring her some interesting things.

I wish you all the best, my dear Timosha. I saw your sisters and your brother-in-law. He's a jolly fellow. Keep well.

Father Aleksei

SOURCE: *AG* 13: 250–1.

148. *To A. M. Kaliuzhny,*[1] *[26 October 1928]*

[Sorrento]

I am most upset that I did not and could not find time to see you, dear Aleksandr Mefodievich. But it turned out that I found myself, quite against my will, in the position of a 'distinguished foreigner', and from the moment of my arrival in Russia I was overwhelmed by a mass of impressions for which I was not prepared and by a noisy commotion of a sort to which I had grown unaccustomed during four years of quiet and solitary living. When I arrived in Tiflis I learned that you were at your dacha and resolved to call and see you on the way to Erevan, but in the end I didn't manage to do so. I am sure that I will see you in the spring if I am able to make my way from here by ship to Batumi or Odessa. One way or another, I will be in the Caucasus; I want to spend some time in Baku and that means I will have to visit Tiflis as well.

I very much want to see you and hear what you have to say for yourself, believe me. Things turned out so strangely: I met hardly any of my old personal friends. The entire trip had a fantastic quality about it, and there were a great many things about it which I could not help but find staggering. People have changed enormously over these six years. They 'hurry to live and hasten to feel' as they surely have never hurried or hastened before.[2] I am not just talking about the places I hadn't been to in twenty or twenty-five years, such as Nizhnii Novgorod. Even the people living in the Crimea, where I spent the summer of 1915, seemed like new people to my eyes—I'm talking of the Tatars.[3]

What struck me most of all was the active and demanding attitude towards life, an attitude which has intensified greatly during these years, in my opinion. Of course, it is possible that one sees only what one wants to see.

Will you write to me? It would be good if you did and it would make me very happy. Otherwise I shall be afraid that you are displeased by my having 'passed you by' on my travels—which, as I have already said, was quite involuntary on my part.

Keep well, A. M.

All the best,

A. Peshkov

SOURCE: *SS* 30: 105–6.

¹ Aleksandr Kaliuzhny (1853–1939) was a political prisoner and a Populist in pre-Revolutionary Russia; in 1892 he encouraged Gorky to begin writing and helped get his first story, 'Makar Chudra', published in Tiflis.

² The quotation is from 'First Snow' ['Pervyi sneg'] by the nineteenth-century poet Viazemsky.

³ In fact, it was the summer of 1916 which Gorky spent in the Crimea.

149. To P. P. Kriuchkov, [5 December 1928]

[Sorrento]

Dear Petr Petrovich,

The enclosed article should be included in the first issue of *Nashi dostizheniia*; it is the more interesting of the two. Either that, or include them both. I'll write about this to Artemii Bagratovich [Khalatov]¹ as well.

Drovianikov very much wants us to publish the reviews of his performances—as it is, he is walking on air because of his success.² I am enclosing the same. Could you place them under 'News' in the 'Theatre and Art' section? The fellow has indeed made amazing progress, and we need to show that he has justified the help given him by our comrades.

I am enclosing my letter to Pogrebinsky together with a letter to Makarenko, which you should read. Please speak personally with P. [. . .] I am most distressed by the dissolution of the colony.³

News: *Rul'* suspects that I am handing over to the GPU the letters which I received from the 'mechanical citizens'.⁴ Those scoundrels have no shame.

The Spanish newspaper *El Sol* reports that a majority of the votes for the N[obel] Prize has apparently been cast in my favour, but they fear that I would hand it over to the State. They are right to have such fears.

Doctor Levin is coming today.⁵ That's also right and proper; something is wrenching inside me—it feels as if it's tearing, but it's in the liver rather than the intestine. It's probably because a lot of things irritate me.

Generally speaking, everything is in order. Maksim and Timosha have got themselves lost somewhere. Marfa says 'hello' to me in a deep bass and with three 'o's. Daria looks more and more like Fersman.⁶ The weather has been cold. Etc.

How are you feeling?

Lutokhin has been to see Khal[atov]. And what about Zazubrin, is it true?⁷ Do you happen to know whether there are any plans to publish the almanacs we talked to A. I. Rykov about?

The *émigrés* are celebrating the 'victory of truth and justice'. They have slandered everything it would seem possible to slander, yet they still go on lying. This habit is no longer 'second nature' to them; it is their fundamental nature. . .

Keep well!

Regards,

A. Peshkov

The materials from *Nashi dostizheniia* still haven't come yet.

Please send the following books as quickly as possible to this address: O. Kuroda, The Osaca—mainichi.[8]

Books published by Federatsiia
Kolokolov's *Honey and Blood* [*Med i krov'*]
Kopylova's *Chimeras* [*Khimery*]
P. Sletov's *The Breakthrough* [*Proryv*][9]

Tell *Izvestiia* not to send me the paper by *registered* mail; it gets through all right by ordinary mail. However, *Pravda* is not arriving, and should be sent registered, even if it is expensive to do so.

SOURCE: *AG* 14: 486–7.

[1] Managing director of *Nashi dostizheniia*.
[2] The singer Vasilii Drovianikov had been sent to Italy to complete his musical education; his concerts there received excellent reviews.
[3] Makarenko had founded a children's colony named after Gorky near Poltava in 1920. He ran into trouble because his pedagogical principles were in conflict with new government policy. Matvei Pogrebinsky was in charge of the GPU's labour colonies.
[4] Gorky had received letters from Soviet citizens unhappy with Soviet rule; he answered them in an article called 'To the USSR's Mechanical Citizens' ['Mekhanicheskim grazhdanam SSSR'].
[5] L. G. Levin (1870–1938), Gorky's physician, later executed for his alleged involvement in a plot to murder the writer.
[6] Aleksandr Fersman, mineralogist and biochemist.
[7] Gorky had been trying to persuade both men to work for *Nashi dostizheniia*.
[8] This is written in the Roman alphabet. The address is apparently that of an Osaka daily newspaper.
[9] These books were by less experienced writers whom Gorky wanted to encourage: Nikolai Kolokolov (1897–1933), Liubov Kopylova (1885–1936), and Petr Sletov (1897–?). Otokichi Kuroda, Japanese writer and translator with whom Gorky corresponded.

150. To A. P. Platonov,[1] [18 September 1929]

[Moscow]

You are a talented writer—that is indisputable—and it is also indisputable that you possess a highly distinctive language. Your novel is extraordinarily interesting; its technical defects are an excessive prolixity, an abundance of 'dialogue', and the concealment and effacement of the 'action'. This is particularly evident in the second half of the novel.

Despite the undeniable merits of your work, I do not believe that it will be printed or published. It is your anarchical frame of mind—apparently an innate part of your 'spirit'—which will prevent this from happening. Whether you intended it or not, you have imparted a lyrical-satirical tone to your interpretation of reality, and this is, of course, unacceptable to our censorship. Despite all the tenderness of your attitude towards people, you depict them ironically, and they strike the reader less as revolutionaries than as 'eccentrics' and 'half-wits'. I do not claim that you have done this deliberately, but it has been done all the same. Such is the reader's (i.e. my) impression. It could be that I am mistaken.

I will only add that among our contemporary editors I see no one who would be capable of judging your book on its merits. A. K. Voronsky might have been able to, perhaps, but as you know, he is 'not at his desk'.[2]

That is all I can tell you, and I am very sorry that I can say nothing else.

I wish you well,

A. Peshkov

Where should I send your manuscript?

SOURCE: *LN* 70: 313–14.

---

[1] Andrei Platonovich Platonov (real name Klimentov, 1899–1951), an important and innovative prose writer. Platonov had sent Gorky a copy of his novel *Chevengur* after it had been rejected by a Soviet publishing house due to its 'counter-revolutionary' implications. Platonov was hoping for Gorky's approval of the work as 'an honest attempt to depict the essence of Communist society'. It was not published in Russia until 1988.

[2] By this time Voronsky had been removed as editor of *Krasnaia nov'*.

151. To I. V. Stalin, [27 November 1929]

[Sorrento]

Dear Iosif Vissarionovich!

I did not manage to share my observations with you before leaving Moscow, and even if I had had time, I would not have been able to express them to you in a sufficiently clear and coherent form. I am not good at speaking, and I will probably do better in writing.

The depiction of Soviet life in the *émigré* press, as in the bourgeois press generally, is based almost entirely on facts of a negative character which have been published by our own press in the pursuit of educational and propagandist aims, for the purpose of self-criticism. The reports by 'staff correspondents' in the bourgeois press are neither as abundant nor as hostile as the facts and conclusions contained in our very own self-denunciations.

By laying such great emphasis on facts of a negative kind, we provide our enemies with a huge amount of material which they are able to use most skilfully against us, compromising the Party and the government in the eyes of the European proletariat, and even compromising the very principle of the dictatorship of the working class. This is because the proletarians of Europe and America are fed predominantly by bourgeois newspapers, from which they are unable to perceive the revolutionary cultural growth of our country, the achievements and successes of industrialization, the enthusiasm of the working masses, and their influence on the poor peasants.

Of course, I do not imagine that the attitude of the bourgeoisie towards the Union of Soviets can be changed for the better, and I know that European life itself is doing its level best to bring about the revolutionary education of the European proletarian.

But I also know that *our one-sided treatment of the life we are creating is exerting a very harmful influence upon our young people.*

Both in their letters and in their conversations with me, our young people display an extremely pessimistic mood. This mood is natural. The young people in the urban centres—and more particularly those in the provinces—have first-hand experience of reality which is both weak and insignificant. The only way they know about the course of events is through the newspapers. And if on any given day one reads two or three newspapers, the mass of facts concerning mismanagement, swindles etc., might quite easily provoke both pessimism and panic in those who lack balance and whose political literacy is low. All too often I am obliged to read and hear such phrases as 'life is disgusting', 'one loses heart', 'to hell with everything', and other things in the same vein.

Unfortunately, it is often the most thoughtful young people who suffer from such pessimism and scepticism, those who have been taught by the experience of old Bolsheviks, by their books and speeches. What they see now is that their teachers are dropping out of the Party one after another, or that they are being declared heretics. This cannot help but disturb them. They are unable to sense the essential contradiction between city and country as profoundly or as vividly as they should, and as it must be sensed and understood by all socialist-industrialists. The historical necessity of forcing the peasant—whose unskilled, and hence rapacious, labour despoils the earth—to work collectively, productively, and economically with respect to the soil: this necessity is poorly understood by young people.

I enclose a cutting from Miliukov's newspaper,[1] which is reprinted from *Komsomol'skaia pravda*. There are dozens, hundreds of such 'letters'. Of course, what they write is not all that they think.

Generally speaking, our young socialists are not as profoundly socialist as one imagines; on the contrary, individualism is achieving some serious victories in their midst. This can be confirmed by hundreds of examples drawn from life and literature.

The Party is not exerting as strong an influence on the education of young people as it could. This can be explained in part by the frictions within the Party itself. In the past, these frictions resulted in 'the selection of the best' and the creation of Bolsheviks. But at present all that is being created is an enormous quantity of two-legged rubbish, including the 'Makhaevites'.[2] The latter are conducting a relatively successful campaign against the old Party intelligentsia and the forces of culture. The Party is clearly not rich in such forces, given that the top cultural positions are being occupied ever more frequently by people of patent mediocrity. Seeing such mediocrity among the bureaucrats, the more energetic and egoistic of our young people—those who are 'greedy for power'—strive to push their way forward, to occupy prominent positions themselves. Their only weapons are revolutionary phrases and the cunning of a fox. You realize, of course, that under such conditions the Bolsheviks will be unable to ensure that they will be replaced by people whose energy and purposefulness are equal to their own. It is my belief, however, that the pupils should always be better—more intelligent, more broad, and more profound—than their teachers, because as time goes by, the demands placed upon the builders of the new world will be all the more severe.

Why am I saying all this and what do I suggest? Very little, and nothing new.

It is essential that we pay more serious attention to the cultural and political development of our young people. First of all, it is essential to ensure that our present-day life is depicted more objectively. The facts of a negative kind which are being published by our press need to be balanced by facts of a positive kind. We are living in a country where, despite all the dusty chaos which has resulted from the destruction of the old days, and despite all the internal and external obstacles, the will of the working class is toiling ever more consciously and energetically towards the creation of new forms of life.

It is necessary that the facts concerning the realization of this will, and its consolidation in life, be illumined not in brief telegrams, as our press is doing at present, but in serious, intelligently written reviews. We must emphasize the initiative of the masses even when it is manifested only in small things.

The fulfilment of the Five-Year Plan must be shown from week to week, from month to month. Facts about slovenliness, laziness, drunkenness, theft, and hooliganism must not be allowed to prevail over facts which contribute to revolutionary and cultural education—the construction of living quarters, factories and plants, bakeries and palaces of culture, canteens and schools; the progress in maternal care and the education of children; the resourcefulness of the working class; the development of hygiene and sanitation; scientific discoveries; the enrichment of the country through the exploitation of precious minerals; the significance of the Pioneer movement; the growth of the press and of book circulation; the growth of collective farms and agriculture, etc.

It is necessary for the press to remind itself and its readers—although not necessarily every day—that the building of socialism in the Union of Soviets is being achieved not by slovens and hooligans, nor by crazy fools, but by a powerful and new historical force—the working class. One must write about this in a simple, sound, and literate manner.

As a practical suggestion, I propose that we introduce into the central organs of the press a new section entitled 'The Progress of State (or Socialist, or Cultural) Construction'. This section would present the reader with a summary of facts of a positive character beside facts of self-criticism, thereby creating a balance between the facts of each type and, in so doing, it would surely serve to reduce pessimistic feelings.

Furthermore, in the interests of a sounder education for our young people and the development of social literacy in the mass reader, it is essential that we publish the journal *Za rubezhom* which I have spoken to you about.[3]

In this journal we should, and we can, counteract any negative facts concerning our life here by supplying facts of a similar nature about the way people live in Europe and the United States of America.

I don't think there is any need to demonstrate the usefulness of such a juxtaposition.

This would provide us with the opportunity to defeat the petty bourgeoisie as we please, since the process of its cultural decay is already progressing furiously. Foreign literature will also serve us excellently in this venture. But the journal will have to be very literate, witty, and easy for the masses to read. As I have already told you, *other than Karl Radek I cannot think of anyone who could successfully organize such a journal.* Radek would find no scope for his 'deviation' in this venture, as its framework is very limited and the aim of the journal extremely simple and clear.[4]

I am, of course, in favour of Voronsky's plan to publish the journal *Voina.* The objective necessity for such a publication is confirmed in particular by our relations with China. I don't know how your conversation with Voronsky ended, but in this case, too, the question of 'deviation' does not appear to me to be one which should lead to an unfavourable decision concerning the publication of *Voina.*[5] As I see it, 'deviations' are something which our working-class life manages to straighten out most excellently of its own accord.

Next. The conduct of atheist propaganda needs to be more soundly organized. We will not achieve much here with weapons supplied by Marx and materialism, as we can see. Materialism and religion represent two different planes; they don't coincide. If a fool speaks from the heavens, and a clever person from the factory floor, they will not understand one another. The clever person has to beat the fool with the fool's own stick, with his own weapon.

For this to happen, it is necessary to organize courses at the Communist Academy[6] for the study not only of the history of religion, but also, and above all of the history of the Christian church, i.e. the study of church history as politics.

It is necessary to know 'the church fathers', the Christian apologists. It is particularly essential to study the history of Roman Catholicism, which is the most powerful and intelligent of the church organizations and one whose political importance is especially clear. It is necessary to know the history of schisms within the churches, of heresy, the Inquisition, 'religious' wars, etc. Against every quotation put forward by a believer, it is quite easy find a dozen or two theological quotations to refute it.

It is essential to publish a Bible containing critical commentaries drawn from the Tübingen school,[7] and books about the criticism of biblical texts, all of which would produce a very useful 'confusion of minds' among the believers.

A popular book on the history of the Taborites and the Hussite movement could play an important role here.[8] Zimmerman's old book *The History of the Peasant Wars in Germany* should also be included. With careful editing, it would prove very useful to the mind.

It is necessary to produce a book on the history of the church's battle against science.

Our young people are extremely poorly informed on questions of this nature. And there is amongst them a very clear 'deviation' in the direction of religious feeling, which is a natural consequence of the rise of individualism. At the same time, they are, as always, in too great a hurry to find the 'definitive solution'.

Add to this the fact that Marxist journals are publishing articles in which—without any commentary—one encounters statements about 'the finger of God' causing fluctuations in the ether, and about the possibility of considering 'the universe as an idea in the mind of the creator', etc.

When a young person who is not very well educated reads in the journal *Pod znamenem marksizma* [*Under the Banner of Marxism*] (No. 1 for 1929, the article entitled 'Usable Energy') the statement: 'Nature or God, depending on which term you prefer', that young person is bound to be rather stunned.

To young people of this kind I am responding with an article which will soon be published and which I sincerely ask you to read.[9]

Next. It is now two years since I first insisted on the need to publish *The History of the Civil War* for the peasants.[10]

The peasants do not understand that history because they do not know its full extent. The peasant needs to know the motives which inspired the working class to begin this war; he needs to know that the workers saved the country from slavery and conquest by foreign capital; he needs to know what bloodshed and loss of life, what economic damage—in figures and pictures—were caused in the land by the Denikins, the Kolchaks, the Wrangels, and Iudeniches, and what role was played in all this by those people-loving SR's, the Chaikovskys[11] and other 'god-men'.

This book must have strong popular appeal. In order that it does so, I believe that we should involve the Revvoensovet and PUR, and have them select a commission to assemble all the material and organize it chronologically.[12] This raw material should then be worked into literary form by our writers. I would particularly recommend Aleksei Tolstoy for this task, as he is well suited to this sort of work, and also Sholokhov, the author of *The Quiet Don*, and Iu. Libedinsky.[13] Of course, their work would have to be edited. The book should be published in a mass edition, so that there would be a copy in every village, where it would be read like a novel.

This, dear Iosif Vissarionovich, is all I wanted to say to you for the time being.

In conclusion, I will inform you of something which bears a direct relation to the business of the documents that were found at the Academy of Sciences.

The Petrograd secret police department was raided on 24 or 25 February 1917. On one of those days a group of young people, led by *a certain Podgorny and a worker from the Parviainen-Aksel factory*, set out from my apartment (Kronverkskii Prospekt, No. 24)[14] with the intention of occupying the Okhranka[15] and seizing its archives. When this group arrived at the Mytishchenskii embankment, it turned out that some other people had got there first. The head of the Okhranka had been killed, the office had been ransacked, files and papers had been thrown out of the windows and some of them had already been set alight. There were not many of these people and they seemed most suspicious, as did their activities. The young people drove the rioters away and put out the fire. The files and papers which had been thrown out on to the street were collected up, loaded on a cart, and sent off to the Academy of Sciences, where they were received by Academician *Sreznevsky*.[16] Among these 'files' was a *very thick volume of 'observations' on Rasputin and another on P. N. Miliukov*. Subsequently I saw both these 'files' in the Police Department, where Zenzinov, I think, was sorting through the Department's archives.[17]

I sincerely wish you good health, good spirits and generally all the best.

A. Peshkov

SOURCE: *Izv Ts K* 1989 (3): 183–7.

[1] *Poslednie novosti* [*Latest News*].

[2] A movement inspired by the Polish socialist W. K. Machajski (1867–1926). It was characterized by its antagonistic attitude towards the intelligentsia, including the revolutionary intelligentsia.

[3] This journal was published monthly in Moscow between 1930 and 1938.

[4] K. B. Radek (1885–1939), prominent figure in the Russian and international Communist movement. Expelled from the Russian Communist Party in 1927 for 'Trotskyite sympathies', he was re-admitted to the Party in 1930 after denouncing Trotsky.

[5] Voronsky was expelled from the Party in 1928 as a Trotskyite. His Party membership was restored in 1930 and he became an editor for Gosizdat. Like Radek he perished in the purges.

[6] The Communist Academy functioned between 1918 and 1936 as an institute of higher education and research into the social and natural sciences.

[7] A school of protestant theologians established by Christian Baur in the mid-nineteenth century.

[8] The Hussites were followers of a Bohemian religious reformer burned at the stake in 1415. The Taborites were one of two opposing parties within the Hussite movement.

[9] The article 'A Reply' ['Otvet'] appeared in *Izvestiia* on 12–13 December 1929.

[10] Two volumes eventually appeared under this title in 1937 and 1942.

[11] Petr Nikolaevich Wrangel (1878–1928), combined forces with Denikin against the Bolsheviks during the Civil War; Nikolai Nikolaevich Iudenich (1862–1933), Commander of White Army in the Baltics.

[12] PUR, Russian acronym for the Political Directorate within the Revolutionary War Soviet (Revvoensovet), organized in 1919 for political work within the Red Army.

[13] Iurii Nikolaevich Libedinsky (1898–1959), prose writer actively involved with the proletarian organizations Oktiabr and RAPP.

[14] Gorky actually lived at No. 23.

[15] The tsarist Secret Police Department.

[16] V. I. Sreznevsky (1867–1936), literary historian and head of the archive section of the library of the Academy of Sciences.

[17] V. M. Zenzinov (1880–1953), an SR who emigrated to France after the Revolution.

152. To I. V. Stalin, [21 December 1929]

[Sorrento]

To Stalin, the Kremlin, Moscow
Congratulations. Warm regards.[1]

Gorky

SOURCE: *SS* 30: 155.

[1] Telegram sent on the occasion of Stalin's fiftieth birthday.

153. To I. A. Gruzdev, [7 January 1930]

[Sorrento]

Dear Ilia Aleksandrovich,
I can say nothing about the 'excision marks' because I don't have any of my books with me. I have given them all away, and even if I had them

here, I just wouldn't be able to find time to check the texts. It's a pity that the legend about Christ and the devils in 'Kalinin' has been spoilt—it was very interesting and unusual.[1] I've lost my original record of it, and in this case I cannot rely on my memory. Generally speaking, I've had 'bad luck' with Christ. In *Confession* the censor cut out the conversation between the Cossack and the monk: the Cossack was arguing that Christ was a 'useless god' because he was 'good and not dreadful'. I feel that the censor has not treated me kindly. There is an excellent Zaporozhian proverb about death:

> Go, good Cossack, follow your eyes,
> Carry your death on your back.
> So long as you live, it doesn't exist,
> But when you die—the devil take you!

L. Andreev imagined death not in the usual form of the skeleton but in the form of a vulva; it seems that he may have borrowed this idea from the artist Alfred Kubin.[2]

I think that people are afraid not so much of death as they are of dying. I have noticed that people with heart disease—and who are thus under sentence of instant death—experience no fear of it and do not trouble themselves by thinking about it. In my view, this fear is provoked by ignorance of what is to come, and it is destroyed completely when one acknowledges that there is nothing at all to come. Atheists die more easily and more simply than religious people—I'm talking of 'cultured' people here. There is reason to think that the Russians generally think about death and fear it far more than people of other nations (perhaps it would be more accurate to say people of other denominations). The Orthodox owe this to the quite exceptional beauty and voluptuousness of their church music and of the funeral liturgy in particular. I stress the word voluptuousness, for church canticles—both the words and the music—were created by the 'black' clergy, who translated all the power of their sexual emotions into religious emotions. The hymns to the Virgin and to the great martyrs are examples of this. Another example is provided by the erotic word-games of the monks, in particular the anecdote about the monk who coupled with Death, who had taken pity on him in his virginity.

Generally speaking, when it is compared with the duration of life and with the splendid intensity of life's tragic element, death is an insignificant moment lacking any significance. And if this is dreadful, it is only because it is dreadfully stupid. Speeches on the subject of 'eternal renewal' etc, cannot conceal the idiocy of so-called nature. It would have been more sensible and economical to have made people eternal beings, in the way that we suppose the universe to be eternal, and thus standing in no need of partial 'destruction and rebirth'. It is essential that people apply their will and reason to questions of immortality and longevity. I'm

absolutely convinced that this will be achieved once their cognitive ability becomes transformed into an instinct.[3] N. Z. Vasiliev translated
Zarathustra in 1893, not 1889–90. He was very keen on Nietzsche during
his work on the translation, but once he had finished it, his interest
cooled. He gave me a thorough working-over with Nietzsche, just as V.
A. Posse subsequently worked me over with Stirner.[4] They worked me
over with rasp-file and rough-plane, but most frequently of all with the
head of an axe. I survived, however. In essence, my past is a humorous
one, and the obituary writers will be in error if they fail to mention this.

Incidentally, about Posse. I read his book the other day.[5] He looks at
himself in a mirror which magnifies and embellishes his figure superbly.
He has forgotten a great deal, much of what he does say is not quite correct, and some things are completely incorrect. But this is the fate of all
those who would see themselves as one of the principal forces by which
'history' is created. In particular, he was incorrect in giving me the credit
for the exposure of the *provocateur* Gurovich. He was exposed by S. D.
Protopopov, brother of the late 'prime' minister.[6] Protopopov learned
about this from an officer of the gendarmerie, and Stanislav Grinevitsky,
the editor of *Nizhegor[odskii] listok*, reported Proto[opopov's] words to me.
I then went to Petersburg, where I passed on the news. It's not true to
say that '*Zhizn'* was destroyed more by what Gorky did than by what he
wrote'.[7] I never organized any conspiratorial meetings in the editorial
office of *Zhizn'*. It was Gariushin who organized them. Savinkov and
Tatarov attended his meetings; at that time the latter was either an illegal or already a *provocateur*, most likely the former.[8] During my interrogation at the Peters[burg] gendarme office in 1905, the head of that
office, M. A. Konissky, an acquaintance of mine from Tiflis, hinted quite
openly that Tatarov was lying low in the *Zhizn'* office, and that this was
what finished [the journal] off. But that is not true either. Skitalets lived
at the editorial office for a while, and he was similar in appearance to
Tatarov. There are many other factual inaccuracies in Posse's book, and
he has forgotten a great, great deal. But this is all in the realm of personal relationships and has no social significance. He was a good man,
Posse. As well as hunting, he apparently also loved horses, and I think
he looked upon me rather as he would have looked upon a trotter. That
is flattering, but inaccurate.

I am writing *Samgin*. It is a very difficult thing. Posse is one of those
contemporaries of mine who particularly dislikes Samgin.

As you see, I am writing a lot. I wish the same to you and I ask you
to write a little article for the jour[nal] *Literaturnaia ucheba* on the subject
of literary technique! Please! I shall be greatly in your debt!

Warm regards,

A. Peshkov

SOURCE: *AG* 11: 210–12.

¹ 'Kalinin', a story from the cycle *Through Russia*. The censored passage was subsequently restored.
² Alfred Kubin (1877–1959), German Expressionist artist.
³ These comments bear the clear mark of Fedorov's philosophy. See Letter 110, n. 3.
⁴ Max Stirner (real name, Johann Kaspar Schmidt, 1806–58), philosopher who stressed the primacy of the individual will in human behaviour.
⁵ See Letter 142, n. 4.
⁶ Mikhail Ivanovich Gurovich (1859–1914), police *provocateur* who infiltrated Marxist groups at the turn of the century. Sergei Dmitrievich Protopopov (1862–1933) was a Nizhnii friend. His brother became the last tsarist Minister of Internal Affairs.
⁷ The journal *Zhizn'* was closed down in June 1901, partly because Gorky's 'Song of the Stormy Petrel' was published there.
⁸ Sergei Andreevich Gariushin, journalist who worked for *Zhizn'*. Boris Viktorovich Savinkov (1879–1925), an SR and one of the most controversial figures in the revolutionary movement. Rumoured to be an *agent provocateur*, he also wrote novels under the pseudonym Ropshin. Nikolai Iurievich Tatarov, another SR and reputed *provocateur*.

154. To I. V. Stalin, [8 January 1930]

[Sorrento]

Dear Iosif Vissarionovich!

There is a report in *Rul'* that a certain journal in Chita has been punished for not having written in my praise.¹ If one counts the Central Committee's reprimand to the people in Novosibirsk, this is the second such incident.² I am quite sure that there will be a third, a tenth, etc. Although I consider this phenomenon both natural and inevitable, I do not think it is necessary to punish those who write about me in an uncomplimentary or hostile manner.

Like you, and all the other 'old-timers', I receive many hostile letters. The crazy ideas and attacks contained in these letters convince me that, ever since the Party set the countryside so decisively on the track of collectivization, the social revolution has begun to assume a truly socialist character. This is an upheaval of almost geological proportions, and it is greater, immeasurably greater and more profound, than anything that has yet been done by the Party. A way of life which has existed for thousands of years, an order which has created people of singular monstrosity, people quite horrifying in their animal conservatism and proprietorial instinct—this order is being destroyed. There are some 20 million such people. The problem of re-educating them in the shortest possible time is an insanely difficult one. Yet it is being resolved in a practical way right now.

It is quite natural that many of these millions are falling prey to a truly violent insanity. They don't even understand the full depth of the upheaval which is taking place, yet they sense instinctively, in their bones, that the very deepest foundations of their antiquated life are beginning to be destroyed. A ruined church can be rebuilt and you can install any God you like in it, but when the ground slips away beneath your feet—

that is irreparable and for all time. So now we find people cursing furiously. These are people who have mechanically acquired revolutionary phrases and a revolutionary lexicon, yet who very often conceal beneath such phrases the vindictive mood of an ancient person for whom 'the end is nigh'. Note that these curses are strongest of all in Siberia and the Far East, and that is where the peasant is strongest too.

But 'names will never hurt me'; they will never keep me from living. As for my work, such abuse serves only as a stimulus. As you know, I am not a Party member, which means that nothing addressed to me can touch the Party or its leaders. So let them curse. All the more so since some people—indeed, many people—curse out of ignorance and a lack of understanding, so that when you explain the crux of the matter to them, they stop. Many people hasten to declare their orthodoxy, thereby hoping to gain something for themselves, and they do gain certain things.

Generally speaking, however, everything is going very well—much better than could have been expected. And so, I beg of you, please do not punish those who curse. Some of them are incurable and not worth thinking about, whereas others are only slightly ill and they will get better. Our life itself is a most skilful doctor.

Let me take this opportunity to congratulate you once again on your fifty years of service to life. Fine service it has been too.

Keep well!

A. Peshkov

Will you write something for *Literaturnaia ucheba*? You should. It would be very useful for beginning writers. Very. Do write something!

A. P.

SOURCE: *Izv Ts K* 1989 (7): 215–16.

[1] The report stated that the Politburo had ordered the closure of *Nasha literatura* [*Our literature*] for its criticism of Gorky and the poet Demian Bedny.
[2] In 1929 A. L. Kurs was dismissed as editor of the newspaper *Sovetskaia Sibir'* [*Soviet Siberia*] after criticizing Gorky, who was attempting to defend Siberian writers from attacks in the press.

155. To I. A. Gruzdev, [May 1930]

[Sorrento]

The suicide of V. V. Maiakovsky[1] came as no surprise to me, Ilia Aleksandrovich. This is not because I considered him a 'tragic' figure, but because from the very first time I met him he most definitely gave the impression of being a broken man. I remember saying to someone at the time that M[aiakovsky] would destroy himself before long, either by his own hand or by having someone else do it for him. This impression was reinforced when he visited me in Mustamäki in the summer of 1914 (or was it 1915?). He recited excerpts from *A Cloud in Trousers* [*Oblako v shtanakh*] and *The Backbone-Flute* [*Fleita-pozvonochnik*] and many of his lyric poems. I really liked the poems, and he read them extremely well. He even burst into tears like a woman, which disturbed and frightened me greatly. He complained that 'man is divided horizontally through the diaphragm'. When I told him that in my opinion he had a great, although probably very difficult, future ahead of him and that his talent would require an enormous amount of work, he gave the sullen reply: 'I want that future today.' Then he added: 'If there is no joy, I have no need for the future; and I feel no joy!' He behaved very nervously and was evidently deeply disturbed. He praised E. Guro highly for her *Celestial Camels* [*Nebesnye verbliuzhata*], but he criticized V. Khlebnikov, even calling him an 'idiot'.[2] And yet that very same evening, after supper, he recited some of Khlebnikov's verses in which death is called 'an enigmatic procuress', and when he read the lines 'I will accept everything that death desires'—or something to that effect—he nearly burst into tears again. And he ended by saying that 'Khlebnikov is probably a genius'. I have grown used to all sorts of people, but with him it was hard going. He would speak in two voices somehow, like the purest lyric poet one minute and in a sharply satirical fashion the next. One had the feeling that he did not know himself, that he was afraid of something. M. F. Andreeva reproached him for his inconsistencies and his excessive rudeness, and he answered her in verse: 'I don't want to know how to be tender' or 'to exude voluptuousness', 'I want to walk about naked' instead—or something like that. At the same time he showed a predilection for verbal tricks:

> The owl turns grey by October,
> As do the claws of Briusov.[3]

And so on and so forth.

This would have been good if it had been done in fun. But it was as if he attributed some serious significance to this contrived word-play, elevating it almost to the level of phonetic mysticism, as A. Bely once put it. One thing was clear, however: this was a man of unique sensitivity, a man of great talent, and yet he was unhappy. *His revolutionary poems were a surprise to me. I never found them moving: they contain a great deal of shouting, but lack pathos. In general, I never believed in Maiakovsky's revolutionariness, nor do I believe in it now. Esenin and Maiakovsky are not the first whose fate it has been to perish in these harsh times. And in the future it will be all the more difficult for people to serve the cause of freedom unconsciously.*

But all the same, Maiakovsky's death did bring a 'lump to my throat'.

Being a one-eyed individual, the person I blame for this death is, of course, Vavila Burmistrov, the savage who strangled the poet Sima Devushkin in *Okurov*.[4]

This is all so hard.

A. Peshkov

SOURCE: *AG* 11: 227–8.

[1] Vladimir Vladimirovich Maiakovsky (1893–1930), leading poet and playwright of the Futurist movement.

[2] Elena Genrikhovna Guro (1877–1913), writer of the Cubo-Futurist group. The collection of poems referred to was published in 1914. Velimir (real name Viktor Vladimirovich) Khlebnikov (1885–1922), poet, playwright, and theoretician of the Futurist movement.

[3] An untranslatable trick of language: in Russian the two sentences are virtually identical in sound although quite different in meaning, viz: *Sedeet k oktiabriu sova,* | *Se deiut kogti Briusova.*

[4] Characters in Gorky's novel *Okurov Town*.

156. *To N. K. Krupskaia, [16 May 1930]*

[Sorrento]

Dear Nadezhda Konstantinovna,

I have just finished reading your memoirs of Vl[adimir] Ilyich [Lenin]—such an unpretentious, charming and sad book. I wanted to congratulate you from here, from afar, although I am really not sure if I should even say thank you for this book. But I do just want to say something and to share the emotion that your memoirs aroused. There's another thing too: D. I. Kursky and Liubimov were here yesterday. Kur[sky] talked about Vogt's work and the structure of Vladimir Ilyich's brain, and afterwards I was thinking all night long: 'That such a beacon of reason should have been extinguished, that such a heart should have stopped beating!'[1] I recalled very clearly my visit to Gorki[2] in the summer of 1920, I believe it was. I wasn't involved in politics at the time but I was up to my ears in 'daily cares', and I complained to V[ladimir] I[lyich] about the pressure of life's trivialities. Among other things, I mentioned the workers in Leningrad who were pulling down wooden houses for fuel, breaking window-frames in the process, smashing glass, and ruining roofing iron—and all for no reason whatsoever. In the mean time, their own houses had leaking roofs, windows covered with plywood, etc. I was distressed by the low value that the workers placed on the products of their own labour. 'Vladimir Ilyich, you think on the broad scale; such trivialities do not affect you,' I said. He walked around the terrace in silence and I reproached myself: I was wrong to have pestered him with such trivialities. But after tea we went out for a walk and he said to me: 'You are wrong to think that I attach no significance to trivialities.

Besides, this is not a triviality: the undervaluing of labour that you indicated is, of course, no triviality at all. We are a poor people, and we must understand the value of every log and every penny. A great deal has been destroyed and we must take very good care of all that remains; this is vital for reviving the economy. But how can you blame the worker for not yet realizing that he is already the owner of everything there is? It will take time for such awareness to arise, and perhaps it will arise only among the socialists.' Of course, I am not reproducing his words literally, but this was the gist of it. He spoke on this subject for a very long time, and I was amazed at just how many 'trivialities' he was aware of and at the striking ease with which his mind would turn from insignificant everyday phenomena to the broadest generalizations. I was always amazed by that ability of his, an ability which he had developed with such remarkable subtlety. I do not know anyone in whom analysis and synthesis operated in such a harmonious way. On another occasion I went to see him with a project for moving retarded children away from Leningrad to remote monasteries, so as to separate them from normal children. The former were having an extremely harmful effect on the latter. But it turned out that Vladimir Ilyich had already thought of this and had spoken about it to some of his associates. 'How do you find the time?' I asked. 'The idea came to me a long time ago when I was in Whitechapel in London,' he said. He was far-sighted. When he was staying with me on Capri, we used to discuss contemporary literature together, and he would characterize the writers of my generation with remarkable deftness. He had a merciless facility for exposing their essence, and he also indicated certain crucial deficiencies in my own stories. He concluded by reproaching me as follows: 'You are wrong to dissipate your experience in small stories; it is time you put it all into one book, a large novel.' I told him that I had the dream of writing the history of one family over the course of a hundred years, from 1813, the time when Moscow was rebuilt, right up to the present day. The family patriarch is a peasant, a village elder, emancipated by the landlord for his exploits as a partisan in 1812; and the family goes on to produce clerks, priests, manufacturers, Petrashevtsy, Nechaevtsy, men of the seventies and the eighties.[3] He listened very attentively and asked some questions. Then he said: 'An excellent topic. It's a difficult one, of course, and it will require a massive amount of time. I think you'll manage to deal with it, but I don't see how you will bring it to a conclusion. Reality has not yet provided such a conclusion. No, you should write this after the revolution; for the time being, you should do something along the lines of *Mother*.' Needless to say, I could not see myself how the book would conclude.

He was always like this—he trod a remarkably straight path to the truth, foreseeing and anticipating everything.

But why am I telling you all this? You walked by his side throughout his life and knew him far better than I, or indeed anyone else.

Keep well, dear Nadezhda Konstantinovna. Warm regards, and a friendly hug.

Heartfelt greetings to Mariia Ilyinichna [Ulianova].[4]

A. Peshkov

SOURCE: *SS* 30: 167–9.

---

[1] Quotation from Nikolai Nekrasov's poem, 'In Memory of Dobroliubov' ['Pamiati Dobroliubova']. Kursky was the Russian ambassador to Italy and Oskar Vogt the German neurologist who dissected Lenin's brain. Isiodor Evstigneevich Liubimov (1881–1939), senior Soviet trade representative in Germany.

[2] A suburb of Moscow. The similarity to Gorky's name is coincidental.

[3] The Petrashevtsy were members of a political discussion group led by Mikhail Petrashevsky (1821–66). Several of them, including Dostoevsky, were arrested in 1849. Sergei Nechaev (1847–82) and his followers were radical political activists of the late 1860s and early 1870s.

[4] Lenin's sister.

157. To K. A. Fedin, [9 November 1930]

[Sorrento]

Dear Konstantin Aleksandrovich!

I have already informed I. A. Gruzdev that I am unable to write anything about A. A. Blok, since I am convinced that I would only write something boorish and unjust. Blok's misanthropy and pessimism are alien to me, and—like his mysticism—these are traits one cannot ignore. Besides, I am presently in a vile state of mind and at odds with the world. I was never particularly attracted to Blok's poetry and it seems to me that he did great harm to 'The Beautiful Lady'—his essence of essences—by endowing her with the degenerate characteristics of a German lady of the late eighteenth century, a lady who, albeit much older, is nevertheless an entirely healthy person.[1] I do not have any 'connection' with Blok in general. That is possibly a failing on *my* part. On these grounds I decline to write; don't be angry with me!

After reading your 'Old Man' ['Starik'],[2] I wanted to write and tell you how well you had done, but I was weighed down with 'affairs' and just didn't get round to writing.

Keep well!

Regards,

A. Peshkov

SOURCE: *SS* 30: 191–2.

¹ Blok's 'Verses about the Beautiful Lady' ['Stikhi o Prekrasnoi Dame'], a poetic cycle of 1901–2, highly mystical in flavour and influenced by the philosophy of Vladimir Soloviev.
² A story published in *Krasnaia nov'* in January 1930.

158. *To Popov,*¹ *[3 January 1931]*

[Sorrento]

You wrote me a very good letter, Comrade Popov. I did not find any 'sharp words' in it; however, I did gain a clear sense of its sincerity and forthrightness. I will answer you in the same manner that you wrote to me.

As far as the villa is concerned, you've been misled. I have never owned one, I do not own one now, and of course I shall never own one in the future either. I am incapable of lying, and it would be a great lie if I were to acquire property at a time when I am rejoicing at the mighty task of building socialism by the working class of the Union of Soviets. I would do far better in terms of the 'acquisition of every comfort'—i.e. the facilities which my age, my work, and my state of health demand— were I to reside in the Soviet Union and not here. I am not having my sons educated in 'bourgeois schools'; I have one son only, and he is my secretary. He is thirty years old and married with two children; they are too young to be going to school yet. It is the bourgeois *émigré* press which has foisted this 'villa' and 'comfort' upon me, and it has done so with a simple aim, which is to compromise me in the eyes of sincere but credulous socialists.

In the Union of Soviets there are, of course, places no worse than Sorrento, but, if I were to live over there, I would live in Moscow. It would make no sense for me to live on the Black Sea, for instance; that's almost as far from Moscow as Italy is. And in Moscow there would be meetings, visits of various sorts, and so on, all of which would interfere with my work. Here I live in total isolation and alone; and this allows me to work in tranquillity for ten or twelve hours a day. In Moscow I would be tempted to go to the theatre and take trips hither and thither; whereas over here I never go to the theatre, and it's even been two months since I last went into town, which is only three kilometres from my apartment.

The 'Italian censorship' cannot cause me any hindrance. I have always written what I know and what I think 'without caution'. There is no reason for them to 'arrest' me, and if I were to be arrested, it would cause a scandal which could only be of value to our cause in the Union of S[ocialist] S[oviets]. So there you have it, my dear fellow!

All the same, I will be coming back to live in the Soviet Union; the times are such that one needs to be at home.

But I will move only after I've finished all the work I have begun here. I shall visit [Russia] again this year, though, in April.

Does my answer satisfy you? If not, then do write to me again and I'll answer.

Thank you for the letter. A very good letter it was too.

Warm regards,

A. Peshkov

SOURCE: *SS* 30: 198–9.

¹ Popov (his other names are unknown) was a factory worker from Leningrad who had written to Gorky complaining of the comfortable life the writer was leading 'in Fascist Italy' and asking him to settle in the Soviet Union.

159. To R. Rolland, [2 April 1931]

[Sorrento]

My dear and ever more respected friend!

Forgive me for sending this letter without a translation into your language, but I wanted to answer your letter quickly, and there is no one here at present able to do a sufficiently accurate translation.

I still do not know anything about a Gorky evening; I think such an evening was arranged on 27 March, on the occasion of my sixty-third birthday.[1]

I agree with you completely that radio reports from Moscow are too narrow in their scope and fail to shed any light on a whole range of phenomena of the most profound cultural significance. For example, by 20 March some 9,800,000 of the 25 million private holdings had joined collective farms.[2] This movement towards the collective cultivation of the land is quite natural. Lenin dreamed of 100,000 tractors, and we already have some 70,000. At this very moment 29,000 tractors purchased in America are being unloaded in our southern ports.

What is the cultural effect of saturating the countryside with machinery? In the first place, the peasants on a collective farm have an income which exceeds that of the private holder by something between three and five times. Moreover, they have plenty of free time—time which they are using to eradicate their lack of education. And although the movement on to the collective farms has been going on for less than three full years as yet, it has already created a virtual book crisis. Editions of 200,000 copies are swallowed up in a month. I'm not just talking of brochures here either; these are 'thick' books. *La Chartreuse de Parme*[3] by Stendhal— 20,000, 30,000, 75,000 copies—and not a single copy of any of these three editions is available any more. Balzac, Mérimée, Gautier, Flaubert, etc. have been more successful still. When I get to Moscow, I'll send you exact figures for publications by the State Publishing House, which, incidentally, is functioning extremely poorly, displaying insufficient skill in the selection of titles, and insufficient energy in their dissemination. The demand in the countryside for fiction and popular science has already created a paper crisis. Not that the factories are lagging behind the countryside, of course; each one has its own newspaper, and at some factories every shop puts out its own little paper. In my home town of Nizhnii Novgorod the Sormovo factory has 18,000 workers and a newspaper which is published in 18,000 copies. Now that must be something of a curiosity! And it is not an isolated instance. My dear friend, can you imagine my pride and joy when I learn facts of this sort? I sincerely wish that one day you might experience what I am feeling now.

I could tell you many things about the growth of culture in the Union of Soviets, about life in the work colonies for homeless children, about the way that 'socially dangerous' (that is, criminal) elements are being re-educated through labour in Central Asia, and about the emancipation of Central Asian women; but I will save all that for when we meet in the summer.

Now, regarding the letter from Professor Henri Sée.[4]

The historian S. F. Platonov is someone I met in 1920. He made no secret of his monarchist convictions even then, during the years of the Civil War. However, in the course of the next ten years nobody touched him. Apparently, his daughters were arrested in 1929 for being members of a monarchist organizaton. I have been told that he himself was arrested for concealing documents of state importance—and for being the organizer of and the inspiration for a group of monarchists which had dealings with Russian monarchists in Paris. I must say that in so far as I know the mood of the masses, all these monarchist conspiracies are academic affairs which are built on sand. The peasants understand the meaning of monarchism perfectly well; that is, they understand that it is based on large-scale ownership of the land. There is not, nor can there be, any force which might turn the peasantry back in that direction. It has already come too far for it to return to what it has fought against so fiercely.

You can inform 'A Farmer' that Abramovich was not in the places which he indicated. This has been established with complete accuracy. It only remains to establish with equal accuracy that he was in Moscow, and this no doubt will be done.[5]

It seems to me that in this instance one has to take into consideration the indignation of Groman, one of the accused, who told the court: 'I am not insane, nor do I suffer from hallucinations. If I say that Abramovich was in Moscow and that I conversed with him there, that means it really did happen.'

Groman is a comparatively decent man, and his repentance is most sincere and most solidly grounded.

Ekaterina Peshkova, my first wife and the mother of my son, is here with me in Sorrento at present. She confirms that Ghezzi is free and at work. I know that all the saboteurs convicted at the trial of the 'Industrial Party' have excellent living conditions in prison and that they are working to repair the damage they have caused. Ramzin is even giving lectures to engineers at the Thermal Institute.[6]

My dear friend! When you go to the Union of Soviets, you will be convinced that something truly great and universal is happening. I am sure that we will meet over there. My warmest regards to a courageous fighter for justice. Keep well!

M. Gorky

SOURCE: *SS* 30: 210–13.

[1] On 28 March 1931 there had been a French-language broadcast from Moscow of an evening in honour of Gorky. The writer was always prone to inaccuracy when indicating his date of birth.
[2] On the collectivization drive, see the Introduction to this section.
[3] Gorky gives the French title here.
[4] The professor had asked about the fate of S. F. Platonov.
[5] Rolland had sent a letter from 'a farmer', in which the evidence given at a Moscow trial of Mensheviks was called into question. Abramovich, one of the Menshevik leaders, was living abroad.
[6] Leonid Ramzin was convicted at the 'Industrial Party' trial of 1930. He was released before his term had expired, eventually receiving a Stalin Prize. Francesco Ghezzi (1894–?), Italian anarchist, arrested in 1929 and exiled, after which nothing is known of him.

160. To A. N. Tikhonov, [before 20 January 1932]

[Sorrento]

To A. N. Tikhonov,

Here are some thoughts regarding a repertoire for the contemporary theatre. As yet there is no such repertoire; it will have to be created.

I proceed from the conviction that in our age, in our unique circumstances, the theatre must assume an exclusively pedagogical responsibility for the sincere, persistent, and tireless promotion of culture for the masses, a responsibility for stimulating class-conscious revolutionary emotions.

In the past the theatre presented monotonous spectacles of family dramas and individual conflicts; whereas today it must reveal the social causes of these dramas and conflicts with the utmost clarity. We must try with all our might to endow this theatre with the utmost clarity of thought, word, and gesture, to endow it with such indisputable ideological and artistic authority as to exclude the possibility of misunderstanding on the part of the viewer and of contradictory interpretations by the critics. This is very difficult, of course, but 'difficulties exist in order to be overcome'.

Our life today imperiously demands that we accelerate and extend the cultural and revolutionary education of the masses in every way. People who do not understand or sense the pressure of this need are either alien and inimical to the masses because of their class background or inner make-up, or else they are quite frivolous and incapable of understanding the decisive significance of the masses in contemporary history—the significance of a force which has itself yet to gain a sufficiently profound self-awareness and which does not know, or has forgotten, the bitter taste of that mess of pottage which was the past.

The masses must be able to see the past so that they can remember it and come to know it; the theatre can show them their ancestral past—that is, it can realize its proper role as political instructor. I think that the theatre could fulfil this role very well once it has forged close working ties with our writers, and once it has worked out with them a plan for a repertoire and has then set about creating it.

It seems to me that we should begin with plays which might illustrate important historical moments in the life of Europe and Russia in the most artistically satisfying manner—moments when coercion by the minority over the reason and will of the majority finds particularly clear and brutal expression. These would include the time of Spartacus, the Dolcinists, the Albigenses, the Taborites etc.

Then we should take historical and biographical material so as to create comedies and dramas, developing such themes as the battle waged against church dogma and the prejudices of the masses by outstanding representatives of investigative and critical thought. There is also the theme of the 'Battle for Individuality'—that is, the fruitless attempts made by individuals to conduct their own battle against the pressures of state and society.

European life urgently suggests a range of very important new themes.

Here are some sample outlines: during the war in France, in the milieu of Balzac's 'thirty-year-old women', many followed the path of skullduggery and easy profit.[1] A typical representative of women of this type is Marthe Hanau with her scheme involving the *Gazette du Franc*.[2] It would be most instructive to portray on stage the figure of an emotionally boorish, cynical woman, greedy for sensual pleasure; she would, as it were, symbolize the bourgeoisie in contemporary France.

One might present Saccard, the hero of Zola's novel *L'Argent*, but in the new and ironic situation of a person who has been crushed by his money.

One might—and indeed one should—present the figure of one of our former socialist ministers, a man who understands the inevitability of social catastrophe and the inescapable destruction of the class-based state, but who nevertheless attempts to repair it. One might also present the doctor who is treating him, even though he realizes that the minister's senile ailments are incurable; and the servant who works for the minister and hates him as if he were his worst enemy and despises himself because he works for his enemy, and yet fears at the same time that the death of that enemy will deprive him of his place in life.

The theatre has yet to touch on the theme of the Catholic priest who tries to build the power of the church on the ruins of society; or of the general who wants to engage in battle, no matter on whose side he might be fighting; or of the chemist who wants to use human subjects in order to test the potency of a gas he has invented.

The present is extremely rich in nightmarish figures. There is no question of creating caricatures here, even if you wanted to. These are figures made for satire, so long as one is speaking of them as material for verbal art.

A. Peshkov

It also seems to me that it is high time to set the theatre against the church, to stage productions of great and staggering power, with music and choruses, with masses of people on stage, so as to depict social tragedies or humorous comedies—for example, life beyond the grave, complete with heaven and hell. The latter would be particularly timely, since nowadays there are people who contend that hell does exist as a place where people endure various *physical* torments, and that the circumstance which makes hell so particularly agonizing is that 'a depraved society prevails there'. Don't get the idea that I've dreamt this up myself; no—this is something which has actually been published.

A. P.

SOURCE: *SS* 30: 231–3.

---

[1] *La femme de trente ans*, one of the 'Scènes de la vie privée' of Balzac's *Comédie humaine*.
[2] A scandal involving the worlds of banking, politics, and the press. It is also mentioned in Gorky's article of 1928 'On This and That' ['O raznykh raznostiakh'].

161. To E. P. Peshkova, [3 February 1932]

[Sorrento]

I haven't written to you, mother, because I haven't had time. There's nothing to write about anyway. There's not much that's any good over here, and I don't feel like writing about the bad things.

Everything is more or less fine at home; the girls are growing by leaps and bounds. Daria is rowdy enough for three, but that is not so very bad;

she is more of a child than Marfukha, who is a young woman inquisitive beyond her years. She may perhaps grow up to be an intellectual, even though life itself demands resolute people.

I am worried about Maksim's health—he has become too nervous and tires too quickly. His organs are all functioning normally, but his nerves play up. He has stopped drinking wine and he doesn't smoke much; it was a hard job convincing him to give up wine and tobacco. Lipa[1] gives him massages and 'electrifies' him with a 'Tephra'[?];[2] that helped a lot, and he has become calmer and more refreshed. But you know what it is I'm afraid of. I'm trying to convince him to leave for Moscow without waiting for me, and I think I may succeed. He must get himself examined and undergo serious treatment there. That's the situation.

Well, what else is there to tell you? Nothing at all. When will you be coming here?

Goodbye for now,

A.

So Uncle Fedia [Nikolaev] has died, has he? That's a shame. He was a fine fellow.

SOURCE: *AG* 9: 283–4.

[1] Olimpiada Chertkova, Gorky's nurse.
[2] Electrotherapy was commonly used at this time for the treatment of many ailments ranging from acne to writer's cramp. By 'tephra' Gorky may have had in mind Tesla, or Nikola Tesla (1856–1943), whose announcement in 1890 about the therapeutic effects of the deep heating caused by high frequency currents applied to the human body led to the proliferation of such devices in subsequent decades.

162. To R. Rolland, [September 1932]

[Moscow]

Dear friend,

I am writing to inform you of the reasons why the Russian delegation could not take part in the congress. As you know, we were not let into Holland at all, and the French government granted only Comrade Shvernik and myself permission to enter Paris, refusing to admit Elena Stasova, Karl Radek, academician Ioffe (the well-known physicist), and Lev Fedorov, one of the most prominent colleagues of I. P. Pavlov at the Institute for Experimental Medicine.[1] Under these circumstances Shvernik and I considered it impossible to avail ourselves of Mr Herriot's so strangely limited courtesy.[2] Moreover, I was unwell. I was running a temperature of 38.8° which is high for me, and Professor Kraus expressed his firm opposition to my trip, for fear that pneumonia might set in. Of course, I would have gone to Paris regardless, had not Mr Herriot deprived the fellow members of our delegation of that same right.

Furthermore, there was some confusion over the selection of a venue for the congress—I am not sure whose fault this was. Willi Münzenberg maintains that he had Herriot's verbal permission for all the delegations to enter Paris without restriction for a period of eight days.[3] But for some reason Amsterdam was chosen. Who did this, and on what grounds, I do not know. As a result of my illness, I have not yet managed to familiarize myself in any detail with the work of the congress or with the resolutions which were adopted there, but it seems to me that in general the congress was a success and that it will be of major significance in the business of organization of anti-militaristic feelings broadly amongst the people.

It seems to me that if members of the congress are going to organize anti-war committees in every country, then their immediate concern should be the publication of a journal with the aim of exposing all preparations for a new war and any attempts to provoke such a war. What are your views in this regard?

I'm sending you the 'Basic Guide-lines' for the second Five-Year Plan, and I'll soon send you some other things as well. I'm also sending several photographs taken by my son on Vaigach Island, inside the Arctic Circle. My son is spending his second summer up there, among exiles whose job it is to mine lead. The working conditions up there are difficult, of course, but one day's work is counted as three, and people are exiled there only after a medical examination to prove that they have great strength and powers of endurance. Some 600 people work there, and even though they have served out the term of their sentence and earned the right to go wherever they please, many of them have chosen to remain on the island as free citizens, sending for their families and building houses which can be acquired on the mainland in prefabricated form. They organize fishing co-operatives, breed reindeer, and generally 'become attached to the land'. They already have a club, an orchestra, and a theatre group; they will get a theatre and a school building in the spring (again in prefabricated form, of course). Generally speaking, the Arctic is rapidly becoming populated by people with a penchant for strong sensations and the 'unusual'. It is apparently true that the North possesses an irresistible power of attraction. Having visited Murmansk and Solovki in 1929, I myself would be pleased to go there again—and for a long period at that.[4] It is said that a person who has witnessed the Northern Lights and has seen the sun remain in the sky day and night for the duration of several months finds it quite easy to become reconciled to the polar night.

Berlin made a very painful impression on me: the profusion of jobless people who perform on the streets as musicians and singers, the groups of prostitutes on every corner, and the despondent children. And right beside them are the impudent countenances of young degenerates in Fascist uniforms, detachments of 'Steel Helmets', the 'German revanchists'. They described themselves to me as such because the majority of the 'Steel Helmet' youths are supposedly the children of those killed in the war of 1914–18. There are probably hundreds of thousands of such children in France as well, and they would probably not be averse to avenging the deaths of their fathers either.

We are living in a terrible time, my dear friend, and great tragedies await us, but what a joy it is to observe at the same time the pride of the young people in my country, prepared as they are for any tragedy, to observe the rapidity of their intellectual growth and of their awareness that they are responsible for life, for everything being created in the world. I know, of course, that young people of the same kind are growing up in Europe as well, and I am firm in my belief that they are the future victors and builders of a new world.

It is a great pity that I have only a little while left to live and that I will not see the days which will follow the victory. But I am profoundly grateful to people and to my destiny for what I have seen, for what I see now, and for still being able to work with those who are so boldly and courageously marching towards the beautiful future, towards the Renaissance of mankind.

SOURCE: *SS* 30: 259–61.

---

[1] The Dutch government had refused the Soviet delegation permission to attend an anti-war congress in Amsterdam in late August 1932. Shvernik, Stasova, and Radek were all prominent Party officials.

[2] Édouard Herriot (1872–1957), French Premier and Foreign Minister.

[3] Münzenberg (1889–1940), German Communist later expelled from the Party for his opposition to Stalin.

[4] For further information, see the Introduction to this section.

163. To V. S. Grossman,[1] [7 October 1932]

[Moscow]

The story 'Three Deaths' ['Tri smerti'] is a frivolous, superficial work. It seems to me that Russian literature already possesses outstanding examples of the emotional treatment of 'death' as a theme—L. Tolstoy ('Three Deaths', 'The Death of Ivan Ilyich'), Chekhov, L. Andreev, *et al.*—and that if this theme is still worthy of attention (which is not even to mention the question of its timeliness), then it will have to be approached from a different point of view. Death is a biological phenomenon, and to write about it without knowing anything of biology is hardly a valuable undertaking. To write solely for the sake of making people 'ponder the inevitable' is only so much idle chatter and mere church business, i.e. it is clearly harmful.

'Glück auf' contains very good material for a novella, but it is poorly 'assembled', too thickly sown with superfluous words, and spoiled by the didacticism of an author who often preaches to the reader in a dry and ponderous narrative—and this at the very moments which call for artistic portrayal and the presentation of ideas through images. Overall it seems to me that the author's skills of depiction are rather weak and undeveloped.

Personally, I do not see any counter-revolutionary tendencies in the novella, but critics could have certain grounds for seeing such tendencies in the author's 'naturalism'. I cannot say that naturalism as a device for depicting reality is 'counter-revolutionary' in itself, but I am convinced that this device distorts our life and is thus inapplicable to it and incorrect. The author says: 'I have written the truth.' But he should put two questions to himself. The first is, which truth? The other is, why tell it? As we know, two truths exist in our world, and while it is the base and sordid truth of the past which predominates in a quantitative sense, there is a different truth—the deadly enemy of that first truth—which has already been born and continues to grow. And we also know that nothing can be understood without taking into consideration the clash, the battle between these two truths. The author sees the truth of the past quite well, but he does not have a very clear understanding of what he should do with it. The author has provided a true and tasteful picture of the obtuseness of the miners, of the drunkenness, the fighting and, generally speaking, of everything which appears to dominate his field of vision. Of course, this is the truth. It is a most vile truth, even an agonizing truth, and one which must be fought and destroyed without mercy. Does the author set himself such an aim?

It is possible that he does set himself such an aim, but naturalism as a device is not suitable for the battle against a reality which is destined to be destroyed. Naturalism 'fixes' the facts, it registers them in a purely technical way. Naturalism is the trade of photographers. The photographer can, for instance, reproduce the face of a person with, let us say, a sad smile. But if he wants to give us this same face with an ironic or a joyful smile, he must take another photograph. All these photographs will more or less contain 'the truth', but it will be 'the truth' only for that moment when the person was sad or angry or joyful. The photographer and the naturalist are quite powerless when it comes to depicting the truth about a person in all his complexity.

In the novella 'Glück auf', it is the material which controls the author, not the author the material. The author examines the facts whilst standing on the same plane as the facts themselves. Of course, this is a 'position' too, yet it would have been to the benefit of both the material and the author had the author asked himself the question: why is he writing? What kind of truth does he assert? What kind of truth does he want to triumph?

He is a talented man and he must resolve these questions.

M. Gorky

SOURCE: *SS* 30: 261–3.

---

[1] Vasilii Semenovich Grossman (1905–64) achieved posthumous fame for *Life and Fate* [*Zhizn' i sud'ba*] and *Forever Flowing* [*Vse techet*]. 'Three Deaths' was never published; 'Glück auf' appeared in 1934.

164. To K. A. Fedin, [21 December 1932]

[Sorrento]

I don't quite understand, my dear Fedin, how the 'mystery' of my merchants can be 'seductive'. The mystery is, after all, quite simple. In the third volume of my endless 'plaintive song' of Klim Samgin, Dr Makarov explains it in terms of the merchant's uncertainty about the stability of his social position.[1] 'His great-grandfathers and grandfathers were resourceful' peasants; they believed in the legitimacy of slavery and they saw clearly the lawlessness which was the freedom of the nobility. Under Catherine they themselves obtained the right to own slaves, a right which they later exercised by purchasing peasants on behalf of landowners. The peasant's thirst for 'emancipation' was a thirst for the right to lawlessness. After all, the advantages of injustice were completely obvious! There is firmly rooted in man a slavishness which has been nurtured over the ages and which the church has reinforced through the idea of servitude to God. And so it is that by 'abiding in servile fear' a man does not believe in the permanence of his 'freedom', but keeps seeking to test its limits, to see if he can do things this way or that. Immersion in the arts and in philanthropy does not satisfy every merchant: Savva Morozov, Gorbunov from Kaluga, Meshkov from Perm, and many others helped the revolutionaries sincerely and not without risk to themselves. Anyway, if it is possible to have 'repentant noblemen', why shouldn't there be 'repentant merchants' too? Furthermore, in Russia, as in the USA, the merchant class has produced a third generation with a large proportion of ignoramuses and degenerates—which is explained by the depletion of biological energy in the pursuit of rapid profit. Just consider the wondrous speed with which the Moscow textile magnates and the Volga timber merchants and shipowners increased their wealth. Indeed, each of these people had to face the question: is everything permitted? And, 'testing the mercy of the Lord in fearful dread', they permitted themselves everything.

Our literature has not concentrated on the merchant. For writers from the nobility the merchant was no hero; for the *raznochintsy*[2] he was only a boss and an enemy. Ostrovsky, even though he 'exposed' the Moscow merchant, was also attracted by him: the man may be a swine, but he's an amusing fellow! Andrei Pechersky, even though he exposed the 'religious schismatic' in the merchant, nevertheless admired him for his 'efficiency'.[3] And who else has written seriously on the subject?

I sometimes imagine that I have succeeded in saying something significant about people of this kind, but when I compare what I've said with what I know, I lose heart, for I know a lot, yet I am capable of little. Besides, it is difficult to find a form appropriate to the tale of the merchant Aleksandr Petrovich Bolshakov, for example. The builder of a church and also its elder, he was a depraved profligate and seducer of under-age girls. When he fell dangerously ill, this man summoned a priest—not his own priest, however, but one from another parish. Otherwise he would have had to confess to his priest that he, Bolshakov, had 'seduced' the man's niece, who was an orphan and a pupil in the church school.

So he summoned the other priest and asked: is it true that I'm a libertine and a dirty swine? The priest confirmed that such was the general view among the people. 'And will the Lord forgive me?' 'If you repent sincerely, He will forgive you, for He is merciful.' 'He'd forgive me, you say? Then you can tell him. . . that if I, Leksandr Bolshakov, were a Turkish or Mordvinian God of some sort, I would smash his ugly face in and tear out his beard for that mercy of his, so to hell with him! He is merciful, he sets no limits—what kind of a God is that? To hell with him!' After he had driven the priest away with his swearing, he ordered his wife and daughter—a half-wit—to take down all the icons and remove them from the room. He died the next day, at the same time that late mass was being celebrated, swearing lustily almost until his last breath. You see the sort of thing I mean? Vaska Buslaev is no invention, he is one of the greatest artistic types in our folklore, perhaps the most significant of all.[4]

Afinogenov reports something quite different—about Paris and a talk by Marina Tsvetaeva on 'Art in the Light of Conscience'.[5] The former lawyer Stremoukhov tells an ancient legend about a soul at the gates of heaven. The gatekeeper Peter asks: 'Are you a thief?' 'I am.' 'Have you killed anyone?' 'I have.' 'Do you repent?' 'I do.' 'Then go to heaven.'

Stremoukhov goes on to distort the legend as follows: it is the soul of the writer Lev Tolstoy or someone like him. He hasn't killed anyone, but he is debauched. He doesn't repent. He will continue his debauchery for two hundred years after his death. Peter sends him to hell. 'You can boil there in pitch for two hundred years.' This is what our *émigré* intelligentsia has come to. And this is what their servile nature is like.

You must excuse me for writing at such great length. How is your health? How were you treated in Leningrad? What new things did you see? How is the *Rape of Europe* of going?[6]

Warm regards,

A. Peshkov

SOURCE: *SS* 30: 266–8.

[1] The passage is actually near the beginning of the fourth volume.

[2] The *raznochintsy* were Russian intellectuals not of gentle birth, who became a moving force in Russian life from the 1840s onwards.

[3] Pseudonym of P. I. Melnikov (1818–83), whose long novels *In the Forests* [*V lesakh*] and *In the Mountains* [*V gorakh*] depicted merchants who were also members of schismatic 'Old Believer' sects.

[4] See Letter 72, n. 4.

[5] 'Iskusstvo pri svete sovesti', an article of 1932 which argued against the use of literature for extra-literary purposes.

[6] *Pokhishchenie Evropy*, a novel of 1934–5, which turned on the opposition between the 'decadent' West and a 'healthy' Russia.

165. To E. S. Dobin,[1] [25 April 1933]

[Sorrento]

I am most upset that it has taken me an entire month to find time to answer your very fine, businesslike letter. I am extremely pleased by the decision of the editorial board to put an end to the wavering of *Litucheba* and to set the journal on a firm and solid footing.

I welcome the intention to combine 'a high theoretical standard in the articles with . . . maximum clarity' and an economy of words.

'Every topic needs to be developed anew,' you write. You are absolutely correct, my dear comrade: 'anew and in a new way'. But what does it mean—'in a new way'? Let us take a look at our work in terms of the lofty goal we have set ourselves. We want to help our young writers to become educated as socialist writers, which means that *Litucheba* must also be *politucheba*. It also means that we should not forget a certain (and rather serious) contradiction between what we desire and what stands against us: in a country which is supposed to be socialist, we were obliged temporarily, due to powerful opposition on the part of the majority of the peasantry and the small landowners, to rely on individualism, 'shock work' and other means of stimulating the work effort by each person.[2] Say what you will, but this is to rely on the 'hero'. When we sing:

No one will deliver us,
Not God, not tsar, nor *hero*,

it is quite possible that the aforementioned hero is grinning to himself.

We are living not only in the epoch of the fall of capitalism but also in the years when Mussolini has given birth to Hitler, and when the petty bourgeoisie expects to find salvation through Fascism. I do not doubt that we ourselves have 'heroes' who take pleasure in reading the reports in *Izvestiia* of the murders of Communists by Fascists in Germany, acts which have gone unpunished. We would be bad politicians if we were unable properly to assess the ancient power of that bourgeois malevolence which is our chief enemy.

Let us return to the question of topics. The basic *emphasis of the journal* should be *specifically on the topics and not on the authors*. We have the habit of overpraising our authors, as a consequence of which their development goes sour. In the course of fifteen years we have overpraised several dozen authors, and these are now a dead-weight on the ship of our literature. This is why I favour treating the beginning author both seriously and carefully. One should neither praise nor censure, but simply teach such a person how to gain a correct understanding of the two realities which exist simultaneously and in a state of implacable hostility to one another. Since the facts of socialist reality are both more prominent and incomparably more striking, we must master them so that they may crush and destroy the multitudinous abominations of bourgeois behaviour.

As we note the merits and defects of the author's formal expression— his use of language and speech (that is, dialogue)—we should pay attention above all to the way he deals with his topic. To what extent has he developed it properly? What has not been said? Where did he burden it with extraneous details? A topic is a fact, a social phenomenon; how thoroughly has the author exhausted and revealed the meaning of that fact? Where, how, and by what means is his socialist treatment of the topic expressed, if it is expressed at all? This is what the teaching of literary work on the basis of facts and real-life material would be like.

The author's personality should be revealed, displayed, and explained to the author himself in exactly the same way—on the basis of his treatment of the topic. This is the easiest way to show what he lacks and what he should renounce as something extraneous or even socially harmful on some occasions. One must not forget that our young people often write neither what they should nor how they should, and that this is simply because of a lack of linguistic material and the poverty of their vocabulary.

I would suggest, therefore, that we select a group of stories on one and the same topic—we don't have very many—and talk about five or seven authors as though they were one. In my view, this would accord fully with the intention of the editorial board to 'include surveys of the work of beginning writers'.

We can talk about all this in greater detail when I come to Leningrad.

As far as the 'debate' and Shklovsky are concerned, it seems to me that we should not clutter the brains of our young people with such trifling matters.[3] But if they themselves were to demand that such trifles be elucidated, then we should provide a serious, factually based article about the 'apoliticality' of Formalism so as to demonstrate how such apoliticality serves as a mask for a particular type of politics, and to show that this is not the first time the bourgeoisie has resorted to this means of 'camouflage'.

'Art for art's sake' is not a bad method of camouflage, it is even quite pleasant in fact—witness Aikhenvald's books, Khodasevich's articles in *Vozrozhdenie* [*Renaissance*], and those of Adamovich in the little shop of words run by Miliukov.[4] One could delve further back into the past—to literary criticism in post-1848 Europe, for example.

I enclose an article for the first issue. I have asked V. A. Desnitsky to write a foreword to Petr Zalomov's[5] interesting correspondence with the schoolchildren.

Comradely greetings. I wish you good cheer and success in your work.

A. Peshkov

P.S. Some Germans—people who love a quiet and comfortable life—have escaped here. Some German Jews have escaped here too, and this is having a certain pedagogical effect on the indigenous democrats. They gloat somewhat: aha, so you've been squeezed out too, have you? And ever more often people are seriously starting to say: there *is* one country in which such abominations are impossible.

Regards,

A. P.

P.P.S. In one of the first issues we should provide an article about descriptive language (Turgenev, Chekhov, Bunin, *et al.*) and about dialogue (Leskov, Ostrovsky, *et al.*).

SOURCE: *AG* 10/2: 314–17.

---

[1] Efim Dobin (1901–77), literary critic, editorial board member of *Literaturnaia ucheba* (1931–6).

[2] The 'shock-worker' movement arose in the 1920s as part of a campaign to improve labour productivity.

[3] Shklovsky had recently published a controversial article ('South-West' ['Iugo-Zapad']) in which he had called upon writers to look towards the West as the source of all innovation.

[4] *Vozrozhdenie* was an *émigré* journal; the critic Georgii Adamovich (1894–1972) wrote for Miliukov's newspaper *Poslednie novosti*.

[5] See Letter 46, n. 2.

166. To I. A. Sokoliansky,[1] [25 August 1933]

[Moscow]

Your conjecture was absolutely correct: I did not receive the letters you sent to Sorrento, and I was waiting with some impatience for a response from you and Olia,[2] since I was convinced that you would tell me something of profound importance and value. I was not mistaken. Your long letter has pleased and excited me mightily.

My dear Ivan Afanasievich, I am a man of superficial and unsystematic learning, and you should believe me when I say that I encroach upon your field of investigation into the most complex and mysterious phenomena of human neural activity neither in order to collect 'scientific wonders'—so as then to display my 'nodding' acquaintance with them—nor to use such wonders as a means by which to improve my personal disposition, in the way that some people do. It is just that I have a great liking for the 'mass individual', for people in general, and that I have an even greater liking perhaps for the heroic and daring power of the investigative mind.

I am excited and pleased by that part of your letter where you talk of the 'capacity of the human brain', of the 'maximum amount of knowledge' which the 'mass individual' can accommodate, of the fact that 'the brains of an overwhelming number of contemporary people have become depraved by the shameful culture of the capitalist economic system', and that 'the fanatical racial theory must be challenged'.

Such wonderful and indisputably correct thoughts cannot help but make one excited and happy, especially when they have experimental confirmation. They must become the property of the 'mass individual', since it is essential to improve his disposition. This individual needs to have a clear conception of the power of his brain, of the broad possibilities for its development, and of the conditions necessary for the freedom of that development. It is necessary for 160,000,000 crania[3] to become more or less equally powerful accumulators of the mighty energy created both by organic nature and by social history in the process of their development—an energy which gradually discovers and subjugates to its will all other energies in the cosmos. I think that it is already possible to speak about cosmic energies. You can see how your letter has inspired me, my dear Ivan Afanasievich. I appeal to you again with an earnest request that you publish your research. Its enormous significance is unquestionable, and the necessity of acquainting our young people with it requires no demonstration. You are wrong when you assert that you 'do not know how to talk about your work'. Your letters to me are proof to the contrary. You should write as if you were having a conversation with a person whom you like very much and then you will be readily understood.

This person is an adolescent not only physiologically but also historically. However, he is beginning to create a new history and deserves every assistance he can be given. Forgive me, I seem to have adopted a 'preachy' tone.

In my opinion, you are quite correct when you point out that the 'notion of over-compensation' is harmful and contains a 'whiff of the divine'.[4] This is a very old notion. You will discover it in the folklore of all nations, and it is possible that it finds particularly clear embodiment in the attitude of our peasants and petty bourgeoisie towards various 'holy fools', 'simpletons', and 'imbeciles'—in other words, towards people who are idiots in all instances except when they are rogues, i.e. pretending to be idiots, like Iakov Koreisha, the 'holy man' of Moscow, and many others of his ilk. That science should acknowledge the supposedly unique giftedness of such organically defective individuals seems to me a very strange thing for scientific thought. The theological nature of such an acknowledgement is perfectly clear. It is a different matter when this acknowledgement has its origin in the superstitious masses who are infected by religious prejudices—in those masses who are dimly aware of the sinfulness of their lives and want to see 'holy men' in their midst. In one of my stories—'Nilushka'—this desire for holiness is explained by one character as follows: 'Once upon a time there lived scoundrels and villains, then they acquired a righteous man.' Crude, but true.

I saw Helen Keller in 1906 in New York.[5] As a matter of fact, it was William James, back in Boston, at Harvard, who advised me to 'become acquainted' with this 'miracle'. He managed somehow to make a most intricate connection between this 'miracle' and his own views—[according to which] a religious sensation of the world is constant reaction by the individual to the cosmos, a reaction which is highly valuable in that it harmonizes the individual. It is possible that my exposition of his idea is not entirely accurate, since I do not speak English and James's words were translated for me. I found this idea elaborated later in James's book *The Varieties of Religious Experience*—a book which is excellently written, yet 'muddled' in a typically American manner and which in essence— although none too deftly—'sanctifies' his own country's experience of a dreadfully hypertrophied capitalism.

The impression that Helen Keller made on me was unpleasant, even painful: an affected, most capricious, and apparently extremely spoilt girl, she spoke of God and of how God disapproves of revolutions. In general she reminded me of the 'simple' and 'holy' nuns and 'pilgrims' whom I have observed in villages and monasteries. She was surrounded by some old maids who treated her as if she were a parrot they had trained to talk. There was a professor, whose name I do not remember, and the Tolstoyan Kennedy, the author of poems published here by Posrednik and a man just as foolish as he was rich.[6] It was absolutely clear that for those around her, Keller was a 'business'. A very unpleasant memory.

Look what a long letter I've written you! I'll write to Olia soon as well. Keep well. I am extremely glad to have made your acquaintance.

A. Peshkov

SOURCE: *SS* 30: 316–19.

[1] Ivan Sokoliansky, director of the Kharkov Institute of Defectology.

[2] Olga Skorokhodova, who was left deaf, dumb, and blind after contracting meningitis in childhood. After learning to read, write, and speak at Sokoliansky's institute she gave lectures and did research on disabilities.

[3] This figure was the approximate population of the USSR at the time.

[4] As the following examples make clear, Gorky is talking about the apparent way that certain people 'compensate' for disabilities.

[5] Helen Keller (1880–1968), American author and lecturer, who became deaf, blind, and mute after an illness when she was nineteen months old.

[6] Gorky apparently means Crosby, a prominent American Tolstoyan. Posrednik [The Intermediary], publishing house set up by Tolstoy and Vladimir Chertkov to provide edifying and morally improving literature for the common people.

167. To I. E. Babel, [late 1933 or 1934]

[Moscow]

My dear Babel,

When you read us your play in Sorrento, you probably noticed that I was unable to say anything sensible or definite about it.[1]

This is probably because at the time your play surprised me but did not excite me. The same is true now that I have read the manuscript of the play for myself. It is a skilful piece of work, its details are most subtle and acute, and their presentation is masterful. But I will say nothing of this, since overall the play is cold, its purpose vague, and the author's goal elusive.

Everyone who has a sincere love of literature—and I include myself in that number—holds you in exceptionally high regard. Given your great talent and wisdom, people expect of you works which are particularly lucid and significant.

This play does not justify the expectations you have inspired. I myself am repelled above all by your Baudelairean passion for rotten meat. All the people in your play, from the invalids onwards, are putrid; they smell bad and almost all of them appear to be infected or enslaved by a bellicose sensuality.

It may be that this is the sensuality of desperate people who, even as they perish, endeavour to leave spots of mould on the walls and floor as a reminder of themselves and as an act of vengeance.

The task of 'significant' art is to show people in all their complexity (which is the business of psychologists), or else as distinctly repulsive (which is the business of critical realists), or even to arouse sympathy and respect for people (which is to romanticize them).

You appear to be essentially a romantic, but it seems that for some reason you cannot make up your mind to be one.

Your penchant for romanticism is confirmed by the final act and by Mariia, whose part in the play is purely 'epistolary'. But that penchant is expressed by characters who do not seem successful and even allow one to think that they have been introduced into the play as a 'concession' to some external demand and not for the purpose of a juxtaposition which has its source in the emotions of the author. The entire final act is tacked on to the play mechanically—such is the impression it creates. Here it is reason which operates exclusively, whereas in the first two acts one senses the presence of intuition.

It is difficult—indeed one is unwilling—to admit that the discord or rupture between 'intuitio' and 'ratio' came to you organically; I am personally convinced that this disharmony is technical in nature.

Although I do not consider myself a 'dramatist', I am capable of writing amusing and reasonably interesting scenes for the theatre—this is the explanation of my theatrical 'success'. I don't think you are a dramatist either, for this is a genre which requires a light, deft hand, whereas yours is heavy. Speaking between ourselves, good, genuine drama is an exceptionally rare thing: of Gutzkow's work only *Uriel Acosta* has survived, from Ostrovsky only *The Storm* [*Groza*], etc.[2] The only dramas that survive are those which are akin to the 'high art' of tragedy. Comedy is quite vital too: this is what the modern theatre should be built upon.

As a man who possesses a sense of humour which turns not infrequently towards sarcasm, you should try to write a comedy, I think. Your dramas are almost always built upon a force which is mighty, yet flawed and broken.

In your play I particularly dislike the figure of Dymshits. He is reminiscent of Grzhebin.[3] You have placed him in a position which will be only too gratifying to the anti-Semites. I imagine that I have not expressed all this so very intelligibly, but I would draw the following conclusion: do not stage the play in its present form. The critics will point out to you that the play is not in harmony with reality, that everything depicted in it is out of date and insufficiently characteristic, in fact, to be worthy of depiction. And they will single out a handful of remarks which would provide those who so desire with the right to make political deductions personally harmful to you.[4]

SOURCE: *LN* 70: 43–4.

¹ Gorky comments on what is apparently an early draft of Babel's *Mariia*.

² Karl Gutzkow (1811–78), German novelist, playwright, and critic. This 1847 play is about religious intolerance.

³ Zinovii Isaevich Grzhebin (1869–1929), publisher and old acquaintance of Gorky from the days of Parus and World Literature.

⁴ The typescript of this letter breaks off at the bottom of a page.

168. To R. Rolland, [26 May 1934]

[Moscow]

My heartfelt thanks, dear Rolland, for your friendly letter. The death of my son has been a truly heavy and idiotically offensive blow for me.[1] The spectacle of his agony remains relentlessly before me. It seems that I witnessed it only yesterday; to the very end of my days I will never forget the disgraceful torture of a man by the mechanical sadism of nature. Maksim was a strong and healthy person, and his dying was painful. He was gifted. He possessed an original artistic talent which resembled that of Hieronymous Bosch in nature; he had a bent for technology, and inventors and specialists took notice of his opinions. His sense of humour was well developed and he had real critical flair. But he was weak-willed; he squandered his energies and did not develop a single one of his gifts. He was thirty-six. I see him as he was thirty-two years ago, in Arzamas, the town where Lev Tolstoy experienced the 'Arzamas horror' of the meaninglessness of bourgeois existence.[2] It was a holiday; the local citizenry had attended church, after which they had gone home to stuff themselves with pies and then fall asleep. A sultry silence bore down on the small town, with its twelve churches and two monasteries for 10,000 people. Frogs were croaking in the ponds. Maksim was sitting alone on a bench by the gateway to the house, singing in his thin child's voice:

> Oh, my will, my will,
> You are my treasure!
> My will is a soaring falcon,
> My will is the radiant dawn!

The child's yearning for will, of which he sang in a dead town full of people who were burdening the earth in vain, was etched on my memory for life. Today Arzamas has a technological institute, two nine-year schools, and is outstanding in its floriculture.

I must say that I was profoundly moved by the response of the Soviet people to my sorrow. I am still receiving letters and telegrams from collective farmers and workers. The crew of the [ice-breaker] *Krasin* even sent their greetings and good wishes from the Arctic Ocean. My dear friend, how I wish that you—courageous and steadfast crusader for justice that you are—could also experience such a fine, profound sensation of a strong bond with your own country. This is a reward you have long deserved.

Of course, I have already settled down to work and seem to be working well. You probably already know that the Academy of Sciences and the All-Union Institute for Experimental Medicine are being moved from Leningrad to the outskirts of Moscow, where these two huge institutions will serve as the basis for a 'City of Science'. In all likelihood, an Institute for the Study of World Literature will also be built there.[3] It has a most interesting programme.

During the current Five-Year Plan particular attention is being paid to issues of culture and the education of children. The entire system of teaching is being reorganized, new textbooks are being introduced, schools are being transformed into ten-year institutions, and a special publishing house has been set up for children's books, with editions of 100,000, 200,000, and even 500,000 copies. Not that I think these quantities will satisfy the demand. In a few days I'll be sending you Marshak's report on the demand for books among our young Pioneers;[4] it is a very interesting report, part of which was published in *Pravda*. The report was put together on the basis of over 5,000 collective and individual letters from Pioneers.

I came across a book today by a person who proposes the destruction of the polar ice cap so as to return Siberia and Canada to the 'heavenly conditions' of the Miocene era.[5] This fantasy bears witness to the stimulation of creative thought directed towards the goal of genuinely 'changing the world'. And, do you know, such fantasies are already being realized in practice over here. For example, we have stopped sharpening all cutting tools, since we have got them to sharpen themselves during their operation. This results in a huge saving of time and metal.

The idea of biosynthesis in the plant kingdom is leading people to work on the creation of long-life wheat, long-life tobacco, etc. There have already been some successes.

There is also much of interest being done in other scientific fields. In general, what this signifies to me is the striving of physical energy to be freed so that it can become transformed into intellectual energy.

I will end this long letter with a firm handshake from afar. I still cherish the hope of being able to hug you, my dear, wonderful friend and fellow warrior.

Cordial greetings to Mariia Pavlovna.

M. Gorky

P.S. My secretary has sent you my brochure.[6] I am not in the habit of sending my books to friends. This is not due to stinginess, although I really cannot say just why it is. It is a 'custom' which embarrasses me for some reason. Perhaps it is because in general I do not have a high opinion of my books.

SOURCE: *SS* 30: 347–50.

[1] On Maksim's death, see the Introduction to this section.
[2] In August 1869, Tolstoy had a terrible psychological experience (which sprang from his fear of death) during an overnight stay in Arzamas.
[3] The following year, 1935, saw the formation of what became known as the Gorky Institute of World Literature.
[4] Samuil Iakovlevich Marshak (1887–1964), children's writer and translator.
[5] E. S. Gernet, *Glacial Lichens: A Popular Account of a New Theory about Glaciers* [*Ledianye lishai (Novaia lednikovaia teoriia, obshchedostupno izlozhennaia)*] (Tokyo, 1930).
[6] In his previous letter to Rolland, Gorky had promised to send him 'On Surpluses and Shortages' ['Ob izbytke i nedostatkakh'], a work published for distribution on collective farms.

169. To I. V. Stalin, [2 August 1934]

[Moscow]

I'm sending you my 'report' and urge you to acquaint yourself with it as soon as possible so that I can include in it any changes you might make.[1]

I enclose letters to me from comrades Mirsky and Jasieński, together with a copy of an article by the latter: this was sent to *Pravda* and has not yet been published.[2] In all likelihood it won't be published there, since Iudin and Mekhlis are men of the same stripe.[3] I know nothing of their ideology, but in practice they are leading towards the formation of a group which wants to take command of the Writers' Union. Possessing the 'will to power' and drawing support from the leading organ of the Party,[4] this group is of course quite capable of assuming such command, but in my opinion it does not have the right to that real ideological leadership of literature which is so necessary today. This is because the group lacks intellectual vigour and displays extreme ignorance regarding the past and present of literature.

The directorate of the Union is being selected from the people indicated in Iudin's article, which I also enclose. In my opinion, Serafimovich, Bakhmetiev[5] and Gladkov are just so much 'exhaust steam'. They are men of decrepit intellect. The latter two are hostile to Fadeev,[6] a man who is himself in a state of arrested development, something which he appears to be experiencing as a personal drama—not that this is hampering him in his efforts to play the role of a lit[erary] leader. It would, however, be better both for him and for literature if he were to study. I consider Mirsky's judgement on *The Last of the Udeghes* [*Poslednii iz Udege*] fully justified, but from what Iudin tells me, Fadeev only took umbrage at it.[7] My attitude towards Iudin is acquiring an ever-more negative hue. I cannot abide the peasant cunning, the lack of principle, the duplicity, and cowardice of a man who admits his personal impotence, yet attempts to surround himself with people even more insignificant than he is so as to hide in their midst.

I don't believe in the sincerity of Panferov's Communism;[8] he is another ignorant peasant who is also cunning and painfully ambitious, even though he is a fellow of great will. He is fighting most energetically against the critical response to *Bruski*; he has enlisted Vareikis in his defence, and someone called Grechishnikov has published a laudatory book about him, in which it is maintained that the 'cognitive significance of *Bruski* is, without any exaggeration, enormous', and which repeats a sentence from Vasilkovsky's article: 'No study, not even one specifically dedicated to collectivization, could ever take the place of *Bruski*.' Of course, there isn't a word in this book about Sholokhov's *Virgin Soil Upturned* [*Podniataia tselina*] or Shukhov's *Hatred* [*Nenavist'*].[9] The excessive praise of Panferov is, quite naturally, having a painful and harmful effect on these other authors.

For me personally, Panferov, [Aleksandr] Molchanov, and the others [of] this group are serving—in literary circles as in literature itself—to champion the peasant, with all his individualistic notions of 'personal ownership'. For them literature is mere 'seasonal work', a springboard from which to leap to high positions. My distrustful and even inimical attitude towards the peasant is not diminished by the fact that the peasant sometimes speaks the language of the Communist. Peasant literature and literature about the peasant require particularly careful reading and particularly acute criticism. More and more often it has become necessary to note that the peasant does not study as avidly as the proletarian. Here is the latest instance of this. Molchanov was offered funds to go to one of the large construction projects, live there for a while and watch the proletariat working towards the revival of the countryside. But he refused, pleading that he is writing a new book. The criticism of his *Peasant* [*sic*] has washed off him like water off a duck's back.[10]

Vishnevsky, Libedinsky, and Chumandrin cannot serve as the leaders of non-Party writers who are more literate than they are.[11] The Communist faction in the Organizational Committee lacks authority among our writers, who can see only too readily the struggle between these various cliques. And I am obliged to say that these cliques have come about thanks to patronage: certain responsible c[omrades] have certain literary figures to whom these 'important personages' offer their particular patronage and whom they praise with a marked lack of prudence. And around each of the literary figures thus favoured by the 'authorities' there is a clique made up of people who are less talented still. It is not even as if these people are organizing themselves around a 'teacher'; it is everyday and narrowly personal motives which operate here instead.

And the 'big names' in their own turn simply play the role of patrons, placing before our publishers the immature 'fruits of creativity' produced by young perch, pike, and other fish of the predatory kind. The 'big name' endeavours to acquire a ration card and an apartment on behalf of his admirer, to whom he refers as his 'pupil', even though he is not teaching him his craft and is even incapable of doing so, since he is an ignoramus himself. One has to add that we are dealing primarily with people who are thirty years of age; that is, with those who experienced 'hard times' in their adolescence and youth. Those hard times have had a most harmful effect on the psyche of many a thirty-year-old: they are people too greedy for the pleasures of life, in too great a hurry to enjoy themselves, and thus unwilling to work conscientiously. And so impetu-ously do some of them 'hurry to live' that they create the impression of people who are not confident that the reality created by the Party is suf-ficiently well established or that it will continue to develop precisely as it is developing now; they think that the peasant is only pretending to be a collectivist, that we have all the pre-conditions for Fascism, and that 'a war could set us back to where we were before the NEP'. If it were only the petty bourgeois and the Philistines who felt like this, it wouldn't mat-ter, but certain 'Party people' feel the same way too, and this is what seems disturbing to me, even though I'm an optimist, as everyone knows.

In addition to this, there are the activities of saboteurs among our youngsters in school. Ivan Makariev has told me about this and he says that he has informed you as well.[12] The c[omrades] from the GPU have told me about another form of sabotage among schoolchildren in the Crimea. I pay a lot of attention to our children and one of these days I will make good my promise to write something about them—I haven't done so yet due to reasons beyond my control.

It is necessary to protect children from being infected with Philistinism—that's the point.

Everything I have said above—albeit most incompletely—convinces me of the need to pay very serious attention to literature as 'the trans-mitter of ideas'. Indeed, I would add not so much of ideas as of senti-ments. My dear, sincerely respected and beloved comrade, it is necessary to place the soundest ideological leadership at the head of the Writers' Union. What is happening at present is the selection of personnel in line with the interests of certain ambitious people, and this signals the in-evitability of petty, personal struggles among the cliques within the Union, struggles not at all in keeping with the organization of literature as a force which might operate in an ideologically unified manner. The cultural and revolutionary significance of literature is not understood by many people. I know that you will be presented with lists of people who are being recommended for the Directorate and the Presidium of the Writers' Union. I don't know who they are, but I can guess.

It seems to me personally that the Union would receive the soundest leadership from the people named in the enclosed list. But even if the proposed composition of the Writers' Union Directorate is confirmed, I earnestly request that I be relieved of the chairmanship of the Union due to poor health and my own lit[erary] commitments. I am not a capable chairman; I am even less able to sort my way through the Jesuitical intrigues of group politics.[13] I will be of far greater use as a worker in literature. I have accumulated a multitude of topics on which I don't have time to work.

Sincere regards, and I wish you a pleasant holiday.

M. Gorky

SOURCE: *LG.*

[1] Gorky's report was written for the first congress of the Soviet Writers' Union and delivered later in August.

[2] Dmitrii Petrovich Sviatopolk-Mirsky (1890–1939), literary critic, author of a renowned history of Russian literature, who returned to Stalin's Russia from emigration. Bruno Jasieński (1901–41), Polish prose writer and Communist. He went to Moscow in 1929 and was appointed to the board of the Writers' Union in 1934.

[3] Pavel Fedorovich Iudin (1899–1968), member of the organizing committee of the Union of Writers; Lev Zakharovich Mekhlis (1889–1953), *Pravda* journalist.

[4] i.e. *Pravda.*

[5] Vladimir Matveevich Bakhmetiev (1885–1963), prose writer, appointed to the board of the Writers' Union in 1934.

[6] Aleksandr Aleksandrovich Fadeev (1901–56), prose writer, literary official, prominent in RAPP, author of the Civil War novel *The Rout* [*Razgrom*], infamous for his support of Stalin.

[7] Mirsky's negative review appeared in *Literaturnaia gazeta*, 24 June 1934.

[8] Fedor Ivanovich Panferov (1896–1960), prose writer of peasant background, appointed to the board of the Writers' Union in 1934.

[9] Mikhail Aleksandrovich Sholokhov (1905–84), Communist, member of the leading group in the Writers' Union from 1934. Awarded the Nobel Prize for Literature in 1965 for *The Quiet Don*. Ivan Petrovich Shukhov (b. 1906), novelist.

[10] Gorky had written critically of Molchanov's *The Peasants* [*Krestiane*] in an article of June 1934.

[11] Vsevolod Vitalievich Vishnevsky (1900–51), playwright; Mikhail Fedorovich Chumandrin (1905–40), prose writer. Both were members of RAPP.

[12] Ivan Sergeevich Makariev (1902–58), literary critic associated with RAPP.

[13] Gorky, of course, was elected chairman. The presidium included those mentioned in this letter as unsuitable—Iudin, Bakhmetiev, Gladkov, Serafimovich, and Panferov—but also a number of people whom Gorky had recommended.

170. *To S. M. Kirov,*[1] *[end of November 1934]*

Dear and Respected Comrade Kirov,

The History of the Civil War has always enjoyed your liveliest attention, and this allows me to hope that you will not deny it your attention on this occasion either and that you will quickly read the first volume.

The work on this first volume was most difficult, although while they were at it, the secretariat also put in a great deal of very valuable work on the selection, classification, and processing of material for the following volumes, and on the creation of an archive for documents etc.

I beg you also to give your attention to the work of the Leningrad editors of *The History of Factories and Plants* [*Istoriia fabrik i zavodov*] which is insufficiently energetic. Why don't you call in Comrade Nizovtsev[2] and suggest that he step up their work?

I wish you all the best and I send my warm regards.

SOURCE: *Izv Ts K* 1990 (7): 222.

[1] Sergei Mironovich Kirov (1886–1934), head of the Leningrad Party organization, member of Politburo from 1930.
[2] P. L. Nizovtsev, member of the Leningrad Regional Party Committee.

171. To K. E. Voroshilov,[1] [1934]

Dear Klimentii Efremovich,

I have been sent a photograph of the design for the Red Army Theatre and the attached decree approving that design signed by you and other comrades.

I am, of course, very grateful for this kind notification that our excellent army will have a theatre of its own and that its cultural work is growing and expanding. Needless to say, this is a fact which requires wide publicity: the soldiers of the capitalists should learn of this and realize its significance.

Needless to say, too, the Red Army Theatre should be a building which will not simply embellish Moscow and allow our soldiers to take pride in the outward appearance of their theatre; its architecture should also reflect the power of the army, thereby stirring certain thoughts and feelings in the soldiers of capitalist armies.

But is the approved design capable of fulfilling this requirement? I think not. The design is somehow extremely reminiscent of a country restaurant—a squat building cheaply decorated with a paling of narrow columns like matchsticks.

I cannot detect or see in it anything which might speak clearly of its profound cultural significance or of the enormous power which it is being called upon to foster. The architects have obviously striven to create a light-weight building and they have produced something frivolous, as if they were planning to perform operettas and vaudevilles in it, and display *étoiles* naked from head to toe.

Forgive me for this bold and uninvited criticism of the approved design. But I am sure that you—perhaps even more than I—would like to see a different Red Army Theatre, one which would be more powerful and severe and which might better correspond to the idea of raising intellectual qualifications in our Red Army, an idea which could arise only in a country with a dictatorship of the working class and where the worker stands at the head of the army.

You have seen the theatre on the site of the Simonov monastery.[2] This is not what the Red Army Theatre should be like, but it is perhaps the best theatre in Moscow in terms of architectural finish, both exterior and interior. I mention this only to say that we are capable of building well when it is understood what is necessary.

Your theatre prompted in me an urgent desire to write a play called *The Orderly Nikonov* [*Denshchik Nikonov*]—a dramatic story about a fellow who was tormented by the officers Neiman and Nesterov. I was witness to this story, I remember it well, and I know a fair amount in general about the attitude of officers towards soldiers, since I once lived for two years in a building which was full of officers' quarters and I was very 'friendly' with their orderlies.

Once again I ask you to forgive me for this belated and inappropriate criticism of the design. I really don't like it at all.

SOURCE: *Izv Ts K* 1991(8): 153–4.

[1] Kliment Efremovich Voroshilov (1881–1969), military commander, member of Politburo from 1926.
[2] The Palace of Culture of the Moscow Automobile Factory, built in the Constructivist style.

172. To A. S. Shcherbakov,[1] [19 February 1935]

[Moscow[2]]

It seems to me that the state of literary criticism and its tasks has been described in terms that are too 'general' and familiar to our writers and critics.[3] Hence they are hardly capable of inspiring lively and urgent interest or of giving rise to a fruitful discussion on the subject either of Socialist Realism as a method and technique of creative writing, or of the aesthetics and ethics of Soviet art.

A great deal has been written and continues to be written about Socialist Realism, but there is no clear or unified opinion about it, which explains the sad fact that at the Writers' Congress the critics did not declare that it exists. What we need is a firmly-prescribed 'working-class truth' sufficiently broad to embrace and illuminate the meanings of all the processes taking place in our country and all acts of opposition to the creative efforts of the dictatorship of the proletariat. It stands to reason that within the limits of this 'working-class truth' certain contradictions are both permissible and unavoidable—and that is why it is necessary to establish the limits of what is permissible and unavoidable with particular firmness and precision. I think that as the starting-point for Socialist Realism we should take Engels's assertion: life is continuous and uninterrupted movement and change. In the natural world the forces of physics and chemistry operate in a mechanical fashion; in human society one has friction, conflicts between class forces, and labour activities directed towards the creation and expansion of a bourgeois material culture which serves class interests. Historical facts show that in bourgeois society intellect has played the role of a 'catalyst' which seeks, with greater or lesser success, to forge links and connections—that is, to reconcile; in the social sphere such reconciliation involves the subjugation of one force by another. It is necessary to show the individualists that under the conditions of capitalism, intellect is concerned least of all with the rate of its own growth, seeking only a state of stable equilibrium.

The realism of bourgeois literature is critical, but only to the extent that such criticism is necessary for the 'class strategy'—for elucidating the mistakes of the bourgeoisie in the struggle to stabilize its power. Socialist Realism serves the struggle against the remnants of the 'old world' and its pernicious influence, working towards the eradication of that influence. But its chief task is to stimulate a socialist and revolutionary outlook and attitude.

It seems to me that thoughts of this kind might lead to objections and annoyance among writers and critics, and hence give rise to a useful debate. For the goals and tasks of literature are the very things that our writers think and talk about least of all—and we must try to stimulate a livelier and more profound interest in the work they are occupied with.

In general we ought to point out the following to our writers as often and as urgently as possible: the predictions of scientific socialism are being realized ever more widely and profoundly through the activity of the Party, and the organizing power of those predictions lies in their scientific nature. The socialist world is being built and the bourgeois world is collapsing precisely as predicted by Marxist thought.

From this the conclusion naturally follows that the figurative thinking of the artist, which draws on a broad knowledge of reality, supplemented by an intuitive urge to impart a more polished form to the material—to supplement the given with the possible and the desirable—that such thinking is also capable of 'foresight'. In other words, Socialist Realist art has the right to exaggerate, to 'conjecture'. The intuitive should not be understood as something 'prophetic', something that precedes knowledge; it is rather that this is what completes experience in those cases where experience, when organized in the form of a hypothesis or an image, lacks certain links, certain details. We should familiarize our writers with the revolutionary hypotheses of science, with the hypotheses of Speransky, which have already been confirmed experimentally and now serve as 'working-class truths'.[4] [. . .] It would be very useful if you were to discuss this matter with Lev Nikolaevich Fedorov, the director of the All-Union Institute of Experimental Medicine, and if you were to ask him while you are at it to draw up a report on the tasks of the Institute—on the necessity for a comprehensive study of the human being.

I direct your attention to the fact that so far nothing has been done regarding a monument to Morozov or an All-Union theatre.[5]

Afinogenov's report seems to me both unclear in its premises and devoid of perceptible conclusions.[6] I doubt that we have the right to talk of the 'victories'—let alone the 'brilliant' victories—of Socialist Realism until it has displayed itself as a method with all necessary clarity. If one is to protect actors from the wilfulness of directors, it has to be indicated that such wilfulness also reflects upon the authors of plays in those (far from rare) instances when the authors themselves present the theatre with what is really only 'raw material', rather than a play which has been developed in full detail. Afinogenov has quite rightly noted that in both the theatre and the cinema we have directors who are better educated than our playwrights and script writers. He should have dwelt on that point. Afinogenov's report will probably provoke an extensive polemic, but one which will be as petty as a kitchen squabble.

Shaginian asks the critics for 'guidance'.[7] That is hardly the right thing to do; one should be asking instead for an amicable combined effort. After all, novelists, short-story writers, and playwrights also provide guidance to the critics by presenting them with material which is typical of the age and developed in images, material from which publicistic (that is, ideological) conclusions may be drawn and a social ethic and aesthetic constructed. The request that a history of literature be written is understandable, but 'separate monographs on every writer' would bring nothing except harm to the writers concerned.

Shaginian's reference to the need for a critical evaluation of Russian literature compared with the literatures of the sister republics is extremely valuable.

M. Gorky

SOURCE: *SS* 30: 381–4.

[1] Aleksandr Shcherbakov (1901–45), leading Party official, elected Secretary of the governing board of the Writers' Union in 1934, when Gorky was elected Chairman.

[2] The archive contains another letter of the same date written to the same addressee. Gorky complains in that letter of the failure of a government official to hand over to the Writers' Union funds set aside for the construction of dachas.

[3] Gorky had received the advance outline of a report to the forthcoming plenary session of the governing board.

⁴ Aleksei Speransky (1888–1961), pathologist and neurologist.

⁵ Pavlik Morozov became a state 'hero' after he was killed by peasants for denouncing his own parents to the authorities. Gorky had earlier proposed the creation of an All-Union theatre to concentrate on plays from the non-Russian republics.

⁶ Aleksandr Nikolaevich Afinogenov (1904–41), playwright, earlier involved with both Proletkult and RAPP. Gorky had received a summary of a report delivered by him on 2 March.

⁷ Marietta Sergeevna Shaginian, prose writer, author of *Hydrocentral* [*Gidrotsentral'*], a famous five-year-plan novel of 1930–1.

173. To A. A. Andreev,¹ [7 November 1935]

[Crimea]

Dear Andrei Andreevich,

In accordance with the division of labour among the Secretaries of the Central Committee, the direction of cultural affairs has fallen to you. And so for the first time I am obliged to trouble you on two important matters.

In Leningrad there is an Institute of Russian Literature—IRLI—which is a part of the Academy of Sciences and of which I am the director, with I. K. Luppol and Oksman as my deputies.² The Institute has a huge library and a large manuscript archive. Now that the Academy of Sciences has moved to Moscow, IRLI has been left without assistance or supervision.

It is in Moscow, too, by a decree of the Central Committee, that LitVUZ is being set up,³ an institution which has been charged with the conduct of scholarly research, along with the training of literary specialists. The director of LitVUZ is, once again, Luppol. But LitVUZ has neither library nor manuscripts. The question naturally arises, therefore, of the merger of the two institutes, IRLI and LitVUZ, all the more so since the practical direction of both institutes is concentrated in the hands of one man. Such a merger would economize on funds, facilitate the selection of personnel, and allow us to close down a number of literary institutions which are collecting the same manuscripts, snatching them from one another and creating unnecessary competition. The only difficulty is that a great deal of space would be required to accommodate this. For the time being, however, LitVUZ (which has already had funds allocated to it) will be able to cope in the new building. It may perhaps prove possible to utilize the former Rumiantsev museum temporarily, seeing that the Lenin Library is apparently soon to move to its new premises.

Whatever the case, the question of merging the two institutions has come to a head.

The second question is very much more complicated. I am referring to the Union of Soviet Writers. It seems to me that the situation there is intolerable. It is characterized by an almost complete absence among the writing fraternity of any consciousness of corporate and collective responsibility for their work, for their social behaviour before the Soviet reader and also before the international reader. In my view, it is this very lack of any consciousness of responsibility that is the cause of all the sins of our literature and the cause of the political ignorance and cultural poverty of its members. The cause lies in their unwillingness to study or to teach young people, the cause lies in their unwillingness to struggle relentlessly against every manifestation in their midst of that Philistinism which is the root of Fascism.

Of course, I understand that the blame for all these sins must rest with the Chairman of the Union, but I am obliged to live far from Moscow and I am overloaded with work which I must finish before I turn up my toes, yet which I fear I won't manage to get done. To a certain extent the blame for the neglected and broken condition of our writers may also lie with the Central Committee of the Party. The Party has installed the labour force of the entire land of the Soviets at the head of humanity; it is now wisely fortifying, developing, and cultivating that labour force and leading the way resolutely towards the great goal—the reorganization of the social structure of the entire world. The Party is devoting considerable attention and assistance to scientific and technical workers, but less to doctors, less still to teachers, and very little indeed to writers, the 'engineers of souls'.[4] The creation of the Union and the provision of a budget of ten million roubles—these are, of course, generous acts of assistance to literature. They are so generous, in fact, that they may even be harmful. The 'big names' in literature are rich. Aid from the Literary Fund is amazing, even improbable at times. Money is often distributed without due care, taking no account of the actual needs of Union members. It is not unusual for a needy writer to be denied assistance, whilst that same writer's sister might be given five thousand roubles. The government gave money for the construction of a dacha settlement, and 700,000 roubles of that sum is vanishing like smoke in the wind. There are many instances of such generosity.

At the same time, there is a writer who lives by the seaside but doesn't go swimming, even though it would be good for him. Why not? Because he doesn't have the three roubles to buy a pair of swimming trunks. And yet he is a very valuable worker in the provinces, he has been working there for twenty-odd years, and in Ivanovo-Voznesensk to boot, a major working-class centre. There are dozens of young writers who have no room to live in. They live in basements and in 'corners'; there are even rumours that they live in graveyards and burial vaults. Can it be a good thing to separate the sheep from the goats quite so sharply? After all, these goats are our young people!

The treatment of our writers is very mixed. 'Patronage' exists, and very often a writer is valued not according to his merits but according to his sympathies. [Pilniak is forgiven for his story about the death of Comrade Frunze, a story which asserts that the operation was unnecessary and was conducted only at the insistence of the Central Committee.[5] Pilniak is forgiven for *Mahogany* [*Krasnoe derevo*] and many other scandalous things. There are, of course, many such facts.][6] And, of course, this all leads to arguments and ill-feeling amongst the writing fraternity.

Com[rade] Marchenko, the Secretary of the Party group of the Union of Writers writes a fulsome review of Galina Serebriakova's book, *The Youth of Marx* [*Iunost' Marksa*] conferring upon the author the honorary title of 'Stakhanovite in literature', even though it's a bad book.[7]

Marchenko's appraisal has provoked a protest from a number of writers in the Party. Of course, Comrade Marchenko's speech has had a corresponding effect on non-Party members too, especially after he announced that non-Party members would be invited to attend discussions 'with discretion'.

I am not against debates, I am for them. But unfortunately, there are no debates in the Writers' Union. The Congress took place fifteen months ago, and yet the differences which surfaced at that time between Comrades Bukharin and Surkov[8] over the evaluation of poetry have not been followed up. The speeches made by Ehrenburg, Malraux, and others have passed without commentary.[9]

We don't have any serious 'criticism', even though a 'critical' journal is being published.[10] 'Friendly' reviews predominate. Comrade Shcherbakov conducts a 'policy of reconciliation', he praises everyone and makes gentle, 'paternal' suggestions. For him literature is an alien affair, and one of secondary importance. He is an optimist, but only because he doesn't like to cause trouble for himself, it would seem.

I have already made concrete practical suggestions on a number of occasions. It has been said that we have no criticism. There has been a lot of chatter but there is still no criticism. We need to assemble twenty or thirty critics and organize them into a continuing seminar devoted to topics of extreme importance, such as 'The history of literature'. Such a seminar is doubly necessary: for one thing, the critics would pick up a little learning, and in the second place, some important questions of literary history would be resolved. With its multi-million budget, it would cost the Union of Writers nothing to spend a few hundred thousand roubles on the training of critics. If the Union of Writers is prepared seriously to set about the realization of this idea, I will personally work out a plan for such a seminar and recommend some people who could run it.

The Union is doing very little towards the training of young writers. At times it seems that the Party's key slogans are passing the Writers' Union by. What has been done to put into effect Stalin's slogan 'The cadres decide everything'?[11] Where are the young people who have been educated by the Writers' Union? We should not limit ourselves to some sort of cottage industry here: it is essential that we centralize the business of training our literary cadres.

I have made many requests that lectures be organized for writers on the philosophy of Marxism, on the history of literature, on current work in Soviet science, on the situation in the West, etc. Nothing has been done. Is this really so difficult?

As a rule, writers don't read each other's books. We ought to organize lectures evaluating book production at least twice a year.

It is essential to keep an eagle eye on regional literature and to introduce reviews of this literature into one of our moribund journals.

It seems to me that it is necessary to reorganize the Secretariat of the Union and turn it into a regularly functioning institution. Its membership could include Comrades Eideman, Luppol, Lakhuti, and one or two other writers.[12] Two more people would be needed besides, one of whom must be a good manager, and the other an organizer of lectures and the person 'in charge of advanced training for writers', so to speak. However, the main thing is that the Secretariat should be a working institution within which there is a business-like division of labour and where strict accountability for all work undertaken is a reality.

I beg you to help us all!

My sincere regards,

M. Gorky

SOURCE: *Izv Ts K* 1990(11): 217–19.

[1] Andrei Andreevich Andreev (1895–1971), Secretary of the Central Committee and member of the Politburo from 1932 to 1952.

[2] Luppol (1896–1943), historian, philosopher, and literary scholar; Iu. G. Oksman (1894–1970), literary scholar.

[3] The Institute of World Literature (IMLI) was formally established by government decree in 1932.

[4] Stalin's notorious description of writers as the 'engineers of human souls' originated at a meeting at Gorky's Moscow apartment in 1932.

[5] *The Tale of the Unextinguished Moon* [*Povest' nepogashennoi luny*] was published in *Novyi mir* in May 1926 and brought the wrath of the Party down on the head of writer and journal alike. Mikhail Vasilievich Frunze (1885–1925), Soviet military leader. *Mahogany* was also the subject of major controversy.

[6] The passage in brackets was deleted by Gorky.

[7] G. I. Serebriakova (1905–80). Her book was the first part of a trilogy entitled *Prometheus* [*Prometei*].

[8] Aleksei Aleksandrovich Surkov (1899–1983), poet and literary official, formerly associated with RAPP, later a secretary of the Writers' Union in the Brezhnev period.

[9] Ilia Grigorievich Ehrenburg (1891–1967), prose writer, memoirist, later prominent in the Khrushchev 'Thaw'. André Malraux (1901–76), writer, art critic, and political figure. Ehrenburg had challenged the idea of 'writers' brigades', insisting on the personal nature of literary creativity; Malraux had emphasized the need for a properly psychological element in the Soviet novel.

[10] *Literaturnyi kritik* [*Literary Critic*] appeared between 1933 and 1940.

[11] A catch-phrase from a speech of 4 May 1935.

[12] R. P. Eideman (Eidemanis) (1895–1937), Lett writer; Abulkasim Lakhuti (1887–1957), Tadzhik poet.

174. To V. M. Molotov,[1] *[January 1936]*

[MOSCOW]

Dear Viacheslav Mikhailovich,

I have received your letter. Thank you very much for your promise to assist the secretariat and contributors to *The History of the Civil War*. The people working on this project are modest and unassuming and hence all the more deserving of attention.

Incidentally, allow me to remind you of my request to unite 'under one hat' the personnel of 'The Civil War', 'The History of Factories and Plants', and 'The History of the Village' ['Istoriia derevni'].

It is with deep emotion that I read the newspaper accounts of the government's continuous, tireless, and wise work on the socialist education of the labour force in factories, collective farms, mines, and transport. Of course, the very broad scale of this work is yielding striking results and it will, of course, inspire the entire mass of the labour force to 'feats of honour, glory, and heroism', giving a powerful boost to the entire economy of the country. The days of this astonishing work are truly historic days. This is the work of true 'engineers of souls'.[2]

I am delighted and happy, but then I remember my own writing fraternity, and I can say without exaggeration that I feel ashamed. What are the three thousand people who have been brought together in the Union of Writers actually doing? In the period between the Congress and this January, I have read several dozen books and manuscripts. The impression was dispiriting. It is quite clear that people are learning nothing, that they don't recognize the need to do their work in a more literate and serious manner. The Volga is praised in verse for bringing to the Moscow River the waters of the Oka and the Kama, and these verses are being published in one of the central organs.[3] They publish rubbish like this: 'When I was a twelve-year-old boy, I hauled bales of cotton'—yet a twelve-year-old wouldn't be able even to budge a bale of cotton since it weighs 350 pounds, sometimes even 400. Or: 'I pinned her throat down with the edge of the spade and, exerting pressure on the spade with my foot, I began to push down on her neck until the spade sank into the soil'. From what follows, it emerges that the spade severed the woman's head completely, which is nonsense: however sharp a spade might be, it is impossible for skin to be cut under its pressure, especially on soft soil. It is difficult to slice through skin on the ground even if you use an axe. In our country, books containing such nonsense are not only being published, but they are even being praised. The author of three books, one of which is being published for the fifth time, writes things like this: 'It would happen that, *the wife and I*, we'd push ourselves to the limit, and in the morning *my husband* would have trouble with his heart.'

In our socialist fatherland, in these historic days of the Stakhanovite movement,[4] one finds sentences such as this: 'To fight your way to equality is as hard as fighting your way out of the terrible power of your equals so as to get ahead'—this piece of sententiousness comes from the author, not one of his heroes.

I have spoken many times of the low level of literacy among our writers. Is it necessary to say it again and again? I don't want to be a fly in the ointment. But I feel shame before the Stakhanovites, many of whom are even now more literate than our writers.

I feel shame before the revolutionary literature of Europe, where our books are being read with ever greater attention. But it is inadmissible to remain silent about these idiocies.

Ultimately, the writer's material is a complex made up of his social sympathies and antipathies; but what social sympathies does this writer display?

I find it hard to understand the reason for the astonishing indifference of our writers towards reality.

During the eighteen months since the Congress there has not been a single discussion meeting for writers in the Union, even though there are a great many things to talk and argue about! What about Ehrenburg's article on Maiakovsky, for example, i.e. on the question of the limits of creative freedom?[5] And I haven't seen the writers getting together with Stakhanovites: the Union hasn't organized a single literary evening for them. What is this—paralysis? Sabotage? It seems to me that these are the days of the spoilt, the sated, and the indifferent.

Of the three thousand people [in the Union] one can count a hundred writers who are working after a fashion and publishing books. But what are the others doing? And what is the Party leadership doing with the Union, what measures is it taking to expand the social horizons of writers? My dear Viacheslav Mikhailovich—I could write a great deal and for a long time on this topic, but you don't have time to read long letters. So let me raise the following question.

Why not have *Komsomol'skaia pravda* attempt to shake up and revive the Union by placing before it a series of questions—concerning the results of its activities since the Congress; concerning what lectures have been organized for the advanced training of writers; concerning their participation in collective literary work; concerning the results of work with beginning writers by the editors of journals; concerning what reports or lectures have been organized in the Union on the subject of the Stakhanovite movement, what questions of literary technique have been discussed since the Congress, and so on and so forth?

I think that it would be of considerable benefit if one were to bombard writers with such questions and that our young Komsomol people have the right to conduct such a bombardment.

It would be really good if you or I. V. [Stalin] could find time to have a talk to our writers, in the same way that you talk to our collective farmers and factory workers.

Wishing you good health and all the best.[6]

SOURCE: *Izv Ts K* 1990(11): 222–3.

[1] Viacheslav Mikhailovich Molotov (real name Skriabin, 1890–1986), member of Politburo from 1926, Chairman of Council of People's Commissars (1930–41).
[2] See Letter 173, n. 4.
[3] The geography is, of course, completely wrong.
[4] The Stakhanovite movement arose in 1935 as a new stage in efforts to promote labour productivity. It was named after A. G. Stakhanov, a Donbas coalminer who set a record for coal extraction on 25 September that year.
[5] The article appeared in January 1936 in *Izvestiia*.
[6] This is a typewritten draft letter with no signature.

175. To I. V. Stalin, [no earlier than 7 March 1936]

[Tesseli]

Dear Iosif Vissarionovich!

Here are my impressions of the meeting with Malraux.[1]

I have heard a great deal of praise and other soundly based comments about him from Babel, whom I consider a man with an excellent understanding of people and the most intelligent of our writers. Babel has known Malraux for some time and while he was living in Paris he carefully followed the growth of Malraux's significance in France. Babel says that government ministers take account of Malraux, and that of all the intellectuals in the Romance countries today, this man is the most prominent, talented, and influential figure. What is more, he possesses a gift for organization. My other informant, Mariia Budberg—you have met her at my place—confirms Babel's opinion. She has long frequented literary circles in Europe and knows all the attitudes and opinions that prevail there. In her view, Malraux is truly a man of exceptional ability.

Having now met him in person, I have formed much the same impression of him: he is a very talented man who has a profound understanding of the universal significance of our work in the Union of Soviets. He also understands that Fascism and national wars are inevitable consequences of the capitalist system, and that in organizing European intellectuals against Hitler and his philosophy, and against Japanese militarism, it is necessary to convince them that a world-wide socialist revolution is inevitable. Comrade Koltsov will inform you of the practical decisions that we reached.[2]

As I see it, Malraux's weaknesses lie in his tendency to go into detail and to say more about trifles than they deserve. A more fundamental weakness is one which is typical of the entire European intelligentsia— 'the individual, his creative independence, the freedom of his inner growth' etc.

C[omrade] Koltsov has informed me that Malraux's first questions were about Shaginian and Shostakovich.[3] My main purpose in this letter is to tell you frankly about my view on these questions. I haven't bothered you on this matter before, but now that we have to concern ourselves with the broader unification of the European intelligentsia, these questions have to be posed and clarified. Last year, in your speeches and your articles in *Pravda*, you spoke more than once of the need to display 'a careful regard for the individual'. These words were heard in the West; they gave us a boost and increased support for us.

But then this incident with Shostakovich blew up. Favourable reports of his opera appeared both in organs of the central press and in many regional newspapers. The opera played with great success in the theatres of Leningrad and Moscow, and it received excellent reviews abroad. Shostakovich is a young man—he is about twenty-five—a person of unquestionable talent, but very self-confident and quite highly-strung. The article in *Pravda* hit him like a ton of bricks; the fellow was completely crushed.[4] It goes without saying that when I speak of bricks, I don't mean the criticism itself but rather the tone of that criticism. Yet even the criticism itself is not convincing. Why is this a 'muddle'? Where and how is this 'muddle' expressed? The critics should provide a technical evaluation of Shostakovich's music. Instead of this, all that the *Pravda* article provided was the opportunity for a pack of mediocrities and hacks to persecute Shostakovich in every possible way. And this is what they are doing. Shostakovich lives by what he hears; he lives in the world of sounds. He wants to organize those sounds, to create melodies out of chaos. What was expressed in *Pravda* cannot be described as a 'careful regard [for the individual]', even though it is precisely such a careful regard that he so richly deserves as the most gifted of all contemporary Soviet musicians.

The decree about Bersenev's theatre also sounds extremely sharp.[5] Of course, Bersenev is stunned too, and it goes without saying that he will acquire the mantle of a man who has suffered innocently.

There are few theatres in Moscow. We need a theatre for children, that much is true, but where is the repertoire for such a theatre to be found? And why—for whose sake—do we have the theatres of the brilliant Meierhold and the no less brilliant Tairov?[6] There is a view in circulation that one of these theatres is required for the actress Raikh, and the other for the actress Koonen.[7]

SOURCE: *LG*.

[1] The meeting, at which Babel and Koltsov were also present, took place at Tesseli.

[2] Mikhail Efimovich Koltsov (1898–1942?), journalist, co-editor of *Za rubezhom* from 1932.

[3] Dmitrii Dmitrievich Shostakovich (1906–75), renowned Soviet composer.

[4] The article, published in the issue of *Pravda* of 28 January 1936, was entitled 'A Muddle Instead of Music: On the Opera *A Lady Macbeth of the Mtsensk District*' ['Sumbur vmesto muzyki: Ledi Makbet Mtsenskogo uezda'].

[5] Probably the decree on closing down the Second Moscow Art Theatre, published in the issue of *Pravda* of 28 February 1936. Ivan Nikolaevich Bersenev (1889–1951), actor and director.

[6] Aleksandr Iakovlevich Tairov (1885–1950), experimental director, severely criticized for his 'Formalism' in the Soviet period.

[7] Zinaida Raikh and Alisa Koonen, the respective wives of these two directors, and both well-known actresses.

176. To R. Rolland, [22 March 1936]

[Tesseli]

My dear friend Rolland,

Yesterday I read your article—as wise and courageous as ever—which was published in *Vendredi* on March 6.[1]

How good it is that Soviet people are able to read your articles and that you are writing letters to citizens and comrades in the Soviet Union! You are becoming more and more liked, more and more highly esteemed. I recently received a business letter from an acquaintance of mine, in the postscript to which he exclaimed: 'How upset Rolland must be by the events on the French border.' I find that exclamation most touching.

Malraux has visited me. He seems an intelligent and talented man. He and I came up with several practical measures which should serve the cause of unifying the European intelligentsia in the struggle against Fascism. Are you personally acquainted with Malraux? I think that in the interests of our common cause it would perhaps be very useful if you were to have a conversation with him.

I am in the Crimea, where the almond trees are already in bloom and the southern spring is in its usual hurry to show off its energy.

I am working hard, but I'm not managing to get anything done. I am devilishly tired, and—just to complete the pleasures of my life—I coughed up a lot of blood today. This is not serious, of course, but as always, I find it quite disgusting, especially when those around me look frightened and some of them even try to reassure me by telling me: 'Don't be afraid!' I am afraid only of one thing: that my heart will stop beating before I manage to finish the novel. In general I have never been afraid of anything, and now that I have lived for sixty-eight years, it would be ridiculous for me to be afraid of anything.

I am irritated by the egotism and hypocrisy of the 'aristocratic race' which inhabits the islands beyond the [English] Channel—I am irritated and feel ill will towards that race. It appears that it is abandoning France to pillage and destruction by the German Fascists. That self-important cockerel Wells is wisely keeping silent, although he ought to feel somewhat ashamed of his countrymen. One could talk for a long time on this topic, but it is better not to do so, since 'there is no salvation in words'.

Keep well, my dear friend, and warm regards. Heartfelt greetings to Mariia Pavlovna.

M. Gorky

SOURCE: *SS* 30: 434–5.

---

[1] A Russian translation of Rolland's article 'Pour la défense de la paix' had been published in *Pravda* on 13 March.

177. *To N. N. Nakoriakov,*[1] *[early May 1936]*

[Moscow]

Dear Nikolai Nikandrovich,

As my knowledge of our poetry is so poor, I cannot serve as the editor of the *Anthology of Twenty Years of Soviet Poetry* that you have undertaken, although I beg you to attend to the following considerations about what the point and the nature of the *Anthology* should be.

These considerations are guided by my firm belief in the international significance of our country's literature and of its poetry in particular. It seems to me that our prose writers and poets are not very clear about the significance of their work, and I think that if they realized what history demands of them, they would be ashamed to compose so much careless and bad verse. We have no shame before our own people, a fact which probably has its source in the conviction that 'man is not a dog—he'll eat anything'.

In publishing the *Anthology*, it would be good if you were to stress the 'internationalism' of our poetry by including in it translations of Armenian and Georgian poets, and poets of other sister republics. Of course, those translations would also be in the form of Russian verse, but this is where issues of plot and imagery come to the fore.

It seems to me that both these elements are conveyed in a manner more rich, more graphic and more 'epic' by the poets of our sister republics. We are living in a country and in an atmosphere where it is precisely the epic, and not the lyric, which is most characteristic. The *Anthology* should thus include the greatest possible number of 'legends' and long poems, such as Bagritsky's 'The Lay of Apanas' ['Duma ob

Apanase'],[2] Aseev's poem about the partisan,[3] 'Ulialaevism' ['Ulialaevsh-china'][4] and Nikolai Tikhonov's verses in the following style:

> If you were to make nails out of these people,
> There would be no stronger nails on earth.[5]

Tikhonov's early poems are not short on heroic sentiments.

I very much insist that the poems should have a plot and concrete, historical content. Our gentlemen poets are excessively keen on the mastery of form to the detriment of content; they have become accustomed to parading and flaunting the said mastery and forget that they will never manage to outspit the French and the English in this domain. The poets will probably insist that this very mastery be demonstrated: you must argue against this.

Mastery must be in evidence, of course, but above all you should have them display sincerity and the power of inspiration. And have them display international themes in their poetry! In this respect, other than 'Grenada',[6] there appears to be nothing. How can this be? They are supposed to be internationalists, yet the life of their proletarian neighbours does not excite them and gives rise to no anger, joy, or hatred. Very strange!

However, there is still time left, and perhaps we will find the poets to make good this shameful deficiency. A most shameful deficiency it is too!

A *History of Soviet Literature* is, of course, a matter much more difficult still than the compilation of the *Anthology*. I do not see who could carry out this task. I cannot imagine that there is anyone at all who could get it done in a period of eighteen months. We have so much new material here for such a *History*, material which nobody has even touched upon yet, that it would take no less than a year and a half just to select and organize it all.

The editors of the thick journals should refrain from publishing thick novels, which should be issued immediately in separate editions, and the space thereby freed up in the journals should be given over to the works of young writers. Hardly anyone is being published in our journals except for famous authors.

Nikolai Nikandrovich, if you need a good, competent translator from English, allow me to recommend the daughter of the writer K. A. Trenev.[7] Her address is: Natalia Konstantinovna Treneva, Moscow, 3 Nashchokinsky Lane, Ap[artmen]t 50.

Keep well.

Warm regards,

M. Gorky

SOURCE: *SS* 30: 441–3.

---

[1] Nikolai Nikandrovich Nakoriakov (1881–1970) was head of the State Publishing House of Artistic Literature (GIKhL) at this time.

[2] Eduard Georgievich Bagritsky (1895–1934), poet, whose manner was often characterized as 'revolutionary romanticism'.

[3] Nikolai Nikolaevich Aseev (1889–1963), poet associated with the Futurist movement. The poem is 'Semen Proskakov'.

[4] Narrative poem by Ilia Lvovich Selvinsky (1899–1968), poet and playwright associated with Constructivism.

[5] The concluding lines of Tikhonov's 'A Ballad about Nails'.

[6] A work of 1926 by M. A. Svetlov (1903–64).

[7] Konstantin Andreevich Trenev (1876–1945), playwright best known for his play of 1926 *Liubov Iarovaia*.

BIBLIOGRAPHY

BARRATT, ANDREW, and CLOWES, EDITH W., 'Gor'ky, glasnost'and perestroika: Death of a Cultural Superhero?', *Soviet Studies*, vol. 43, 1991: 1123–42.

BERBEROVA, NINA, *Zheleznaia zhenchchina* [*The Iron Lady*] 2nd edn. (New York, 1982).

BOTSIANOVSKY, V. F., *Maksim Gor'kii: Kritiko-biograficheskii etiud* [*Maksim Gorky: A Critical-Biographical Sketch*] (St Petersburg, 1901).

BYKOVTSEVA, L. P., *Gor'kii v Italii* [*Gorky in Italy*] (Moscow, 1975).

CHUKOVSKII, K., *Dnevnik 1901–1929* [*Diary 1901–1929*] (Moscow, 1991).

GOR'KII, M., *Kak my pishem* [*How We Write*] (Leningrad, 1930).

—— (ed.), *Belomorsko-Baltiiskii kanal imeni Stalina i Istoriia stroitel'stva* [*The White Sea-Baltic Canal in the name of Stalin and the History of its Construction*] (Moscow, 1934).

—— 'The Letters of Maksim Gor'kij and V. F. Xodasevič, 1922–1925', *Harvard Slavic Studies*, no. 1, 1953: 279–374.

—— *Letters of Gorky and Andreev*, ed. P. Yershov, trans. L. Weston (New York, 1958).

—— *Letters*, trans. V. Dutt (Moscow, 1966).

—— *Nesvoevremennye mysli. Zametki o revoliutsii i kul'ture* [*Untimely Thoughts. Notes on Revolution and Culture*] (Moscow, 1990).

—— *Neizvestnyi Gor'kii* [*The Unknown Gorky*] (Moscow, 1994).

GRECHNEV, V. Ia., *Gor'kii v Peterburge-Leningrade* [*Gorky in St Petersburg/Leningrad*] (Leningrad, 1968).

GRUZDEV, I. A., *Maksim Gor'kii: Biograficheskii ocherk (po novym materialam)* [*Maksim Gorky: A Biographical Sketch (Based on New Materials)*] (Moscow, 1925).

HOLTZMAN, FILIA, *The Young Maxim Gorky 1868–1902* (New York, 1948).

IVANOV, VIACHESLAV, 'Pochemu Stalin ubil Gor'kogo?' ['Why did Stalin Kill Gorky?'], *Voprosy literatury*, no. 1, 1993: 91–134.

KAUN, A., 'Obituary: Maxim Gorky', *Slavonic and East European Review*, vol. 15, 1937.

KHODASEVICH, V. F., *Izbrannaia proza v dvukh tomakh* [*Selected Prose in two volumes*] (New York, 1982).

KHODASEVICH, VALENTINA, and MARGOLINA-KHODASEVICH, OLGA, *Unpublished Letters to Nina Berberova* (Berkeley, 1979).

Lenin and Gorky: Letters, Reminiscences, Articles, trans. B. Isaacs (Moscow, 1974).

MURATOVA, K. D., 'Epistoliarnoe nasledie M. Gor'kogo' ['The Epistolary Heritage of M. Gorky'], *Russkaia literatura*, no. 2, 1988.

POSSE, V. A., *Moi zhiznennyi put'* [*My Life's Path*] (Moscow–Leningrad, 1929).

SLONIMSKY, M., 'Dnevnikovye zapisi, zametki, sluchai', ['Diary Notes, Comments, Events'] *Neva*, no. 12, 1987.

SPIRIDONOVA, L., *M. Gor'kii: dialog s istoriei* [*M. Gorky: Dialogue with History*] (Moscow, 1994).

TRENEV, K. A., 'Moi vstrechi s Gor'kim' ['My Meetings with Gorky'], *Maksim Gor'kii v vospominaniiakh sovremennikov v dvukh tomakh* [*Maksim Gorky in Contemporary Reminiscences in two volumes*], comp. A. A. Krundyshev (Moscow, 1981).

TREPLEV, A. A., 'Kak M. Gor'kii nachal svoiu kar'eru' ['How M. Gorky Began his Career'], *Biulleteni literatury i zhizni* [*Bulletins of Literature and Life*], no. 3, 1913.

TRIFONOV, N. A., 'A. V. Lunacharskii i M. Gor'kii (K istorii literaturnykh i lichnykh otnoshenii do Oktiabria) ['A. V. Lunacharsky and M. Gorky (On the History of Literary and Individual Relations leading up to the October Revolution)']. *M. Gor'kii i ego sovremenniki* [*M. Gorky and his Contemporaries*], ed. K. D. Muratova (Leningrad, 1968).

VENGEROV, S. A., *Russkaia literatura XX veka 1890–1910* [*Twentieth-Century Russian Literature, 1890–1910*], vol. 1 (Moscow, 1914).

INDEX OF RECIPIENTS

The numbers refer to the letter numbers employed in the body of the text.

GENERAL INDEX

The titles of Gorky's works are to be found under Gorky, M., Works. All other works are indexed under their authors.

Subheadings are arranged chronologically in the case of events, and alphabetically in all other cases.

Page references in **bold face** indicate that the person is the addressee of a letter from Gorky.

Topical entries appear in bold face and indicate Gorky's interest in or opinion on the given topic (e.g. **anti-semitism**; **realism**).